DATE DUE

Feb 05				
GAYLORD				PRINTED IN U.S.A.

THE POLITICAL ROLE OF INTERNATIONAL TRADES UNIONS

The activities of the international trades union movement extend far beyond the narrow confines of collective bargaining. They play a crucial, if less public, role in the conduct of international relations. Union organizations are, in virtually every nation, a major political force. Their leaders are intimately involved in political parties and frequently assume high governmental offices. Unions provide the backbone of innumerable socialist, social democratic and communist parties. Throughout their histories, the trades unions of Europe and North America have participated in the political process. In the Third World their role has been even more political. During the nationalist campaigns for independence the unions provided an alternative for nationalist activities when political parties were banned. Scores of Third World leaders (among them Gandhi, Touré, Mboya and many others) rose to power through the vehicle of their national unions.

Inevitably, this close relationship between unions and the political process has attracted the attention of competing intelligence services seeking to influence the political affairs of those nations in which the unions are active. One of the major battlegrounds of the Cold War has been the international union movement. As the unions seek to establish a role in the face of the new demands of the multinational corporations and the strong economic challenges posed to unions by the spread of free trades unionism in Eastern Europe, they have sought to build new institutions of international labor co-operation.

This book describes the development of the international trades union movement in Europe, Africa, Asia, Latin America and North America and the competing political influences which played a major part in this process.

Dr. Gary K. Busch is Chairman of Multirees Ltd, the London consulting company. He graduated BA from Cornell University in 1961 and was awarded the certificate in international studies from the London School of Economics in 1963. He received a PhD in international relations from the American University in Washington, DC, in 1969.

Dr. Busch was Research Director of the International Affairs Department of the United Auto Workers' union from 1964 to 1970. From 1970 until 1974 Dr. Busch was a Professor and Director of the Center for Labor–Management Education at the University of Hawaii in Honolulu. He went to Geneva, Switzerland, in 1974 to become Assistant to the General Secretary of the International Chemical and General Workers Federation (ICF). In 1975 he established Multirees Ltd.

Dr. Busch is a member of the Labor Panel of the American Arbitration Association and the (US) Federal Mediation and Conciliation Service. He was the host of the nationwide radio program *A Look at Labor* and the host and executive producer of *Rice and Roses*, a weekly half-hour television series on Public Television. He has researched several documentary television programs for major television companies in North America and Europe.

He is the author of *Political Currents in the International Trade Union Movement* (two volumes) and *Pan-Africanism and Pan-African Trades Unions*, and has published more than fifty specialized studies for the international trades union organizations for whom he acts as a consultant. He is a frequent lecturer at universities, business schools and international agencies.

THE POLITICAL ROLE OF INTERNATIONAL TRADES UNIONS

Gary K. Busch

University of Charleston Library
Charleston, WV 25304

St. Martin's Press   New York

© Gary K. Busch 1983

All rights reserved. For information, write:
St. Martin's Press, Inc., 175 Fifth Avenue, New York, NY 10010
Printed in Hong Kong
First published in the United States of America in 1983

ISBN 0-312-62447-6

Library of Congress Cataloging in Publication Data

Busch, G. K.
  The political role of international trades unions.

  Bibliography: p.
  Includes index.
  1. International labor activities. 2. Trade-unions—
Political activity. I. Title.
HD6475.A1B87   1983   331.88′091   82-16818
ISBN 0-312-62447-6

For Carol

Contents

Acknowledgements	ix
Introduction	1
1 The Development of Political Internationalism	6
2 Early Trades Union International Organisations	15
3 The Labour–Government Nexus	31
4 International Labour in Postwar Europe	42
5 The Background to Third World Unionism	73
6 The Development of African Unionism	83
7 The Development of Asian Unionism	101
8 The Development of Latin American Unionism	134
9 The Rise of Euro-unionism	181
10 Current Problems in International Labour	227
Notes and References	264
Glossary of Commonly-used Abbreviations	266
Select Bibliography	272
Index	280

Acknowledgements

I am very grateful for the assistance and guidance given to me in the research for this book to a list of trades unionists, academics and friends far too numerous for me to mention by name. However, certain of these have played such a major role in my education that they cannot escape mention. Principal among these are the Reuther brothers (Victor, Walter and Roy), who first gave me a chance to participate in international unionism. Through them and my fellow workers in the International Affairs Department of the UAW, Guy Nunn, Lew Carliner, Ed Torres, Ceferino Rodriguez, Stan Greenspan, Herman Rebhan and Collin Gonze, I was able to catch a glimpse of the outlines of the international labour movement. Thanks, too, must go to Chip Levinson of the ICEF, John Löfblad of the IFBWW, Heribert Maier of the FIET and my colleagues at the International Metalworkers. No one can ever forget the dedication and sacrifices made on behalf of the trades union movement by men like Reuther, Otto Brenner and Dirck Klosterman.

I am grateful to Sarah Wood of the Economist Intelligence Unit for permission to use some portions of their *Special Report 75*, 'Political Currents in the International Trade Union Movement' and to several labour intelligence officers for their insights. These have had to remain nameless.

Above all I am grateful for my introduction to trades unionism by my grandfather, William Siegel, who struggled so hard for workers' rights in his native Russia and later in the United States, which offered him refuge; and to my mother, who carried on that tradition. I am no less grateful for the support and encouragement offered to me in preparing this book by my wife, Carol, whose critical judgements and insights were of major importance, and to my son, Tristan, who assembled the bibliography.

Needless to say, the opinions and prejudices in this book are mine alone.

G. K. B.

Introduction

One of the most important of the international non-governmental voluntary organisations is the international trades union movement. Except for the transnational corporation there has been no international organisation which has been more active or played such an important role in international relations than the international labour movement. This has not been solely a result of the vitality of the union organisations which constitute the international trades union movements or their broad international perspectives. Rather it is because throughout the history of this movement, governments and political parties have used the international labour movement as one of the principal vehicles for their covert interactions with political parties and governments in foreign nations. The international trades union movement has been, and continues to be, a vital tool of governments in the shaping of the political destinies of foreign political parties and states and is an important part of most nations' foreign policy system.

One of the barriers to the appreciation of the key role played in international affairs by the trades unions is the difficulty in perceiving labour activities within the domestic political and economic scene as a model for union activities abroad. Since there are, with some minor exceptions, no international negotiated collective agreements it is difficult to perceive just why, how and with whom trades unions interact on an international basis. This difficulty is compounded by the ambiguity of the term 'trades union' itself; a noun which can be used to mean several quite different things. Understanding the differences in the various meanings of the term is an important step in appreciating the role of trades unions internationally.

Trades unions exist on several levels of abstraction. The most concrete, and perhaps the most familiar, is an organisation which exists to police the agreed working practices and compensation schemes within a plant or office on behalf of those members of the workforce who have delegated to a trades union their right of representation. On this level, the actual work practices and compensation within the plant are the main focus. The grievance procedure is the main source of interaction between the trades union and the employer, only occasionally augmented by interaction with the national union or its regional branch office for the purpose of collective bargaining.

At the second level of abstraction, trades unions exercise their functions as national organisations joining together unionists in their respective areas of jurisdiction (autoworkers, engineers, farmworkers, etc.) for the purpose of mutual representation and collective bargaining. At this level the trades unions speak for whole industries or sectors of the nation's economy, often bargaining with large national employers or employers' federations. In order to pursue these aims, trades unionists at this level often have a role which extends beyond the narrower confines of shopfloor economics; extending to the area of political interaction with government agencies and planning bodies concerned with their particular sector of the economy.

There is yet a higher level of abstraction of labour activity in which the term 'trades union' is used: the level of the national centre. These national centres are voluntary political organisations of the sectoral unions which have been created to promote regular interaction with their governments and national political parties in support of economic, social and political goals. These national centres (e.g. the British Trades Union Congress; the American AFL–CIO; the German DGB, etc.) are federations or confederations of national unions sharing a common ideology and economic programme. They derive political power as a result of the economic power of their constituent unions. In only rare cases do these national centres involve themselves in the process of collective bargaining. Their economic role consists mainly in participating in tripartite government bodies or commissions in the creation of schemes of broad economic planning, employment policy or other social legislation.

Their most important role, however, is that of representing the political ambitions of their constituent unions in their interaction with governments or government agencies. The nature of the trades union national centre is largely determined by the political system in which it operates and reflects the historical process through which it attained legitimacy. In highly centralised economies in which the state directly determines the allocation of resources, as in Eastern Europe and many nations of the Third World, there tends to be only one recognised national centre. In other states, where there are a multiplicity of political parties and ideologies, there tends to be a number of trades union national centres. In those states in which there is one national centre, despite the existence of a number of contending political parties, this phenomenon often reflects the series of compromises made by rival political movements during the struggle for trades union recognition which helped promote that recognition.

A principal reason behind the importance of the trades union movement in the political process has been the weakness of political parties. For most nations outside of Eastern Europe political parties are not strong. They frequently lack funds, manpower and organisation. They are capable of generating interest and support from their constituencies during the electoral campaigns but soon after, their continuity and direction is left in the hands of their parliamentary parties. The maintenance of their continued interaction with their membership is most often left to the activities of the voluntary organisations with whom they are associated. These voluntary organisations (trades unions, corporate groups, civic associations or religious groups) maintain the continuity of contact at national level between the members and the parties between elections.

Most often the trades unions have been linked with Labour, Socialist, Social Democratic, Communist or Christian Democratic parties. Indeed, for many years, membership in most of the parties of the left was based on affiliation to the party through the trades union or co-operative movement. These parties only rarely permitted direct personal affiliation. The trades union movement acted as a surrogate for a national party structure between elections.

Because of this close relationship between the political parties and the trades union movement, the work of the national centres has been almost exclusively political. Trades union leadership at the national level has been deeply involved in sustained interaction with the processes and offices of government. There has been a flow of trades union leaders away from the national centres into high political posts, especially when their party has assumed the responsibility of office. This centralisation of political power in the hands of the national centres has not precluded a strong political role played by lower-level union 'barons', but the day-to-day liaison with the political forces of the state has been conducted largely through the medium of the national centres.

It is precisely because the trades unionism practised by the national centres is so intimately involved with the political forces of the state that there has been such an interest in the growth of international trades unionism. The strategic role of the trades union movement within the political and economic life of the nation has proved to be a tempting target for outside interests seeking to intervene in or influence the party and state with whom the national centre interacts. There are few nations which have not sought to influence the policies of their neighbours and still fewer which have not feared the effects of such intervention in their own affairs. The area of intervention in the domestic political and economic relations of nation states through the vehicle of the trades union movement is one of increasing concern and attention.

In addition to the political links which exist between trades and trades unions and parties, there are other compelling reasons for a nation to use the vehicle of trades union intervention as a method of extending its outreach. In most nations of the world there are trades unionists active, outside their trades union role, in the conduct of private and public business as workers or employees. There is probably no better source of commercial intelligence than the workers employed in the plants and offices of the company. The trades unions have a legitimate 'need to know' vital information such as sales, markets, suppliers, types of products, production processes and similar matters often regarded as confidential by management. With the growth of increased participation by the representatives of the workforce in the management of commercial enterprises, this problem has become more acute. Access to this fund of critical knowledge by external powers can often be crucial in economic, political and military planning.

Access to trades unionists at shopfloor level, in industry and in governmental agencies, can often provide a form of insurance for those seeking to alter the system in which these unionists operate. Throughout the industries and government departments of the world there exist 'sleepers'; agents waiting to carry out vital tasks in the event of conflict. These sleepers and their contacts stand ready to disrupt war supplies, halt energy production, cut transport and communication links and generally assist in disrupting the defence apparatus.

It is hardly surprising then that the subject of international trades union activity has been a matter of active concern for the intelligence and security arms of national governments. There is probably no area of concern, outside of military intelligence, which is more vital to the security of a nation than the activities within and through the international trades union movements. Importantly, the very obscurity in which this international union interchange takes place makes it more attractive to governments. For a very long time, and most vitally since 1948, the international trades union movement has been the arena of the most open Cold War struggles. First in Europe, and later in the Third World, this competition and conflict between the Cold War protagonists has not diminished despite moves towards 'détente' in other spheres. The conduct of national foreign policy through the medium of the international trades union movement has written many chapters in modern political history. It is hard to think of a major change of government in recent years in which the activities of the trades union movements in those nations and internationally did not play an important role.

There have been few weeks during the past twenty years in which there have not been international meetings of trades unions taking place. Trades unionists sent overseas by their national centres and unions are scattered in fairly large numbers across Africa, Asia and Latin America. It is difficult to make a firm estimate of the number of trades unionists engaged in full-time international activity, but the number must be at least seven to eight thousand people. To this total should be added the number of unionists not engaged in full-time international activity but who attend the meetings of international trades union bodies or study in one of their numerous training programmes. Together, the total of unionists engaged in international activities amounts to well over twenty thousand people.

To a large extent these unionists are seeking to strengthen the international trades union movement by assisting unions abroad to organise, negotiate and to build political power. A key feature of this movement has been the growth of international union assistance and development agencies offering funds, training and self-help projects to unionists across the globe. There have been scores of housing projects, medical clinics, research centres and humanitarian aid schemes undertaken by labour organisations on behalf of overseas unionists. Vast amounts of technical assistance have been made available to union organisations towards these ends. Occasionally, the funds for these international activities have come from the resources of the trades union movement itself. Most frequently, however, this assistance has been made available to the international trades union movement as a result of government donations to national centres or directly to the organisations of international trades unionism. The annual resources and cash turnover of the institutions of international trades unionism in the development field alone total tens of millions of dollars. It is an active force.

The dispensing of international aid and assistance by the trades unions is carried out through the fourth level of trades union abstraction: the international labour organisations. These international labour bodies provide the structure for international activity and are important vehicles for the political aspirations of the key protagonists. The origins and development of these internationals provides an important guide to the present-day structure of international unionism.

1 The Development of Political Internationalism

The first stage in the development of an international trades union movement was the creation of international links among the political organisations which claimed to speak on behalf of the European working classes. For the most part, these European socialist and anarchist political movements were instrumental in forming trades unions within their nations. Only in Britain, whose trades unions had united to form the Trades Union Congress (TUC) in 1868, did the unions antedate the political party. The TUC was in existence and politically active fully seventeen years before it voted to create its own party. Elsewhere in Europe, though, it was the parties who created the unions.

These socialist and anarchist parties had suffered during the wave of repression which followed the 1848 uprisings. Many survived underground. There were large numbers of political exiles. An important number of anarchist and socialist activists met in London in 1864 to found an international organisation to co-ordinate their efforts at gaining recognition from their own and foreign governments. This new organisation, the International Workingmen's Association (better known as the First International or the Black International), was inspired and led by two formidable activists who personified the forces within the European left: Karl Marx and Mikhail Bakunin. It was Marx who wrote the drafts of the inaugural address and its provisional rules.

The delegates to this first international were a motley assembly. The most numerous were the British unionists, hostile to socialism, anarchism and revolution; deeply involved in Liberal politics. There were delegates from the republican democrats of France; followers of Mazzini from Italy; Proudhonist anarchists from the Jura; and exiled revolutionaries and activists from all over Europe. The two main streams of ideological thought centred around the persons and programmes of Marx and Bakunin. The anarchists, led by Bakunin, rejected the demands of the socialists for a highly structured and centralised organisation, but the Marxian socialists initially gained control of the international at its first official congress in Geneva in 1865. The anarchists continued to gain support within the international and Marx, fearing a takeover by the anarchists, moved the headquarters to New York in 1872 to keep it out of their hands. The First International lingered on in New York until 1879 but played a very minor role once it moved out of Europe.

The accomplishments of the First International were negligible. This was not only because the political activists and their parties were weak and disorganised, but also because the range of ideologies included in its membership virtually guaranteed disagreement on any matter of policy. The First International could not even get a clearcut agreement on whether it should support the rise of the Paris Commune 1871. It did serve, however, as a first step towards linking the Left across national borders and provided a useful starting-point for subsequent efforts at 'solidarity'.

The disappearance of the First International did not mean that trades unionism was dead or retarded. It reached a high pitch of activity across Europe and North America in the 1880s. It was in this period that the often disparate national unions began to join together to form national centres. A prime area of growth was the United States where the Knights of Labour were very important in that, for the first time, a labour organisation was formed which accepted into membership both skilled and unskilled workers. The Knights became a potent political force within the US and began organising international branches. In the mid-1880s the Knights of Labour set up assemblies in England (Sunderland), in Belgium (Charleroi, Jumet and Brussels), in Australia, New Zealand and in Ireland.

The success of the Knights in building a strong national organisation in the US was viewed as a threat by the craft unions and their municipal assemblies. These craft union bodies followed the political lead of Adolph Strasser and Samuel Gompers and united to form a Federation of Organized Trades and Labour Unions. This new organisation was anti-socialist, anti-Knight and careful to remain non-partisan in political activities. In 1886 this Federation joined with the Carpenters' Union of Peter McGuire in calling for a peaceful demonstration of support for the introduction of the eight-hour day. They met at the McCormick harvester plant in Chicago where a clash between demonstrators and the police left four dead. The following day labour radicals called a protest demonstration in Haymarket Square at which a bomb exploded and the police opened fire. The demonstrators fired back. There were seven policemen killed and sixty-seven wounded. Four workers were killed and some fifty wounded. Although no one knew who threw the bomb, several anarchist leaders were arrested and sentenced to death. Six were executed and two were given long sentences. A wave of sympathy towards these men and their supporters swept across the world. Telegrams and letters seeking a stay of execution poured into Chicago from trades union, socialist and anarchist groups from around the globe. Despite their lack of success in staying the execution numerous groups on the Left adopted the day of the Haymarket explosion, 1 May, as a day of worker's solidarity.

One other result of this international campaign to support the Haymarket anarchists was the renewal of the idea of creating an international structure to co-ordinate the campaign for socialism. Despite aborted attempts between 1881 and 1889 towards this end, the May Day demonstrations provided the link which united the various socialist organisations in a Paris congress which built an International Socialist Bureau. This new international, best known as the Second International or the Socialist International, united the European socialist and social democratic parties in a loose confederation.

The Second International was created during a period in which European socialist and social democratic parties were emerging into legitimacy and power. These parties, except in Britain, were also the dominant powers in their national trades union movements. Membership in the unions was contingent upon membership in the party. In Sweden, for example, the constitution of the trades union federation required compulsory membership in the Swedish social democratic party. Throughout Europe the socialist and social democratic parties were umbrella organisations for a host of socialist organisations. In countries like Austria or Germany the socialists built their own separate societies: with socialist book clubs, hiking clubs, singing societies, socialist housing co-operatives and cultural societies. There were socialist newspapers, socialist drama societies and socialist schools. For many of the socialist unionists, the trades union was only one of a number of socialist organisations to which they belonged.

Within this context, the socialist parties of Europe, except for Britain and the 'Hirsch–Duncker' unions ('bread and butter unions' of Germany), dominated and directed their trades union movements. The trades union movements were seen as fulfilling an economic role in the regulation of the workplace and a political role in turning out bodies for demonstrations. There was considerable movement between the leadership of the union and the party but with promotion leading to political posts rather than conversely.

As more members began to join unions this balance between trades union and party began to alter. Workers soon discovered that they had an economic interest in self-help and solidarity which focused their concentration on the first two levels of trades unionism; the workplace and the national union. Workers with economic interests at stake grew unwilling to stop work or occupy their plants in the cause of an abstract political principle or cause. The trades unions found that they had real interests distinct from party interests. They began to create national centres as a method of pressing forward their separate identities.

As early as 1886 the craft unions in the US formed the American Federation of Labour (AFL) as the major national centre. The French General Confederation of Labour (CGT) was formed in 1895. In 1898 the Belgian Labour Party created its own national centre. The German social democratic unions formed a general commission in 1890 which provoked the formation of a Catholic workers's federation in 1894. The programme of the German socialists developed in Erfurt in 1891 became a guidebook for socialist parties across Europe and set the pattern for union–party relations.

In Britain, the pattern was different. The conservatism of the more purely craft union leadership altered after the dock strike of 1889. New unions were formed which united skilled, semi-skilled and even unskilled workers into the new general workers' unions. Trades union and socialist activists demanded that the TUC adopt a programme which would include creating a socialist party, but these pleas were rejected on the grounds that the interests of the working classes were already represented within the Liberal Party. After the Taff Vale decision and the introduction of a broader ideological appeal to socialism by the Fabians and their allies, the British unions voted for a Labour Representation Committee in the 1906 general election. The election of several candidates created a Parliamentary Labour Party. Membership in this Labour Party was by membership in the unions and the co-operatives with no provision for individual affiliation. Dues were collected by the unions and the TUC directed and supported the Labour Party. It seconded its leaders to party offices and nominated candidates for parliamentary seats.

The Second International attempted to create a unity among these diverse political parties. At its inception it joined together the powerful socialist parties of Germany, Austria, Sweden and the British Labour

Party along with the socialist national organisations of Belgium, Holland and France. There were scores of smaller socialist factions from Eastern and Southern Europe which attached themselves to the Second International in an effort to gain recogniton and support in their internecine political battles. The power in the organisation lay with the British, Austrian and German parties.

Power within international and national trades union and socialist organisations is largely dependent on membership, or at least paying membership. Each national delegation is accorded a certain number of delegates based upon its claimed membership. Dues, as well, are assessed on the claimed membership totals. This has meant that those national bodies willing to claim and pay on a large membership have more votes than those with a smaller membership. This has often meant that the largest and wealthiest of the national organisations constitute the governing bodies or committees which actually run the organisations between congresses. It was most frequently they who determined the policies and priorities of the organisations.

This was true of the Second International. The large British, Austrian and German parties were the dominant parties and largely determined the policies of the international. However, the strength of these parties proved to be the weakness of the organisation. One reason behind the strength of the British, Austrian and German parties was that they had gradually become intimately involved in their domestic governmental processes. Their leaders held important positions within their national assemblies. As the situation in Europe became grave and war seemed imminent in 1913-14, the parliamentary representatives of the major socialist and labour parties voted for the provision of war credits for their national governments. They chose to fulfil their national obligations rather than to obey the strident calls for socialist internationalism and pacifism issued by the more radical elements of the socialist movements.

These radical socialists who advocated voting against the war credits were mainly revolutionary socialists operating in exile and powerless within their own nations. Not only were they opposed to voting war credits, they were opposed to not being asked. They demanded more militantly revolutionary policies from their fellow socialists to assist them into power. They met at Zimmerwald in 1915 and at Kienthal the following year under the leadership of Lenin to try and build a revolutionary international.

Revolutionary socialism was not a new phenomenon. Periodic outbreaks of political violence were a fairly familiar occurrence, but

Development of Political Internationalism 11

never on a truly mass scale. The forces of reaction were always more powerful than the forces of revolution, principally because they included the armed forces and the police. This situation changed dramatically when the forces of revolution had a state, complete with an army and police force, it could call its own. The chaos of the First World War was compounded by the revolution in Russia and the civil war which followed it. Socialist and revolutionary parties in many nations were galvanised by the success of the Russian revolutionaries. Many sought to support the revolutionaries in their struggles.

As early as 1916 the 'Revolutionary Shop Stewards' of Berlin led political strikes to persuade the Kaiser to grant concessions to the Russian revolutionaries suing for peace. They led similar strikes in support of the Russian position at the treaty signing at Breast–Litovsk in 1918. Similar strikes were undertaken by revolutionary socialists in Vienna and Budapest the same year. The success of the Russian revolutionaries changed the political topography of Europe – most especially for non-communist socialists.

Efforts to restore normalcy within European politics after the war were made more difficult because of the Russian revolution. In Bavaria, Eisner and Landauer attempted to emulate the Russian example by creating a short-lived soviet state in Germany. Romanian troops marched into Hungary to suppress the abortive soviet state declared by Bela Kun. The naval mutiny at Kiel in 1918, which forced the abdication of the Kaiser, ushered in a period of revolutionary radicalism in Germany. Workers' and soldiers' soviets sprang up to sieze control of several German municipalities. The German Social Democrats were gradually able to restore order and hold free elections only at the cost of alienating the more revolutionary wings of their party. These revolutionaries of the Spartacist movement, led by Karl Liebknecht and Rosa Luxemburg, attempted to set up their own government. It was brutally supressed by the army and the Freikorps.

Throughout Europe the socialists and social democratic parties which had played such an important role within their national assemblies before and during the First World War were faced with deep schisms within their own movements as to how they should best proceed. They were torn by the need to continue their progress towards the goal of control of their governments through the democratic process and the conflicting demand by substantial sections of their own movement to abandon parliamentary gradualism in favour of revolution. This choice was often difficult.

The fear of revolutionary contagion was very strong in Europe as many nations agreed to build a 'cordon sanitaire' around Russia in an effort to isolate communism of the Bolshevik type within Russia. For the most part, the European trades union movements were willing to cooperate with their governments in this programme. It was they who had the most to lose by revolution. They would lose their jobs, their gains, and their legitimacy as the spokespersons for the working classes. By then the communists had made it clear that the enemies of communism were not only the capitalists and their minions but also the non-revolutionary socialists who were competing with the communists for the right to speak on behalf of the working classes.

In March 1919 the Bolsheviks called an important international congress of revolutionary parties and communist supporters, designed to build a new international political organisation: a communist international. This new international, the Third International (better known as the Communist International or Comintern) met in Moscow and was attended by delegates from the various Russian republics and two foreign delegates (Eberlein of Germany and Steinhardt of Austria). Despite the opposition voiced on behalf of the foreign parties by Eberlein, the new Comintern adopted a fiercely sectarian programme. It issued a manifesto demanding the dictatorship of the proletariat and the need to do battle against the socialist parties of Europe.

Russian communists set out to do battle with the European socialist parties, singling out for attack the British Independent Labour Party, the German Social Democratic Party and the French Socialists. The Comintern pressed for ideological conformity among its adherents and set itself up as the spiritual guide for all parties of the left. The Comintern's manifesto included a twenty-one point programme which had to be adopted by all its affiliates as a requirement for their admission and continued membership.

The most important of these points dealt with the need for communist parties and organisations to do battle with the socialists for control of the trades unions. Communists were required to fight against reformism and sever any ties between them and reformist parties or groups. They were directed to form communist nuclei within existing trades union organisations to gain control of these organisations and to prevent their participation in any international union organisations organised by the socialists. They were told to agitate against their armed forces and to refuse to produce or transport munitions or supplies destined for enemies of the soviet republic. Communists were required to form unions in the colonial territories and to agitate ceaselessly against colonialism.

There were strict organisational requirements as well. Even in those nations which permitted a legal communist party to operate, the Comintern directed that the communist parties create and maintain a parallel covert party organisation 'capable at the decisive moment of fulfilling its duty to the revolution'. Similarly, the parties had to agree to periodic purges of the membership of those elements unwilling to follow the political line laid down by Moscow. This policy of 'democratic socialism' also meant the purge of all bourgeois elements from party posts and membership. To assure strict control over these programmes the Comintern assigned a representative, known as the 'Moscow rep', to each major national party. It was his task to assure party discipline and to mediate factional disputes. In those cases in which the Moscow rep found himself unable to restore discipline the Comintern sent out orders for the disputants to come to Moscow where the Russian party was the final arbiter.

The aims of the Comintern in setting forth the twenty-one points were clear. Their primary concern was the use of foreign communist parties to split the forces of socialism into parties loyal to Moscow and those who were not. By this they sought to secure the safety of the new communist state in Russia by either provoking revolution elsewhere or by severely diminishing the willingness of Russia's enemies to contemplate military action against Russia, by threatening internal disruption by forces loyal to and directed by the Russian Communist Party.

Throughout the history of the Comintern there was one clear policy which transcended its many shifts in policy and direction: the primacy of the Russian Communist Party and the needs of the Russian state. The Comintern and the many organisations under Comintern control (the communist 'front' organisations) were established, funded and directed as an integral part of the soviet Russian foreign policy. The controversies which emerged in the international communist movement arose primarily when national Communist Party policies and aspirations conflicted with soviet foreign policy objectives.

The forces of socialism reacted quickly to this challenge by the Comintern. At the request of the British Labour Party, an international conference of socialist parties was convened in Berne where the Second International was reconstituted. This Second International played an important role in the Versailles Peace Treaty negotiations and succeeded in creating an International Labour Organisation (ILO) under the auspices of the League of Nations. The debate within the European socialist parties over whether to accept the twenty-one points of the Comintern or to rejoin the Second International led to many splits and divisions. One important group of European socialists, including the remnants of the dwindling numbers of European anarchist movements, attempted to bridge the gulf between the socialists and the communists. This 'Marxian centre', led by Friedrich Adler and Otto Bauer of Austria, Leon Blum of France and Otto Hilferding of Germany, was able to cobble together an international organisation of its own. This new international, the International Association of Workers (best known as the Two and One-Half International) had a membership of about two hundred thousand with affiliates in Spain, Germany, France, Holland, Sweden, Portugal and the US. Its attempts to bridge the two rival currents of socialism and communism failed and the organisation dissolved in 1923. Most of its members rejoined the Second International. The rest, primarily the anarchists, joined the Comintern.

These political internationals provide the background for the development of the formation of the international trades union movement.

2 Early Trades Union International Organisations

Even as national centres were growing in the late 1880s, craft unionists attending the meetings of the first and second internationals discovered that there were issues of mutual concern which they shared with fellow craft unionists from foreign nations. Across Europe, employers were introducing new techniques of production, new systems of work assignment and new methods of compensation. These craft unionists first began to meet informally at these larger union gatherings to discuss their union's response to the new challenges. Then they began to create international information clearinghouses to disseminate their shared information to other unions within the same craft. These new organisations were called International Trades Secretariats (or ITSs for short). Each major craft developed its own ITS. By the beginning of the First World War there were thirty-three of these international trades secretariates in operation.

These ITSs were known as 'postbox internationals' because their major role was to collect and disseminate information about the latest developments in the trade to its affiliates. The affiliates of the ITSs were not national centres: they were national (or occasionally regional) craft unions with jurisdiction in a particular trade or craft. Despite the fact that most of them were socialist or social democratic in orientation, their activities within the ITS structure were designed to promote practical and pragmatic projects, rather than the achievement of some ideological goal. They shared information; they extended assistance during strikes; they prevented their workers handling struck goods; they created international mechanisms for recognising union membership cards (of considerable value for workers in transport and itinerant crafts). Some ITSs maintained a hiring centre for qualified journeymen. Others, especially in international shipping and transport, enforced minimum standards or wages and working conditions for those employed in their trades.

The first stirrings of an international trades union movement based on national centres emerged from the Copenhagen labour congress in 1901. There the several Scandinavian union delegates were joined by leading trades unionists from the national centres of Germany, Belgium and Great Britain, who were invited as fraternal delegates. These national centre discussions, separate and apart from the deliberations of the Second International, were considered very useful and an appeal for a further meeting of representatives of national centres was held in Stuttgart the following year. The unionists meeting in Stuttgart decided to create an international organisation of trades union national centres parallel to the Second International. The German hosts, once they were convinced that this new organisation would not be in conflict with the Second International, agreed to take the necessary steps for the founding of the organisation. They created a temporary secretariat which worked for a year to plan the organisation: a plan which they presented to the establishment meeting in Dublin. This new organisation, the International Trades Union Secretariat (ITUS), was attached to the German trades union national centre under the leadership of Karl Legien. It was headquartered in Berlin and drew much of its resources from the Germans.

The relationship between the ITUS and the Second International was very close, primarily because the ITUS unions were drawn from the ranks of the socialist and social democratic unions. This closeness diminished as the unions gradually established their separate identities from the political parties. This gradual separation between union and party was hastened by the expansion of the national centres to include unionists whose political loyalties lay elsewhere than the Second International. In France, for example, the new French national centre, the CGT united the Marxian socialists with the strong French syndicalist movement. Together they agreed the Charter of Amiens in 1906 which established the CGT as an independent organisation, free from any ties to any particular party or ideology. Even in the very heart of socialist orthodoxy, the German trades union movement, the party and the unions signed the Mannheim Declaration which effectively gave equal footing to the national centre and the SPD.

This ITUS was, initially, a purely European affair. The organised unions of the US affiliated to the AFL were chary of joining an international labour body which included socialist parties and revolutionary socialists like those of the French, Italian or Spanish national centres. The AFL rejected socialism and revolution not only on ideological grounds but also for the immensely practical reason that the socialists, and revolutionary socialists in particular, were competing with the AFL unions for control of US labour. The peaceful growth of the craft unionism of the AFL contrasted sharply with the increasingly bitter battles of the emerging industrial unions forming outside the AFL in brewing, coal mining, metal mining and the railways. These industrial unions were considered a threat to the AFL. At the turn of the century the AFL was the recognised spokesperson of US labour although it represented only about 5 per cent of the wage labour force. There were almost as many workers organised in non-AFL unions.

The battle for recognition by these non-AFL unions was frequently a battle not only with the employer but also with the forces of the state, in the form of the armed forces or the police force. The battle at the Homestead Steel strike in 1892 saw armed clashes between locked-out workers and armed Pinkerton guards. Later the same year, at Coal Creek, Cour, d'Alene and Tracy City armed strikers fought armed company guards. The most significant battle which had the effect of radicalising large sectors of the US workforce was the struggle by Eugene Debs' American Railroad Union (ARU) and the Pullman Company in 1894. Their attempt to use union muscle to prevent the railroads from using struck Pullman carriages led to Federal intervention with troops: an intervention that left over thirty strikers dead in one day in Chicago. When Debs asked the AFL railroad unionists for support and asked the AFL to call a general strike, Gompers told Debs that the AFL was neutral. In the aftermath of the radicalisation of many workers in the turmoil of 1894, a new labour organisation was formed as a rival to the AFL: the Industrial Workers of the World (IWW).

In 1905 the labour radicals of the Western Federation of Miners, the leaders of its parent union the American Labour Union (ALU) and the two socialist party factional leaders, Debs and Deleon, met to form the IWW, a militantly radical union dedicated to continuous confrontation with the capitalist system. Its radicalism contrasted sharply with the AFL's policy of 'rewarding our friends and punishing our enemies'. The conflict between the IWW and the AFL was intense as each accused the other of dual unionism and unfair tactics.

The IWW did not restrict its organising to the US alone. It was very successful in Canada where it set up the 'One Big Union' movement. It sent its organisers around the world in an effort to assist radical unionists in their efforts to build industrial unionism. The labour histories of countries as diverse as Argentina, Australia, South Africa or India are replete with examples of IWW organisers paying visits and remaining to found chapters of the IWW. The IWW made contact with socialist movements in Europe and particularly with the more revolutionary socialists of the French, Spanish, Italian or Russian national labour movements. Through them, they began to participate in the work of the ITUS and the Second International.

The initial welcome extended to the IWW by the European socialists and trades unionists disturbed not only the AFL but also the British TUC and the German national centre. The British, just beginning to assert themselves as an important domestic political force in the newborn Labour Party did not want the spectre of labour revolution to be attached to the organisations in which it played such an important role. The Germans, too, did not favour the idea of labour radicalism. These two groups persuaded Gompers to attend the ITUS Congress in 1909 as a fraternal delegate (a visitor from a non-affiliated organisation). The AFL was under strong pressure to affiliate, if only to keep the IWW from being accepted into membership. When it came to a vote, the powerful battalions of the British and Germans lined up behind the AFL and affiliated the first non-European member to the ITUS. Since only one national centre from each nation was permitted to affiliate (a rule designed primarily against the Christian unionists), the IWW was left outside. One of the first acts of the AFL was to demand a name change away from the term 'secretariat' which they said was unknown to the US unionists. They wanted a federation in which each nation's autonomy was guaranteed. At the next congress, in Zurich in 1913, this was agreed and the organisation became known as the International Federation of Trades Unions (IFTU).

The IFTU suffered severe difficulties from its inception. For a major trades union international, headquartered in Berlin and under the control of Karl Legien of the German national centre, the outbreak of war between Germany and much of the rest of Europe posed severe internal difficulties; not the least of which was Legien's contention that there was no problem at all. When the Dutch national centre demanded that the secretariat be moved to a neutral country for the duration of the war, Legien refused. He offered a compromise which would grant special powers to Jan Oudegeest to act as a neutral intermediary between the IFTU and those nations with whom Germany was at war. The British and French leaders disagreed and, with the support of Gompers of the AFL, demanded that the IFTU be moved to Berne immediately. Legien continued to refuse so the trades union leaders of the French,

Belgian, Italian and British national centres met in Leeds in 1916 and set up a separate bureau in Paris.

With the entry of the United States into the war and the increasing involvement of the AFL in a national programme of co-operation with the Wilson government, the battle between AFL unionists and the socialists in the US became intense. The socialists, most of whom remained adamantly anti-war even after the US entry, became even more of a threat in the eyes of the AFL after the victory of the Bolsheviks in 1917. The 'foreignness' of many of these socialists and their nascent industrial unions left them open to severe repression by the forces of the government. The passage of legislation like the Espionage laws led to a major crackdown on the activities of the socialists, the IWW, and their union bodies. This was coupled with vigilante activities on the part of local law enforcers. The Federal government made a wholesale arrest of the top 166 leaders of the IWW. This presaged the famous Palmer Raids where government forces raided union and socialist party offices in an effort to suppress Bolshevism. The record arrest was the one night total in New York of over 5000 workers whose offences fell into the extremely broad category of misdeeds covered by the Deportation Act of 1918. As might be imagined, much of the militant unionism which characterised the pre-war era went underground: the IWW was virtually dead due to decapitation, and the surviving AFL grew even less willing to associate itself with socialist or radical unions.

The national centres of the allied powers were interested in building a role for themselves in the creation of a framework for the eventual peace negotiations. They chaired many joint study committees on inter-allied war aims and participated in their own national political arenas by eliminating holdups in war production. In September 1918 they met in London to endorse the Fourteen Point proposal by President Wilson. This co-operation with other national labour movements, however, did not dissipate the strong AFL antagonism to socialists or other political organisations. When the British Labour movement (both the trades unions and the party) called for a meeting in Berne after the armistice to reconstitute the IFTU and the Second International, the AFL refused to attend, basing its disagreement on the pairing of the two. Gompers said that trades union internationalism was not a 'side-show' and that much as Lenin had challeneged world socialism when he created the Third International, the AFL was challenging world socialism by demanding a purely trades union international.

The conference at Berne took place with the Americans and Belgians absent. The allies proposed a labour international conference to be held in Amsterdam in July 1919. At the Amsterdam conference there was the reconstitution of the IFTU as a major labour body. Attending the Amsterdam congress were the national centres of Austria, Belgium, Czechoslovakia, Denmark, France, Germany, Great Britain, Holland, Luxembourg, Norway, Spain, Sweden, Switzerland and the US. All but the US national centre affiliated. Appleton of the British TUC was made President; Jouhaux (France) and Martens (Belgium) were made Vice-Presidents; and the two Dutch unionists, Fimmen and Oudegeest, were named international secretaries in the new headquarters in Amsterdam. This Amsterdam congress also gave approval for the participation of its delegates in the peace-making process and the deliberation which would accompany the debate on the peace treaty.

Labour did participate in the peace treaty discussions. The leaders of the allied powers appointed a fifteen-man commission to study the problems of labour and social policy in the treaty. This commission, on which sat four prominent trades unionists (Jouhaux – France; Vanderveld – Belgium; Barnes – Britain; and Gompers – US), recommended the creation of a separate international organisation responsible for labour and social policy. It became an autonomous organisation under the umbrella of the League, composed of four delegates from each nation affiliated to it. On it were two representatives from the national government and one representative each from the employer and union organisations chosen by the government. These delegates have one vote and pass conventions on labour and social policy which are sent to their national parliaments for ratification. This new organisation, the International Labour Organisation (ILO), has continued in this form until the present. What is especially important in the way in which the ILO is constituted is that it permits groupings of workers and employers to form which transcend national limits. There are Workers' Groups on a number of topics as well as Government and Employers' Groups. The ILO is one of the very few areas in which the several competing trades union political factions meet, interact and share a common platform on issues which affect working people. The ILO and the other UN bodies are important areas of interaction for the international trades union and other non-governmental bodies.

While the IFTU was being reconstituted, the Christian unions in Europe were under pressure from Catholic and Liberal parties to expand their international ties. The political parties under Christian control in Germany, Italy, Belgium, Holland and France encouraged their Christian national centres to create a Christian international labour movement. In the early days of 1908 they formed an

International Committee and an International Secretariat. In 1919 the Christian unionists of Belgium, Italy, Latvia, Lithuania and Spain met in Paris to try and reconstitute the international committee. Later that year in Lucerne, the German, Austrian, Dutch and German-speaking Swiss joined together for a similar aim. Under the aegis of the Dutch unionists a conference was called in the Hague in 1920, which united these two groups into the International Federation of Christian Trades Unions (best known by its French initials – CISC). The CISC attempted to build rival ITSs in the various crafts and sought, with no success, to gain direct representation at the ILO (since the IFTU had control of the labour seats on the governing body). The CISC upheld the doctrine of Christian justice. It condemned socialism and communism. It advocated systematic collaboration of the classes. Although, with the exception of Holland, Christian unionists never won a majority of the workers organised in trades unions, they nonetheless were important organisations by virtue of their close ties with their parties. They were a constant thorn in the side of the affiliates of the IFTU and weakened the credibility of the socialist unions in their efforts to become recognised as the sole voice of the working classes. The Christians and socialists competed for members, for recognition by the employer, and for control of the votes of the European working classes.

This competition for members and influence was not the only challenge to the IFTU affiliates. A far more dangerous foe was created in July 1920 when the leaders of the Comintern called a meeting of the revolutionary trades union organisations of Russia, France, Spain, Italy, Georgia, Bulgaria and Yugoslavia in Moscow. There they created a new organisation of international trades unions, the Red Trades Union International (best known by its Russian appellation – Profintern). The Profintern convened in Moscow in 1921 under the auspices of the Comintern and constituted itself as an international of communist and, initially, some anarcho-syndicalist, unions dedicated to the creation of the dictatorship of the proletariat, the struggle against reformism in trades unions, the battle against the IFTU and the ILO, and the building of communist party cells in trades union organisations around the world. They endorsed the twenty-one conditions of the Comintern and called for the establishment in every country of a practical liaison between the red trades unions and the Communist Party. Like Comintern, the Profintern was created to be the labour arm of the Soviet foreign policy apparatus.

The activities of the Profintern consisted primarily of trying to 'bore from within' in the trades unions outside Russia to build a communist cell loyal to the dictates of the Comintern leadership which could effectively block any attack being mounted against Russia. In the words of Lenin, the Profintern recommended 'the use of all strategems and artifices, the adoption of illegal methods, occasional silence, occasional concealment of the truth, for the sole purpose of penetrating the trade unions, staying there and still carrying out the communist assignment'.[1]

In fact, despite a great deal of rhetoric and excitement over the many and often startling reverses in the direction of the party line, the effects of Profintern policies were negligible. The main effects of the successes were in the early days of Bolshevism when the shop stewards organised a viable, albeit temporary, opposition within the plants to the unions which they ostensibly represented.

The revolutionary shop stewards of Berlin were soon crushed but the growth of the British Shop Stewards' Movement in the early 1920s created a precedent for the derogation of local power by the unions to their shop steward organisations: a condition which still applies in some contemporary British unions. In other cases, the shop stewards and loyalists of the party cells acted as espionage agents for the Russian state, relaying information on the types of production, production designs, and levels of orders in their plants, factories or offices to their local Moscow 'rep'. A good example was the 'Fantomas Affair' which came to a head in 1932.[2] Then it was revealed that the Profintern had developed a network of 'correspondents' of over 3000 in number in France, who reported to the *Parti Communiste Français* (PCF) various information about their workplaces. In the course of such reports the 'rabcors' (from the Russian term for labour correspondents) revealed classified information which would be passed directly back to Moscow. In the 'Fantomas' affair a prominent PCF leader and local Moscow rep, Jacques Duclos, was revealed as the leader of this network.

The ideological conflicts which divided the unions of the IFTU, the CISC and the Profintern were important in the later formation of trades union internationalism but were not really as debilitating as problems of the world-wide depression of the 1930s. Until 1935, internationalism played only a secondary role in the development of trades unionism. Internationalism among trades unions, largely as the result of Bolshevik rhetoric, was used as a convenient albatross to hang around the neck of any unionist incautious enough to raise it as a cause. The events in Germany, Italy Austria and Spain in the mid-1930s had a profound effect in reuniting the fissures in the international trades union movement and gave a new respectability to the activities of this movement. Faced with the forcible dissolution of trades unions in these nations and the likelihood of another world war developing, the nations of the West and the Soviet Union drew closer. The AFL rejoined the IFTU in 1937 and the Profintern dissolved. The Russians ordered their communist adherents around the world to seek an alliance with the forces of socialism and social democracy. They formed Popular Fronts against fascism. This cohesion lasted as long as it took Stalin to agree to the pact with Germany in 1939.

The ambivalent role which communist unions played was best illustrated in France. There, the CGT, which had been reunited in the wake of the Popular Front, soon split again over the Russian invasion of Poland after the signing of the Russian–German Pact. The PCF unionists sabotaged French war production, militated against national defence, and sought to assist the Nazis even when France itself was occupied. When the Nazis occupied Paris and suppressed the free operation of political parties and trades unions the PCF won the right to resume publishing their daily paper *L'Humanité* which the French government had banned in 1939. The role of the PCF in the period 1939–41, as well as the role its adherents played in the CGT, is now largely forgotten by the French working classes. When French Resistance fighters attacked the German occupation forces in the early days of 1940, the leaders of the PCF publicly deplored the Resistance and issued declarations against it which the Nazis circulated. The CGT and the Christian CFTC refused to allow the PCF unionists to participate in their activities in the Resistance until late 1943. The PCF supported the Nazis and the German occupation until 22 June 1941 when Hitler invaded the Soviet Union, thus breaking the former pact. The attack on the Soviet Union by the Nazis signalled a rapid 'about face' by communist parties and unionists across the world. Then, fascism became the enemy and communists began to participate in the resistance movements.

During the war the socialists and the communists joined together, albeit unwillingly, in the underground movement to overthrow fascism. In this effort they were aided by the governments of the allied powers. This aid was substantial and included funds, printing machinery, weapons, radio equipment and implements for sabotage. Trades union experts were drafted into the military intelligence corps of the US, British and Commonwealth armies. The Soviets already had labour experts employed in this function. These allied trades union experts operated covertly in occupied Europe and openly in the headquarters of the several armies in Britain and Russia. The experiences already gained by these labour experts in the efforts to win the support of the Spanish working classes during the recent Civil War served them well in these new European operations. The Axis powers also created a special department which dealt with labour problems in the occupied nations, both in the overt side of drafting forced labour into German industry as well as in a more covert side which dealt with the smooth operation of Nazi-like labour fronts in these areas. Most importantly, a special section of the military intelligence set-up was directed at covert penetration of allied labour movements to gather defence information, to sabotage production when necessary and to provoke labour unrest in an effort to slow up production. Some surprising personages became identified with this effort, not the least well-known of whom was John L. Lewis of the United Mineworkers of America (UMW).

The outbreak of war saw the IFTU lose its major affiliates in Spain, Germany, Austria, Czechoslovakia, as well as in the conquered nations of France, Belgium, Holland, Poland, Norway, Finland and many others. ITSs lost the bulk of their affiliates. The IFTU and the ITSs moved to Great Britain where they received funds and support from the British TUC (as well as funds from the British and US governments). By the end of 1940, the British TUC had become the virtual custodian of the international labour movement.

The British TUC, despite its strong support for the IFTU and the ITSs, also engaged in some major international labour activities outside the sphere of these organisations. The TUC General Secretary, Walter Citrine, who was also president of the IFTU, had arranged an Anglo-French Trades Union Council in 1939 to assist the French CGT. The occupation by Germany soon ended the effective work of the committee. In 1941, shortly after the attack on Russia and Russia's late entry into the war, the British TUC called for a meeting with the Soviet AUCCTU (All-Union Central Confederation of Trades Unions) in order to exchange views and information on problems. Meeting in Moscow in October 1941, they formed an Anglo-Soviet Trades Union Council. At the second meeting in 1942, the TUC suggested that the AFL be approached in an effort to include the leadership of the American unions in the work of the council. In the actual wording, however, the invitation spoke of 'representatives of the American Labour Movement', a term which then did not necessarily include only the AFL.

By 1940 the AFL was not the only recognised trades union national centre in the US. In the face of the great depression in the 1930s in the US, a wave of organisation of industrial unions began; a militant organisation of workers who used sit-down strikes and the threat of class war to build a union movement which was organised by the industry, from the sweepers up to the tool-and-die men. By 1935 the AFL could not tolerate their continuous rank-and-file strikes and called for a vote of its affiliates on whether they should maintain craft union status. The majority voted to stay a craft organisation and the minority, under the leadership of the UMW's John L. Lewis, met with the leaders of the Typographers' Union, the Ladies Garment Workers' Union, the Hat and Millinery Workers' Union and created the Committee for Industrial Organisation. The Mine, Mill and Smelters' Union and the Oil Field Workers joined with them. The following year, at the Tampa Convention, Matthew Woll and William Green of the AFL ordered the suspension of the opposing unions. The same year these unions organised themselves as the Congress of Industrial Organisations (CIO). The rivalry between the two bodies was intense. Each organised against the other. New unions were formed where no unions had ever succeeded: in steel, in the auto plants and in the rubber plants. These new industrial organisations staged sit-ins at Akron and at Flint. By 1938 CIO membership was over four million.

In May 1942, when Citrine came to the US to approach the US labour movement with a proposal to join in the work of the Anglo-Soviet Trades Union Council, he met with both the AFL and the CIO representatives. As he expected, the AFL wanted no part of any organisation in which communists, especially Russian communists, were members. Equally, it wanted no part in any joint membership with the CIO or the independent Railroad Brotherhoods. The AFL offered to create an Anglo-American Union Committee on which the British and American unionists would have equal representation. When this proposal was presented to the Anglo-Soviet Council it was rejected by the Russians who wanted a direct tie with the US and who wished to foster closer links with the CIO which was making a major effort for world-wide recognition as the legitimate voice of US labour. Citrine returned to the US in 1943 and tried to get the AFL to agree to a joint committee with the CIO, the Railroad Brotherhoods and the UMW. This the AFL flatly refused so Citrine agreed to the convening of a Joint Anglo-American Trades Union Committee on which the AFL was the sole member. When Citrine tried to justify this to the CIO he was told that the difficulties between the AFL and the CIO were a matter of internal US concern and that the TUC should not interfere. Accordingly, the General Council of the TUC tabled any action on the Joint Anglo-American Committee.

While these manoeuvres were proceeding, the CIO had also been active in attempting to set up its own international contacts. It attempted to affiliate directly to the IFTU, only to be blackballed by the AFL. When the CIO tried to become part of the ILO delegation, the AFL used its powerful political muscle with the government to reserve the ILO spot for an AFL representative. After 1941, however, the CIO and the AFL proceeded to lower the tensions which divided them and to work for a unity of sorts. The prime movers in this were the leaders of the communist-dominated unions of the CIO (the Mine, Mill, the Fur Workers, and the Maritime Workers). The CIO constantly pressed for a major conference of all allied labour movements which would join together the Soviet trades unions with the IFTU unionists in exile. The key to this lay in the TUC. Both the Russians and the CIO attacked Citrine for his apparent agreement to limit US labour involvement to the AFL. At the next meeting of the Anglo-Soviet Council the Russians demanded that an international trades union conference be called which would bring together all the trades unionists from the allied nations as well as those unionists representing the occupied nations (Yugoslavia, Poland, France, Czechoslovakia, Belgium, Holland, Norway, Greece). Citrine was outvoted in the TUC General Council and was instructed to send out invitations to fifty-five trades union national centres and unaffiliated national centres in thirty-one countries, to the IFTU, to the Latin American Confederation of Workers (CTAL) and to the sixteen ITSs.

It was important that the TUC issue this invitation as the IFTU and the ITSs could not call together unionists which were not affiliated to them. The TUC invitation was clear in stating that the conference was designed to be consultative and not binding. It was an effort by the TUC, with the strong support of the British government, to contain the demands for an Anglo-American-Soviet labour alliance (which would be dominated by the Russians and the CIO) and to attempt to recreate the IFTU. The meeting, called originally for June 1944, was delayed when the allied landing in Normandy took place. A new date was set for meeting: 6 February 1945. The AFL decided not to attend and, at the next meeting of the Anglo-Soviet Council, the Russians demanded that a Preparatory Committee consisting of TUC, AUCCTU and CIO delegates be charged with preparing the conference agenda. Although the TUC was able to maintain its position as the host of the conference, it did give way to the creation of the tripartite preparatory committee.

Before the actual World Trades Union Conference was scheduled to meet in London on 6 February, the General Secretary of the IFTU, Walter Schevenels, took the opportunity of calling together his affiliates who were in London for a meeting to discuss the future of the IFTU. The enmity of the AUCCTU, which accused the IFTU of being unrepresentative, and the enmity of the CIO, which accused the IFTU of being divisive, was coupled with the enmity of a new source, the French CGT. During the Resistance, the PCF cadres in the underground CGT were able to gain effective control of the movement. The final allied push on to Paris to effect its liberation was aided by a general strike called by the CGT and the CFTC, an event which saw the CGT assume the role of militant nationalist partisans; especially the PCF cadres within the union who attacked the former Vichyites for their collaboration. The PCF cadres had access to funds, to the journals of the movement, to a voice in the new coalition government and to trained manpower which had stayed behind in France. It was soon able to take charge of the executive committee of the CGT. This newly constituted CGT was hostile to the IFTU because it had rejected the approaches of the AUCCTU and had proven less than welcoming to communist unions.

As soon as the IFTU meeting began the CGT delegate attacked Schevenels for the lack of support given by the IFTU to trades unionists working underground during the war. Schevenels, supported by the TUC delegate, Hallsworth, rejected this charge which was also an attack on the TUC into whose care the IFTU had been consigned. The IFTU attempted to pre-empt the decisions to be taken later at the World Conference by offering to reconstitute itself by admitting the AUCCTU, by permitting more than one national centre, and by integrating the ITSs into the new organisation in an organic manner rather than in their customary consultative role. These compromises were not acted upon as the delegates did not wish to commit themselves until after the World Conference had met.

The Preparatory Committee had proposed some major changes in the structure for the World Conference. The TUC, as host of the meeting and as titular head of the IFTU, had assumed that there would be only one president at the meeting. The AUCCTU and the CIO demanded that there be a *troika* of the three national centres, reserving three vice-presidencies to France, China and Latin America. Whereas the British had continued to support the call for consensus voting, the AUCCTU and the CIO demanded a change in the Standing Orders which would permit three delegations to demand a roll-call vote in which each delegation would have one vote. This virtually ensured that the AUCCTU–CIO–CGT coalition could force a roll-call vote on any issue. While not very important in itself, the ability to call for a roll-call vote gave a legitimacy to a resolution passed which transcended the consultative nature of the conference. If the *troika* decided to create a new international organisation it would have, at least, the presumption of sanction for this from the assembled delegations.

The delegates from the world's trades union national centres met in London from 6 to 17 February 1945. They represented, or at least claimed to represent, over 50 million workers around the world. There were 135 delegates from forty national centres plus thirty observers. The IFTU, the CTAL and the ITSs had another seventeen delegates present, plus one observer. The neutral countries sent nine observers. The largest delegation was that of the AUCCTU which had thirty-five delegates and ten observers. The CIO, then claiming a membership of 6.2 million sent most of its top officers to the meeting. The twelve CIO delegates, led by Sidney Hillman, were split fairly evenly between communist and non-communist tendencies but the group of lawyers and public relations specialists who accompanied the delegation were largely from the circle of communist intellectuals which had attached itself to the CIO. The AFL, of course, did not attend.

The first item of business at the meeting was especially divisive. The AUCCTU demanded that the newly formed trades union national centres of Hungary, Romania, Finland, Bulgaria, Italy and 'Lublin' Poland be recognised and admitted. The CGT and the CTAL supported the Russians but the CIO was able to refer the matter to the Credentials Committee, thus blocking a divisive roll-call vote. Sidney Hillman took the floor and proposed the immediate creation of a new World Federation of Trades Unions. In this he was supported by the AUCCTU, the CGT and the CTAL. The TUC attempted to buy time to prevent an immediate dissolution of the IFTU and the ITSs. Citrine proposed a drafting committee for the new organisation to develop an acceptable constitution, effectively delaying action until later that year. The new World Trades Union Conference Committee which emerged lacked an established secretariat but power lay with the CIO–AUCCTU–CGT. It convened a congress to adopt the draft constitution for Paris in September 1945.

The Conference Committee at its first meeting in Paris in March 1945, created an Administrative Committee to press on with the draft constitution. This committee elected Louis Saillant of the CGT as its chairman. Saillant, though initially a member of the socialist wing of the CGT had, during the days of the Resistance, become closer to the communist CGT leadership. They convened again in Washington, DC and moved on to Oakland, California where the United Nations was being formed. Largely due to opposition by the US and the British government delegations to the UNO, the World Trades Union Conference was refused representation at the UNO except in a consultative capacity and was rejected for a place in the non-governmental ranks of the Economic and Social Committee. In Oakland, the Administrative Committee won agreement on the terms of the new constitution except for the controversial Article 13 which required the ITSs to subsume their status into departments of the new organisation. The leadership of the ITSs, especially J. H. Oldenbroek of the International Transport Workers' Federation (ITF) was very reluctant to go along with this development.

Meeting from 25 September 1945 to 3 October 1945, the 187 delegates from sixty-five organisations in fifty-six countries joined with the representatives of the ITSs, the CTAL, and the leadership of the Christians' CISC to pass the new constitution. Once this constitution was passed, they reconvened as the first congress of the World Federation of Trades Unions (WFTU). The CISC had left by this time, refusing to join in the organisation.

The WFTU claimed a membership of over 67,000,000. A large chunk of the membership was derived from the sudden creation of full-blown trades union movements in the wake of the Soviet occupation. Citrine was acerbic in his criticism of how, 'Phoenix-like from the ashes, there spring up trades unions with hundreds of thousands of members where formerly those particular countries counted their members only in hundreds'.[3] The TUC was caught between the British government on the one hand and the increasingly large contingent of the communist unionists within the TUC on the other. The position of the TUC was to delay activities. The TUC had long been working with the AFL and the allied intelligence organisations in providing assistance to trades unionists fighting underground in Europe, particularly through the ITF under the aegis of the former TGWU leader, Ernest Bevin, now Minister of Labour. The TUC was cautioned by the British government to move slowly in any open hostilities against the Russians for three reasons. The first, and probably the most important, was the tenuous position of the British on the 'colonial question'. The week before the February 1945 meeting in London the British TUC had called together a colonial trades union conference to try to gain recognition for these colonial trades unions in the new international structure. At the Paris meeting which created the WFTU the British brought with them unionists from the Empire. In fact, much to the disquiet of the AFL, fifteen of the WFTU's thirty-five founding countries were British colonies or dominions, seven of whom, at least, had no trades union movement at all to speak of (Sierra Leone, Northern Rhodesia, Gambia, Cyprus, Jamaica, the Gold

Coast and British Guiana). However, these affiliations did prevent the communist unions hurriedly organising trades unions in these nations and pressing their affiliation to the WFTU. The TUC's strategy was to pre-empt the affiliation of hostile unions from these nations. The question of British vulnerability on the colonial issue was made more intense as the nations of the Empire, notably in Asia, pressed for independence. Throughout its participation in the WFTU the TUC sought to shield the colonial labour and social policies from international scrutiny.

A second reason why the TUC was under pressure from the government not to anger or needlessly upset the Russians was the delicate position of the allies in finishing the war and in dividing up the liberated territories. The repression of the communist labour movements in Greece and Iran by pro-Western governments was raised in the WFTU but the TUC was able to mute the harshest criticisms. The third area of concern was the recognition that Britain, as an occupying power in Germany, would have to face serious confrontation with communist and pro-Russian trades union efforts in their occupation zones. They hoped to use the labour unity of the WFTU to assuage these problems.

Citrine demanded that the WFTU keep on the staff of the IFTU and fought against moving the headquarters to Paris, but to no avail. Shortly after, the General Council of the WFTU met to elect a general secretary. The TUC pushed for Schevenels to continue from his IFTU post but the CGT–AUCCTU–CIO alliance demanded that Saillant be named to this post. The TUC backed down when the *troika* promised to find a job for Schevenels. He was given the job of assistant general secretary along with two others (John Brophy of the CIO and Mikhail Tarasov of the AUCCTU). The WFTU located in Paris and began operations in November 1945 without the membership of the ITSs.

Almost from the outset, the WFTU was riven by the political strife of Cold War. The pressures of ideological confrontation outweighed any counter-pressures towards unity and the organisation foundered on the rocks of the Cold War. The international labour movement grew more intimately enmeshed with the growth of the labour–government nexus.

3 The Labour–Government Nexus

The intensification of the struggle between the communists and the other allies in the reconstruction of Europe and in the Third World was influenced, to a high degree, by the close co-operation which emerged during the Second World War between the forces of national unions and their respective governments. Unless this close working relationship on external policy is perceived, much of what has occurred since then in the field of international labour will be virtually unintelligible.

With the defeat of the allied armies on the continent in 1940, the headquarters of the IFTU and numerous ITSs were moved to London and set up their operations in Transport House. This put the TUC and its constituent union leaders in a very strong position. In July 1942, those ITSs which were still operating joined with the IFTU rump in London to form the Emergency International Trades Union Council (EITUC), a body which co-ordinated the wartime union effort out of its London headquarters. The TUC general secretary, Citrine, was also president of the IFTU and the EITUC. The major ITS still in operation was the International Transport Workers' Federation (ITF) which maintained contacts around the world out of its London headquarters.

The co-operation between the TUC and the government was not limited to the attempts at promoting a more efficient method of achieving high levels of war production. The presence in London of scores of European trades unionists in exile with contacts on the continent made another avenue of co-operation also attractive. The British, and later the other allies, created a network of undercover activities on the continent utilising exiled unionists and making good use of their contacts in key areas of the European economies. This included assembling intelligence on road and rail transport, weapons production, labour bottlenecks and the whole range of intelligence subjects necessary for the conduct of a war. Scores of unionists and socialist party workers, later followed by communists, were recruited to British intelligence and played a vital role in the war effort. The close relationship between British intelligence and unionists in the British colonies was not left untapped. Many overseas and colonial unionists played their part in attempting to prevent the war in the Pacific from degenerating into a series of national liberation struggles in colonies like India, Malaya, Burma and Singapore. As London became the heart of international intrigue during the war, trades unionists took on an ever-increasing role in the struggle for the liberation of Europe, Africa and the Pacific area. The trades unions, and the TUC in particular, assumed an important diplomatic role in the conduct of diplomacy between the nations.

As early as 1939, Citrine had established, on behalf of the British government, a closer link with the French labour movement – especially since the socialists of Blum were in power. The TUC and the French built an Anglo-French Trade Union Council, theoretically under the wing of the IFTU. With the occupation of half of France and the dissolution of trades unionism under Vichy, many of the French trades unionists joined the nascent Resistance and acted as important intelligence sources in France and in the French North African colonies. When the Nazis invaded the Soviet Union, the TUC was asked to attempt to re-establish contact with the All-Union Central Confederation of Trades Unions (AUCCTU), the Soviet national centre. They agreed to meet and, in Moscow in 1941, they formed an Anglo-Soviet Trades Union Council. This new Anglo-Soviet Council attempted to link up with the trades union movement of the US but met with a major obstacle: the refusal of the AFL to have any contact with the communist labour organisation.

The close government–union ties of the British TUC grew even closer with the Labour victory in the postwar election; especially as Ernest Bevin emerged as Foreign Secretary. These close ties resembled the very close working relationship between the AFL and the US government.

The ties between the AFL and the US government stretch back to the period of the earliest days of the AFL. Samuel Gompers, the 'father' of the AFL was instrumental in developing a programme for the mainstream of American labour which avoided any close ties between the trades unions and the political parties. Avoiding ties between parties and labour did not mean avoiding ties between labour and government though. Gompers was on close terms with Woodrow Wilson and acted for Wilson in some major international diplomatic efforts, including support of the Root Commission in its mission to support an anti-Bolshevik programme in Russia: later using the American Alliance for

Labour and Democracy to channel vital assistance to the new government of Kerensky. Gompers assisted in setting up the ILO and pursued an active anti-socialist and anti-communist policy by keeping the AFL away from any entanglements with international labour bodies led by socialists or social democrats. The AFL did not affiliate to the IFTU until shortly before the First World War and then only because the IWW looked as if it was going to be allowed to join. Its major area of activity in this early period of union–government co-operation was in Latin America. Much of the current AFL – CIO policies in this area can be traced to the early interactions of US labour and government in Latin America.

Gompers and the AFL were instrumental in setting up the Anti-Imperialist League, an organisation opposed to the US annexation of the former Spanish possessions of Cuba and the Phillipines. Although the Anti-Imperialist League lost the battle against annexation, Gompers sent out union organisers to the Phillipines, Hawaii and Puerto Rico to assist unionists there. This experience in building unions on the AFL model in the newly annexed territories spurred the AFL to expound a 'Monroe Doctrine' for labour in Latin America. Gompers and the AFL played a very important role in the development of Latin American unionism, particularly in Mexico, and, as a result of its successes (often against the wishes of substantial segments of the American government) won the confidence of Latin American governments and the leading sectors of the US government.

With support from the AFL, Santiago Inglesias of Puerto Rico and Carlos Loveira of Mexico called together the leaders of the Latin American labour movements to a meeting in Laredo, Texas, 18 November 1918. There were seventy-one delegates from Mexico, and three from Central American states. This meeting created the Pan-American Federation of Labour (PAFL).

The PAFL was primarily an international union co-ordinating body linking the AFL and the newly unified Mexican national centre, the Regional Confederation of Mexican Workers (CROM), under the leadership of Luis N. Morones. The PAFL was established during wartime and was designed to keep unwanted influences out of Latin America and Latin American labour which might be threatening to US interests. Recognising the key role of labour in Latin American policies and needing the support of Gompers in Europe, the President of the US, Wilson, granted money and support to the AFL for its overseas work and for the PAFL in particular. On 17 July 1918 the AFL leaders met with the Secretary of Labour, the head of the War Labour Policies

Board, the Committee on Public Information chief, and the head of the American Alliance for Labour and Democracy. The AFL and these Administration leaders approved the plans for the PAFL and allocated government money to assist its formation. The subsidy of the PAFL, like the government subsidy of the AALD, was kept confidential. The Committee on Public Information allocated fifty thousand dollars from the President's special fund to the PAFL.[1] The PAFL was given the franking privilege. The AALD and the Committee funded the 'Pan-American Labour Press', the PAFL publication. Monies for this journal were handled by Bernard Baruch as part of the responsibilities of the War Industries Board. This pattern of confidential US government funding of US labour activities in Latin America through tripartite bodies like the AALD was one which has survived until the present.

In the interwar period, the US was concerned with the threats of extremism from both the right and the left. The victory of the Bolsheviks and their creation of the Comintern and the Profintern threatened to radicalise the political debate in nations across the world. The US was worried, in particular, about the chances for success of the left within the US and throughout Latin America where the US had vital economic, political and strategic interests. In pursuing a policy designed to thwart the efforts of the left, the US government's interests overlapped with the interests of the AFL. The AFL was in competition for members and influence with the Industrial Workers of the World (IWW) whose militant unionism was attracting new members in the US west, in the mines, mills and logging camps, and in Canada. The US government felt that its policies were threatened by the militant anti-war stance of the US socialists and, later, the communists, and took severe steps to repress political and trades union dissent. In this, the government was assisted by vigilantes who felt that the government sanctioned their policy of lynchings, and repression of socialists, anarchists, communists and unionists. Hundreds of these dissidents were deported or jailed. The AFL supported the government in its crackdown on the left.

This activity overlapped into Latin America where the US feared the spread of socialism, communism and Christian socialism among the workers of the continent and their union organisations. The PAFL was designed to be the vehicle for conducting a campaign of support for anti-revolutionary forces. In the words of its key officer, the PAFL promoted constructive Latin unionism, 'saving the American trade union movement from a continuing battle at its back door with a most destructive and revolutionary labour movement'.[2] The AFL, the backbone of the PAFL, fought leftist unionism and political activism through Latin

America by supporting Latin unions and governments which followed the basic US government line. It fought against any outside unions or international union bodies like the IFTU, the Profintern or others having contact with unions in Latin America or in affiliating unions or national centres from these lands. Within the ITS structures the AFL tried to create regional (Western hemisphere) bodies of the ITSs which it could control.

The basic position of the AFL was that its model should be the one followed in Latin America. The model allocated to the unions a purely economic function, leaving political action to the political parties. For a developing region like Latin America, whose urban unionists were often, outside of the military and landed aristocracy, the only major domestic political force, this policy was hard to follow.

With the growth of the CIO as a rival group within the US seeking to organise trades unions in competition to the AFL, the domestic struggle for recognition by the US government became heated. A principal arena of this competition was Latin America. Just as the AFL supported the Mexican CROM of Morones through the PAFL, the CIO began to develop important contacts with the rapidly expanding rival Mexican Labour federation, the Mexican Confederation of Labour (CTM) led by Vincente Lombardo Toledano. The CTM, supporting the new Mexican president, Lazaro Cardenas, in his expropriation of British and American oil interests in Mexico in 1938, won the support of the CIO. The AFL and the CROM opposed these policies, as did the US government. The centrist unions of the US and Mexico supported the PAFL while the CIO and the CTM joined to form a rival Inter-American federation, the Confederation of Latin American Workers (CTAL). An interesting aspect was the ties between some labour leaders of the CIO and the CTM with the German *Abwehr*, whose major goal in Latin America was to pre-empt vital war supplies to Britain and the US. Covertly, the labour arm of the *Abwehr* attempted to assist this effort; although there is some question as to how aware these unionists were of the links with Germany. When the war broke out in Europe and when Germany invaded the Soviet Union, both the right and the left united in preparing a trades union challenge to the axis powers.

The close ties between the US trades unions of the AFL and the US government did not develop out of some coercive power of the government exerted against the unions. Rather, the unions and the government had shared values and aims. Each saw in the other a useful vehicle to achieve mutually desirable goals. In Latin America, in particular, it was the AFL who frequently led the way in the government–union relationship. For an essentially isolationist government like the US, the AFL, in its support of non-political unionism in Latin America, seemed a daringly activist partner. Frequently US–Mexican relations were shaped by the AFL with only reluctant support of the US government. However, this interaction with labour did not amount to very much in terms of actual financial support of Latin unionism on anything like the scale the rhetoric would lead one to believe. When the Second World War began, however, this changed. The AFL and gradually the CIO began to take an active role in proposing and staffing labour–government programmes throughout the world and not limited to Latin America.

In 1940, the head of the International Ladies Garment Workers' Union (ILGWU), David Dubinsky, joined with the head of the Photo Engravers' Union, Matthew Woll, to form a committee to support war relief and trades unionists world-wide: the Labour League for Human Rights. Their first task was to aid European trades unionists attempting to escape the clutches of the Gestapo. The League sent out observers into Europe and lobbied in Washington for visas for the endangered unionists. They were able to save a number of important trades unionists. When Citrine visited the US in 1942 the League set up another committee, the American Labour Committee to Aid British Labour, which raised funds and bought supplies for British unions. In March 1941, the ILGWU locals in New York raised over $300 000 to rescue unionists under threat in German-occupied Europe. A Jewish Labour Committee, joining together many New York AFL unions and organisations, like the Workmen's Circle, were responsible for handling these sums.

The CIO, although active in pursuing an international policy, especially in Spain, was unwilling or unable to co-operate fully in the international relief work of the AFL until the invasion of the Soviet Union in 1941. A study group set up to explore co-operation among the US unions, the American Labour Conference, started the dialogue in 1943, but it was soon supplanted by a far more activist group formed in 1944, the Free Trade Union Committee (FTUC).

The new President of the AFL, William Green, and his secretary–treasurer, George Meany, joined with Dubinsky and Woll to form the FTUC. Dubinsky, who had the most experience in these efforts, took over control of the FTUC and worked closely with Meany in arranging its operations. Its leadership was placed in the hands of Jay Lovestone and his assistant Irving Brown.

Lovestone and Brown were assigned to work with the ILGWU and

Dubinsky. Through Dubinsky, Lovestone met and befriended George Meany, then the AFL secretary–treasurer. At the request of Meany, Lovestone was asked to draft a resolution on international labour for the 1944 AFL congress. This resolution called for the formation of a Free Trade Union Committee to be the overseas arm of the AFL, which would raise one million dollars to promote free trades unionism abroad and render direct assistance to the allied forces. Dubinsky turned over to Lovestone, as head of the FTUC, control of his agents abroad who had been working with the Labour League for Human Rights and the British Committee. The FTUC was recognised as labour's official liasion organisation with the Office of Strategic Services (OSS). The FTUC began to work overseas in sending aid and advice to unions attempting to rebuild.

Largely as the result of the militant anti-communism of Meany, Lovestone, Woll and Dubinsky, the AFL refused to join in the WFTU or any of the discussions which preceded it. Meany frequently attacked the British TUC in his denunciations of the WFTU, commenting that the organisation was a weird blend of British imperialism and Soviet communism. Meany attended the TUC convention in September 1945 and attacked the British unions for making pacts with Soviet labour.

Under the guidance of Lovestone, American labour of the AFL wing (and later with the active participation of the CIO) established a close working relationship with the OSS, the wartime US intelligence service. Lovestone, once described as 'a real mystery man, whose personality is part cloak and dagger and part cloak and suit'[3] established strong ties with European trades unionists operating underground on the continent during the war and established ties with Third World unionists in Asia, Africa and Latin America. The medium was the OSS.

The OSS, started under the guidance of the British, was largely the product of 'Wild Bill' Donovan. It brought together specialists from all areas of the political spectrum in an organisation dedicated to fighting the Axis powers. An OSS colonel, Herbert Blankenhorn, suggested that a vital area of activity should be the labour movements around the world. He won the support of Donovan and began recruiting for the OSS Labour Division, based at 72 Grosvenor Street in London. In the early days of 1942, Blankenhorn enlisted the talents of George Bowden who brought with him, as his assistant, the CIO's chief counsel, Arthur Goldberg. By March, Goldberg was operating as OSS labour chief out of Allen Dulles' office in New York. Goldberg began to hire hundreds of trades unionists and labour attornies to work with the labour branch. Gerry Van Arkel, one of those so employed, was sent to North Africa, where he set up penetration and political intelligence networks among the exiled European socialists who had fled the continent.

In mid-1942, Goldberg and Bowden met with Omar Becu, the general secretary of the International Transport Workers' Federation (ITF). The ITF had moved its entire operations to London into Transport House where, in co-operation with the former ITF president, Ernest Bevin, it collaborated with British intelligence in providing information on transport movements and labour conditions in occupied Europe. Becu met with Goldberg and urged him to establish a working relationship with the anti-Nazi union cells across Europe through contacts in London. Goldberg and George Pratt came to London to set up the labour operation.[4] Pratt stayed in London to run the labour branch, meeting regularly with German socialist and labour refugees. He paid them small retainers so that they could survive. The OSS labour branch decided that their trades unionists could penetrate Germany itself.

To conduct this penetration of Germany the OSS enlisted the support of a gifted trades unionist: the research director of the ILGWU, Lazar Tepper. Tepper, born in Russia in 1924, had studied at the Sorbonne and Johns Hopkins in the US. In the mid-1930s he joined forces with Dubinsky and became the ILGWU's research director. In 1943, Tepper reported for duty in Grosvenor Street to head Project Bach, the code name for the creation of labour agents who could operate behind German lines in Germany itself, reporting on conditions in Germany, supervising sabotage activities there.[5] Project Bach drew upon the services of the trades unionists in London, the several ITSs, and the rump of the IFTU to enlist volunteers to return to Germany. During the rest of the war, these labour agents were parachuted or infiltrated into Sweden, Belgium, Holland, Italy, France, Poland and Germany itself. These conducted numerous successful operations and provided American intelligence with virtually their only reliable hard information from within Germany. Many set up elaborate stay-behind nets for reactivation after liberation.

The OSS attracted a large number of key American unionists who served in virtually every theatre of the war. In Latin America, the work of the unionists was placed under the control of the Office of Inter-American Affairs (OIAA) headed by Nelson Rockefeller. Rockefeller recruited labour men like Dave Saposs and John Herling to co-ordinate US labour initiatives throughout the hemisphere. Among the most active and successful OSS agents assigned to work in the labour field in Latin America was Serafino Romualdi. He was the first hired to work on building support for US policy within the numerous Italian communities of Latin America. Then, after a stint in Italy where he succeeded in keeping the Italian socialist unions away from the communist unions, he returned to Latin America to work for the FTUC as its Latin American representative.[6]

The ties which bound US labour to the US government were strengthened by the creation of a mutual programme of support in the immediate postwar years. The creation of the Marshall Plan provided many ex-OSS labour staff with important roles in postwar Europe where the Cold War battles were beginning in nations like Greece, Czechoslovakia, Finland and Poland. The FTUC and the US government gradually came to adopt a similar position on the restructuring of Germany into a divided state, one-half communist one-half democratic. In Asia the US Occupation Forces were augmented by labour specialists in places like Japan, Korea and China where they worked with the authorities to build anti-communist unionism.

The immediate postwar reshuffle of the OSS into first the Central Intelligence Group, and then the Central Intelligence Agency (CIA) resulted in many OSS labour specialists being placed in key positions in the new agency; people who valued the support of the labour movement in the waging of the Cold War. The fairly straightforward conflict between the forces of the communists and the anti-communist forces within Western Europe were relatively easy to co-ordinate among the allies as, for the most part, the concerns of the British, French, West Germans, Belgians and the Americans were similar. In the Third World these concerns were very different. The government–union nexus which had emerged among the unions of the West and their governments during the war years, involved these unions in serious conflict with each other in the postwar world, especially on what policies ought to be pursued in the nations of Africa, Asia and Latin America.

The development of a close relationship between the national trades union movements and the national governments was not limited to the TUC, AFL or the Soviet unions. In the immediate postwar years numerous Western European governments were formed in which socialist, social-democratic and Christian-democratic parties played a key role. In this domestic political endeavour they were assisted by their respective labour movements. Under the new governments prominent unionists took on governmental responsibilities. There was an expansion of the institutionalisation of labour–government co-operation. This co-operation extended as well into international relations. The trades unions took an active role in shaping and effecting international trades union programmes. They formed study groups, foundations, tripartite international assistance bodies and a variety of other agencies to promote the national interests of their states.

Although particularly true in the nations where colonialism was still in force (France, Britain, Belgium and the Netherlands), the cooperation which developed between the national centres and their governments in the immediate postwar world was particularly close. In nations like West Germany, Sweden, Norway, Denmark or Switzerland the ties which grew between the national governments and the trades unions expanded into massive programmes of international assistance under the aegis of the international labour movement, or through bilateral assistance programmes. Additionally, the security organs of these states, both individually and through co-ordinating committees in organisations like NATO, took an active interest in, and occasionally participation in, international trades unionism. This interaction took the form of counter-intelligence which sought to prevent the domestic movements from being penetrated and manipulated by agents of a foreign state, as well as positive intelligence efforts at penetrating foreign labour movements to gather vital intelligence or to influence decision-making there.

For a nation like the new-born West German state, in whose territory numerous East German intelligence operatives function with great ease, the duties of counter-espionage were easy to see. The competition between West and East Germany in the nations of Africa and Asia generated a tremendous pressure for positive intelligence efforts in these areas. It was this effort at pre-emptive intelligence and national security which created a whole series of trades union–government interactions in the postwar world. For no state was this more true than the close ties between the Israeli state, its intelligence organisations and the Histadrut (the Israeli national centre).

In the immediate postwar world one of the main activist nations in the development of international relations conducted through the medium of the international trades union movement has been Israel. The Histadrut set up a series of training schools in Israel (the largest was the Afro-Asian Training Institute partly funded by the AFL–CIO), where Third World unionists were sent to study on government scholarships. Local trades union-to-trades union schemes were set up across the world by the Histadrut–government nexus, especially in Africa.

Just as the nations of the Eastern bloc set up trades union schools for the Third World unionists in East Germany, the Soviet Union, Hungary or Romania, the US set up training programmes in the US, the British set up programmes in Britain or overseas (as in British Guiana), and the Israelis, Taiwanese and others set up training schools and programmes. With the victory of the communists in the postwar reorganisation of China, the Chinese government, and its labour subsidiary the All-China Federation of Trades Unions (ACFTU) also actively involved itself in inter-Asian trades union initiatives.

This labour–government nexus among the great powers and middle-level power was not the only example of union–government activity. Perhaps the most active, if less well funded, programme of international labour activity emerged from among the Third World nations themselves. As early as the mid-1950s the Argentine leader, Peron, built up an *Agrupación de Trabajadores Latino Americanos Sindicalistas* (ATLAS) as an important element in Argentine policy. It united pro-Argentine Latin American unionists into a 'Third Force' trades union confederation. With the independence of the Gold Coast, the new Ghanaian trades union leadership created a special overseas labour assistance arm, promoting inter-African subversion and intrigue. The Egyptian Confederation of Labour, under the tutelage of Nasser, attempted to build Pan-Arab and Pan-Maghreb trades union organisations. The Cuban government, under Castro, has developed a major programme of international trades union assistance throughout the world. In all of these efforts, the vulnerability of nations to intrigue conducted through the medium of the trades union movements has been exploited. There are few nations anywhere in the world whose security forces do not have some part of their efforts targeted at positive or defensive programmes relating to labour union activity.

The development of this situation has been a direct result of the very important role played by trades unions in the reconstruction of Europe after the Second World War. There, the battle for control of the unions was the first battlefield of the Cold War.

4 International Labour in Postwar Europe

The growth of the labour–government nexus, originally developed as an extension of the war effort, soon took on an even greater significance in the immediate postwar struggle to rebuild Europe. The interactions between governments and trades unions in Europe became crucial in two concurrent struggles. The first was the struggle to rebuild the war-torn economies of Europe by renewing the productive capacity of the nations. The second was the struggle to win hegemony within the political arena in order to shape the political destinies of the European states. The creation by the allies of 'zones of influences' in Europe at the Potsdam and Yalta talks presaged the division of Europe into two hostile camps. In this process of division trades unions played a vital role.

European politics in the interwar years was characterised by the strained compromise between the forces of the Liberal, Christian Democratic and Smallholder parties of the right and centre and their competitors among the forces of the Socialist and Social Democratic left. The rise of Fascism and Nazism decimated the European left; many of whose leaders were imprisoned and killed. The parties of the right and centre found themselves ousted from effective governmental participation or taken over by their more extreme factions. The fragile compromise and balance of the interwar years between the two competing democratic systems was largely destroyed during the war, leaving in its wake a vacuum in which the control of armed bands became more useful than a compelling ideology.

In the aftermath of the destruction of the Axis powers, much of Europe was occupied by the victorious allied armies. To administer these nations the occupying forces set up governments of occupation designed to rebuild the economies of these nations and to ensure that the 'zones of influence' agreed to at Potsdam and Yalta became a reality in practice. Each of the allied occupation forces sought to create in its area of occupation a new national governmental and political system, congenial to its form of government and under its effective control.

One of the principal vehicles used by the allied powers during the occupation was the national trades union movements. These movements held the key to the peaceful restoration of industry and production and served as nuclei of the process of political rebirth. For most of Occupied Europe the system of free political parties had not survived the war. Political parties were forbidden in much of Europe in the early days of occupation. Only the trades unions still had the ability to function as national organisations, having re-established contacts with regional and local union bodies. The battle for control of the unions was a microcosm of the battle for control of the nation.

During the war unions, for the most part, had continued to function, albeit as part of Labour Front organisations run by the Germans. These Labour Front organisations were created by the Nazis to maintain high levels of war production. Many of the pre-war trades unionists, including some of the old socialist and social democratic unionists, collaborated: some on ideological grounds; some out of greed; some as part of the Resistance; and some as a result of fear of the consequences of opposing the Nazis. Nonetheless, the very fact of their collaboration proved difficult to deny during the reconstruction. It was a positive advantage to the communist unionists who, after the invasion of Russia, had opposed Nazism and had been so ruthlessly suppressed that they were barred from open collaboration during the war. To this must be added the fact that many communist unionists had fled their native lands to sanctuary in Moscow and had returned with the occupying Red Army to be placed in key posts in the trades union movements of their newly 'liberated' homelands.

The occupying powers found that one of the principal problem areas in the reconstruction of the political and economic structure of Europe was the battle for control of the trades unions. One of the best examples of the struggle was the battle for control of Czechoslovakia.

In Czechoslovakia the wartime conflict had not destroyed much of the industry or its relative prosperity. Czech political relations with the allied powers in London were especially good. In May 1945 the Czech government in exile of President Benes returned to Prague to govern, with the approval of the allies (even the Soviet Union to whom the Czechs had surrendered their eastern province of Ruthenia in January 1945). Once the Czechs succeeded in expelling their German and Hungarian minorities there were many unoccupied farms and the demand for skilled labour was great. The political party structure, however, was virtually non-existent. Only the communists had maintained a functioning relationship with its cadres during the war years and the early days of Soviet occupation. The largest party, the National Socialists, which had rejected both the Second and the Third International's offers of membership, was decimated during the war (only Jaroslav Stransky was left of the old executive committee and the new leadership included the London group and followers of Petr Zenkl and Vladimir Kraina – militant anti-communists). The Catholic People's Party kept its pre-war leader (Monsignor Jan Stramek) but was split between rival factions. In the worst shape was the Social Democrats whose leadership was dead or too old to rebuild the party to its former strength. The new leadership was left to young radical socialists, led by Zdenek Fierlinger, who pledged themselves to co-operation with the communists.

The Czech trades unions were badly split before the war. Each party had had its own trades union affiliate. With the German occupation, they were united into two national labour fronts: the first was for industrial workers; the second for white-collar employees. These unions were collaborationist organisations run by the special section on foreign labour questions of the German ministry. The Czech workers were treated comparatively well by the Germans who valued their high productivity. By spring 1945 there were over 500 000 Czech workers paying dues to the German-sponsored unions. With the return of the new government in May 1945 the Red Army placed the communists in control of the German-sponsored unions, renamed them the *Revolucni Odborove Hnuti* (ROH), and placed a communist, Antonin Zapotocky, at their head. The Russians flew in their man Josef Kilsky from his place of refuge (Kilsky had been a key organiser in the old Profintern) and made him organisational secretary.

The ROH was a pyramidal structure with the leadership firmly in the hands of the communists, assisted by some social democrats who were pledged to co-operation (among these was Evzen Erban, the General Secretary). Its controlling organ was the *Ustredni Rada Odboru* (URO), the Central Council of the Unions led by Zapotocky. The URO became almost part of the government and had the right to participate in governmental meetings and to send delegates to all bodies performing a social function. The URO was charged with drafting the decrees on nationalisation. Its power was made even greater because it was given control over the quasi-autonomous works council structures which represented workers in each plant or office.

Theoretically representing all workers, not only trades union members, these works councils participated in day-to-day decision-making in the plants. In fact the ROH drew up the election slate and the works councils voted them in. The key element in the power of the works councils was not in their ability to influence decision-making, but rather in their control of the armed factory militia (a force set up to protect factories during the liberation). After the liberation these factory militia retained their weapons and continued drilling under their new bosses. In the initial phase of reconstruction the trades union militia were an important element in establishing domestic order and tranquillity under the close control of the communists.

Gradually, as the trend in international communism moved from a policy of co-operation with the bourgeois parties to a policy of more direct confrontation, the Czech Communist Party began to lose its appeal to the Czech electorate. This reached a peak when Stalin reversed Czechoslovakia's decision to participate in the Marshall Plan. The communists were severely embarrassed and were losing support. They first sought to gain lost ground by arranging a merger with the Social Democrats; a merger agreed to by Fierlinger but rejected by others in the party. These ousted Fierlinger, supplanting him by Bohumil Lausman.

The other parties drew together into a National Front. In the face of attacks by Klement Gottwald's Communist Party the National Front resisted. Through their control over the Ministry of the Interior the communists kept discovering 'plots' against the regime; plots which tried to discredit the other parties. The date for the new elections in 1948 was drawing nearer and the communists were still losing control. They decided that they should use their most potent weapon to wrest control of the country from their opponents; they decided to use their control over the unions to bring down the government. Following a ten-day ultimatum on deciding for new elections issued by the Constitutional Committee of the government, the communists realised they had to act quickly. They used the discussions on an outstanding pay claim for civil servants as their instrument.

The Social Democratic minister, Vaclav Majer, favoured a straight percentage increase across-the-board; the unions demanded a weighted increase of an absolute sum which would favour lower-paid workers. When the minister won the point the communists siezed the issue. Zapotocky announced that the URO had called a major conclave on industrial policy for 22 February 1948 of the ROH and the works councils. The other parties protested vehemently against the calling of the works council congress. The communists used their control over the Ministry of the Interior to order the national police (who were also organised into unions and works councils) to assist the works council meetings. The democratic parties ordered Nosek (the communist Minister of the Interior) to rescind his order calling for the replacement of regional police officers by communists. The Prime Minister, Gottwald, tabled all motions and dicussion on the issue and Nosek was diplomatically ill at the next cabinet meeting. When Petr Zenkl demanded that Gottwald give some reply on the police issue, Gottwald evaded the answer but brought up the details of yet another 'plot' discovered by the police which implicated Zenkl's party. The National Socialists resigned as did the People's Party and the Slovak Democrats. Only the Social Democrats and the two ministers without party affiliation, Jan Masaryk and General Ludvik Svoboda, decided to stay on.

This breakdown of the government occurred two days before the works council congress was scheduled to begin. By 17 February, the party secretary in charge of the trades unions, Rudolf Slansky, had already put the factory militia at a state of readiness. When Slansky ordered that the workers be vigilant against a 'reactionary coup' the militia and trades union security patrols were placed on a twenty-four hour alert. The armed forces of the unions were turned into an effective alternative army run by the communists, under the leadership of a general staff composed of regional commanders. On the night of 23 February 1948 a convoy of trucks escorted by the police, brought 10 000 rifles and 2000 machine guns from the Zbrojovka factory in Brno to Prague where they were distributed to the trades union offices. On 25 February the party distributed the arms from the other factories to 6500 militiamen in key factories across the country used as fortified operational bases. Before this the communists had used their power to bring the capital to a halt. On 21 February the ROH called a demonstration in Wenceslas Square of over 100 000 which demanded a change of government. This was echoed the following day at the congress of the works councils. The next day, 23 February, the communist print union refused to supply newsprint for the non-communist newspapers and communist-led truckers refused to distribute non-communist pamphlets. On 24 February the unions held an impressive one-hour general strike at noon. On the 25th the communist coup was successful and a massive rally was held to celebrate the victory. The final capitulation of the Social Democrats under Fierlinger marked the end of the Czech experiment in democracy. The communists had won effective control over the country and took over all the cabinet offices. Zapotocky became Vice-Premier. In May, after elections, Gottwald became President and Zapotocky Premier.[1]

Without the trades unions the Czech coup would not have been possible. A good deal of the credit for the communist victory went to the efforts of Valerian Zorin, formerly Soviet ambassador to Czechoslovakia until September 1947. By a strange coincidence Zorin, who had returned to the Soviet Union to become Deputy Minister of Foreign Affairs, had arrived secretly in Prague on 19 February, ostensibly to distribute Soviet wheat. His movements were concealed but later it was shown that he, and some members of his staff, were the co-ordinators of the Czech communist victory. This victory in Czechoslovakia caused a major upheaval in what was already a deteriorating situation among the former allies and heightened the tensions which were leading to a full-scale Cold War.

The events in Czechoslovakia were not the product of unique or especially Czech circumstances. The pattern of East European communist intervention in national affairs through the medium of trades unions after the war was the rule rather than the exception.

The Czech pattern was the one that was most frequently followed in Eastern Europe. A new government of national unity was installed; a coalition of centrist, socialist and communist political parties. The communists took control of the Ministry of the Interior. Infiltration and control of the trades unions enabled communists to win important roles in the unions. Mass demonstrations in support of political aims succeeded in the winning for the unions a role in national economic planning. The Ministry of the Interior appeared to find numerous plots against the state by members of the non-communist parties. The unions then refused to print opposition newspapers and refused to transport provincial papers to the capital. They precipitated strikes which, because of their political nature, effectively split the socialist movement into factions allied with the communists and those opposed. The trades unions then created a crisis into which the communists could step as the party able to heal the breach. The communists and the left socialists formed a government together, ousting the centre and right parties. Then after an interval, the communists purged the government of the socialists. This pattern is one which was repeated in virtually every nation in Eastern Europe. The control of the trades union movement by the communists was the lever to make the transition from a government of national reconciliation to one firmly under communist control.

This pattern was followed with only minor variation. In Hungary the unions were placed under communist control and given the right to decide which civil servants would loss their jobs in the postwar reorganisation. A tripartite committee of government and union representatives drew up 'B' lists of redundancies; a process which effectively permitted the communists to purge the civil service. The unions were periodically called out into the streets to demand that the government purge non-communist leaders like Sulyok or Bela Kovacs. They boycotted the opposition newspaper, *Holnap*, when it attacked the communist control over the unions. After their success in grasping the reins of power, the trades union boss, Kossa, became Minister of Industry.

In Bulgaria the pattern was not much different. The unions were placed under communist control. The opposition paper, *Narod*, was siezed by the print unions. The unions demonstrated for the removal from power of the non-communist political leaders and for their execution as 'traitors'; first Petkov and then Lulchev. By mid-1948 the communists had taken complete control of the government. This process was repeated in Romania. Only in Poland was there much of an effective union opposition to the communist initiative in seizing power, largely because of the long history of socialist control of the union structure.

Polish unionists returning to Poland after the war had kept in touch with the indigenous Polish unionism which had survived under German occupation by liaison with the government in exile in London and through joint activities with the British TUC and the AFL's Free Trades Union Committee during the war. These unionists returned to Poland and took up their old positions in the Polish trades unions. When the venerable Socialist Party (PPS) was banned and its leadership hunted down by the communists, the socialist unionists joined the Polish Socialist Workers' Party (RPPS – which had been orginally created as a communist splinter from the PPS in 1942). The socialists proved very successful in this party and won many key union offices. This RPPS and its trades union arm were able to win numerous union and works council elections. Their strength won them a place in the Cabinet where they challenged the communist's claim to be the main party in the government coalition.

Gomulka, the communist party chief, had come to office after serving as a minor functionary in the chemical workers' union and was attuned to the potential power growing in socialist hands through their domination of the trades union wing of the RPPS. He invited a left-wing socialist, Kazimierz Rusinek, former head of the Seamen's and Dockers'

Union of Gdynia and a close colleague of the left socialist Cyrankiewiecz, to return to Poland and become head of a unified Polish trades union movement. The Soviets called a meeting between the PPR and the RPPS in Moscow and forced an agreement between the two to collaborate in the upcoming elections to the Sjem in January 1947. This agreement bound the two parties to create a popular front against the Polish Peasant Party of Mikolajczyk. Cyrankiewiecz became premier and the RPPS was given six ministries. The PPR (the communists) kept only five cabinet seats but appointed vice-ministers in all other ministries. This arrangement was opposed by the non-communist unionists. They were supported in this opposition by many Western European union organisations – especially in Britain and the US. Their efforts rebounded as the new government then accused the socialist unionists of treason and espionage as a result of their collaboration with the Western unionists. In mid-1947 the unionists Zulawski and Puzak, along with many of their followers, were liquidated by the communists on the grounds of treason. The Polish workers remained calm because they felt that the presence in government of the remaining socialists of the RPPS would exert a moderating force. They were mistaken. On May Day 1947 Gomulka demanded the merger of the RPPS with the PPR. Despite protests by the socialists (and the purge of Gomulka) the merger of the two parties was achieved in December 1948 when a new, united party, the United Polish Workers Party (UPWP) was created under virtually total communist control. It was not so much a merger as it was an enveloping of the socialists (reminiscent of the phrase coined by Lenin's rival, Martov, of the process resembling the 'merger' of a hungry man with a piece of bread). By 1948 Polish independent unionism was dead, but the spark of dissidence remained. The Western powers and the trades unions in the West were virtually powerless to prevent this destruction of non-communist political parties and unions in Eastern Europe. They sought, unsuccessfully, to raise an opposition to this process through the Allied Control Commission and within the WFTU but met with a series of Soviet vetoes.

In other nations, however, the abilities of the Western organisations to deal with the attempts by the Soviets to extend their influence were less hindered by the impediment of a resident Soviet military presence. In these nations, the battle lines were drawn and the trades unions and their respective governments joined together in a unique form of cooperation. This growth of union–government co-operation first manifested itself in the struggle for control of Greece[2] and the important role played by the trades union forces in the civil war there. Perhaps the most dramatic illustration of the trades union role was that which surrounded that reconstruction of the German state.

Like the creation of the West German state itself in 1949, the unity of the trades unions into a single DGB was the product of a compromise among divergent and competing systems. Traditionally, German unionism was divided along religious and political lines; with a strong Social Democratic Party (SPD) supporting its own unionists and the Christian Democrats (CDU) supporting the two types of Christian unionism. The non-affiliated Hirsch–Duncker unions and the white-collar federations played only a relatively minor role in Weimar unionism.

The rise of the Nazis virtually destroyed the German traditional unions. Despite its appellation as a National Socialist German Workers' Party, the Nazis were ruthless in their suppression of genuine trades unionism. Trades unionists were exiled, imprisoned or executed for their activities. In place of the Weimar unions the Nazis created a German labour front (DAF) which imposed a corporate structure on the unions, uniting them into one central union in which all tendencies coalesced. This type of labour front was under direct control of the Nazi party apparatus.

The partition of Germany by the allies as a result of the Yalta Conference in February 1945 created three zones: administered by the British, the Russians and the Americans. The British zone lay in the West; the Russian zone in the East; and the American zone in the Southwest. Later, a French zone was carved out of the British and American zones. The initial efforts to prevent German rearmament led to a policy of retribution in which a policy of reparations was instituted and in which Germany was to become a 'pastoral nation'. Within the Russian zone the first stage of occupation saw the massive removal of whole factories and productive capacity to the Soviet Union. The Red Army installed its occupation troops throughout the east and in their sector of Berlin. These worked closely with the security organs to assure the ascendancy of communist party (KPD) loyalists into administrative positions. The Russian occupation was immediately effective in that the first economic policy of the occupation was the freezing of all bank accounts. This policy guaranteed that, apart from the black market, no German in the Russian zone could afford not to work since there was no other source of money.

Since all Germans were forced to work to survive, the loss of a job was a matter of critical importance. The workers found that their ability to get work or to keep working was very much a factor of whether the local plant representative liked them or approved of their politics. Since these plant representatives were chosen by the Red Army administrators working in liaison with the teams of labour specialists sent from Moscow, they were a powerful organisational tool for the KPD in the Russian zone. As early as 10 June 1945, the Russians announced the formation of a new German trades union national centre, called the Federation of Free German Trade Unions (FDGB), headquartered in the Russian zone of Berlin and claiming jurisdiction over the whole of German industry. The WFTU was invited to set up its offices in Berlin. It recognised the efforts of the FDGB to extend its influence into the other zones. The AUCCTU and the WFTU made available large sums of money to the FDGB to hold interzonal conferences and to press for recognition of the FDGB as the legitimate national centre. The legitimising role of the WFTU in this effort was crucial as it linked together the trades union national centres of the occupying powers (the TUC, the AUCCTU, the CIO and the CGT). This WFTU support was used to justify the acceptability of the FDGB in the non-Russian zones. The FDGB was created from the top down as what the Germans called an *Eintopf* (goulasch) union. This meant that there were divergent ideologies and strains accepted by the FDGB but the party loyalty was to the KPD. The political control over the FDGB at its centre was repeated on regional or local levels. Each industry was represented as a separate committee of the FDGB rather than as a separate union.

The conflict in the rebuilding of the German labour movement was essentially one in which the centralised, Soviet-dominated FDGB claimed representation for all of Germany while the other zones permitted, and encouraged, the separate development of trades unionism for each of their zones. The importance of this was not only that trades unionism was governed by this policy but also that the political structure was directly affected. During the early days of the Occupation political activities among the Germans were banned. The only permissible vehicle for political agitation and activity were the trades union movements representing the SPD, CDU and KPD factions. The struggle for trades union control and unity was a surrogate battleplace for the struggle for political unity and control. Whereas the Russians were perceptive enough to realise the political implications of the battle on trades union structure, the other allies seemed less aware or less willing to face the challenge.

The French occupation of Germany was, for a time, more debilitating and destructive of German industry than even the Russian. The French, too, packed up industries and carted them to France. They took art treasures, livestock and raw materials from Germany back to France.

These they kept or sold on the world market at a substantial profit. The French insisted that Germany be kept disunited and constantly pressed for separation of the Saar, the Ruhr and the Rhineland. The trades unions in the French sector were guided by the trades unions of France; especially the CGT. The PCF financed a mass immigration of German exiles, the Free Germany group, from France where these *émigrés* had worked closely with the CGT during the war in Resistance groups. These Free Germany unionists were largely KPD exiles who were returned to Germany under CGT and PCF guidance to create a trades union movement close to the CGT position. As long as the postwar coalition in France survived (until the dismissal of the PCF ministers from the government in 1947), the CGT was successful in keeping control of the trades unions in the French zone in communist hands.

In the British zone, the occupying administration permitted and, eventually, encouraged the rebirth of German unionism. They were aided in this by the return to Germany of many of the key trades union exiles who had spent the war in Britain or Sweden. Many of these were ex-Operation Bach personnel, as were those who rose to prominence in the American zone. One of the most important of these returnees was Hans Boeckler, the former head of the metal workers' union and the leader of the underground trades union movement in Germany during the war. Boeckler had barely escaped from the Nazis when he was sought for his important role in the July plot of 1944 in which Count von Stauffenberg attempted to assassinate Hitler. Boeckler and August Schmidt of the coal miners' union initially pressed the British authorities for permission to reconstitute the old DAF organisation in the British zone, but under democratic auspices. The British, while favouring a strong trades union movement, feared that the creation of another *Eintopf* union would be politically unwise. The strength of the KPD unionists in the works council had raised the possibility that the unified national centre might fall victim to an organised assault by the political cadres. They told Boeckler and Schmidt that this type of union structure was unacceptable. They suggested a new structure.

The British authorities sent a TUC delegation to advise Boeckler. The delegation was composed of Will Lawther of the Miners' and Jack Tanner of the Amalgamated Engineering Workers' Union (AEU). These met with Boeckler and Schmidt in 1945 and suggested the creation of a trades union movement composed of a single united national centre including both social democratic and Christian unions, and made up of thirteen nationwide industrial unions. These thirteen were expanded to sixteen when the teachers, railwaymen and postal workers demanded their own separate industrial unions. This was agreed to by the British. The zonal federation was created in 1947. This structure later became the structure of the DGB when West Germany was created in 1949. Hans Boeckler became the first DGB president.

The progress towards the development of an effective trades union zonal federation in the British zone was not matched by similar progress in the American zone. In March 1945 a group of thirty-five returning trades unionists in the American zone met in Frankfurt to create a provisional organisation committee for a zonal trades union centre. The American Military Government (AMG) refused to permit this and blocked its formation for a considerable time. Although the Potsdam Agreement clearly permitted, and encouraged, the formation of unions during the occupation the American authorities behaved somewhat idiosyncratically in their interpretation of the rules. The AMG set up elections for the shop stewards and works councils in its zone. Each election was limited to a choice of steward or councillor from the ranks of those employed in each factory. No one who was not then employed could run or vote. While on the face of it a democratic measure, it effectively blocked most genuine trades unionists with experience and political contacts from taking union office. Since these trades unionists had been exiled or driven underground during the war they were not employed in the factories in the early days of the occupation, so they were barred from participating or running for union office. Those who were elected were either naive or tainted by association with the DAF structure.

Although the CIO participated in the general debates on German policy, it played a relatively low-key role in the efforts to shape US policy in its zone. On the other hand, the AFL and its committees were very active. The Commander of the US Occupation Forces, General Lucius Clay, was not very sympathetic to unions or unionism. He turned down a request by the AFL to set up an office in Stuttgart, saying that granting such a request would open the door to the WFTU requesting similar privileges. The AFL was determined to build an opposition to the WFTU and the FDGB. Matthew Woll demanded that the AFL be granted representation rights in all the zones, but was refused. The AFL carried the battle back to Washington.

The AFL declared that the reason for the ineptitude and misdirection of AMG labour policy was the subversion of the AMG's Manpower Department by communists occupying a number of key positions in the AMG. They identified as a member of the communist group George Shaw Wheeler, Allocations Director of the Manpower Division and directly concerned with trades union development. Wheeler, who soon after defected to Czechoslovakia, promulgated a rule which created a two-year waiting period before a trades union could be recognised by the AMG. It was one of Wheeler's deputies who ordered the dissolution of the Hesse Federation of Labour. He also unilaterally expanded a union committee by adding twelve communists to the committèe to achieve 'greater representation'. Newman Jeffrey, the CIO representative, was dismissed from the Manpower Administration because he objected to Wheeler's policy of preventing plant-level unions from merging into zònal unions or forming a central labour organisation. The AFL attacked Mort Wolf of the Amalgamated Clothing Workers and Joe Gould of the CIO Office Workers for supporting Wheeler. The AFL demanded participation in AMG labour policy. One of their stalwarts, Joe Keenan of the International Brotherhood of Electrical Workers (IBEW), was sent as a labour secretary to General Clay. Additionally, the AFL set up representation in the American zone, led by Henry Rutz of the Typographers Union. He was under the direct control of the newly appointed US labour representative in Europe, Irving Brown.[3]

The AFL and its affiliated committees (the Free Trades Union Committee and the Labour League for Human Rights) began to play an active role in AMG policy. It was able to get some of the further left members of the AMG Manpower Division removed and began to send vital assistance to German unionists. The first battle concerned the return of confiscated trades union property under Directive 50 of the AMG. Under Directive 50 trades unions could reclaim the assets which the Nazis had confiscated: the old socialist union funds. Despite resistance by the AMG and the effects of the revaluation of the mark, these funds were eventually returned to the unionists. A zonal federation was formed on lines similar to that of the British zone. Under AFL prodding, and with the support of the Reuther caucus of the CIO, the AMG gradually returned union property and made available to the unions the same type of facilities that the Russians were making available to the FDGB: gasoline, cars and tyres. The Free Trades Union Committee and the Labour League (which was a founding member of Co-operative for American Remittances to Europe – CARE) sent a regular supply of food parcels to German unionists and Austrian unionists.

Another requisite of the German union movement was paper and printing materials which enabled them to compete with the extensive subsidised propaganda campaign being waged by the FDGB. The

AMG got the War Asset Administration to provide a continuous volume of paper, presses and ink which was made available to the unions. The AFL supplemented this by shipments of a thin paper suitable for printing propaganda which could easily be smuggled into the Russian zone.

The victories of the communist *Einheit* union in Berlin in 1947 indicated that AFL opposition on a unilateral basis was not as productive as had been hoped. The AFL then enlisted the support of a number of valuable allies, the International Trade Secretariats. The AFL urged that the German unions in the new Bizonia (formed by the union of the American and British zones) affiliate directly to the ITSs for their respective industries. By this, the ITSs (which were also fighting to keep their autonomy from the WFTU), could provide necessary aid to their German affiliates and could provide a defence for the accusations of splitting. Many German unions did affiliate to their respective ITSs and received financial, propaganda and political help from them. The ITSs received funds for their work in Germany from most of the Western European national unions affiliated to the ITSs. Assistance came from Belgium, Sweden, Norway, Switzerland, Denmark, Holland and Britain, as well as from US. This multilateralising of the union assistance supported free German unionism. Gradually, with the introduction of the Marshall Plan, the split in German labour, and in Germany as a whole, widened.

With the creation of the Marshall Plan, and its opposition by the Russians and their allies, the West and the Western unions had a powerful weapon in their effort to rebuild Europe along the political lines they favoured. As part of the international political initiatives by the governments, the Marshall Plan administrators created a trades union advisory organisation which formed the nucleus of the organisations which later disaffiliated from WFTU. Before 1948, though, the AFL and the ITSs were the main supports of free trades unionism in Germany. Although many European trades unionists saw the dangers of continuing co-operation with the communist unions in the WFTU, they were largely constrained by domestic political developments from deviating from that course. The TUC was riven by internal dissension from left-wing caucuses and the Labour Government was cautious about playing too forceful a role overseas which might jeopardise the toleration of British colonial policies. The CIO was jealous of the favoured position as the lone representative of US labour internationally; the French and Italians were undergoing massive internal political struggles; and others were battling between the forces of right and left at home. The growth and strength of German unions owes a great deal to the assistance of the ITSs and the direct support by the AFL.

The use of the term 'support by the AFL' is perhaps a euphemism. While the AFL did support and pressure the AMG for a restoration of German trades union democracy, the large bulk of the funds which were disbursed and the assistance given was provided by the US government agencies through the Free Trades Union Committee, the League for Human Rights and similar agencies.

The old OSS Labour branch, like the rest of the OSS, was disbanded on 20 September 1945 and its functions scattered to different departments. Gerry Van Arkel, the head of the reorganised Labour Unit (in Secret Intelligence), moved from Switzerland to take up residence in Wiesbaden after the occupation where he took control of operations directed at the German trades unions. He and his associates helped direct the flow of support to the German unionists and helped the AFL to gain access to vital supplies. They helped the AFL continue to publish their *International Free Trade Union News* and to circulate these throughout Germany. Initially US policy against maintaining a strong peacetime intelligence service debilitated this effort, but the gradual restructuring of the US intelligence community, first through the Central Intelligence Group and later the Central Intelligence Agency (CIA) in 1947 restored labour to a high priority position in US tactics in the Cold War battle.

The creation of an independent West German state owes a great deal to the success of the labour policies. This success was not repeated in the efforts to build a free trades union movement in France and Italy. In those nations, where a splitting of the nation into two parts was not feasible, the fission produced a divided and conflicted trades union movement.

There are probably no better examples of the direct intervention of external forces in the struggle for the control of the labour movements than France and Italy. In these two nations over the past thirty years billions of dollars and roubles have been spent in an effort to support one or more factions of the labour movement in an effort to shape national political and economic policies. Although the process of delivering this assistance has grown more sophisticated, the basic structure remains largely unchanged.

In the aftermath of the liberation of France the CGT, under PCF control, purged the union of those unionists who had stayed on under Vichy and collaborated with the Germans. Most of these were SFIO (French Socialist Party) members and, to a large extent, with right-wing histories. The general election of 1945 saw the formation of a government resembling the old Popular Front, with the SFIO sandwiched in coalition between the PCF and the Catholic *Mouvement Republican Populaire* (MRP). Within the CGT the PCF elements took control. Although the return of Leon Jouhaux from prison in Germany permitted him to regain the presidency of the CGT, a new post of General Secretary was created in March 1945 and Benoit Frachon, PCF loyalist, was named to the post. The new Minister of Labour, Ambrose Croizat, retained his post as head of the CGT metalworkers. Industrial production was in the hands of Marcel Paul, another PCF minister. Following the directives of the Soviet Union to build a wide postwar coalition with the bourgeois parties the PCF adopted a strategy of commitment to production. The PCF and the CGT denounced the use of strikes 'as a weapon of the trusts and enemies of the working class'. The CGT miners voluntarily gave up their holidays to secure greater production of coal. The PCF and the CGT introduced a system of piece-rate and production incentives. This policy of enforced production did not sit well with the bulk of the CGT members and spawned a number of opposition groups within the union, especially amongst the SFIO remnants. A centre of anti-PCF agitation in the CGT developed around the journal *Résistance Ouvrière* and its editor Robert Bothereau.

This group around the *Résistance Ouvrière* attracted the attention of the American labour representative in Europe, Irving Brown. Brown, representing the AFL in Europe, made contact with the Bothereau group and with Largentier, head of the print workers' union, in an effort to organise an anti-PCF caucus within the CGT. Brown sent urgent requests back to the Free Trades Union Committee for funds which would permit the two opposition groups to operate. Initially the FTUC and the AFL put these funds into the account of the Jewish Labour Committee from which Brown allocated them to the French unionists.[4] Despite these funds the anti-PCF unionists faced a severe setback at the April 1946 CGT convention, where the PCF succeeded in reducing the CGT Secretariat from nine members to four (Jouhaux, Saillant, Frachon and Pierre Reynaud). All, except an increasingly ineffectual Jouhaux, were PCF members. Brown continued to attempt to split off the anti-PCF elements from the CGT. Those unionists who were loyal to the SFIO were largely the white-collar and professional unionists. Most of the industrial unionists remained loyal to the CGT and the PCF leadership. Despite receiving funds in order to split the CGT the French unionists were reluctant to split and to carry the onus of dividing the French labour movement. By this time Brown was supporting the railway unionists, the miners and the postal workers who remained outside the CGT and the Bothereau elements and the printers within the CGT. The funds came from sources outside the labour movement and supplemented the contributions that the FTUC was providing. These funds, coming from the CIA, amounted to around two million dollars a year according to Tom Braden who disbursed them.

On the other hand, massive sums of money were made available to the CGT through the PCF from the Soviet Union and the nations of communist-controlled Eastern Europe. These funds were delivered to the party and union treasuries as credits and deposits to the *Banque Commerciale pour l'Europe du Nord* (BCEN), the French bank owned by the Russian state banks. 99.7 per cent of the shares are owned jointly by the Gosbank and the Vnestorgbank of Moscow (the State Bank and the Foreign Trade Bank, respectively). The party and the union keep numerous accounts at the BCEN as do the several industrial and trading companies run by the PCF and the CGT. As necessary, the accounts of the PCF and the CGT were credited with new funds.[5] Massive overdrafts were written off by the Moscow shareholders when the party and the union required cash for operating. This connection was frequently denounced in the French Chamber of Deputies when the PCF moved away from a policy of co-operation with the bourgeois parties and adopted a policy of confrontation in the wake of the deterioration of East–West relations in 1947.

When the Truman doctrine was announced in March 1947 the East–West conflict entered a new phase. The wars in Greece and Turkey, the struggles in Iran and in Austria, had sufficiently exacerbated the conflict between the two blocs that conflict seemed inevitable. The first signs occurred when the CGT metalworkers called an unofficial strike at the Renault–Billancourt plant. When the CGT ordered the men back to work, they refused. The CGT suddenly did an about-face. It took over the strike and declared it legal. Under Soviet pressure, the PCF took an anti-government line and voted against the government's wage policy. On 5 May 1947, the PCF ministers were dismissed from the government and the PCF went into opposition. In June a wave of strikes spread across France. The same month the Marshall Plan was announced, followed by Molotov's walkout of the Paris Marshall Plan talks in July, and his warning to Bidault and Bevin that if they participated in the ERP they would suffer industrial disturbances at home. The CGT called a nationwide general strike in November 1947 against the wishes of many of its members. By December the nation was at a virtual standstill with the pits, ports, post, chemicals, textiles and engineering workers all out.

During this strike, the non-communists rallied around Jouhaux and the journal *Force Ouvrière* and issued anti-CGT and anti-strike agitation, especially in the coalfields. By the end of December these unionists were ready to leave the CGT. Following the end of the general strike the anti-PCF unionists held a meeting and declared themselves unwilling to continue in membership in the CGT. On 19 December 1947 these unionists resigned from the CGT. The CGT assets (buildings, presses, bank accounts, etc.) remained with the PCF loyalists. When these unionists formed their own national confederation in April 1948, as the *CGT-Force Ouvrière* (CGT-FO) they started with virtually no assets.

Just as the CGT-FO received substantial support from the US and its clandestine services, the CGT received massive assistance from the forces of the newly formed Cominform through the BCEN. The French Minister of the Interior, Jules Moch, stood up to denounce the funds pouring into the BCEN from Romanian, Polish and Hungarian unions for the CGT. The Czech unions supposedly donated the equivalent of one month's wages to their comrades in the French mineworkers. The Czech miners sent 250 million francs to the mineworkers; the Romanians sent more than 10 million. The Minister declared that all these funds were really sent by the Soviet Union to promote a policy of opposition to the European Recovery Programme (ERP) and to disrupt France. Jacques Duclos, for the PCF, denied that these funds, amounting to over 68 million francs in two months, were anything but friendly assistance from brother unionists.

By the creation of the FO, the CGT was effectively split. However, the bulk of the French organised working class still remained in the CGT rather than the CGT-FO. This division was further complicated by the survival of the Christian federation, the CFTC. Remaining largely aloof from the CGT and CGT-FO conflict, the CFTC declared itself against political participation and adopted a resolution which declared the incompatibility of union and political office. After 1947 the demand for a more activist policy led the CFTC to begin a gradual programme of deconfessionalisation in which the overt links with the Catholic Church were dissolved. This process led it, eventually, into total deconfessionalisation and the adoption of a new name, the *Confédération Française Démocratique du Travail* (CFDT) at its congress in 1964. In its latter incarnation the CFDT succeeded in becoming the second largest union federation in France. The CGT-FO group attempted to win the support of the CFTC in battling the CGT, but with little success. Under the guidance of Irving Brown, the FO unions began a campaign to contain the CGT and to keep French industry operating. The severest battles occurred on the docks where PCF unionists, determined to block the entry of Marshall Plan aid, refused to unload American ships. Using money supplied by Braden, Brown hired a squad of strongarm men, under the control of the Corsican leader, Pierre Ferri-Pisani, who attacked the dock unionists and forced the opening of the ports to US aid. This group, known as the Mediterranean Committee, broke the CGT strike and took control of the French ports. This was not an unmixed blessing for the French port authorities as these Corsicans tended to stay on and run the ports long after the political battles were over, exchanging their political activity for a more traditional form of endeavour: gun-running, drug smuggling and the protection business.

It wasn't only the AFL, however, which maintained a presence in France. The CIO also maintained an office in Paris, under Elmer Cope, to provide liaison with the WFTU which was headquartered there. Before 1951, and the arrival of Victor Reuther in Paris to run the CIO office, the CIO refused to become involved in any meaningful sense with French unionism. The main support for the anti-PCF struggle was borne by the ITSs and supported by the AFL and other Western unions. The CGT–FO unionists were affiliated to their respective ITSs but the CGT unions were barred because of their political affiliations.

It is a general rule within the ITSs that, although many unions from a single nation are permitted to affiliate, the affiliation of new unions from that nation is subject to their acceptance by the existing affiliates. The early acceptance of the CGT–FO unions into the ITS structures gave them the unofficial power of blackballing the CGT, or indeed, the CFTC unions from their respective ITSs. This had the effect of isolating the national unions of the CGT (the metalworkers, the chemical workers, the food workers, etc.) from direct organisational links with unions in similar industries in other nations. International activities took place on the level of the confederation or through the confederation's participation in the WFTU. This isolation of the French national unions affiliated to the CGT from the ITS structure was used, and continues to be used, as a powerful weapon by the opponents of the CGT, particularly as the ITSs became more directly involved in developing a response to the multinational corporations. The unity and co-operation between national centres as conducted through the WFTU and the ICFTU has been at a sufficiently abstruse level as to be largely irrelevant to European industrial relations. On the other hand, the level of interaction among the national unions within the ITSs has had a marked effect not only in matters of international industrial relations, but also in the development of specific corporate industrial policies. The locking out of the CGT from this type of interaction greatly strengthened the appeal of the CGT–FO.

The struggle for power within French unionism which led to the splitting of the CGT was not much different than the simultaneous struggle for the control of the Italian labour movement. Many of the principles involved were the same; many of the issues were the same; and much of the funding for this conflict derived from the same sources.

It is very difficult to isolate the special characteristics of political activity in Italian trades unionism, largely because there has been very little of anything else in the history of Italian unions. Unlike most of the other nations of Western Europe, Italian unionism tends to have had only a marginal involvement with the industrial relations system of the nation. Italian unionism is an integral part of the system of political patronage of the country. Union offices and functions are generally bestowed on loyal party cadres as part of the *cursus honorum* of Italian politics.

When Italy was liberated there had not been independent unions there for almost twenty years. The fascist corporate unions of Mussolini had supplanted the existing socialist, communist and confessional unions and forcibly integrated them into the bureaucratic nexus of Italian fascism. Trades unionism existed only among the exiles. This fact was an important determinant of later trades union development as there was no existing, legitimate body of unionists who could assume the role of local or regional unionists, nor was there a central organisation which could claim the mantle of trades union support. This was exacerbated by the somewhat unusual form of the Italian liberation.

When the allied landing in Sicily in 1943 led to the deposing of Mussolini by General Badoglio and the signing of the Armistice in September 1943, much of Southern Italy went over to the allies. The Badoglio government led by the army, police and the fascist civil service under a monarch, had something less than a wide appeal among the Italians. In the north, where the Germans had reinforced their positions, the battle continued. There, a coalition of the anti-fascist parties created a six-part coalition, the *Comitato di Liberazione Nationale* (CLN) composed of the Socialists, the Communists, the Christian Democratic, the Christian Action, the Liberal and the Democratic Labour parties. The CLN, after the liberation of Rome, created a political union to co-ordinate and direct the anti-Nazi guerrilla campaign in the north: the *Comitato di Liberazione Nationale Dell'Alta Italiano* (CLNAI). While the Badoglio government ruled in the south, the CLN–CLNAI ruled in the north.

As part of their war effort the CLNAI, with assistance from the British and American secret services, organised strikes and massive industrial unrest in German-occupied Milan, Cremona, Genoa, Mantua and Turin. The CLNAI, dominated by the communist (PCI) and Christian Action guerrillas, had taken effective control over northern Italy. The political ties which bound the six parties in the CLNAI coalition were very often strained by competition among them for the aid and assistance of the Americans and the British, neither of whom could agree on which section of the partisan movements should be aided. The British and Americans agreed in December 1944 to aid all factions and the CLNAI agreed to accept allied directives. This became a little difficult later when the OSS and the Special Operations Executive (SOE) were negotiating the German surrender without telling the CLNAI and, by this, depriving them of an outright CLNAI victory.[6] When the Mussolini Salo government collapsed in early 1945 the CLNAI refused to take over the reins of power largely because Comrade Ercole (the *nom de guerre* of PCI leader Palmiro Togliatti) insisted on fulfilment of the terms of unconditional surrender.

Under the Allied Military Government which took over in June 1945, the CLNAI broke up into its several parts. The parties, following the lead of the PCI, entered into a new government under Victor Emmanuel and Ivanoe Bonomi as a popular coalition. The delicate negotiations which determined the nature of their popular coalition divided political control and patronage among the six parties. Among the key areas of patronage were the labour unions. Instead of dissolving or reshaping the old fascist unions, the coalition agreed to take them over. One result of the negotiations for the forming of the coalition government was the creation of a new national labour centre, the *Confederazione Generale Italiana del Lavoro* (CGIL) formed in June 1944 by the Pact of Rome. By this pact, the six parties agreed to divide the jobs and patronage of the CGIL among themselves, declaring that the CGIL was non-political and non-denominational. Each of the party caucuses appointed party adherents to CGIL posts. This paralleled the division of the other spoils of victory among the six government parties.

Italy under the fascists and in the immediate postwar reorganisation boasted an impressive degree of parastatal and nationalised industries, directed by the *Istituto per la Ricostruzione Industriale* (IRI) after the fall of fascism. The IRI administers enormous industrial enterprises and banks. The government of the day appoints the leadership of these giant parastatal companies and this leadership appoints lower levels of leadership. This division of the key, and most lucrative, jobs is a major party political task. Each of the trades unions participate in this sharing of power and most important trades unionists hold, in addition to their union office, both a political position and some role in a parastatal company or as an adviser to the government's radio or television networks. Since very little collective bargaining takes place at anything other than the level of the confederation in its negotiations with a confederated employers' federation, the task of the unionists is made relatively easy. Bargaining other than for local grievances, is a matter to be decided by political compromise between party appointees in the companies and party appointees in the union leadership. Italian industrial democracy is too well organised to be left to the unforeseeable whims of a rank-and-file electorate.

This six-party coalition was put to the test when the Christian Democrats arranged a crisis in November 1945. After prolonged negotiations they succeeded in putting De Gasperi, their candidate, in as Prime Minister. In the first major elections, in June 1946, the Christian Democrats emerged as the largest parliamentary party. The Socialists and Communists remained in the Cabinet although in reduced numbers. The PCI was so interested in remaining in office that they agreed to incorporate the fascist Papal Concordat of 1929 into the new Italian constitution, against the advice of the overseas communist parties. The PCI was determined to maintain the important patronage jobs and the power which these jobs gave the party despite the rightist course of the government in which it participated. The crisis came when De Gasperi visited the US and was informed of the allied agreement about the beginning of the Marshall Plan. He was told that throughout Europe the communist parties were attempting to block this type of endeavour and, if Italy were to participate, it ought to remove the PCI from its powerful position. De Gasperi returned and, when forming a new government in May 1947, removed both the PSI and the PCI ministers from the Cabinet, leaving the Christian Democrats to govern on their own.

Within the trades union movement the effect was immediate. The PCI moved to take control of the CGIL. In June 1947, at the Florence CGIL congress, the PCI faction abandoned the prior division of power among the parties and put its representative, Di Vittorio, in as General Secretary. Prior to this the three major parties' union caucuses (the PSI, the PCI and the *Associazione Cristiani dei Lavoratori Italiani* – ACLI, representing the Christian Democrats) each had a CGIL General Secretary. Now these were demoted to assistant secretaries. Di Vittorio joined the board of the WFTU as the representative of Italian labour. The PCI remained relatively moderate before the 1948 elections.

Nonetheless, pressure from the East led to a growth in PCI militance, sufficient to cost both the PCI and its allies in the PSI a lot of votes in the April 1948 general elections. The Christian Democrats won an outright majority for the first time. This victory had a profound effect on trades unionism.

At the meeting to discuss Europe-wide participation in the Marshall Plan (ERP) held in London in March 1948 (attended by forty-eight trades unionists from eleven of the sixteen participating states), the CGIL refused to send an official delegate, as did the CGT. The CGT–FO and the CFTC were represented as were the ACLI faction of the CGIL, led by Guilio Pastore. Even the German unions attended. Pastore was joined by Giovanni Canini of the socialists and Enrico Parri of the republicans. While nothing of great magnitude emerged from the ERP–union conference, it marked the first stage of the deterioration of the WFTU and marked a significant split developing in the CGIL. The unions formed an advisory committee, the ERP–TUAC, to perform a co-ordinating role during the administration of the ERP. The non-PCI union groups within the CGIL participated in this TUAC as did, for the first time, a joint US coalition of the AFL and the CIO.

The problems within the CGIL started in earnest when the delegation returned home. A crisis occurred when an assassination attempt was made on Palmiro Togliatti, leading the CGIL to embark on a wave of strikes which, at times, appeared to threaten the state itself. The PCI, itself surprised by the vehemence of the strike, moved to take control of the strike committees and to prevent the planned takeover of the power plants, the newspapers and the army barracks. Under PCI direction the CGIL turned the strike into a protest against the ERP. The strike took on a distinctly political tone. The Christian Democrats, and the ACLI faction in the CGIL demanded that the CGIL call off the strike. This had little effect, so the ACLI national council declared that the PCI–CGIL activities had violated the principles of the Pact of Rome and called for the establishment of a new confederation to supplant the PCI-dominated CGIL. At a special ACLI congress in September, delegates created the *Libera Confederazione Generale del Lavoro* (LCGL) largely made up of ACLI unionists. The socialists and the republicans, too, decided to pull out of the CGIL and withdrew to form the *Federazione Italiana del Lavoro* (FIL). Between 1948 and 1950 general confusion dominated the Italian labour scene as each party sought to use its labour arm to win political points. In this the Italian parties were aided from outside by the provision of funds, printing supplies and similar assistance. The US provided assistance through Irving Brown and the

Free Trades Union Committee, ostensibly from union funds but primarily from the CIA. The Russians and the Cominform also provided massive aid to the PCI–CGIL through the donation of money from the WFTU, assistance from the East European unions and indirectly through the extensive network of banks, trading companies and travel offices which make up the large financial empire which is the PCI–CGIL. Some estimate that the US and the Russians each provided around seven or eight million dollars a year to the Italian unions in an effort to keep their own allies in power. Through assisting their allies in the labour movement they were able to strengthen their political party friends without have to deal directly with them.

After the founding of the International Confederation of Free Trades Unions (ICFTU) in 1949, Irving Brown was sent to Italy to try to effect a compromise between the LCGL and FIL. He called together Pastore and Canini and helped them to merge. In May 1950 they joined together to form an anti-PCI coalition, the *Confederazione Italiana Sindicata Lavoratori* (CISL). The CISL, although officially non-denominational, was heavily influenced by the Christian Democrats. The social democrats and the remaining republicans soon rebelled at the confessional aspects of the CISL and broke away to form a new confederation, the *Unione Italiana del Lavoro* (UIL). An appeal to the AFL to stop this split from happening by the ACLI was not successful. By mid-1950 Italy had three national confederations, the CGIL, the CISL and the UIL. Each had its own set of national unions. The CGIL, while suffering from the split in its ranks, nonetheless retained the largest membership. As in France and CGIL unions were prevented from affiliating to their respective ITSs. In most cases both the CISL and the UIL unions affiliated to the ITSs and were supported by a wide range of European national union groups.

The co-operation pact agreed to between the CISL and the UIL in 1953 led to a more active industrial policy being undertaken by the two unions. For the first time trades unions, as opposed to the ubiquitous *commissione interne* (an Italian version of works councils), began to have a presence in the plants. The CGIL soon found that it, too, had to play a more direct role in industrial relations.

The conflict within the Italian labour movement, while largely supported by outside agencies, reflected domestic Italian political machinations and rivalries. Although the Cold War aspects were very important and the CGIL played its part in the struggle against the ERP, the CGIL tended to have far more concrete goals than the communist unionists of France or Germany. They tended to moderate their dependence on external support when it began to cost them important votes nationally. One of the reasons for this policy was their alliance with the Nenni Socialists (the PSI) with whom they shared control of the CGIL.

The fact that Italy occupied a strategic area of Western Europe, virtually guaranteed great power rivalries over control of the nation. The Cold War aid found ready recipients among the Italian political parties, and none more willing than the unions.

The break-up of the postwar labour coalition of the WFTU seemed inevitable as the Cold War struggle reached its peak in the days which followed the Czech coup. From the middle of 1948 until early 1949 the clock was ticking for European labour unity. By 1949 it was dead, and the WFTU dissolved in the pressure cooker of Cold War tensions in the labour movements.

With the growth of the Cold War the cohesion of the WFTU in its existing form was doomed. During the winter of 1947–8, one of the coldest and most miserable winters on record, the dependence of Europe on food and assistance from the US was critical. Despite the strong pressure applied by the Russians within Eastern Europe and on their communist party allies in the West to resist the influx of American goods and assistance, the bulk of Western Europe, and indeed Czechoslovakia and Poland initially, decided to make use of the assistance forthcoming through the ERP. ERP delegations were set up across Europe and technicians and administrators came over from the US to work with their European counterparts to administer the ERP. The communist parties rejected the ERP as 'an imperialist venture of capitalistic interests' and condemned the trades union organised in the ERP–TUAC as collaborators with the forces of Wall Street and monopoly capitalism.

The first signs of the rift in the WFTU came at its Executive Board Meeting in November 1947 when the CIO attempted to raise the question of WFTU's role in opposing the ERP. Jim Carey of the CIO demanded that the question of the ERP be placed on the agenda. The Dutch delegate, Evert Kupers, had earlier tried to get the ERP on the agenda but Saillant and Arthur Deakin (of the TUC) had opposed any such effort. Carey demanded the right to read into the record a statement indicating the CIO's support for the ERP but Deakin refused any debate on the statement. Deakin's compromise (letting Carey read his statement but refusing debate) did not satisfy Di Vittorio (CGIL), Sidorenko (AUCCTU) or Saillant. Saillant, who as General Secretary retained control of the propaganda organs of the WFTU, began publishing article after article condemning the ERP, including letters from Romanian unionists, Polish local committees, etc., all purporting to be unsolicited communications. Attacks by the CGT, the Chinese Association of Labour and the AUCCTU on the ERP were repeated in full in the WFTU media. Personal attacks were made on Western unionists and against Irving Brown in particular.

This attack on Brown coincided with his efforts on behalf of the ERP-TUAC. When Brown tried to convene an ERP-TUAC meeting under the auspices of the AFL he ran into opposition from the TUC, the CIO and the Dutch Federation of Labour (NVV). Brown was able to persuade the Belgian national centre to act on his behalf so that AFL dominance would be muted. The TUC, CIO and the NVV agreed that the discussions on the ERP could proceed through the WFTU but, under strong pressure from Kusnetsov of the AUCCTU, Saillant refused to call any WFTU meeting to discuss it. Kusnetsov claimed that he was too involved in negotiating a new Soviet nationwide collective agreement to attend.

The timing of the WFTU meeting to discuss the ERP was important because both the CIO and the AFL wanted to demonstrate to the US congress that the European labour movements supported the Marshall Plan which was scheduled to come to a vote in congress in April 1948. When Saillant announced, in January 1948, that no WFTU meeting would be held, the TUC quickly announced that it would host a union meeting on the ERP for London in March. This meeting brought together most of the non-communist Western European centres, and a joint delegation from the AFL and the CIO, into the ERP-TUAC. The following month, at the WFTU Executive Board Meeting, the CIO and the TUC protested against the WFTU May Day message to the world which had condemned the ERP.

What was behind much of the growing disenchantment of the Western unions towards the WFTU was the support being provided by the Soviet Union to forces hostile to the development of an effective European recovery, to factional movements within their union ranks, and to political factions opposed to the democratic system. Perhaps no policy was more divisive than the Soviet effort to use the CIO to promote the campaign of Henry Wallace for the US Presidency on the Progressive ticket. Despite the coolness which had developed between the right and left wings of the CIO in late 1947, matters did not come to a head between the two factions until the CIO's Executive Board voted to support Harry Truman for a second term as President in the upcoming 1948 national elections. This support for Truman immediately was denounced by the CIO left and eleven CIO unions vowed to fight this endorsement at the upcoming CIO convention. Their support for Wallace was coupled with a denunciation of the ERP and support for the WFTU. They went to the CIO convention looking for a fight. When these unionists were defeated by the Reuther–Murray faction they vowed to continue to support Wallace's third-party candidacy. Lee Pressman, the CIO's general counsel, resigned to work with Wallace as did the CIO's chief publicist, Len de Caux. The close ties between the communists and the Wallace campaign paved the way for the expulsion of many communist-dominated unions from the CIO in 1949. Integral to their efforts was their agitation against the ERP and their support for continuing CIO affiliation to the WFTU.

The pressures for changing the WFTU were growing stronger after the Czech coup and the intensification of the Greek civil war as European and North American unions increasingly polarised between the US and Soviet camps. The splitting of the French and the Italian movements and the continuing conflict with the German trades union movement (especially during the Berlin blockade) made fission virtually inevitable.

The British unions, too, were under pressure from their government to ease themselves away from the organisational ties which linked them with the Soviet unions in the WFTU. The TUC decided in October 1948 to press for the dissolution of the WFTU but, having learned the lessons of the CGT–FO in France did not want to just quit the WFTU and leave behind the money, the assets and the presses of the rump organisation in the hands of its opponents. The TUC proposed that one representative each from five major WFTU-affiliated nations (the TUC, the AUCCTU, the CIO and two others) be appointed as trustees of the WFTU. These would act in lieu of the WFTU during an agreed year-long hiatus. This 'cooling-off' period was put to the CIO and agreed to by Jim Carey. At the next session of the WFTU Executive Bureau, in January 1949, the TUC delegation (Deakin who had succeeded Citrine as President of the WFTU when Citrine moved to the Coal Board and Tewson who had taken Citrine's job as TUC General Secretary) presented the plan for the 'cooling-off period'. After two days of heated debate Deakin, who was in the chair, declared that he was going to put the motion to a vote. Liu, Kusnetsov, Saillant and di Vittorio demanded the floor on points of order, privilege, etc., but Deakin was not willing to prolong the debate. He said that they should vote there and then. With much screaming and waving of the constitution in Deakin's face they refused to be swayed. Deakin got out of the chair and walked off. He was followed by Tewson, Kupers and the CIO delegation. The WFTU was effectively split.[7]

When the British, the US and the Dutch walked out of the WFTU they were followed by most of the other Western European unions, except the CGT and the CGIL. After their disaffiliation from the WFTU, these unions continued to meet under the ERP–TUAC framework. Deakin and Tewson visited the US to lobby for the creation of a new labour international; one which would include both the AFL and the CIO. By May of 1949 it was agreed that the two US unions would participate. This was facilitated by the expulsion of the CIO's communist unions in mid-1949. After agreeing that the CIO would not challenge the AFL's pre-emptive right to control the selection of delegates representing US labour in the ILO, an arrangement was made by which the federations would co-operate in the new labour international. The British gathered together their European colleagues in Geneva in July 1949. This international trades union conference was attended by fifty delegates from thirty-eight national centres. The ITSs were represented as were the Christian unionists of the CISC. This Geneva conference agreed on the basic form for a new labour international and created a preparatory committee to hold the inaugural conference. Meeting from 28 November to 9 December 1949, 261 delegates from 59 countries sat in London to create the International Confederation of Free Trades Unions (ICFTU).

The ICFTU was in direct competition to and opposed to the WFTU. There were serious problems for the ICFTU in terms of organisation, ideology and cohesiveness. The most important area of conflict was its struggle to create a positive ideology with wide appeal, while still maintaining its opposition to the WFTU. This centred around the battle over how militantly anti-communist the new organisation should be.

The unionists of the AFL were, perhaps, the most hard-line anti-communists of the lot. Their experience in working with the OSS labour branch and the CIA's covert action specialists in Germany, France and Italy had created a commitment to anti-communism which frequently dismayed their allies in the Western European movements. They recalled, as well, the attacks over the years by the AFL against socialism and socialists, even those who were anti-communist. The policies of George Meany and, especially, Jay Lovestone, dominated the external relations of the AFL and kept it on the path of militant anti-communism. With the deep commitment of a convert, Lovestone created an anti-communist network of labour representatives, labour attachés and allies dedicated to confronting communists in or near the trades union movement. Lovestone was able to gain control over the US State Department labour policy and virtually named the labour attachés. His colleague, George Philip Delaney, moved from the union movement over to the State Department to co-ordinate the State Department labour efforts. Later, after being cleared of McCarthyite charges brought against him, Cord Meyer, former leader of the United World Federalists and the American Veterans Committee, took over the Covert Action Section of the CIA from Tom Braden, and worked closely with Lovestone and Mike Ross, head of the CIO's International Affairs Department, in building up a network of labour, student and cultural groups covertly funded by the CIA to oppose communist efforts in these areas.

The anti-communism of the AFL frequently upset their allies, who feared that it would prevent organising new unions into the ICFTU, especially in Asia, Africa and South America. The AFL's continuing battle with the ICFTU about anti-communism was witness to the depth of this antipathy. This conflict mirrored the internal conflict in the US delegation between the AFL and the CIO leaders.

Meany argued passionately for an official ICFTU anti-communist crusade against a 'Worldwide totalitarian conspiracy [which] aims to foist on the workers of all free countries a system of economic exploitation and political oppression . . .'[8] Other US labour leaders took a more moderate position. The most prominent of these was Walter Reuther whose views approximated the basic European labour position. The fight, according to Reuther, for the ICFTU was as much against the right, represented by unrestrained and untrammeled capitalism as it was against the totalitarian left. He said, 'We do not believe that our choice in the world today is between Wall Street and the Kremlin. We do not believe that the choice is between Stalin and Standard Oil.'[9] He urged that the ICFTU develop a positive ideology and a programme of organisation and support.

The British position was ambivalent. While seeking to avoid the open politicisation of the ICFTU it attempted to safeguard the leadership role it had won for itself in European unionism. Primarily, though, it was anxious to support its associated Commonwealth unionists whom it had brought to the meeting. Indeed, in the eyes of the AFL's observer in the Far East and others the reason for the British and Dutch walkout from the WFTU was not because of their support for the ERP or solidarity with the AFL, but rather because of the fears of a communist-inspired deterioration in their Asian colonies. The origin of these fears arose as a direct result of a communist youth congress in Calcutta in January 1948 which ordered guerrilla uprisings in Asia and on the Indian subcontinent. The French, British and Dutch colonies were at once affected; indeed, the richest source of dollars in the British Empire – Malaya – was stricken in June 1948 by a civil war. The uprisings in Indonesia, Indo-China and the Indian subcontinent persuaded the Dutch, French and British governments that the ties with communist union, student and cultural groups ought to be dissolved. This 'colonial' issue was one that later served to further divide the ICFTU.

One further point of controversy arose early in the discussions on the structure of the ICFTU. Although the preceding labour international had been dominated by the German and subsequently the British labour organisations, the split in the WFTU witnessed the rise of a strong, wealthy and powerful US delegation. The Preparatory Committee had not been able to achieve consensus on a location for the ICFTU headquarters, nor on a suitable presidential candidate. The TUC wanted London for the headquarters and a British unionist for the presidency. Although the Europeans feared British domination if the ICFTU was headquartered in London, they also rejected as foolish the AFL's proposal of Paris. A compromise was reached: Brussels became the headquarters. The AFL and the CIO insisted that the ICFTU President and the General Secretary come from a union movement not associated with one of the 'Great Powers'. This was partly on the grounds of expediency and partly because they feared the British preoccupation with colonial problems would involve the ICFTU in defending colonialism.

In the event, Paul Finet of the Belgian labour federation was elected President and J. H. Oldenbroek of the ITF was elected General Secretary. Another controversy emerged over whether the admission of the Christian unions to the ICFTU should be encouraged. The Christian unions of the CISC had already reorganised themselves in 1946. Although they had attended the first meetings of the WFTU they maintained their independence from it. When the Geneva conference was planning the ICFTU inaugural meetings the US unions, seeking to form as broad an anti-communist coalition as possible, asked if the Christian unions should be invited. The Preparatory Committee addressed itself to this question and declared that if the non-Christian national centres didn't object, then affiliation by the Christians would be permitted. The Swiss, Belgian and Dutch unions refused to permit their Christian colleagues to affiliate and only the French CFTC was invited to attend. At London, however, Dave Dubinsky of the ILGWU rose to request that all Christian unions be asked to attend and affiliate. This was referred to the Credentials Committee which agreed that the Christians could join if they agreed to disaffiliate from the CISC within two years. Only the Belgian Christian union attended the London meeting and it decided to remain affiliated to the CISC. Both the ICFTU and the CISC agreed to co-operate but this has proven more difficult to achieve than originally planned.

Similarly, the ITSs were invited to attend the ICFTU meeting. There they were enjoined to arrange a close, but informal, association with the ICFTU. They retained their autonomy but agreed to create a ITS–ICFTU Liaison Committee to co-ordinate their efforts. There were seven ICFTU vice-presidencies created, filled by: Leon Jouhaux (CGT–FO), Arthur Deakin (TUC), Hans Boeckler (DGB), Eiler Jensen (Danish LO), William Green (AFL), Philip Murray (CIO), and Bernardo Ibanez (Chilean TUC). The ICFTU moved to Brussels and began operations late in 1949. The tensions and frictions which emerged within the ICFTU mirrored the foreign policy conflicts among the governments of NATO formed the same year. A major force in this conflict was the AFL who, within two years, was boycotting the ICFTU and threatening, once again, the unity of the non-communist labour movement.

The period of the early formation of the ICFTU was dominated by the strong political and financial presence of the AFL. By the mid-1950s though, this dominance was rejected by an increasingly large number of ICFTU affiliates. The main focus of this resistance was the unions forming in the nations of Africa, Asia and Latin America and the regional organisations created to service them within the ICFTU.

5 The Background to Third World Unionism

Although trades union organisations have existed in the nations of Africa, Asia and Latin America almost as long as they have existed in the nations of Europe and North America, they did not play a major role in their national economic or political life until well after the First World War. The first recorded industrial action in Africa took place as early as 1793, when Nova Scotian settlers in Freetown struck against the Sierra Leone Company for higher wages. A similar strike took place in Freetown in 1874. These early unions were formed by European workers who brought with them their traditions and institutions of workers' self-help organisations. In 1881 the Amalgamated Society of Woodworkers created a recognised union in South Africa; the French national trades union centre the *Confédération Général du Travail* (CGT) set up a trades council in Algeria in 1885; the British Rhodesians created a labour council in 1896; Portuguese unionists formed a union in Mozambique in 1898. These unions were restricted, for the most part, to European workers. The earliest unions of non-European labour in Africa can be found in the history of British West Africa where a strike by canoemen in the Cape Colony in 1896 and a trades union of carriers and porters in 1898 succeeded in winning certain rights from the colonial administrators. The first substantive non-white union, however, was created in Lagos in 1905 when indigenous civil servants banded together to form a recognised union. Despite these early developments, union growth and function in Africa, except for white European unions, tended to be slow, evanescent and largely unrecognised.

Trades unionism in Asia, too, tended to appear first among the several groups of Europeans employed in the colonies, only later spreading to indigenous workers in the civil service, sea transport and especially the railroads. In Indonesia, for example, the first trades union, as such, was the *Staatspoorweg Bond* formed in 1905 among the railroad personnel (including indigenous employees).

It was soon disbanded in favour of a new union, in 1908, formed under the tight control of Dutch socialists, the *Vereeniging van Spooren Tramweg Personneel*. Although self-help organisations of a craft nature in India were created by Indian workers, the first indigenous Indian trades union did not appear until B. P. Wadia formed the Madras Union in 1918. Although there were stirrings of labour organisation in Japan in 1896, they were repressed by the government, only to reappear in 1912 when Bunji Suzuki formed his *Yuaikai* (Friendly Society) as a trades union organisation. Settler unions were formed relatively early in Australia and New Zealand as branches of the parent British unions. Settlers migrating to Palestine from Eastern Europe brought with them the seeds of labour co-operatives such as the *Hovevei-Zion* (Lovers of Zion) movement of 1882.

A form of settler unionism grew as well in Latin America. There craft unionism growth paralleled the expansion of similar types of craft unionism in North America. These Latin American unions first emerged among the immigrant communities from Europe and only later spread to the indigenous, largely Indian, working classes. Latin American unionism, with the exception of Mexico, demonstrated that the greater the proportion of immigrants in the community (Argentina, Uruguay, Chile and Brazil) the greater the growth of workers' organisations. Although mutual aid societies were fostered by the rise of Liberal governments in the mid-1840s, the trades unions which formed tended to divide on craft and racial lines. The unions which formed occasionally grew into regional or national federations, however ephemeral. One of the first, and perhaps the largest, to form was the *Federacion Regional Argentina* (FORA) in 1901 only to split into anarchist, socialist and syndicalist factions soon after. The *Federacion Obrera Regional Uruguaya* (FORU) formed in 1896 met a similar fate, as did similar organisations in Paraguay, Brazil and Chile. Individual craft unions, as distinct from regional or national federations, were able to survive and maintain an identity, especially among typographers, port and railroad workers. These unions often allied themselves with large inter-American labour organisations, such as the International Maritime League, and affiliated to regional branches of these organisations. As early as 1892 Latin unions in the port and maritime trades hosted regional and international meetings of the unions to which they were affiliated. The remaining unions were concerned primarily with maintaining craft restrictions in industries like tobacco, textile weaving, milling and skilled mineworkers.

The unions were relatively small, but they were industrially active. In the period 1884-9 Chile witnessed about sixty strikes. There were general strikes in Sao Paulo in 1906, 1907 and 1912. The textile strike in Rio de Janeiro in 1903 involved tens of thousands of workers. In Mexico, under the Diaz regime, although strikes were illegal, the Mexican workers called general strikes and local strikes involving thousands of workers. There were at least 250 strikes in this period. In Argentina the pattern was similar. In the Buenos Aires general strike of 1907 there were over 93,000 workers in sixteen organised trades out on strike.

Clearly, trades union development in Latin America was of a different type and order of magnitude than the trades union movements in Asia and Africa during the pre-world war period. The most important factor in this distinction was the effect of colonial control on the political and economic forces operating within Africa and Asia, and the inevitable overlap between the economic and political activities of the labour movement and currents of insurgent nationalism and anti-colonialism. In the colonial repression of the forces of nationalism many political leaders of the nations of Africa and Asia faced long prison terms or exile. Those political leaders who managed to remain active in the anti-colonial struggle were most often those who had achieved a position in the trades union movement.

This political burden on the nascent trades unions in colonial territories had a profound effect on their activities, structure and leadership. It generated a movement much larger than a more purely economic analysis would predict, while also severely debilitating that movement by generating diffuse and often unreachable goals. Membership tended to ebb and flow; dues' collections were low and irregular; and the leadership of these unions tended to be highly political, attracting to themselves an elevated level of personal loyalty which mitigated against continuity and organisational stability. Much as Latin American unions were characterised by innumerable splits and factional fights over points of doctrinal controversy. Asian and African unions tended to be characterised by intense personal rivalries among their leaders which promoted disunity and incoherence.

For a labour movement to grow and prosper there appear to be certain basic requirements. First, there must be some elemental feelings of solidarity among the workers; the development of a sense of group affinity or coalition behaviour. This process is relatively easy to achieve on a small scale but progressively harder as larger goups become involved. If, for example, a single plant or office employs workers recruited from the surrounding area there is a high likelihood that the majority of those employed come from the same tribe, clan or other self-conscious ethnic grouping. Communication was easy within the group and a carry over of external political arrangements was manifest within the work environment. As two, three or more plants or offices tried creating a unity of workers for a specific purpose, the very strengths of the unions at local level became their weakness in coalition activities. Traditional distrust of 'outsiders', language and communication difficulties, and personal rivalries among the leaders frequently served to deter or inhibit the growth of solidarity among the workers.

A second requirement for success is the continuity of the leadership cadres in creating and maintaining union policies. It has been a traditional source of weakness for nascent unions in the developing world that the union leaders often do not stay very long in their union posts. Since the requirements of union office at any middle or upper level included basic literacy, numeracy, fluency in a language understood widely in the nation and by the colonial power, high-level union jobs attracted educated men. These men had received their education largely because they were members of the narrow band of elite within their nation which participated in educational programmes. As national economic and political developments broadened the opportunities for employment, these trained and experienced union officials were often tempted to leave the labour movements for better opportunities elsewhere. Throughout Asia and especially Africa the trades union movement has served as the training ground and starting-point for innumerable prominent politicians. Among these are Tom Mboya, Sekou Touré, Siaka Stevens, Rashidi Kawawa, Cyrille Adoula, Joshua Nkomo and many others in Africa. Others, like Gandhi or Nehru in India or a succession of PhD economists in Sri Lanka, held important union posts. These men, often coming from the highest social castes or classes in their respective societies, found many doors open to them. With a few exceptions, these leaders left the labour movement for other careers. This turnover in leadership has posed long-term problems for the development of effective unionism.

A third requirement for effective union organisation, or if not a requirement then at least a traditional precondition, is the growth of industrialisation. For much of Africa, Asia and to a lesser extent Latin America industrialisation has proceeded slowly. Beyond subsistence agriculture, the pace of industrialisation in pre-world war colonial nations was extremely slow, except for extractive industries. What money employment did occur was on the railroads, in the ports, in the mines and in government services; to this must be added the largely sedentary and unorganised sector of plantation labour. When unions did form they formed among the workers employed by or servicing governmental agencies: in the railroads, ports, government offices, or as craftsmen supplying government requirements. There were very few private entrepreneurial efforts in Africa and Asia; and even these tended to be quasi-governmental (the British South Africa Company, etc.). Trades unionism or representation of workers' interests tended to consist of political approaches to a governmental employer. Industrial organisations had to wait for industrialisation.

A fourth requirement for union growth is the ability of local institutions to gain recognition on a national scale as legitimately speaking on behalf of the workers organised into these voluntary organisations. Throughout Asia, Africa and Latin America trades union legitimacy on other than fairly narrowly defined craft lines, was restricted by the governments; first, because they posed a threat to colonial policies, and secondly, because they created potential or immediate political difficulties for post-colonial governments. The process of codified industrial relations systems was very late to develop and, even when it did develop, it tended to create an industrial relation format for expatriate or settler employees.

A composite of all these difficulties, the lack of cohesion, the discontinuity of leadership, the late industrialisation and the lack of a recognised industrial relations system which legitimised union development could be found in all areas and was compounded by the most characteristic aspect of the Third World unionism, the high level of politicisation of the trades union movements. The political role of labour in the developing nations was an inevitable consequence of the impediments listed above. Politics were the *raison d'être* of labour organisation, with economic results and achievements dependent on political success.

One important aspect of Third World unionism was the fact that through a large part of its formative period it was controlled by political and economic forces external to the nations in which it operated. Until well after the Second World War, the nations of Asia and Africa and the Caribbean were largely under colonial domination and subject to the labour legislation and political systems of Western European nations like France, Britain, Belgium, Holland, Spain and Portugal. It is a general rule of colonial administration that political and economic institutions created by them in their colonies rarely were better constituted or more efficient than similar institutions in the colonial country. Thus, since Spanish and Portuguese metropolitan unionism was impeded by their governments, the development of strong trades unionism within Spanish or Portuguese colonies was highly unlikely. When ideological splits divided the unionism of Belgium, France or Holland then these ideological splits tended to spread to their colonies, and unions there split among socialist, Christian, anarchist and communist factions, often with ludicrous effect.

Trades unionism, where it emerged, was largely the result of efforts made by the colonial governments, or the individual efforts of national centres operating within the metropole: occasionally both. In 1929 the British passed the Colonial Development Act which, in addition to creating funds for overseas assistance, provided that colonies eligible for receiving these funds must insure that fair labour standards were created in the colony. The Colonial Secretary, Sidney Webb (Lord Passfield) sent a message to all the colonial governors in 1930 informing them that trade unionism was a policy favoured by the government and should be encouraged. The British TUC, whose Labour government was now in office, sent out experienced unionists throughout the colonies to assist local unions in their efforts. By 1938, these informal overseas missions were regularised and the post of labour advisor to the Colonial Office was formed. A social services department within the Colonial Office was created to handle labour questions. Labour officers were sent out under Colonial Office auspices to build colonial unions and the post of labour attaché was created in the High Commissions. The TUC loaned or seconded numerous unionists to serve in this capacity; they also sponsored indigenous unionists to come to Britain for labour training. By 1940 a new act, the Colonial Development Act, was passed. It went further than the 1929 Act by stating that to be eligible for development funds the territorial governments must provide for and maintain a local trades union movement. Trades union national centres sprang up across Asia, Africa and the Caribbean. These were under the close tutelage and control of the labour attachés sent out by the Colonial Office. The linking of trades union development and the provision of developmental grants to the territories made union office very attractive to aspiring politicians. Many joined the growing labour movement in key posts.

When the Popular Front was formed in France in 1937, the reunited *Confédération Générale du Travail* (CGT) was permitted to extend its activities throughout the French colonial empire. Although the right to organise indigenous unions was granted to Algeria and Tunisia in 1932, the other colonies had to wait until 1937. Even then, membership in those unions was restricted to those who were literate in French and possessed an elementary school diploma. These restrictions were not lifted until 1944, when a government decree abolished the literacy requirements and opened the way for large-scale organisation of workers. After 1944, the CGT sent down numerous labour advisors to the indigenous national or regional unions. They set up a large number of labour schools for unionists (especially in French West Africa). Jointly the CGT and the PCF set up schools, called *Groupes d'Études Communistes*, in Dakar, Abidjan, Conakry and elsewhere to teach basic trades unionism and political action. The graduates of these schools became the backbone of early French African unionism. The split in the CGT in France saw the creation of similar CGT–FO and CFTC schools throughout the French colonies, but with less success.

The right to form unions within the territories administered by the Belgians was denied to Africans until after 1946, although unions of European workers had been allowed since 1921. An effort by the Belgian metropolitan Christian federation to promote multi-racial unionism in the Congo soon led to a split along racial grounds. The socialist federation of Belgium, the FGTB, was not able to build a multi-racial federation in the Congo until 1951; it too fell apart on racial lines soon after.

The development of unions within the British-administered areas of East Africa, despite the Passfield memoranda, was severly retarded by colonial practice. A Labour Trade Union of East Africa founded in 1937 was banned as was its successor the East African TUC founded in 1949. A general strike in Nairobi in 1950 was crushed by the army and over three hundred unionists were imprisoned. Many unionists left their union ranks to join the Mau Mau movement which pressed for independence.

The colonial legacy in Africa, in the British colonies, was one in which the colonial authorities promoted a highly centralised trades union movement, watched over by visiting officers of the British TUC, and which was controlled by the ability of the colonial administration to register and deregister unions. Within the French areas, a far more diffuse trades unionism was fostered, with ideological constraints on national or regional unity developing as a result of the replication of the metropolitan union competition. In Belgian areas trades unionism was primarily a concern of Europeans, while in Spanish and Portuguese territories trades unionism was barely tolerated. In the only area where trades unionism was a potent force, the Union of South Africa, trades unionism was divided on strictly racial grounds. Prominent Indian and African unions developed there as did a strong white labour movement dedicated to fighting non-white labour and preventing them from threatening white jobs or wage levels.

The conflict between racial groups within the South African labour movement presaged much of the subsequent social history of South Africa. The Indian nationalist leader, Mohandas Gandhi, helped create some of South Africa's first Indian political and labour organisations through his Natal Indian Congress, and was a testing ground for his technique of passive disobedience. The Africans' indigenous unions formed primarily in the Rand and in the service industries supplying the Rand. Their efforts, notably in the Industrial and Commercial Workers' Union (ICU), were assisted by organisers and tacticians from overseas, especially the Industrial Workers of the World (IWW) who set up a South African, multi-racial branch. As African and Indian unionism grew more strong, unions of white workers, both Nationalist and communist, joined together in the Rand in a racist General Strike in 1922; a strike which almost led to a full-scale uprising. This strange coalition of Boer Nationalists and white communists marched under the banners of 'White Workers of the World Unite' and 'Workers of the World Unite and Fight for a White South Africa'. In March 1922, Smuts had to call out the army. They attacked the strikers leaving 230 dead and many wounded. By then, however, although the white workers' strike was ended, the handwriting was on the wall for non-white unionism. Although the ICU was recognised as having 100 000 paid up African members at its zenith, the pressures of racism soon destroyed it. Following the Rand Strike the poor whites effected a political coalition between the Labour Party and the Nationalist Party in 1924 and formed a government. This government dedicated itself to the reduction in opportunities for non-whites, especially in the trades union movements. By 1930, non-white trades unionism was virtually dead or underground. Non-white trades unionism became, as in most colonial areas, the spearhead of national independence movements.

One of the first areas of national consciousness to emerge from colonialism was trades unionism, especially in the fields of transport where indigenous workers came in contact with foreign workers already engaged in union activity. These unions joined with the rising self-consciousness of civil servants and government employees. These essentially urban, literate workers formed both the backbone of the trades union and nationalist movements. As they grew in strength, the colonial authorities first attempted to crush the unions; then they moved to crush the political parties. By the time they moved against the parties, the unions had found a way to continue operating. When the colonial government exiled or imprisoned the political leadership, the trades union leadership served as alternative nationalist leaders. The party and union became linked.

A second development was the growing dependence on external assistance by both nationalist movements. Particularly within French colonial areas (but not limited to these) the early postwar political developments of the Cold War era saw the Soviet Union supporting nationalist independence movements under the control of indigenous communist parties or communist-led trades unions. Frequently, this support involved the splitting of nationalist political and trades union organisations into communist and non-communist factions. When the US, without a major colonial history and sense of colonial obligation, became active in support of the nationalist political trades union struggles, it often found itself in conflict with its Western allies in France, Britain, Belgium and Holland. The organisations of international labour found themselves competing for the support they could give to Third World unionists caught up in the struggles for national self-determination. This competition was made even more intense since the US and Canadian unions frequently supported different nationalist organisations than the CGT–FO, the Belgian FGTB, or the Dutch NVV. The US and the TUC frequently fought over which factions of the nationalist/union movements deserved support.

The process of decolonisation which followed the end of the Second World War immensely complicated the relationships between the US and its European allies; a relationship already strained over the growing Cold War divisions in Europe and the creation of the European Recovery Programme (ERP). The European colonial nations, Britain, France, Belgium, the Netherlands, Spain and Portugal were reluctant to speed up the process of decolonisation. They felt that they should repair the ravages of war within their own nations before embarking on a programme of decolonisation.

The nations of the West were convinced that the Soviet intentions were much more aggressive and expansionary than had been previously thought likely. The fires of Asian nationalism which had been stoked in the Pacific war created an upswell of movements pressing strongly for national liberation. Within nations like Burma, the Phillipines, India, Malaya and China the nationalist trades union movements had become actively engaged in political activities (and occasionally military operations) designed to speed up the process of decolonisation. The European colonial powers sought to re-establish their control over their Asian colonies in order to counter what they saw as an effort at subversion by the nations of the Soviet bloc. They strengthened their military and civil forces there. They used their votes within international organisations to prevent support to the nationalist movements. The governments sought, as well, to use their national labour centres as agents to restore labour tranquillity in their colonies. Frequent TUC and French trades union missions were sent out to Kenya, Indo-China, Malaya and Burma in an effort to dissociate the trades unions from the nationalist struggle, or at least keep out the communist unionists who threatened to take over the movements.

These activities were not viewed with much satisfaction by the US government or its domestic trades union allies. There has always been a strong anti-colonial bias in the rhetoric of US diplomacy and many political figures in the US argued that the war was not won to restore colonial control by the Europeans. They argued that the perpetuation of colonial rule would inevitably cement the ties between the communist forces and the forces of nationalism in Asia and Africa; ties which would ultimately be damaging to Western long-term interests. The US and the US unionists argued that in the light of the Cold War division of the world into two competing systems, the struggle for national self-determination should not be allowed to promote adherence by the newly emerging states to the communist bloc. Anti-communist nationalist movements should be encouraged and nurtured. This conflict between the two groups in the West had a marked effect on the development of the schisms between the union movements of the US and the rest of the international labour movement, particularly as the trades unions were increasingly locked in the throes of the Cold War struggle.

6 The Development of African Unionism

The importance of African unionism was not merely its role in the expanding industrial and service bases of the nation but also the important role played by these unions in the process of national self-determination. The African labour movements played a vital role in creating a sense of national identity. They worked closely with the nationalist political parties in pressing for a rapid decolonisation. They developed ties with trades unions in other African states and with inter-African political groupings. Within the French colonial areas of the AOF (French West Africa) and the AEF (French Equatorial Africa) these inter-African ties were strong. Gradually, especially in East Africa and Central Africa there were increased links among trades unions operating within the British colonies. For a long time, however, there were few links between anglophone and francophone African unionists.

The developments of African unionism cannot be separated from the political, military and economic developments which took place in other colonial areas, largely because the colonial policies of the metropolitan nation were rarely developed on a colony-by-colony basis. What affected one colony often had a direct bearing on the colonial policy towards other colonies. Some of the momentum which led to the rapid expansion of self-determination in Africa derived from colonial struggles elsewhere, especially Asia. The experiences of Cold War struggles in territories on the fringes of Europe, especially in Greece, Turkey and Iran, and the role of the trades unions in these struggles had made most colonial nations wary of the power of trades unions. They tended to view the unions in Africa, Asia and Latin America as potentially vulnerable. This was not, of course, because they were fantasising a threat from the Cominform but rather because the Cominform, the WFTU and the various 'front organisations' were quite explicit in advocating the immediate overthrow of colonial rule. The East provided leadership, funds, public platforms and support for anti-colonial forces throughout the Third World. That is, they provided this support to those movements which they felt were most amenable to the strategic interests of the Soviet Union; not necessarily to the most representative of the broad spectrum of nationalist interests.

The West, in seeking to counter this thrust by the forces of the Eastern bloc in the colonial areas was itself divided between colonial nations and the United States, each of whose foreign policy goals called for different programmes. Also important was the concomitant development of African institutions of political and economic unity: for example, the thrust towards Pan-Africanism. As African states won their independence they tended to form links with other like-minded independent African states and, gradually, inter-African political and economic institutions were developed to carry forward these mutually agreed policies. These inter-African groupings were themselves divided between right, left and centre although virtually all professed non-alignment.

By 1949 it had become clear to the WFTU that after the walkout by the Western unions it would be very difficult to maintain a large number of affiliated unions in the colonial territories. They recognised that the colonial powers would not permit this and would actively discourage any expansion of the WFTU influence. They made a decision to cut their losses in Africa and to seek to work through indigenous organisations with whom they could build and maintain a firm liaison. They also sought to pre-empt any expansion of the trades union work of the ICFTU or the Christian CISC by making the issue of non-affiliation a yardstick by which the degree of non-alignment could be tested. Since the WFTU could not have any major number of African affiliates, it sought to deny the ICFTU and the CISC affiliates by making disaffiliation an issue in the test of African nationalist legitimacy. The postwar growth of African trades union internationalism was riven on the issue of disaffiliation. The left unions insisted that any organisation to which they belonged must be purely an African, or in some cases Afro-Asian, organisation without any official ties to international union organisations to which the unions of Great Powers belonged. On the other hand, the right and centre unions demanded the right to choose whatever organisation with which they wished to affiliate. The history of Pan-African labours had been largely a battle over this issue. The first postwar conflict affecting the trades unions in Africa was the extension into French Africa of the turmoil caused by the split in the CGT in metropolitan France. The split between right and left within the French national centre had a profound effect in Africa.

In late 1947, the French trades union scene was dominated by the giant general strike which rapidly was adopted by the French communists as a test of strength with the new government. The communists gave their support to their CGT allies in the strike which caused an almost total disruption of the ports, pits, post, textile and chemical industries in France. As a consequence non-communist unionists in France united to split the CGT into two factions: the communist-dominated CGT and the non-communist CGT–Force Ouvrière (FO). Foreign communist parties donated massive sums of money to the CGT to sustain it in its struggle and to the PCF (whose leaders had left the government). Some of this money which poured into the PCF–CGT coffers made its way to Africa where it was used to turn a legitimate labour dispute among workers on the major rail line in French West Africa into a political strike in support of the CGT battle in France. The PCF expanded its alliance with the inter-territorial AOF political party, the *Rassemblement Démocratique Africaine* (RDA).

There had been two small general strikes in Dakar in 1945–6, but the major industrial unrest was on the railroad linking the AOF territories. The African unionists of the CGT in the AOF had demanded a single union structure incorporating both black and white workers with a single rate for the job. The government and the unions of white workers opposed this. The Africans staged a protest demonstration at the arrival of the French President in Dakar in April 1947, and won agreement on the creation of a single union. When the railroad board refused to honour the agreement, the African workers went on strike. In November, the African unionists, supported by the CGT, struck and closed down the Dakar–Thies railroad;[1] it stayed closed for 82 days. Over 19 000 workers stayed on strike. After the strike it was found that the CGT in France had intervened in this African union struggle and had prolonged it for French domestic political purposes. They prolonged the strike and supported the strikers through massive infusions of funds and by support from visiting organisers. The metropolitan CGT donated 500 000 CFA francs; the local CGT organisations gave hundreds of thousands of CFA francs more; the RDA donated over 350 000 CFA francs. Some of this money was given to the CGT from sources external to France. Other funds, estimated at over 20 million CFA francs, were given to the strikers from undisclosed sources.[2] The strike ended with a mediated compromise which, while not satisfactory to all was still better than the results the CGT achieved in France.

The first area to feel the pressures from France was the political party affiliation between the RDA and the PCF. When the French Socialist

Party (SFIO) joined the government in 1947 and helped to promote the CGT–FO split in the CGT, it also embarked on a campaign to drive a wedge between the forces of African nationalism and the CGT in Africa. Strong pressure was put on the RDA by the colonial authorities. The SFIO African delegates formed their own inter-territorial federation, the *Indépendents d'Outre-Mer*, to compete, with their union allies in the CGT–FO, against the CGT–RDA–PCF nexus. In this they were supported by the AFL. By 1950 the RDA dissolved its ties with the PCF and reconstituted itself as an autonomous African party. This break in the political field was not followed by a similar split in the labour field.

The African labour movements retained their affiliation to the CGT which called a number of inter-territorial meetings to co-ordinate the African labour response to the proposed changes to the French *Code du Travail*. In Bamako, in October 1951, the CGT gathered delegates from fourteen countries in French Africa, setting up two regional co-ordinating committees (one at Dakar for the AOF; and one at Douala for the AEF). When the new *Code* was passed, the African unionists demanded that it be enforced in Africa. They called a meeting in Dakar in October 1952 and demanded its implementation.

Unfortunately, although the French agreed to enforce the *Code*, French administrators set about emasculating its reforms. They reduced the hours of work as provided for in the legislation from 48 to 40 hours per week, but also reduced the wages by 20 per cent. Enraged, the Africans called a second conference in Bamako in March 1953, where they agreed strike action. Strikes broke out across all of French Africa. The longest, and most bitter, strike took place in Guinea, beginning on 21 September and lasting until 25 November. This strike pushed Touré into national and territorial prominence.

By 1955 pressure had been building up among the CGT African affiliates to dissolve the ties which bound them to the French parent confederation. Disappointed by the CGT's lack of support on anti-colonialism the Africans began to discuss disaffiliation. At the RDA meeting in July 1955, Touré put forward a resolution calling for the disaffiliation of all trades union and youth movements from French and international ties. He felt the trades union movements should direct their energies at the most pressing African problem, national independence. The unions began to dissolve their ties with the CGT.

In November 1955 the Senegalese and the Mauritanian CGT unions disaffiliated from both the CGT and the WFTU, creating, under Bassirou Gueye, an autonomous centre. The CGT met to discuss the matter in January 1956 when Bassirou Gueye, Touré and the Malian unionist, Seydou Diallo, announced that they were creating an independent, non-affiliated labour organisation, the CGT Africaine (CGTA). Touré was expelled from the CGT. During the next six months many CGT unions disaffiliated from the CGT and joined the CGTA. These ex-CGT unionists in the CGTA were joined by some African CGT–FO affiliates and some Christian CFTC affiliates. The CGTA remained unaffiliated to either CGT or the WFTU, although friendly with both.

In July 1956 the Christian unionists of the African branches of the CFTC in France met in Ouagadougou to form their own autonomous African labour group, the *Confédération Africaine des Travailleurs Croyants* (CATC) linking, first CFTC unionists in the AOF, then CFTC unionists in the AEF.

An abortive attempt by Abdoulaye Diallo of Mali to hold together a loyalist CGT died as most union bodies switched their affiliation to the CGTA. Five months or so after the creation of the CGTA, Abdoulaye Diallo resigned his position as a Vice-President of the WFTU and joined with Sekou Touré in calling for a meeting of all French African unionists. In January 1957 the meeting which had been scheduled for this unity was held in Cotonou. Attended by both the CGTA and the CATC unionists (as well as the independent railwaymen and CGT affiliates) the trades union bodies joined together to form a new organisation, the *Union Générale des Travailleurs d'Afrique Noire* (UGTAN).

The UGTAN dedicated itself to promoting the struggle for national independence and also pledged itself to remain autonomous from any international labour affiliation. The CATC unionists, although they participated in the founding of the UGTAN, had serious reservations on the disaffiliation issue; they did not want to disaffiliate from the CISC.

By the time of the founding of the UGTAN there were developments elsewhere in Africa which had a profound effect on the development of African unionism. In the British colonial areas of West Africa a degree of normalcy had been restored at war's end. Trades unionists seconded to the Foreign and Colonial Offices were sent to the colonies where they kept a close watch over the development of unionism. Their major power lay in their ability to advise the local colonial administrators on which unionists and unions were to be recognised. The labour advisor supervised labour legislation and labour policy. He was used as a mediator and conciliator in local disputes. He served as a local liaison between African unionists and their British counterparts, often providing educational assistance for local unions or travel grants for African unionists to study trades unionism in Britain (often at Ruskin College, Oxford).

Despite some initial effort to maintain an informal link between British colonial unions of Africa and the WFTU, most union activity took place within the confines of the British colonial policies and the ICFTU. After Suez, the debate between the British TUC and the AFL–CIO (newly united in 1955) over the speed of decolonisation became heated and intense. Disappointed with what they considered the ineptitude and lack of judgement displayed by the British and the French governments in the Suez Crisis, the AFL–CIO was determined that it would use its strength in the ICFTU to promote a rapid disengagement of colonial control by both the British and the French.

The ICFTU had developed a low-key presence in Africa since 1951, when it held an African conference in Douala, attended by the national centres of its affiliated states in Senegal, Ivory Coast, Dahomey, the Cameroons, Gambia, Sierra Leone, Gold Coast, the British Cameroons and the nations of the AEF. Those attending were from the French CGT–FO affiliated bodies or those linked to the TUC. Subsequently, the ICFTU established a West African Information and Advisory Centre in Accra in 1953. A similar advisory centre was established in Nairobi the same year. These advisory centres did little more than act as co-ordinating bodies. This development of an ICFTU presence in Africa did not emerge without substantial controversy between the American unions and the colonial nations.

This conflict between the US unionists and the unions of France and Britain over the pace of decolonisation grew stronger and more public. In Milan, in 1951, at the ICFTU's second congress, matters reached boiling point when Meany and the new ICFTU president (Tewson of the TUC) clashed over a whole range of policies. Key among these was the British imprisonment of Michael Pissas, the leader of the Greek Cypriot labour movement, and the French actions in Tunisia. At the root of the conflict, however, was the lack of a visible anti-communist commitment by the ICFTU; or at least a commitment which would satisfy the AFL. The AFL withdrew from active participation in the ICFTU after the Milan meeting and issued a Bill of Particulars against the organisation in 1952, charging it with being soft on colonialism and for entertaining such notions as affiliating Yugoslav unionists or Italian socialists. By 1953 the AFL had succeeded in manoeuvring Omar Becu (a project Bach participant) into the ICFTU top job and rejoined the Europeans to work from within.

However the AFL refused to abandon its unilateral international aid programmes. These aid programmes were a continuation of the trades union assistance programmes set up between the OSS and the FTUC. The US government had set up an inter-agency labour advisory programme to co-ordinate international trades union programmes. This was headed by Meany himself and administered by John Meskinen of the Brotherhood of Railroad and Airline Clerks (BRAC) within the Foreign Operations Administration (FOA) of the State Department. The AFL was given control over selections to the labour attaché programmes and approval of any delegations of trades unionists to and from the US. Some US unions began to receive funds from government sources for overseas union work. These funds were often used to help create and expand their activities in the Third World. Other sums were allocated to the host national centre, out of US government P. L. 480 Title II local currency balances, for use in 'in-country' development programmes.

As the AFL expanded its overseas programmes on a unilateral basis it increasingly irritated the European unionists and the unionists of the CIO. Among their differences was the AFL's reaction against the growth of neutralism and non-alignment while also offering support to the Third World against European colonialism. At the 1955 Vienna congress of the ICFTU Meany declared that the ICFTU should support a boycott of all products produced by slave labour: for example, all goods produced in nations under Soviet or colonial domination. Meany was supported in this by the colonial unionists but opposed by them when he denounced neutralism and non-alignment; especially along the lines suggested at the recent conference at Bandung.

Any opportunity for working towards a mutual ICFTU–AFL programme was virtually dead after the 1955 congress. A proposal was made to hire a Director or Organisation for the ICFTU to promote Third World unionism, but wrangling over who was to get the job caused a long delay in finding a suitable applicant. In the event, it was decided that Charles Millard, former head of the Steelworkers' Union of Canada (USWA), would take the post. Lovestone opposed the nomination of Millard on the grounds that he spoke no Spanish, that he was trying to take control of the ICFTU regional programmes (especially in Latin America) away from the AFL and return them to the ICFTU, and that he was trying to bar any union from taking money or support directly from the AFL or its FTUC. Meany and Lovestone disowned Millard and set up their own AFL–CIO $500,000 African regional fund which would dispense assistance to African unions directly.

This conjunction of AFL–CIO displeasure with the ICFTU and its

African regional efforts came at a very important period in African history. By 1956-7 a major watershed in African development was reached. With the upcoming independence of the Gold Coast, the independence of Tunisia and Morocco and the Mau Mau efforts in Kenya, the handwriting was on the wall for colonialism in Africa. Independence fever began to grip the continent and politicians, trades unionists and colonial administrators braced themselves for the rapidly accelerating pace of self-determination. Parallel to this development, the trades union movement of Africa began to expand its Pan-African ties.

Coinciding with the independence celebrations of the new state of Ghana in January 1957, the ICFTU held its First Regional Conference for Africa in Accra. At the meeting were most of the leaders of the major Western trades unions affiliated to the ICFTU. Chairing the conference was John Tettegah, head of the Ghanaian TUC and member of the ICFTU Executive Board. Among the other resolutions passed at the meeting was the demand for the creation of an African Regional Organisation (AFRO) for the ICFTU, similar to the ICFTU's regional organisations in Asia and Latin America. The national centres of several African states affiliated to the ICFTU including Algeria, the Federation of Rhodesia and Nyasaland, the British Cameroons, Gambia, Ghana, Kenya, Libya, Madagascar, Morocco, Nigeria, Sierra Leone, Somalia, the Sudan, Tanganyika, Tunisia and Uganda.

Meanwhile, the UGTAN had continued to insist on all its affiliates disaffiliating from any extra-African body. The CGT-FO affiliates resisted this (especially as they were important members of the AFRO). In February 1958, these CGT-FO unionists met in Abijan to create an organisation which would unite them into a Pan-African body similar to the UGTAN or the Christian CATC. They agreed to form a *Confédération Africaine de Syndicats Libres-FO* (CASL-FO). They soon dropped the FO suffix. Thus by early 1958, there were three major Pan-African trades union bodies operating in French Africa; the unaffiliated UGTAN, the Christian CATC and the CASL.

These divergences became part of the wider struggle for independence. When a referendum was held in the AOF and the AEF, the party leaders of the RDA and the PRA supported the proposed constitution which promised eventual self-rule to the French colonies. The trades union movements affiliated to the UGTAN and the student movements of the RDA and the PRA compaigned for a 'no' vote in the referendum. Touré, with the financial backing of the Ghanaian government, led the unions to demand an immediate end to colonialism. The UGTAN was unable, despite this support, to build sufficient agreement among its allies in territories other than Guinea. After the referendum only Guinea had voted against the proposed constitution; only Guinea was given its independence immediately. This failure to unite resulted in the break-up of the UGTAN. Union leaders of the separate territorial UGTAN units in each state were forced to choose between maintaining ties to the UGTAN and thus separating themselves from their ruling parties or renouncing UGTAN and seeking greater domestic power. Most chose to renounce their ties to UGTAN; some remained as dissident UGTAN factions in a non-UGTAN state. When Guinea won its independence in October 1958 it used the remnants of the UGTAN organisation to promote, with Ghana, an anti-French and anti-AEF and AOF policy. An abortive Ghana–Guinea political union cemented a close working relationship between the labour section of the *Parti Démocratique du Guinea* (PDG) Politburo and the Ghanaian Bureau of African Affairs (BAA) in promoting splinter labour groups and parties in their neighbouring African states.

Touré and Nkrumah, using large infusions of outside cash and supplies, supported dissident exile groups from many African nations. The Ghanaians, in particular, became very active in promoting inter-African intrigue through their support of the trades union Pan-African endeavours. These splinter political and dissident groups from across Africa were invited, in December 1958, to Accra to participate in the first All-African Peoples Organisation (AAPO). Heading the AAPO meeting was the Kenyan trades unionist/political figure Tom Mboya. Mboya had risen to prominence through his key role as head of the Kenya Federation of Labour (KFL) and as a leader of the newly formed Pan-African Freedom Movement of East and Central Africa (PAFMECA). PAFMECA was an organisation formed in September 1958 at Mwanza, Tanganyika, uniting labour, nationalist and co-operative movements in a search for liberation and Pan-African unity. At the AAPO meeting Mboya was joined by African dissidents like Patrice Lumumba, Holden Roberto and Felix Moumie. The AAPO set up a permanent secretariat in Accra and established a Freedom Fighters Fund which would provide assistance throughout Africa to nationalist movements. In Accra, the AAPO and the Freedom Fighters Fund became the inter-African operating arm of the Ghanaian Bureau of African Affairs. Money, supplies and advisors were sent from Accra throughout Africa promoting unrest and pressing for independence.

This creation of a permanent secretariat for the AAPO still left the Pan-African trades union movement without a central focus. Touré called an UGTAN congress for January 1959, in Conakry, where it committed itself to the anti-colonialist struggle. Its first non-French affiliate was the Ghanaian TUC which had disaffiliated from the ICFTU. The UGTAN declared itself a Pan Aftrican labour organisation and required all its affiliates to disavow other affiliations. The French government and the local authorities were quick to quash any mass affiliation to the reconstituted UGTAN and within a few months the UGTAN disappeared in any meaningful sense.

The Christian international (CISC) held a meeting to rally its affiliates into a Pan-African body, in January 1959, when the individual unions of the CATC in the AEF and the AOF joined to form a Pan-African Christian federation, the *Union Pan-Africaine des Travailleurs Croyants* (UPTC) under the leadership of Gilbert Pongault. The UPTC became the regional affiliate of the CISC.

The ICFTU had not been totally inactive in this period. In 1958, the ICFTU set up a Regional Training College in Kampala. Under pressure from many West African unions the ICFTU called a meeting in November 1959, in Lagos, where it finally agreed to form an African Regional Organisation (AFRO) as part of the ICFTU. The funds for this activity and the college were provided as the result of the creation of an International Solidarity Fund (ISF) within the ICFTU, administered by a separate committee. The decisions taken at the Tunis Congress in 1957 creating the ISF did not result in any reduction in bi-lateral assistance programmes but provided a mechanism by which the major donors could 'ear-mark' specific grants to go through the ICFTU.

The success of the ICFTU in creating an African regional organisation was resented by the former UGTAN unionists. They met in November 1959 in Accra, under the auspices of the AAPO and the rump UGTAN to plan an All-African Trades Union Federation (AATUF). Attending were delegates from Ghana, Guinea, Gambia, Sierra Leone, Nigeria, Morocco, Algeria, Egypt, Uganda and South Africa. They spent a lot of time criticising the AFRO and the UPTC as imperialist stooges. The problem came when the ICFTU-affiliated unionists attending the meeting as AAPO delegates (notably Tom Mboya) objected to Nkrumah's suggestion that affiliation to the new Pan-African labour body should entail immediate disaffiliation from the ICFTU. Despite this a trades union meeting was held later in November 1959, in Accra, attended by delegates from the trades union movements of Morocco, Tunisia, Kenya, Togo, Nigeria, Rhodesia, Uganda, South Africa and representatives of the UGTAN and the newly created Pan-Arab labour federation, the International Confederation of Arab Trades Unions (ICATU). These unionists agreed to form a provisional secretariat under Majoub Ben Seddick of the Moroccan UMT and to prepare for the inaugural congress of the AATUF in May 1960.

Tensions grew as the trades unions divided among the three confederations.

The parallel growth of what was being called the Brazzaville and Casablanca Groups had a strong interaction with the trades union conflicts. The Ghanaians spent massive sums of money attempting to split the national centres of the nations which opposed the Ghanaian unity call. The best example was in Kenya whose trades union leader, Mboya, was a principal opponent of the Ghanaian–Guinean control of the Pan-African labour organisation. The Ghanaians sent in money and organisers to Kenya to finance Arthur Ochwada in his attempt to create a Kenya Trades Union Congress (KTUC). In the period before the creation of the AATUF the Ghanaian trades unionist, John Tettegah, was made a roving ambassador by the Ghanaian government. He roved across Africa spreading his philosophy of unionism and dispensing cash to his adherents. Ochwada was not successful in topling Mboya and incurred the wrath of many in the KFL. He (and Mamadou Jallow of the Gambia) were placed on the payroll of the Bureau of African Affairs. These two were sent off on a mission across Europe and North America in an effort to drum up support for a 'hands off' policy on African labour. This mission was less than successful. It generated, instead, sufficient distrust among the major Western unions as to prompt Ghana to postpone the AATUF's inaugural meeting.

In response, the KFL called a meeting of its supporters at its congress in June 1960 where it reaffirmed its desire to maintain its affiliation to the ICFTU and denounced the provisional AATUF. Mboya delivered a major address which cited all the intrigue and covert plotting by Tettegah and the Ghanaians. At this time as well, the Conference of Independent African States was meeting in Addis Ababa. There the polarisation between the Ghanaian philosophy and the adherents of the more moderate Nigerian philosophy split the organisation into two rival groups: the Casablanca and the Brazzaville groups. Each of these adopted the trades union movement most closely identified with its position as its labour standard bearer and supported its labour efforts against the rival group. The Casablanca Group supported the AATUF while the Brazzaville Group supported the ICFTU's AFRO. The AFRO called another organisational meeting in November 1960, in Lagos, which set out the working procedures for the organisation and stressed the need to maintain freedom of choice on international affiliations. It stated that international ties did not rule out Pan-African legitimacy. The chairmanship of the AFRO was won by Alaji Adebola of Nigeria; Ben Ezzidine of Tunisia became Vice-Chairman. The offices were set up in Lagos under Nigerian control. The AFRO suffered from its lack of a major francophone membership but continued to receive support from the ICFTU. It soon ran headlong into a major series of battles with the AATUF.

Initially the crisis was one of claims and counter-claims about Pan-African legitimacy. This was expanded when the newly formed AATUF circulated a document purporting to be the annexe of a British Cabinet paper entitled 'The Great Conspiracy Against Africa'. This document was a clever piece of disinformation. It stated what a British Cabinet paper might very well have said had such paper actually been written. The document alleged that there was a direct secret relationship between some top union leaders in Britain and the US and their respective governments and intelligence services and that the rivalry between the two nations' unions for control of Africa was harming British interests. The text was printed in full in *Trud* the AUCCTU journal, accusing the US of taking 'advantage of the difficult situation in which the United Kingdom and other European powers find themselves and to replace their influence and interests by direct U.S. penetration in Africa using the machinery of ICFTU and American contacts that have been built up with African leaders for this purpose'.[2] In particular, the document cited the alleged covert support by the US for African unionists like Mboya, Alioune Cisse, N'Gom, Mbilla Marcous, Macrae and others. The document condemned the ICFTU for working with the Americans, and Oldenbroeck in particular for being part of the ITF co-operation with the British SIS during the war. It singled out Irving Brown as the key instrument of American penetration of the ICFTU. The paper stated that a new model of African unionism should be created; based on 'John L. Lewis (or Ernest Bevin) in their early days and not Hoffa or Anastasia in their later days'.[3]

As might be imagined, this supposed Cabinet paper caused havoc within the international labour movement. The Americans and the British denounced the document as a forgery. Tom Mboya issued a bitter statement denouncing the implications and attacking AATUF for circulating the document. He said that the ICFTU was not, as stated in the document, a colonial endeavour by the NATO states but rather a genuine international labour effort independent of governments.

The planned meeting to officially inaugurate the AATUF was rescheduled for Casablanca in May 1961 at a time when another meeting was scheduled to see if unity could be agreed between the Casablanca and Brazzaville political movements. Ultimately, the Casablanca powers did not attend the political meeting, leaving the largely francophone Brazzaville group in alliance with the more moderate anglophone states (notably Nigeria and Liberia) who formed a new Pan-African grouping, the Monrovia Group. At Casablanca, however, trades unionists from forty-two African states or colonies met to inaugurate the AATUF. Attending as foreign guests were representatives from the ICFTU, the French CGT, the Italian CGIL, the Chinese ACFTU, the Czechs and the Poles. A charter was submitted to the meeting which required total non-affiliation by its members to any international. By the end of the debate, over one-third of the delegates had walked out (Kenya, Uganda, Nyasaland, Nigeria, Southern Rhodesia, Tanganyika, Somalia, Congo (B), Cameroons, Mauritius and Madagascar). AATUF headquarters were established in Casablanca under the presidency of Majoub Ben Seddick. Other officers included Maachou (Algeria); Tettegah (Ghana); Kaba (Guinea); Awab (Morocco); Sissoko (Mali); and Salema (UAR Egypt). It was a replication among unions of the Casablanca political group.

The ICFTU and its AFRO affiliates denounced the AATUF as unrepresentative and government-dominated. It questioned where AATUF funds were coming from, and called for vigilance on the part of non-AATUF states against covert intrigue in their nations conducted under AATUF auspices. Tettegah issued a reply to the call for vigilance. He stated that there would be total war between the AATUF and others: 'We shall isolate them and enter their countries and form AATUF unions there. It is as simple as that – total war.'[4]

The non-AATUF unions feared this was not an idle threat. The AFRO unions, especially the weaker Christian UPTC unionists, decided that they too must band together for mutual action. They called for a non-AATUF unity meeting to be held in Dakar in early 1962 where the representatives from forty-one African unions from thirty separate countries formed a new organisation, the African Trades Union Confederation (ATUC). These unionists agreed that affiliation to the international trades union bodies was permitted and called for the independence and autonomy of each union from national or international domination. Tlili of Tunisia was made President and Soumah (the Senegalese president of the UPTC) was made administrative secretary. The newly formed ATUC leadership flew to Lagos at the end of the meeting to attempt to win recognition from the Monrovia Group powers who were meeting there, but they were refused this status.

This formation of ATUC was met by hostility from the AATUF. AATUF decided to pursue a policy of confrontation with ATUC affiliates in every African country. They announced that they were starting to publish monthly journals in three languages; they were opening labour colleges in Morocco, Ghana, Guinea and Egypt to train unionists in their role in Africa's struggles; and they announced the creation of a solidarity fund to assist weaker unions. Throughout Africa large sums of money arrived from AATUF sources. Union journals were subsidised by the AATUF. Jeeps, Land Rovers and public address systems appeared in union halls donated by the AATUF. By the end of 1962, an important battle was being waged for the hearts, minds and political support of African unions.

This rivalry and conflict between the AATUF and the ATUC came at a particularly unfortunate time for the survival of independent African unionism. With the rapid decolonisation of Africa and the growth of domestic self-rule the role of the trades unions in Africa had dramatically changed. During the independence struggles the union movements had proved a valiant ally of the nationalist movements. With the achievement of independence these same movements were increasingly viewed as potential political and economic threats to the new African elite. The new governments were faced with integrating the unions' consumptionist urges with the need for domestic austerity and central planning of the economy. Since most of the organised labour force was white-collar civil servants and service workers, they were often the elite of the nation's labour force, with high wages and even higher expectations. With the achievement of independence they felt that they deserved an improvement in their living standards. As expatriate colonial officials vacated their jobs indigenous workers moved into their positions, expecting to move into the wage and benefit status which accrued to these positions. In almost every case they were disappointed. Pressure was brought by the new governments on their unions to help keep down wages, and even to reduce existing wage patterns for the cause of national development. The unions fought against any reduction in the living standards of their members and campaigned against the rising corruption and misuse of power which independence too frequently generated within African states.

Unlike examples in Asia and Latin America, the ally of the African labour movements tended to be the army. African army structures, especially in the immediate post-colonial period, often were distrusted by the general public in that they had had a tradition of conflict with the nationalist movements during the colonial era. Many African soldiers had fought and died defending the colonial empires of Britain and France against anti-colonial uprisings and civil disturbances. Many, if not most of the African armies had been recruited either from tribes with a long military tradition or among illiterate minority tribesmen from remote corners of their nation. The British had followed a policy of tribal quotas for their colonial armies; a policy which filled the armed forces with a tribally unbalanced set of forces. In Nigeria and Ghana, for example, the great majority of the ordinary soldiers were recruited from northern Muslim areas while the officer corps came from the southern non-Muslim areas. In other areas, like Kenya, the British recruited minority tribes into the army. Out of nearly 6000 African ranks in the Kings African Rifles 34 per cent were Kamba and 34 per cent were Kalenjin. The largest tribe, the Kikuyu, were barely represented. The French concentrated on recruiting from among tribes with low levels of literacy but with a strong warrior tradition for their recruits and NCOs, and from among the Europeanised ethnic groups for the officer corps. With independence, despite the discipline inherent in any army structure, there was a great gulf between the military and civilian leaderships in the African states. This was accentuated as the new civilian leaderships attempted to broaden the tribal base of their armies and to curb the power of the officer groups.[5]

Similarly, the governments began a campaign to co-opt the trades unions into their vision of a 'productionist' model. The governments co-opted the union leadership into political posts. They made union membership contingent on party membership in the ruling party. They exiled, banned or imprisoned union leaders. They created splinter labour groups which they favoured with government recognition. They disallowed the dues checkoff systems. They gave the unions the role of quasi-governmental entities in the provision of social services. For example, in Mali in 1962 the government passed legislation giving unions the right to establish provident schemes, to run experimental farming stations, and to determine curricula development. In Ghana the GTUC was charged with establishing technical training centres. The Tanganyikan centre (NUTA) was given the responsibility of creating adult education programmes. Most importantly, the unions, especially on the level of the national centre, were charged with the task of acting as agencies for capital accumulation. Many unions were requested to set up savings funds or similar capital schemes which would help spur domestic savings which could be made available for investment.

In Tanganyika, Ghana, Mali, Senegal and the Ivory Coast the unions were permitted (some say required) to create small-scale commercial undertakings in agriculture or housing projects. This development of government-directed worker capitalism was resented by the union's rank-and-file. A good example of this was the bitter strike in 1961 at Sekondi–Takoradi in Ghana. The strike developed largely as a protest against a government scheme to deduct 5 per cent from the wages of all workers with incomes over 120 pounds per year. The deducted monies were to have been invested in development bonds earning 2.5 per cent per annum, but whose principal and interest were not touchable for ten years. The strike lasted for twenty-one days and involved over 10 000 workers. It took a direct government intervention (Nkrumah ordered in the police and jailed forty-eight strikers) to end the strike. It is some measure of the resentment by the workers of this savings scheme that they were willing to face a hostile government and a vehemently hostile trades union leadership to press for an end to the savings plan.

It is small wonder then that the new African governments sought to minimise contact between their unions and unions overseas, especially those who might protest the destruction of trades union rights on the continent. It is equally clear that the ruling political leaderships, across the full ideological spectrum, had little interest in fostering a genuine Pan-African trades union organisation. Despite the creation of the Organisation of African Unity (OAU) in 1963, into which the Monrovia and Casablanca groups subsumed their separate identities, no such unity was forthcoming in the African labour movements.

It was no accident that those unions most active in promoting disaffiliation from the internationals and in promoting intrigue within other nation's union movements, were those unions most totally under domestic political control. As a result of this fundamental conflict relations deteriorated further between the AATUF and the ATUC. Periodic efforts aimed at creating a united Pan-African movement were made but faltered on the rock of the disaffiliation issue. Another meeting was arranged for AATUF–ATUC unity in Dakar in 1970. Unfortunately for the proponents of unity the ATUC delegation was self-elected and not representative of the organisation. The OAU intervened and issued a draft constitution for a united labour movement. It called another meeting in November 1972. The ATUC did not attend but, on the third day of the meeting, the OAU was able to persuade Ben Ezzidine of Tunisia to attend. Robel of the Malagasy Christian federation also arrived. They were presented with a constitution which was virtually identical to that drafted by the AATUF in 1964.

In April 1973 they succeeded in persuading many of the African national centres to agree to form a new, united organisation, the

Organisation of African Trades Union Unity (OATUU). Discussion on the affiliation issue was postponed until the next congress. This was held in Tripoli, Libya, in 1976, where no real decision was reached. What occurred was a conflict between the several national centres from each country. Each was seeking to become the sole recognised national centre from their nation. The Steering Committee made several unpalatable rulings on admission to the OATUU and caused deep disagreement in a number of cases. Most ludicrous of all was the election of officers for OATUU. The Senegalese Minister of Labour (not the trades union leader but the Minister) was called to the rostrum. He proposed the Libyan unionist, Nefishi, as President, Dennis Akumu of Kenya for Secretary–General and E. Odayemi of Nigeria as Treasurer. He then listed all the other jobs and who should fill them. When he was finished the Tanzanian Minister of Communications endorsed the nominations. The elections were declared closed with no vote taken. The next OATUU meeting was scheduled for 1980, but postponed.

The achievement of Pan-African labour unity through the medium of the OATUU indicates the low level to which African unionism has descended. Once a forceful and dynamic movement active in the nationalist struggle, it has been largely reduced to a branch of the ruling political party in each state. The process of this reduction of importance was primarily due to the general reduction in democracy in almost all aspects of African political and economic life. The post-independence flirtation with parliamentary democracy soon ceased in the face of waves of military coups and counter-coups. As African nations became one-party states, one-man states, or military domains the survival of voluntary, independent organisations, like trades unions, was often doomed. Although the trades unions themselves frequently participated in bringing about these changes by allying themselves with the military, they most often found that they had won temporary victories as their new allies became as repressive as those whom they had replaced.

The period from independence to 1964 in Africa was largely one of attempting to make the parliamentary system work. From 1964 to 1967 many African governments were forcibly changed as the people in the armed forces, the trades unions and the student groups saw that parliamentary democracy did not necessarily guarantee that corruption and mismanagement ceased. They overthrew the first generation of political leaders in an effort to purify the system and they eliminated the divisive forces which threatened national dissolution or bankruptcy. From 1967 to the early 1970s African nations discovered that national dissolution could be averted only at a price; often only by accepting military rule. With a few exceptions, military rule has not been associated with the flourishing of domestic liberalism. 'Military democracy' is essentially a contradiction in terms. The military, and especially within those military-dominated states where one supremo commands the loyalty of the armed forces, found it had appetites of its own. Trades unionism, or at least free trades unionism, did not fit their diet. In this aspect, the African unions resembled the developing Asian labour movement.

7 The Development of Asian Unionism

The interaction of politics and trades unionism within Asia was no less important than similar interactions in Africa. To some degree, Asian unionism found it had to confront the same impediments as those which were so debilitating to Africa. Asia, too, suffered from a lack of a large urban industrial mass during the early stages of its development. Rural agriculture and peasant culture were the main attributes of the labour force. It was often employed on foreign-owned plantations. The national political scene was dominated by a colonial presence or foreign occupation which bought forth a nationalist movement with whom the unions became linked. Also true was the strategic role of the interaction between indigenous unionism and overseas unionists keenly interested in the political configurations being shaped by the trades union and the political party in the Asian nation. As in Africa, the leadership of the trades unions and political parties tended to merge and overlap, with the unions frequently providing a stepping-stone for ambitious leaders to move into national political prominence. Also, as in Africa, ethnicity and caste played an important role in the career opportunities for unionists. Union office required literacy, familiarity with the colonial language and discretionary time. This dependence on an intellectual or social elite for the leadership of the union movements is a prime characteristic of Asian unionism; especially in the case of Sri Lanka or in the Phillipines where most of the union business is conducted by union lawyers.

Asia, of course, had many differences which distinguished its political development from that of Africa, not the least of which was the effect of the Second World War. Under the Japanese Greater East Asian Co-Prosperity Scheme, much of colonial Asia was turned upside down. Most Asian countries were occupied. Many were directly in the war theatre. Still others were occupied after the war, or were 'pacified' after nationalist insurgencies. An even more potent force was the growing might of the Peoples Republic of China which, in 1949, fell under the domination of a militant communist party. The presence of tremendous numbers of overseas Chinese throughout Asia, coupled with the support by mainland China to communist factions in Asian civil wars (in Indo-China, Malaysia, the Phillipines and Korea) created a ferment in the area. In other areas, the Red Chinese were extremely active in seeking to promote local political movements sympathetic to its control, as in Burma, Cambodia and Japan. The proximity of the Red Chinese to the nations of Asia and its role as an activist supporter of national insurgent movements made conflict between East and West much more open than in Africa.

For a long time the Chinese role appeared to be congruent with the aims and desires of Soviet foreign policy. The Chinese were seen as Asian surrogates for the Soviet Union. However this phase did not last. By the late 1950s and early 1960s, the Chinese course veered sharply away from that of the Soviet Union and took a line of its own. After 1960, it was very difficult to speak of a communist line in Asia. There were at least two communist lines. Each claimed to be speaking on behalf of the Third World. The Chinese, speaking as non-whites, had a tactical advantage over the Russians but were only really able to exploit this non-white advantage in Asia. The Chinese alternative became attractive to Asian politicians of the left. The controversy between the Soviet Union and the Chinese first came to the world's attention through their open breach in the WFTU. It is a little ironic that the WFTU should be the venue for an ideological split between the Russians and the Chinese since each had long since relegated their respective trades union movements to the role of transmission belts of party policy. It does illustrate, however, the key importance placed by the Russians and the Chinese on front organisations.

It is difficult to overstate the importance placed on front organisations by the communist movement. Throughout communist history the forces opposing the rise of communist parties have sought to ban contact between domestic political parties and foreign communists and their parties. In many nations communist parties were banned; communist organisers killed or jailed for long periods. For many national governments the appellation 'communist' has been synonymous with 'traitor' or 'spy'. Throughout Asia, Africa and Latin America, governments have used the term 'communist' as a term of opprobrium. In many nations, including the non-aligned and neutralist states, communist parties still are banned and ties between nationalist parties and home-grown communists are forbidden. To overcome these hurdles the communists created front organisations: organisations which they dominate, ostensibly promoting a useful goal but in which membership in a communist party was not required. In the postwar world, in particular, these front organisations flourished. The World Peace Council, the World League of Democratic Youth, the International Union of Students and the WFTU provided a venue for communists which was only moderately useful in Africa, but which played a key role in the development of Asian unionism.

The front organisations gave a plausible cover for meetings with neutral and non-aligned student and labour bodies. It gave the communists access to those in need of financial or other assistance whose own governments would not have tolerated contact or aid between those in need and the communists. Most importantly, it provided an acceptable organisation which could hold meetings and training courses to which foreign unionists could be invited. If there is one outstanding identifying characteristic of trades unionists in the Third World, it is their desire to attain credentials. Because the early leadership of Third World unions was drawn from the educated elite, those who sought to follow in their footsteps realised that some form of academic or trades union institute credential would be vital to their upward mobility. If they were to rise in the labour movements, they had to be able to demonstrate that they could fill the jobs of those whom they sought to replace. As a result of this tremendous demand for education, training and credentials the trades union global internationals, ITSs, and front organisations have organised large-scale training colleges, short-programmes and residential instruction in the rudiments of unionism across the Third World.

With the formation of the communist front organisations the governments of the non-communist world established front organisations of their own in competition with the front bodies of the East. They created parallel organisations in the student, cultural and trades union spheres to compete with the communists. Just as there arose a major and fundamental conflict between the Europeans and the Americans in organisations like the ICFTU, similar divergences split the WFTU, when the Chinese and their followers widened the rift between them and their Soviet opponents over the direction and control of that movement. In fact, for both communist and non-communist states it was much easier to use the front organisations to engage in conflict with their rivals than to engage in government-to-government confrontation.

A mistake or a step too far at that level might see missiles over the Ussuri. A polemical fight in the front organisations provides a surrogate forum for real warfare.

After the walkout of the Western unions from the WFTU in 1949, and the formation of the ICFTU, the WFTU was entirely in the hands of the communists. It was directed by the Soviet unionists pretty much along the policy line of the Soviet Union. When, in 1956, the Soviets marched into Hungary to put down the rebellion which threatened to engulf Eastern Europe, the Chinese were emboldened to test out their independent line. The death of the 'hundred flowers' campaign had shifted the Chinese line far to the left, and the Chinese complained that the Russians were threatening bloc cohesion. China sought support from other Asian nations and from Albania. The first international confrontation came at the June 1960 meeting of the WFTU at Peking where the Chinese formed an opposition group to the Soviet line. This was followed by a wider breach at the Fifth WFTU Congress in Moscow in December 1961. There the Chinese and Albanian leftist line was opposed by the ultra-right Italian CGIL which demanded national autonomy for unions and parties and the expansion of organisational contacts with non-communist organisations like AATUF. The Chinese line attacked peaceful coexistence and demanded, along with the South East Asian unionists, a full-scale commitment to the anti-imperialist struggle against the US.

Relations worsened and, at the 1965 Sixth WFTU Congress, the speeches of the Chinese delegates were greeted by shouts from the Soviet unionists of 'Go home!' Pro-Chinese Asian delegations supported the Chinese effort to gain control of the WFTU, but succeeded only in wresting virtual Asian autonomy from the WFTU. The Chinese and others had not paid up their full dues and the AUCCTU had to cough up as much as four million roubles to get the WFTU back in the black. Relations have worsened since then. What was important about this split is that it had a profound effect within Asian union movements. From the early 1960s there has been a growth of pro-Soviet and pro-Chinese labour unions throughout Asia, each of which has been competing with each other for influence and control on the left. This has weakened many Asian movements.

On the other hand, the Western forces have been less divided. This was not the result of any major coalescence of ideological positions between the Americans and the others; rather it testified to the abandonment of Asian unionism by the non-American unions. The interaction of European trades union bodies with Asian unions through the ICFTU or bi-laterally has dropped off dramatically. To some degree this was the result of the lack of longstanding ties between Asian nations and much of Europe. Additionally, with the British abandonment of an East of Suez presence and with the dramatic US involvement in Asian political destinies in Vietnam, Cambodia, Thailand, Laos and South Korea, the field has not been left open for many bi-lateral European initiatives. Except for Hong Kong, where British influence remains strong, the non-communist Asian union programmes have been largely the result of efforts made by the US unions (either bi-laterally or through their respective ITSs) or by the increasing spread of Japanese unions' Asian programmes.

A principal cause of this drop-off in aid and interaction has been the gradual loss of Asian trades union autonomy in the face of a campaign by Asian governments to take over control of their labour movements. There are very few unions in Asia, except for Japan, which are more than extensions of the national political party under another name. The takeover of Asian unions by the government forces and their tight control by government administrators was a common feature of Asian unionism. This was not always the case. Asian unionism played a vital role in the struggles for national self-determination. They played a role in the developing of a national consciousness and a sense of nationhood from among often warring and divided ethnic groups. Their close relationship with the national and international forces in Asia have been the strength and the weakness of Asian unionism.

It was a little ironic that the first trades union bodies to fall under the almost complete control of the political forces were the urban unions of China, especially in Shanghai. In China, after the republican revolution of 1911, trades unions began to form among the urban masses of China's large cities. With the formation of the Comintern, numerous unionists were sent to China to help strengthen the nascent Chinese communist unions and parties. Mikhail Borodin's famous mission was only one of a large number of Comintern missions. Nonetheless, power still remained firmly in the hands of the local warlords whose *min t'uan* (private armies) controlled much of the rural areas. By far the most important development emerged in 1923, when the workers, students and peasants began to form national parties. Among the first was the *Kuomintang*, or Nationalist Party. The other major party was the *Kung Ch'antang*, the Communist Party. Interestingly the *Kuomintang* found a close ally in the communist party of the Soviet Union which sent down instructors and advisers to shape the *Kuomintang* into a disciplined party. The Soviets demanded that the *Kung Ch'antang* merge itself into the *Kuomintang*. In the meantime, the *Kuomintang* became a model in miniature of the Bolshevik party. The Soviets sent advisers to instil communism in the military forces and set up the Whampoa Military Academy. The Russians shipped in arms and instructors to bolster the *Kuomintang* forces. The *Kung Ch'antang* remained a left faction within *Kuomintang* and worked to strengthen the *Kuomintang* on Moscow's orders.

The Chinese communists were successful in recruiting the urban workers of Canton and Shanghai and were able to set up communist-led peasant organisations in Hunan. They built strong unions among the railroad workers and miners in Hunan and, through their control over the Independent Division of the Fourth Army in Hunan, were able to control the industrialised areas east of Changsha. The leadership of the *Kuomintang* devolved on the director of the Whampoa Military Academy and the hero of the northern campaign, Chiang Kai-shek. Having won control of Canton he began a march to the south. In support of the *Kuomintang* the workers in the communist unions of Shanghai began a series of major strikes. At the height of this demonstration more than half a million workers went out on strike in Shanghai, backed by an armed workers' militia of more than five thousand. On 26 March 1927 Chiang Kai-shek marched into Shanghai, welcomed by the striking workers as their liberator. Chiang had barely been in the city when he contacted the leaders of the compradors and the notorious Green Gang to make a deal with them. Allied with these forces, Chiang began a purge of all the communists, especially the unionists. On 12 April 1927 he and the local gangs turned their forces on the communists in the unions. More than five thousand communists lost their lives. When the strikes ended in May, communist control had been wrenched from the unions by the *Kuomintang*. A brief attempt at an urban uprising based on the unions in the 1930s was ruthlessly put down by the *Kuomintang*. The Russians had succeeded in creating a *Kuomintang* which had devoured the local communist party. It was Trotsky, in fact, who had warned of the dangers involved in making the communists join the *Kuomintang*. He wrote that 'the policy of a shackled Communist Party serving as a recruiting agent to bring the workers into the *Kuomintang* is preparation for the successful establishment of a Fascist dictatorship in China'.[1] He was not wrong. The *Kuomintang* set about obliterating the communists, driving them from the cities to their stronghold in Hunan.

The Chinese communists, led by the son of a wealthy Hunanese peasant, Mao Tse-tung adopted these lessons to the communist struggle in China. He decreed that the peasantry should form the basis of the revolution. Only after the peasant revolution would there be need for control of the urban masses. In addition to making a virtue of necessity, this line abandoned the unions in the cities to the less than tender mercies of the *Kuomintang*. During the war with the *Kuomintang* numerous workers' units joined Mao's Hunan army and participated in the Nanchang uprising. The largest union support came from the iron miners of Hanyehping in Wuhan. In fact, the First Red Army was largely composed of workers. When these troops were destroyed in battle with the forces of the *Kuomintang* the first generation of trades unionists in China was virtually eliminated. The 1937 start to the war with the Japanese finished off most of the others. When, after the end of the war, there was a brief interlude of relative calm in China, the US and the OSS forces active in China sent in a large number of American unionists and labour specialists in an effort to rebuild a strong Chinese trades union movement. Dick Deverall of the FTUC attempted to set up labour programmes in China.[2] John Shulter and his colleagues in the US Labour Department tried to foster free unionism in Peking, Shanghai and Canton. But with the gradual ascendence of the Chinese communists under Mao, the forces of the *Kuomintang* were driven from mainland China and the US missions were terminated. The All-China Federation of Trades Unions was recreated under tight party control and became similar in function to the AUCCTU of the Soviet Union. The ACFTU was a founding member of the WFTU and remained an important member in it after the ICFTU split in 1949.

The destruction of free unionism in China had a number of important effects throughout the rest of Asian unionism. On the one hand, it created a party-dominated activist force throughout Asia anxious to advance the Chinese national interests in the area. It promoted the creation of anti-Soviet communist unionism among Asian unions. Most importantly, the Chinese union/party leaders learned the lessons of the dangers of temporary alliances with a powerful nationalist organisation. As the Russians, depending on the current party line, frequently insisted on their Asian party affiliates joining with their ideological enemies in a Popular Front (as in India, Burma and Indonesia), the Chinese supported these local parties in avoiding taking these decisions. What the Russians frequently condemned as an 'ultra-left' line being taken by the Chinese was, to a large degree, the result of the Chinese memory of their own union/party history. Unions and parties supported by the Chinese were reluctant to adopt the Soviet-inspired strategy of 'going underground' and maintaining a clandestine communist party while professing unity with other forces on the left in public. Sometimes, as in

Indonesia and Malaya, this strategy did not succeed any better than the Russian programme, particularly when ethnic Chinese could be seen to be the controlling cadres of the party or unions.

This intermixing of communist parties and trades unions was a major factor in the development of Indian unionism. As in many other Asian countries trades unionism and the rise of nationalist parties was shaped by important interactions with foreign unionists and political leaders. India, under British imperial rule, was an amalgam of British-controlled territories and quasi-independent princely states. There was widespread poverty, famine and disease aggravated by the harsh stratification of a rigid caste system. India was largely an agricultural country with over 70 per cent of the population living in small villages, tilling land leased from the rural money-lenders, the *zamindars*. The major industry was the textile industry located in Bombay. It was not in the interests of the British to create local industries which could compete with British domestic manufacturers so industry was never really encouraged. Before 1920 there were virtually no unions or peasant organisations, although within some cities a type of craft guild began to appear. The political structure was the exclusive preserve of the wealthy and educated classes – mainly Brahmins. Almost every prominent Indian political figure, from Congress Party to the Communist Party, was the product of British education and came from the upper classes.

The most important political grouping in India was the All-Indian National Congress, founded in 1885. It was a sprawling, amorphous body embracing a catholic assortment of political philosophies. Its rather nebulous goals were first challenged at the turn of the century by Tiglak and Ghose, but its most powerful champion and unifying force was Gandhi, who rose to power in the Congress after 1915.

Gandhi, having returned from South Africa, created an organisation which combined Hindu mysticism and revivalism with strident nationalism. His weapons were the *satyagraha* (non-violent direct action), *swadeshi* (boycott of non-Indian goods) and the *hartal* (the closing of shops). Gandhi sought Dominion status for India; local autonomy under the imperial umbrella. He seemed uninterested in pressing for complete independence; a failing which irked many of his Congress colleagues. As industrial organisations grew and trades unions emerged these representatives of the urban proletariat pressed for a less nebulous policy for the Congress and provoked a series of splits within the nationalist movement.

The British government was less than tolerant towards the nationalist politicians and the leaders of the nascent unionism. Indian nationalists found a welcome outside of India. The roots of Indian militance emerged in the large emigré communities in Europe, Asia and America, as well as amongst the terrorist groups of Bengal and the Punjab. The Ghadr Party in San Francisco, the Home Rule League in New York, the important Berlin Committee, and the various 'governments-in-exile' in Britain, Japan and Afghanistan all provided leaders and support for militant Indian nationalism. A large amount of the largesse for these emigré groups came from the Imperial German Army who donated funds, arms and training to the Indian dissidents in the hope of causing difficulties for the British, and in promoting German ambitions in Afghanistan. It was not until the success of the Bolshevik revolution and the creation of the Comintern that anti-British activities among unionists and nationalists in India took a leftist direction. One of the principal Comintern missions sent to accomplish this was that of the ubiquitous Borodin, who contacted a Bengali terrorist-in-exile, M. N. Roy (strangely enough a founder of the Mexican Communist Party) with whom the Comintern decided to set up operations in India.

The impetus for Indian unionism came with the rapid industrialisation brought about by the First World War. The textile mills expanded, railway lines were extended and jute mills were set up across India. Workers from all over India, from the disparate cultures, language groups and societies were uprooted and settled in the cities like Bombay, Madras and Calcutta where they formed pockets of foreignness in the local community. The very low wages and the difficulties of communalism caused an explosive situation. The first act of workers' self-help came when B. P. Wadia formed the Madras Union in 1918. Although based on textile labour membership, the Madras Union was not restricted to textile workers. Wadia, a prominent member of the Indian Home Rule League, pressed for representation of workers and better wages. His organising efforts were encouraged by the employers who used the fact of unionism and its organising efforts to promote a series of lockouts across India. This effective union organising on the part of the employers, however unintended, gave impetus to unions in other parts of India. Wadia himself was prosecuted and an injunction was served against the Madras Union in 1920. By then, however, unionism had already spread to other industries and cities in India. In 1918 seven new unions were formed: four in Madras, two in Bombay and one in Calcutta. Another ten were organised in 1919. By 1920 there were scores of unions across India. When the ILO was set up in 1919 and held its inaugural meeting in 1920, the Indian unionists, under the guidance of the British Labour Party, had united to form the All-India Trades Union Congress (AITUC) to which were affiliated sixty-four Indian unions with a membership of almost 150 000.

The role of the British unionists in this development of Indian unionism was most interesting. It comprised a two-pronged effort. On the one hand, the British unionists were sent to India to help build strong textile unionism; not by the British Government but by the textile unions of Lancashire. These feared for their jobs if Indian production was too high and was able to undercut British prices. On the other hand, the British Communist Party (CPGB) was anxious to spread trades unionism in India as a means of strengthening the emerging Indian Communist Party. The AITUC under its appointed leader, Lala Lajpat Rai, the veteran nationalist leader who had spent many years in New York working with the American socialists, was close to the Congress Party. It appointed Rai as their labour spokesperson, linking the AITUC firmly to the Congress Party. The communists sought to drive a wedge between the unions and the Congress and especially to provide an alternative leadership to Wadia, N. M. Joshi and Rai.

The Profintern had offered the AITUC the right to join as the sole representative of India but the AITUC refused. The communist line at that time in India was to create Workers and Peasants parties throughout India as their vehicles for national, political and economic power. They sent support to Indian unionists to create a base among the urban workers. S. A. Dange built and led a major union in Bombay; Muzzafar Ahmed built a political and economic base in Calcutta. These two men together with M. N. Roy were able to promote the widespread growth of these Workers and Peasants parties and won a voice in municipal politics and the trades unions in many of Indian's key cities. The Sixth Comintern Congress laid down the role of the unions in the nationalist cause. Trades union militance was the order of the day. Strikes, often violent and prolonged, broke out across India in 1928–9. The Bombay textile strike lasted from 16 April to 6 October and was characterised by much violence.

The British government decided to crack down. On 20 March 1929 the British CID arrested thirty-one of the key union and WPP leaders in India. In addition to S. A. Dange and Muzzafar Ahmed they arrested Shaukat Usmani, the WPP leader. Most importantly, they arrested the British communists active in organising Indian labour unrest. Phillip Spratt, Bill Bradley and Lester Hutchinson were arrested and stood trial with their Indian comrades at what was known as the Meerut Conspiracy Case. At the trial it was shown that the Comintern had sent in money and advisers from England and the continent to form and shape Indian militant unionism and that the strikes were provoked by the communists against 'the sovereignty of the King Emperor in British India'. The sentencing in 1933 saw all but four of the thirty-four accused sentenced to long terms of imprisonment or transportation. What was also important was the reaction of the younger non-communist nationalists to the trial. Among the attornies for the defence (who served without pay) were Jawaharlal Nehru, Farid-ul-huq Ansari and Kailash Nath Katju. These used the long trial to read out prepared statements denouncing British colonial rule and propagandising for independence and home rule. The dissolution of the top leadership of the communist unions and the WPPs did not destroy the movement. The orders from Comintern to go 'underground' were followed and the communist Party of India (CPI) began to withdraw from any contacts with 'bourgeois elements'. The WPPs were abandoned. Within the trades union movement the CPI attempted to wrest control of the AITUC from the more moderate Congress unionists.

When the tenth AITUC meeting was held at Nagpur in December 1929, Nehru was in the chair. He was in difficulty trying to hold off the pressure from left-wing unionists like S. V. Deshpande, Mrs S. Nambiar and Abdul Halim to affiliate the AITUC to the communist front organisations like the League Against Imperialism, the Pan-Pacific Trades Union Secretariat and the Workers' Welfare League of India. The communist unions were able to get the affiliation of the AITUC to these bodies by artificially jacking up their claimed membership in AITUC and thus gaining greater voting strength. They succeeded in passing resolutions forbidding the AITUC from co-operating with the Royal Commission on Labour and promoting an AITUC boycott of the ILO. The moderate unionists in the AITUC, knowing that the funds from the Comintern to the left-wing elements in the AITUC had permitted them to pay dues on a grossly inflated claimed membership figure, recognised that they could not stay in the AITUC. In 1930, N. M. Joshi took out the moderate unions from the AITUC to form a new organisation, the National Trades Union Federation. The AITUC, with twenty affiliates, remained in the hands of the CPI.

The Comintern sent in numerous agents to influence the unionists to remain aloof from the Congress. As soon as Spratt and Bradley were arrested they sent in a new batch. S. Saklatvala, a British MP from the CPGB was sent to India. J. W. Johnstone of the American Communist Party, and J. Ryan of the Australian Communist Party were sent to India. A Russian-trained Indian, Prem Lal Singh, visited India for a six-month visit. William Kweit and his wife, Helen Howlen, arrived from the US party along with Harry Somers. These were deported in September 1930. Henry Lynd, the American paymaster for the Comintern arrived in 1931, bringing with him 12 000 rupees in cash. Amir Haidar Khan, John Magnus Clark, William Bennet and Mrs Constance Sargent followed. All, except Haidar, were caught quite quickly.[3] The CPGB and the Comintern were able to use the front organisations to which the AITUC was now affiliated to send in more funds. Gradually, with the British government cracking down on the CPGB, Saklatvala was kept from playing an activist role in India. His position as Comintern specialist on India was taken by Rajni Palme Dutt.

The CPI, however, took activism a step too far, even for India. They organised a railroad strike which failed dismally. When Deshpande, the CPI leader of the AITUC, refused to convene the AITUC regular congress in 1931, the opposition nationalist forces still within the AITUC, under the radical nationalist Subhas Chandra Bose, called their own congress in July 1932 in which the Credentials Committee reduced the communist voting strength by investigating their inflated membership figures. Bose took over as leader of the AITUC and the communists pulled out to form their own unsuccessful Red Trades Union Congress. The Red Trades Unions joined forces with the remnants of the trades unions still loyal to M. N. Roy (who had just returned from a disastrous mission to China where he observed the destruction of the Chinese unions by the *Kuomintang*) to call a nationwide textile strike. Starting in Bombay the strike soon spread across India. The British government thought this was a good opportunity to call a halt to left-wing militance. It arrested the strike leaders, banned the CPI and some twelve CPI-unions and stopped much of the activity of the various front organisations. By 1934 the CPI and the communist movement in the unions was in total disarray.

This difficulty on the part of the communists was an opportunity for the more moderate leftists of the Congress Party. The Gandhi campaigns of *satyagraha* and *hartals* in 1930 and 1932 had caused problems for the British government. The left wing of the Congress led by Nehru and Chandra Bose grew restive under the leadership of Gandhi. They formed their own faction on the left of the Congress, called the Congress Socialist Party (CSP). The CSP claimed to speak for all the factions on the left and attempted to forge an alliance with the Red Trades Unions, then operating underground. The ultra-left, under the leadership of Jayaprakash Narayan, agreed to participate with Nehru and Chandra

Bose. In 1935 they worked out a 'mutual non-aggression' pact in the unions. This preceded the vote at the Seventh Comintern Congress which changed the communist line world-wide to one of united fronts. Then communists world-wide formed alliances and mutual aid pacts with those unions and socialist parties which, only weeks before, they had been denouncing as 'social fascists'. The fundamental opposition by the communists to the forces of nationalism will be remembered in India as a result of a dramatic display by the communist unions at a demonstration at the Chowpathy Sands. There the communist union leader, Ranadive, marched across the sands with his supporters to tear down the flag of India to replace it with the red banner. The enraged Indian nationalists attacked the communists who were able to escape with their lives only when they threw away their red banner, shed their red shirts and scarves, and raced from the scene.

With the abandonment of the ultra-left line by the communists the Comintern ordered the CPI and the Red Trades Unions to enter into an agreement with the CSP. Together with the CSP, the CPI and the unions were directed to attempt to oust the Gandhiites from leadership of the Congress and the nationalist movement. In 1936, at Lucknow, the CPI and the CSP signed an agreement creating a united front. By the end of 1937 the CPI and the trades unions under CPI control had succeeded in taking control over Kerala, Andhara Pradesh and the Tamilnad. This growth of the CPI was viewed with alarm by some in the CSP but Nehru and Bose thought that they could use the apparent strength of the CSP to take over the Congress as a whole. They pressured for a showdown. At the Tripuri Congress in 1939, Nehru and Bose made the election for the presidency of the Congress into a vote of no-confidence in Gandhi. Nehru nominated Bose for the presidency. In the election Bose won. Gandhi and his supporters refused to serve under Bose and threatened a split. The CPI, under strict orders from the Comintern to avoid a split, changed its support and voted for Gandhi against Bose and the CSP. The CSP repudiated the Lucknow Agreement and purged the CPI and the unions from its midst. The CPI and the unionists, while at first supportive of Gandhi, again joined forces with the CSP to protest the British involvement in what they called an 'imperialist' war against Hitler. Unlike the situation in Britain and France where the CPGB and the PCF were viewed as subversive for opposing the war effort, in India the CPI was viewed as supportive of nationalism when they joined the Congress in opposing Britain's declaration of war. When Britain declared war in 1939, it announced that India was also a belligerent; an announcement made without consulting the Indian Legislative

Assembly or any other Indian officials. The nationalists demanded that the price of Indian belligerency be a commitment to Indian independence after the war.

This the British refused to do, and the Congress leaders resigned their offices in the national and state bodies. They refused to support the British war effort and called *satyagrahas* and *hartals* in support of the 'Quit India' campaign. Subhas Chandra Bose went even further. He helped to form the Indian National Army which co-operated with the advancing Japanese forces to attack the British in India. The Congress leaders were eclipsed by the strident leadership of the communists. By mid-1940, the communists had taken control of many of the trades union posts in India and had won important seats in the Indian students' movement. By 1940 the communists were riding high on a heady mixture of leftist militance and strident nationalism in their campaign against the British.

Suddenly, all was changed. The Nazi forces had invaded the 'Soviet motherland' and the imperialist war now became a 'people's war'. All communist parties and unions were directed to co-operate with the allied powers in pursuing the war effort. Harry Pollitt of the CPGB sent a letter to the central committee of the CPI, most of whose members were languishing at His Majesty's pleasure at the Deoli Detention Camp, ordering the CPI to abandon all efforts at opposition to the British and to turn their efforts to controlling the trades unions to maximise war production. In a humiliating move, the letter from the CPGB to the CPI was hand-delivered by Sir Reginald Maxwell, then British Home Secretary in the Government of India. The British government in India made a pact with the CPI and released the communists from detention. It made the communist party legal and encouraged the communists to take over control of the trade unions from the militant Congress unionists. The British made money and supplies available to the CPI to start papers and journals in India; the largest was the English-language *People's War*.

Britain's only allies in India were the communists. P. C. Joshi and Sir Reginald Maxwell formed an alliance with the CPI Politbureau which placed at the disposal of the Government of India the services of the CPI and the AITUC. The British Army Intelligence Department set up a separate section to liaise with the Indian Communists and the CID to provide information on planned strikes by the nationalists and to provide blacklists of nationalist agitators. The communists even offered to provide troupes to entertain conscripted soldiers fighting in Burma.

During the period up to the end of the war virtually every non-communist nationalist or trades union leader was in detention or operating underground. The AITUC, with the support of the British, had been totally taken over by the communists. The communists had been successful in creating or penetrating innumerable front organisations in virtually all areas of national activity. At the end of the war the communists lost power and influence. At the first elections to the Central Legislative Assembly in 1945 the Indians repudiated communist leadership; the CPI or its adherents did not win a single seat. In the trades unions the communists decided to try and hold on to their control of the AITUC. Their hold on the national unions was challenged by the Congress forces. Rather than try to challenge the AITUC directly, Gandhi and the Congress formed the Indian National Trades Union Congress (INTUC) in 1947, and gave government sanction to its efforts. The Congress Socialists which had reformed into a separate party from the Congress following independence, created its own national union federation in 1948, the *Hind Mazdoor Sabha* (HMS). The AITUC was a founding member of the WFTU, while the INTUC was a founding member of the ICFTU; joined later by the HMS. A smaller union federation, the United Trade Union Congress (UTUC) formed in 1949, soon disappeared. The close ties between the unions and their parent parties hampered trades union independence.

Inevitably, among the first to suffer was the AITUC. The CPI central committee was split between adopting the more militant line on industrial relations and those who wished to see a continuance of co-operation with the central government. Ranadive, of the militant wing of the AITUC, demanded that the party support the unions in a violent campaign of guerrilla insurrection. Inspired by the success of the Mao Tse-tung uprising in China, Ranadive led his unionists in an attack on the Congress leadership. In Telengana, the Ranadive wing started a virtual civil war. Arson and massacres took place in Nalgonda and the Warangal districts. Violent disturbances broke out in Andhara Pradesh, Assam, Manipur, Uttar Pradesh and the Ahmednagar district of Bombay. This campaign of violence was horrific. It included throwing opposing workers into burning furnaces and a campaign of mutilations of their opponents. It was to be crowned by the calling of a nationwide railway strike. The strike did not come off and the party was once again declared illegal. Ranadive was arrested; S. A. Dange, head of the AITUC and a WFTU vice-president, was picked up and detained, as was S. S. Mirajkar, another unionist. By August 1949, there were about 2500 communist unionists and their followers in detention. Another attempt by the railwaymen to push through a strike resulted in 600 of them being arrested.

The CPGB tried to intervene in the Indian party and R. Palme Dutt sent down advisors and instructions to the party and the unions to abandon their 'left-sectarian' policies. By 1951 there was such disunity that Dange, Ajoy Ghosh, Rajeshwar Rao and Basava Punniah were summoned to Moscow, where Stalin and Molotov hammered out an agreement between the rival factions. The main aspect of this line was the concentration of the party and the unions on the labour movement. The AITUC was instructed to adopt a policy of united front with INTUC and HMS, but both of these refused to have anything to do with AITUC. They were able to set up co-operative efforts only with the evanescent UTUC. For the most part the AITUC was isolated, although the UTUC agreement permitted the CPI to claim that it had found allies in the labour movement.

It is interesting to note that the creation of the INTUC by the Congress did not necessarily lead to labour peace. One of the problems confronting INTUC has been the strength of the Indian employer group within the Congress. Much of the support for the Congress came from wealthy Indian industrialists and landowners. They were quick to try to damp down labour unrest by supporting a system of industrial relations which placed most of the power in an elaborate network of industrial courts. The HMS, while trying to promote collective bargaining, complained that INTUC was too closely tied to the Congress. It was unable to find a safe niche for itself as long as the Socialists, later the Praja Socialists, remained out of power.

When, in the early 1950s, the troops of Red China made their first appearance on the Himalayan border, they were made welcome by a substantial section of the Indian populace. The slogan of *Hindi-Chinee Bhai Bhai* (asserting the brotherhood of India and China) was soon dropped when the Chinese crossed the Indian border in 1962. The reaction of the AITUC was to split into a pro-Soviet and a pro-Chinese faction following the Soviet support for India.

In the ensuing years the Russians and the Chinese battled for allies in the Indian labour movement and for power in the front organisations. A complicating factor has been the growth of local parties in the Indian states which control or dominate the legislatures. Often, as in Kerala or West Bengal, these parties are Marxist or Marxist–Leninist. During Indira Gandhi's 1975–7 Emergency, many of the dissident factions of the trades union and regional parties were squelched. The end of the Emergency and the Janata rise to power saw a prominent trades unionist, George Fernandes, put in as Minister of Labour. Unfortunately his successes were minimal and the proposed reforms of India's industrial relations scene drawn up by the Janata were rejected by both sides of industry. The victory of Indira Gandhi in the general election, in a pact with the pro-Soviet communist parties, was hoped would lead to a diminution of industrial unrest. In 1979 industrial unrest in India topped 40 million man days. Industrial production in 1979 was less than 50 per cent of capacity. In 1979 there were numerous strikes across India in industries like the banks, where many banks were struck for as much as 200 days. Cheques were only cleared through Indian banks on slightly more than half the working days. In Calcutta strikes closed the port for 150 days, and there were disruptions of commerce on an additional sixty days. Absenteeism, 'gangsterism', go-slows, work-to-rules (*gherao*) and sabotage have been the main features of current industrial relations in India.

The reason for this upheaval in Indian industry have not been the purely economic causes of low wages, unsatisfied demand and fear of rationalisation and mechanisation. The underlying cause has been the political role of the unions as stalking horses for the parties. It was no accident that the INTUC, the main Congress union body, agitated and disturbed Indian commerce during the run-up to the general election. They were assured of Congress support and were used to provide leverage against the incumbent Janata government. Political rivalries were fought in the unions even on the regional level. In West Bengal, where the local affiliate of the Communist Party–Marxist held power, its trades union body, the Centre for Indian Trades Unions (CITU), battled for recognition and support with the INTUC and the HMS. Throughout Indian industry the CITU, the INTUC, the HMS and the smaller federations continued to agitate for their parent political parties. The fear of most of these unionists was that Indira Gandhi, whose Congress Party–Indira is now in power, would reinstitute the controls over labour which characterised the Emergency.

These fears were not imaginary. In August 1981 the Parliamentary Affairs Minister introduced nine ordinances to control labour. The most important was the Essential Services ordinance banning all strikes in 'essential services'. These include railroads, electrical power, the post office, telephones, air transport, banking, petroleum products and refining, hospitals and defence industries. The government was empowered to ban strikes for an initial six months and to extend this strike ban to further six-month periods. The Opposition parties walked out of Parliament in protest and trades unionists demonstrated across India.

These ordinances not only ban strikes but also prescribe severe punishment to those instigating or advocating strikes. This punishment includes prison terms of up to six months and heavy fines.

The AITUC called for immediate resistance to the ordinances and strikes and protest demonstrations swept India. The INTUC unions, supporters of Mrs Gandhi, were more muted in their response as they feared the effect of their protest on the Congress–I party. Their role was not made any easier by speeches from prominent Congress–I business leaders, like Naval Tata, head of the largest owners' federation who said the unions had brought it on themselves. He called upon all chambers of commerce, employers' organisations and trades unionists to support Mrs Gandhi.

By all indications the stranglehold on the Indian labour movement imposed during the Emergency has been reintroduced. This time it will be even harder to return to what passes for normalcy in the Indian industrial relations scene. The ICFTU's modest programme among the rural poor in India was already facing severe difficulties. It will be even more difficult to function in India with the new ordinances. At one time, however, the influence of the ICFTU was quite strong.

In its heyday, the ICFTU college was extremely active in training Indian and other Asian unionists in a residential training college in Calcutta. The Calcutta facility was opened in November 1952 as part of the education programme of the Asian regional organisation of the ICFTU (ARO). The ARO had been formed a year earlier in Karachi just before the ICFTU's second congress in Milan. Since Asia was clearly financially incapable of funding its own programmes the ICFTU decided to raise funds for providing assistance to Asian unions. It set a target of $700 000 for the first three-year period and these funds were soon pledged. To administer the fund a special committee was formed by the larger unions, under the leadership of Tewson of the TUC along with Victor Reuther of the CIO and Albin Karl of the DGB. This regional activities fund was soon paying out funds at an alarming rate owing to the incredible costs of transport and expenses in the Asian region. A second call to the ICFTU affiliates was made in which each union was asked to pledge one US cent per affiliated member for one year to raise sufficient funds to begin major operations. From July 1955 to December 1956 the special appeal brought in over $400 000 of which more than half was spent in Asia. A major activity was the trades union college in India.

The Calcutta College attracted unionists from all over Asia and lecturers from the US, Britain, Sweden and Africa. Because of an initial lack of funds, they only conducted seven long courses during the first two years. On the other hand, it sponsored numerous short courses of ten days or so all over Asia. By 1956, the Calcutta College had graduated only 275 students. In the following years, there was a continued reduction in the college's output. While only three twelve-week courses were held between 1957 and 1959, there were numerous short courses held. By 1964 there were only 667 ICFTU ARO college graduates from their long course. Moving the college to New Delhi in 1965 was a small improvement. This did not really meet the need or the demands of the Asians. Another aspect of Asian dissatisfaction was that the Asian unionists considered the courses too theoretical. Khatib of the All-Pakistan Confederation of Labour criticised the long courses because they were taught by 'professors and not trades unionists'. He preferred to send his students on short courses. Bhatt of INTUC reiterated the complaint and said that the use of English as the sole language of instruction created a system whereby the best workers were not often able to participate. Only educated workers could participate since it was they who had learned English. Narayan of Malaysia criticised the college as an 'Anglo-American organisation' and demanded courses in Asian languages. In 1959 the college began to offer a variety of short courses in the Asian languages.

Affiliations within the Asian area to the ICFTU grew. By 1959 there were thirty-two unions from fourteen countries affiliated to the ICFTU. This did not mean that the ICFTU was strong or united since many of the Asian unions, like INTUC and HMS in India, were so divided that missions from the ICFTU were sent to try and calm hostilities between the affiliates. In India, Oldenbroeck, Geddes of the TUC and Irving Brown of the AFL–CIO were sent on a mission to reduce hostility between the affiliates. Similar trips were undertaken to Japan. In some cases the ICFTU made an inspired choice for a delegate. Gerry Daniels of the UAW–CIO was sent as ICFTU representative to Okinawa where he was extremely successful in negotiating the reduction of tensions between Okinawan labour and the US occupying military forces. Howard Robinson, another American unionist, was assigned to Korea, but the US government and the Korean government made it almost impossible for him to rebuild Korean unions after the end of the Korean War.

A major problem in the Asian region was the low level of unionisation among eligible Asian workers. The fact that the WFTU and the local communist unions were faring no better was hardly solace. The ICFTU increased its contributions to Asia after 1960. With the creation of the

International Solidarity Fund (ISF) the ICFTU stepped up payments to the Calcutta College and to other regional programmes. In 1960 direct ICFTU assistance to Asia totalled $275 000. This amount doubled in 1961 and doubled again in 1962. Between 1960 and 1962 the ICFTU sent a little under $1 000 000 to promote Asian unionism. This increase in payments was not matched by an increase in affiliates: in fact, affiliations dropped. By 1964 there was a retrenching in Asian unions.

Philippine unionism emerged in the last days of Spanish colonialism when craft workers, especially in the printing trades, joined together to form local, regional and eventually national labour organisations. Under the leadership of Cruz and de los Reyes, the printers' union was able to form a national union of the crafts in 1902, the *Union Obrera Democratica Filipina* (UODF). The formation of the UODF coincided with a rash of strikes which were intended to win concessions from the newly arrived American forces occupying the Philippines. Using the provisions of the Spanish Penal Code, the American authorities jailed de los Reyes and the top leadership of the UODF. The Americans feared the growth of Philippine trades unions and their close ties to the emerging nationalist movements. Further strikes were put down and the leaders jailed. When de los Reyes left the labour movement to participate in civic and church politics his place was taken by Dominador Gomez who linked the UODF with his newly formed *Partido Nacionalista* and led them both in an effort to win Philippine autonomy. He too was jailed.

The political fervour of the unions was dampened in 1907 when a Philippine Assembly was formed. The creation of tolerated nationalist parties by the American authorities (under Governor William Howard Taft) established the franchise for all Philippine nationals who met fairly rigid literacy and property qualifications. This building of a politically liberated, educated elite caused severe problems for the trades unions. The leadership of the unions, so dependent on their interlinking with the nationalist parties, was formed from among the literate and propertied Philippinos. The lower classes, those who had participated in the rebellion which led to the ousting of the Spanish, were effectively barred from political and trades union leadership roles. Middle-class, professional leadership cadres for both the unions and the parties has been the rule throughout Philippine history.

With the union leadership safe in the hands of the middle classes the US authorities relaxed their vigilance on the trades unions and created an atmosphere in which the economic role of unions was able to flourish.

Unions were encouraged to set up co-operatives, mutual welfare schemes and similar benefit plans. The AFL established fraternal contact with the UODF through the Anti-Imperialism League and sought to assist the Philippine unionists in their efforts in Washington. One of the motivators for these efforts was the threat of the gradual splitting of the Philippine union movement by a militant socialist faction under the leadership of Evangelista. The UODF had reorganised in 1913 to form a more representative national trades union centre, the *Congreso Obrero Filipino* (COF) which grouped some of the rapidly expanding agricultural worker groupings within the organisation. These agricultural unionists, formed under the influence of Evangelista and his *Katipunan ng mga Anak Pawis* (Society of the Children of Sweat) were more interested in the equitable distribution of land, the problems of land tenure and better working conditions of the plantations than collective bargaining. With the success of the Bolsheviks in 1921, and the creation of the Comintern, ties were established, covertly, with Philippine peasant groups. These peasant organisations were instrumental in the founding of the *Partido Obrero* (the Labour Party) in 1925 and the *Partido Comunista* in 1930, led by Evangelista and Pedro Abad Santos. Through these links between the peasant unions and the militant socialist parties, often directly encouraged by the Comintern through agents sent to the Philippines, the left was able to capture control of the COF which it affiliated to the Comintern's Pan-Pacific Trades Union Secretariat in 1927. This growth of labour peasant militance posed a serious challenge to the newly created Philippine Commonwealth Government which, after the constitution was ratified in a national plebiscite, established home rule under President Quezon in 1935.

The new government took strong steps to put the trades union movement under tight government supervision. It created labour legislation under which unions had to be registered by the government. All disputes were to be submitted to compulsory arbitration before a government-appointed industrial tribunal. Through the Secretary of Labour the government reined in any independent union initiatives. This emphasis on legalism, the pleading of union cases before industrial tribunals, had a marked effect on trades union leadership. These new trades union leaders were drawn from within the legal profession in the Philippines. Often the union would be headquartered in the law office of the head of the union. He would represent the union in its day-to-day activities and would deal with other union lawyers in federation or confederation business. These would also provide the linkage to the political parties whom they also served – often as legislators. Between

1936 and 1953, the trades union movement, outside of the plantation and peasant unions, was run by and through lawyers.

After the restoration of order in the Philippines in the immediate postwar period the split between left and right was an important factor in the political and trades union life of the nation. Following the orders given at the 1948 Calcutta meetings, the armed peasantry of the Philippines organised into a militantly left-wing organisation the *Hukbong Mapagpalaya ng Bayan* (Peoples Liberation Army). They began an armed uprising against the Philippine government. The Huks, led by the leaders of the old socialist and communist parties, among them Pedro Abad Santos, were engaged in a major guerrilla campaign, especially in Luzon. The trades union national centre most closely allied to the Huks, the COF, was the subject of government scrutiny. Its registration was revoked and the organisation banned. Luis Taruc, and his fellow communists, were denied their seats in parliament and went off to the mountains to fight. The new government, under Magsaysay, received massive US military assistance to help fight the Huks. Colonel Edward Lansdale was sent to co-ordinate the anti-Huk campaign.

In 1953, the government passed a series of liberal labour laws, encompassing much of the US labour legislative procedures contained in the Wagner Act and the Taft–Hartley Act. It provided for collective bargaining and greatly diminished the role of the labour courts, although not disposing entirely of the industrial tribunal. This liberalisation of the industrial relations scene was accompanied by the dramatic shift in the type of unions recognised by the government and which were permitted the benefit of the labour legislation. With the banning of the COF and the passage of the 1953 labour acts, the government also banned all farm and peasant unions. Before 1940 these peasant and agricultural workers unions accounted for almost two-thirds of the organised labour force. After the early 1950s these unionists were disenfranchised. The unions left in the business of collective bargaining and recognised as such were encouraged to avoid politics. They were assisted in becoming 'bread and butter' unions; or at least the Philippine equivalent, 'rice and fish' unions.

These unions scrambled to put the name 'free' in front of their title. Formed out of the industrial unions, a number of confederations attempted to seize the mantle of the COF to become a national centre. Cipriano Cid established the Philippine Association of Free Labour Unions (PAFLU); Felixberto Olalia formed the National Association of Free Labour Unions (NAFLU); the government, under the Secretary of Labour, Jose Figueras, set up its own confederation, the National

Confederation of Trade Unions (NACTU). The Christian unionists set up the Federation of Free Workers (FFW) and later a Federation of Free Farmers (FFF). The close ties between the government and the unions of the NACTU were criticised by the other unions. By 1954 it had metamorphosed into the Philippine Trades Union Council (PTUC). This merger was followed by several other permutations within the trades union movement largely on the basis of personalities and patronage rather than ideological affinities.

From late 1954 the PTUC was the sole ICFTU affiliate. The Philippine Labour Centre (PLC) formed from centre unions in 1965 was also permitted to affiliate to the ICFTU. The FFW remained an important affiliate of the Brotherhood of Asian Trades Unionists – the Christian WCL regional organisation. With it was linked the FFF which offered the peasants a form of local organisation. The left was controlled by the National Association of Trades Unions (NATU) and the Free Farmers Union. The leaders of the lefter federations, along with Oca, formed the core of the socialist movement in the Philippines.

The whole system changed in 1972 when President Marcos announced the state of martial law. Many unionists were detained; many political party leaders opposed to Marcos found their civil liberties curtailed. In fact, there were so many prominent politicians and unionists in detention that a number of the unionists who had not been detained came to Manila to plead with the government to detain them. They feared the loss of credibility as unionists if they were not immediately placed under arrest. Still others took to the radio on the trades union station to play martial music and to interrupt this patriotic music festival by recorded messages of loyalty to Marcos.

The introduction of martial law led to a reorganisation of the union and of the industrial relations structure. The government instituted what might be called the Singapore model of unionism, tripartite discussions on how to promote economic development. The labour court and the industrial tribunal system was restored. The labour movement was united into a single national centre, the *Kapulungang Anak-Pawis ng Pilipinas* (Philippine Congress of Industrial and Agrarian Workers), later called the Trades Union Congress of the Philippines (TUCP). The TUCP, led at first by Oca and then by Democrito Mendoza after Oca's death, has been tightly under the government's wing. Strikes are banned; compulsory arbitration is the rule. The trades unions are roughly back in the position from which they emerged in 1936. Their international ties consist primarily of bi-lateral assistance between AAFLI and the TUCP, supplemented by relations between the national unions and the

ITSs under AAFLI guidance or through funds provided to the ITSs indirectly by the US government through the American ITS affiliates. The political control over the unions by the government is virtually total and the trades union lawyer-leaders are increasingly accepting high political posts concurrent with their trades union offices. There has been some unrest among the local level unions and some of the regional federations but the scope for acting out their discontent is very limited. The restoration of free union rights in the Philippines is unlikely for the foreseeable future.

Perhaps the only Asian country in which free unionism has taken root and flourished has been Japan. Just as the postwar growth of strong democratic institutions in Japan brought about the perpetuation of democracy in the political sphere, the growth of strong trades union institutions has perpetuated the growth of independent labour organisations. The two processes were closely linked and each helped shape the other. Politics and unionism in Japan are closely linked, but the expected links between the unions and the government are absent. The Japanese trades unions are very important participants in political party activity, but they do so without either controlling or being controlled by the government. The Japanese political and union interaction illustrates the importance of distinguishing among the several layers of trades union abstraction.

The origins of the Japanese labour movements can be traced to the early experiences of Japanese students living in San Francisco at the turn of the century. In 1897 they formed the *Rodo Kumiai Kiseikai* (the Association to Organise Labour Unions) modelled on the AFL. Led by Sen Katayama the organisation launched the first labour newspaper in Japan, the *Labour World*, in 1897. The organisation did not prosper as the AFL model of craft unionism did not match Japanese labour reality. Unions were formed by metalworkers, printers, locomotive engineers, teachers and firemen. By 1900 they reached their peak membership of around 8000. These nascent unions attempted the occasional strike but were soon put out of business by the Security Policing Act of 1900 which, *inter alia*, banned strikes, forbade unions, forbade any mutual aid societies among workers and forbade organising. The penalties were severe, including six months' imprisonment.

The repression of these largely Christian activists in the trades union movement by the forces of the state left the way open to a more politically conscious movement. The humanist intellectuals gave way to the politically active intellectuals who, with the help of some IWW organisers from the US and Australia, were able to build an anarcho-syndicalist group within the remnants of the labour movement. Led by Kotoku Shusui, these unionists rejected the politics of party and programme. They chose instead the propaganda of the deed. They gave priority to the call for a general strike and conducted revolutionary terror against people and property. With the discovery of a conspiracy to assassinate the Emperor Meiji in 1911 these groups were crushed and Kotoku Shusui was executed. By then, however, the First World War was bringing with it the fruits of industrial expansion. The time was ripe for another effort at building a trades union movement.

In 1912 Bunji Suzuki established a circle of intellectuals to study the labour question. Suzuki, a Unitarian social worker, formed this initial small group into a broad movement, the *Yuaikai* (the Friendly Society). Operating under the severe restraints of a hostile government the *Yuaikai* initially masqueraded as a moral and cultural organisation. By 1920 membership had reached 30 000. The following year it changed its name to the *Nihon Rodo Sodomei* (Japanese Federation of Labour – JFL). Membership in the JFL did not include all Japanese unions as there were considerable numbers of small individual unions across Japan. These reflected the nature of Japanese enterprises: small, diffuse and local.

This JFL maintained a low political and industrial profile. It was first challenged on the left by the anarcho-syndicalists of Sakae Osugi but the socialists and communists rallied together to oust the anarchists from control. The socialists and the communists were unable to agree on who should control the unions. In 1925 the JFL kicked out twenty-three unions under communist control who grouped themselves into a new organisation, the *Nihon Rodo Kumiai Hyogikai* (the Japanese Council of Labour Unions – JCLU). These two national centres competed with each other for members. When the government passed legislation outlawing the communist party and its several front organisations in 1928, the JCLU was forced to go underground, where it continued operations with the communists as the *Fenkyo* (the National Federation of Japanese Labour Unions). The JFL itself was split the following year when the socialists broke off from the reformers to create their own organisation, the *Nihon Rodo Kumiai Zenkoku Domei* (the National League of Japanese Labour Unions). Thus, by the beginning of the Second World War there were three major factions in Japanese labour. On the far left were the communists of the underground *Fenkyo*; in the centre were the socialists of the *Domei*; and on the right were the social democrats and reformers of the JFL.

These union bodies did not represent a major section of the Japanese workforce. These were grouped within the giant business conglomerates, the *zaibatsu*, which increasingly dominated Japan's economic life. These corporations were united into a powerful, if paternalistic, employers' federation which controlled the economic and political life of Japan. This organisation, the *Kyocho-kai* (the Harmonisation Society) was led by Iyesato Tokugawa, a direct descendent of the famous Shogun Ieyasu Tokugawa, and second in prestige only to the Emperor. The *Kyocho-kai* promoted not only modern business methods, but the creation of a strongly patriotic political and trades union movement which closely resembled the corporate fascist syndicates of Mussolini. In the late 1930s it created the *Sangyo Hokoku Undo* (the Movement in Service to the Country through Industry), known as the *Sampo*. The *Sampo* was recognised within the workplace as the legitimate representative of labour. The other unions were crushed. The last to disappear was the JFL in 1940. By then the process of industrial relations was in the hands of the *Kempeitai*, the security police, who sat *ex officio* on the compulsory arbitration boards and enforced their judgements with the full sanction of the state.

The pre-war development of Japanese unions was characterised by intense ideological activity in which one faction or another was closely allied with the political movements which struggled for power. It was largely confined to small industrial concentrations and never achieved any major success in establishing collective bargaining. Those contracts which did exist were almost exclusively those of the seamen's union. The political system in pre-war Japan was not conducive to a strong labour input. The growth of successful political parties after the Meji restoration largely reflected the narrow desires of the four powerful groups: the military, the industrialists, the landlords and the civil servants. Politics consisted of these four pressure groups seeking long and short-term advantages through coalitions. The role of an organised labour movement was seen as antithetical to all four groups. It was only the destruction and havoc which accompanied the end of the Second World War which effectively destroyed at least three of the four major elements of Japanese political life, which fostered unionism.

The end of the war saw the occupation of Japan by the forces of the United States. These occupation forces were intent on creating a democratic system in Japan; not only in the political arena but also in Japanese industry. They felt that the power of the industrialists, along with the military, had played a key role in precipitating the war in the Pacific. To help provide a counterweight to a resurgence of Japanese corporate strength they encouraged the formation of unions. The immediate postwar period was characterised by the passage of numerous laws which created a climate favourable to the unions. In December 1945 the Labour Union Act was passed giving unions the right to organise, bargain and strike. These provisions were echoed in the new Japanese constitution of November 1946.

Trades unions began to form and regroup across Japan. One of the principal reasons for this formation of unions was that the unions offered the embryonic political parties of the left and centre a ready-made national organisation with contacts and organisation stretching down to the grass roots. In August 1946 the JFL reconstituted itself. Another federation, the *Sanbetsu* (the All-Japan Congress of Industrial Unions) formed the same month. Each attempted to recruit new unions. These recruiting drives were often accompanied by strike action. Nonetheless, these were tolerated by the authorities. The problems emerged with the increasing militance of the public sector employees. Under the legislation which enfranchised unionism public employees were given the right to organise but were urged not to strike. When the public servants attempted to strike for higher wages and the control of prices in February 1947, the famous '2–1 strike', the Occupation policies began to change. It shifted direction on the permissibility of untrammelled unionism. It feared the intense politicisation of the union movement by militant leftist forces, especially with the rise of communist insurgency in India, Burma, Malaya and China. When in 1948 the left of the Japanese labour movement attempted a general strike, the government intervened to ban it. This action evoked a strong anti-communist policy directive to the Japanese government by MacArthur, which was followed by the Red Purge soon after. The government passed the Labour Relations Adjustment Act in 1949, which excluded managers from unions, prohibited public employees from striking, and required advance notice if a union planned to strike. The outbreak of the Korean War led to an increased anti-communist militancy by the forces of government.

The Japanese unionism which emerged from the immediate postwar reconstruction was substantively different from unionism elsewhere. The basic unit of Japanese unionism is the enterprise union. An enterprise union is a union formed exclusively among the employees of a particular company. Membership usually includes all the permanent workers in the company regardless of job title or responsibility; both white collar and blue collar. It is the enterprise union which bargains with management. The enterprise unit is the main focus of the economic aspects of unionism. In multi-plant enterprises a representative council of the plants often negotiates with top management. Only very rarely is there any government interference. This process of collective bargaining concerns itself with a fairly limited number of issues, mainly wages and bonuses, but leaves other traditional union concerns to an institutionalised dialogue with all levels of management through workplace procedures which do not necessarily involve the unions *per se*.

To a more limited degree there have emerged national unions. These national unions are not entirely industrial unions but rather serve as co-ordinating bodies for the several enterprise unions in an industrial sector in their ties with a national centre. For example, there may be a number of textile enterprise unions joined in a national union. These form a single national union which affiliates to a national centre and constitutes the sectoral union for that national centre. The national union co-ordinates the activities of the several enterprise unions on political matters. There are very few national unions which engage in any form of collective bargaining. They have few resources; they cannot call or ban strikes; and they do not enter negotiations or approve contracts. They maintain the loyalty of the affiliated unions by co-ordinating their interactions with a national centre.

The role of the national centres is purely political. These national confederations have as affiliates the national unions, not the enterprise unions. These national centres have a minor economic function outside of the public sector and represent the labour arms of the political parties. Traditionally, postwar Japan has seen the division of the national centres between support for communist or socialist political parties. These national centres mobilise support for the political programmes of the major national parties and turn out bodies for demonstrations, marches and elections. These parties which are supported by the union national centres, although they have had some success in regional or urban elections, have not succeeded in forming a national government. This prerogative has been given to the Liberal Democratic Party, essentially the party of the employers. Nonetheless, the national confederations have taken strong positions on Japanese disarmament, the Mutual Security Treaty with the US, the banning of nuclear weapons and testing, and a host of purely political issues. To a large degree, the union national confederations represent the national party organisations with access to unionists and others at the base through contacts with their affiliated national unions.

As might be expected, there is more than one national confederation, much as there is more than one socialist party. The national confederations reflect the ideological currents in Japanese political life. They have split and reformed over time as one current or another came to the fore. Each are clearly delineated according to their ties with a particular party or policy. With the realignment of the trades union movement in 1950, the unions at the base, essentially the enterprise unions and some national unions, rejected the intense politicisation of the two national centres and created democratisation leagues within their organisations. They built a movement known as *Mindo* (the Unions' Affiliated League for Democratisation) which pressed for a series of reforms within the labour movements moving towards a more responsive political position on the part of the national officials; primarily an end to the calling of political strikes. In July 1950 the *Mindo* (largely formed of *Sanbetsu* unions) joined with the left wing of the JCL and some independent unions to form a new confederation, the *Nihon Rodo Kumiai Sohyogikai* (General Council of Trades Unions of Japan – *Sohyo*). *Sohyo*, which had started as a democratic movement against the left-wing policies of the *Sanbetsu*, soon became caught up in factional problems of its own.

The problems which faced *Sohyo* derived from the preponderance of government and public sector unions affiliated to it. By law these unions were forbidden to strike. Since these unions comprise more than one-half of *Sohyo*'s membership, action on the economic front involved putting political pressure on government bodies sufficient to win from these bodies the economic gains unwinnable through strikes. *Sohyo* pioneered the movement for an all-industry wage offensive. Each spring the national unions would co-ordinate the programme of wage increases demanded by the enterprise unions so that there were relatively common goals. The co-ordination of this *Shunto*, or spring wage offensive, would give to the union negotiators a form of consolidated pressure which no individual union could produce on its own. Incidentally it put pressure on the public sector to match the increases won through the *Shunto*.

Sohyo, however, was itself challenged by political conflict as the leadership of the organisation moved increasingly leftwards. The *Sohyo* leadership adopted what they called the Four Principles of Peace (a final peace treaty with the US; strict neutrality for Japan; no US bases to be permitted in Japan; and opposition to any rearming of the Japanese military). The non-left in *Sohyo*, appalled by the adoption of what was considered a pro-communist political line by the leadership, was unable to stop Minoru Takano of the left wing from taking over as secretary-general. Takano's victory confirmed the left's control of *Sohyo*, and the domination of the organisation by public workers. His successors, Iwai and Ohta, were no less committed to leftist programmes. One, in fact, was awarded the Lenin Prize for his trades union efforts. According to trades union legend he invested the Lenin Prize money in a factory in southern Japan and retired from trades unionism.

Following the victory of Takano the non-leftists split off from *Sohyo* to form a new coalition with the remaining unions in the JCL. This new organisation was called *Zenro* (Japanese Trade Union Congress), formed in 1954. Soon after it reconstituted itself as the national centre, the *Zen-Nihon Rodo Sodomei* (Japanese Confederation of Labour) known as *Domei*. *Sohyo*, supporting the Japan Socialist Party, and *Domei*, supporting the Democratic Socialist Party, continue their rivalry today. The only major change has come with the introduction of a trend towards industry-wide unionism as the result of the efforts of the International Metalworkers, the metal ITS, to build a co-ordinating body for their affiliated Japanese unions. This IMF-JC which was created provides valuable research and co-ordination for all the metal unions.

There are, as well, two separate non-affiliated groups of unions, the *Shinsanbetsu* and *Churitsororen*, but these play a minor political role. In Japan the three levels of trades union abstraction have brought about a situation in which economic power is largely left within the lowest level of organisation. Political activity takes place at the top. This has meant that to a large extent political strikes are few, industrial unrest is localised, and except for the public sector, political unionism is separate from collective bargaining. International activities are conducted by the national centres. *Domei* is an important affiliate of the ICFTU while many *Sohyo* unions are WFTU members. On the other hand, there are *Sohyo* unions affiliated to the ITSs which play an important part in their activities. Japanese unions on the national and confederation levels are increasingly playing a role in Asian unionism. They have been sponsoring meetings, hosting conferences and forming aid and assistance programmes for Asian unionists, especially in those nations in which Japanese enterprises are active. Japanese unions have not yet rivalled the strong presence of US overseas union activity in Asia, but they are certainly expanding their role and activities.

The success of free unionism in Japan is an aberration within Asian unionism. For the most part, unions, especially the national centres, exist under government suffrage and domination. Their political role has been relegated to mobilising party and government support. Their international ties have largely been cut by hostile governments fearful of outside forces interacting with domestic organisations. The rise of the power of the Asian military has further dampened Asian ardour for free unionism. The ICFTU has continued to promote a form of Asian unionism through its ARO but it has been hampered by its need to deal with the national centres which make up its affiliates. A lack of funds has not helped. The disaffiliation of the AFL–CIO in 1968 had a profound effect on Asian union development. It eliminated a source of funds for the ICFTU and created a rival body to interact with Asian labour, the AAFLI. Equally as important, the question mark over the sources of the funding and politics associated with these US labour initiatives has seriously diminished Western union credibility in Asia, much as it has in Africa. The exposure in the US press, echoed world-wide, of the government–union nexus of covert subsidies to the unions for overseas labour activities has seriously diminished the receptiveness of the host governments to international union activity. The revelations of CIA and other government agency funding of a wide range of US labour bodies, student bodies and cultural activities has compromised labour internationalism. Equally, the sudden profusion of funds available through these government-subsidised labour assistance arms has operated a Gresham's Law of trades union assistance; cheap and plentiful programmes have driven out the expensive and infrequent programmes of the ICFTU, the Christian Brotherhood of Asian Trades Unionists and the bi-lateral assistance of the Swedish, German and British unions.

The AAFLI was set up late in 1968 by the AFL–CIO after discussions with the State Department about the difficult situation in Vietnam. At one time there had been three trades union centres in South Vietnam, led by Buu, Kuu and Vann. Tran Quoc Buu, the leader of the Christian national centre, the CVT, was closely tied to the leaders of the Thieu regime and was providing the local CIA organisation with important support in keeping the docks open to permit the landing of vital supplies. In the regions his unionists were co-operating with the CORDS and the Cheiu Hoi programmes. Kuu and Vann soon found themselves out of business. The CVT dropped its Christian ties and was recognised as the sole legitimate union body in South Vietnam. The AFL–CIO formed the AAFLI which set up its first Asian office in Saigon, donating money and creating training programmes with Buu and the CVT. Other offices followed in Thailand, Korea, Indonesia and Manila.

The AAFLI works through the national centres which approve all projects. Since the bulk of the funds provided for these programmes is US government money, host country government approval is required. These funds were not insubstantial. By the time of the US pullout from Saigon AAFLI had spent over $1 million of US government money in promoting free unionism in South Vietnam. These AAFLI projects often involve providing needed equipment and resources to Asian unions and in providing training programmes 'in-country' and in schools in the US. The travel of Asian unionists to the US for study was pioneered much earlier. In the mid-1950s the Rockefeller Foundation brought numerous Asian unionists from countries like Indonesia to the US to study. A committee to help choose which unionists were most acceptable for these opportunities was set up between Dean Rusk of the foundation and Jay Lovestone of the FTUC. A similar arrangement was made for Africa except that the continent of Africa was left to the Ford Foundation. Initially the directorship of the AAFLI was in the hands of Gerry O'Keefe of the Retail Clerks' Union, after his triumphs in British Guiana, but was put on a permanent basis when Morris Paladino, who had left the ICFTU when the AFL–CIO pulled out, took up the post of Executive Director. The AAFLI remains an important force in Asian unionism. It has supplemented its direct efforts by beginning joint AAFLI–ITS meetings in the area, largely among those ITSs whose budgetary shortfalls had been made up for previously by the ICFTU.

The AAFLI and the American unionists have not merely contented themselves with passing on trades union skills to Asian unionists; they have immersed themselves in the challenging business of advising the US and foreign governments on what was acceptable policy in Asia and what was not. In the minutes of the Labour Advisory Committee on Foreign Assistance (a body chaired, until his death, by George Meany and composed of representatives of the State Department, AID, Labour Department and other interested parties) there are frequent references to the strong political leadership of the US unionists. At one meeting Jay Lovestone demanded that the State Department notify the Indian government that a trades union delegation containing AITUC members would not be received in the US. In Vietnam the US unions were so closely involved in shaping Vietnamese political destinies that Lovestone was recorded as advising Dr Phan Quang Dan to drop his call for negotiations with the NLF. He ordered Dr Dan, a member of the Saigon Cabinet, to cable the text of his remarks to the Premier, Tran Van Huong. A copy of the clarifying telegram is appended to the minutes of the labour advisory meeting.[4] Soon after, Dr Dan was dropped from the Cabinet. The AAFLI gave direct aid to the CVT to buy fertiliser. During the pacification programme the CVT was the largest organisation distributing fertiliser in Vietnam. Clearly, there was more than plain trades unionism at work.

This rapidly diminished scope for labour action on the part of non-US unions (with the exception of the Friedrich Ebert Stiftung which keeps its own country teams in Asia) has been accelerated by the spread of military rule throughout Asia. The paradigm case for this politicisation and internationalisation of trades unionism, however, has been Latin America. In Latin America, all the diverse political forces which have shaped African and Asian unionism have had a full run. What has emerged has been the most highly political trades unionism of all.

8 The Development of Latin American Unionism

There has been no more important factor in the development of Latin American trades unionism than the relations between the movement and the forces of political activism on the continent. Much as in Africa and Asia, the leadership of the Latin unions has come from the educated and largely middle-class strata of the society. The prime differences which distinguish Latin American unionism from the unionism of Africa and Asia has been that, for a large part of its formative period, Latin unions were formed almost exclusively from among immigrant groups from Europe. These immigrants formed the unions and radical political parties which they also led. For the bulk of the indigenous workers of Latin and Central America the politico-economic forces unleashed by militant unionism passed them by, and continue to pass them by. In much of Latin America the national language, Spanish or Portuguese, is spoken by a minority of the inhabitants as their first language. Indian languages, dialects and *linguas franca* suffice for the bulk of the rural population. Only very rarely have there been efforts made by trades unionists or radical politicians to proselytise or organise in languages like Quechua which, in some countries, is the major national language. In fact, in most of Latin America the formative period of unionisation was conducted through recruiting drives, propaganda and organising strikes conducted in Italian, German, English and only later Spanish. Unionism was brought by immigrants and recruited immigrants.

These immigrants came primarily from Europe. Spurred by the failure of the revolutions of 1848 and the destruction of the French Commune in 1871, numerous Latin Americans who had been in Europe participating in these events were joined in their nations by refugees from these political upheavals. The radical ideas they brought to Latin America were primarily the political philosophies of anarcho-syndicalism and utopian socialism. The creation of the First

International (the Black International) under Bakunin led to a large-scale effort to build anarcho-syndicalist unions in Argentina, Uruguay, Colombia, Brazil and Mexico. These anarcho-syndicalist unions rejected a highly centralised system of unionism and did not build the elaborate bureaucratic administrative structures of their Marxist opponents. They did, however, build national organisations to co-ordinate the efforts of their regional and local federations. Among these were the *Federacion Obrera Regional de Argentina* (FORA) and the *Federacion Obrera Regional de Uruguay* (FORU) which reached a peak in membership between 1900 and 1912.

The FORA was primarily built through the efforts of the Italian anarchists. They sponsored a visit by Enrico Malatesta, the noted Italian anarchist. Malatesta, and later Pietro Gori, established important groups of Italian workers in Argentina which joined with the Argentine groups of French, German and central European anarchist federations to form the FORA. By 1900 there were more than a million new immigrants in Argentina. They proved a fertile ground for organising. These also joined to form a Socialist Party in Argentina in 1896. Then socialist and anarchist movements were challenged for control of the working classes by the increasing efforts of the Church to spread the doctrines of Christian unionism. After the publication of *Rerum Novarum* in 1891 the Church urged the formation of workingmen's organisations, primarily to compete against the radical doctrines of socialism, anarchism and communism which threatened Church prerogatives. The Catholic social reformers were able to set up a National Catholic Congress in Mexico in 1903 which created workingmen's circles. The Chilean Church built Catholic unions which it grouped into the *Federacion Obrera de Chile* (FROCh). The FROCh was soon taken over by the socialists. An early attempt to set up workers' circles in Brazil soon faded as did similar efforts in Bolivia. Only in Argentina did the movement pick up a lot of strength. By the turn of the century there were over sixty Catholic Workingmen's Circles in Argentina in a Federation of Workingmen's Circles.

The anarchists were also strong outside of Argentina. In Uruguay, Spanish immigrants, like Adria Troitino, arrived to help build the FORU. In Brazil, foreign unionists from Germany, Portugal, France and Italy built a national centre, the *Confederacão Operaria Brasilieria* (COB). Cuban unions, too, grouped around foreign anarchist leaders like Arevalo. A major factor in the success of these union efforts resulted from visits by anarchist sailors putting into foreign ports and proselytising. The IWW of North America had organised a union of sailors in the

Pacific, and later the Atlantic, which encouraged missionary work. The IWW set up a regional office in Chile to co-ordinate organising on the continent. The Argentine and US sailors of the IWW built trades unionism among the port and transport workers of Paraguay, the *Federacion Obrera Regional de Paraguay* (FORP). By the beginning of the First World War anarchists had a firm hold on Latin American trades unionism. There were frequent and often bitter strikes against the local industrialists and government bodies. The governments' reaction was to pass laws permitting the swift deportation of foreign agitators.

The outbreak of the First World War had a major impact on Latin American unionism. The stable exports of raw materials from Latin America continued throughout the war, but the importation of manufactured products from Europe was impeded. Local import substitution industries developed throughout the continent. The postwar slump left many workers unemployed. Adding to the miseries of an already overcrowded job market in most Latin American cities was the rapid rise in the cost of living which threatened to reduce the standard of living of even those workers who were employed. This slump, and the concurrent rise in labour militancy coincided with the victory of the Bolsheviks in Russia. The newly formed Comintern and its labour counterpart, the Profintern, sent teams of organisers to Latin America. M. N. Roy was instrumental in forming the Mexican Communist party; Sen Katayama of Japan helped to form unions and parties on the continent as did the ubiquitous paymaster of the Comintern, Borodin. The American party sent Joe Zack to Latin America. These Comintern agents built loyal cadres within the national federations and attempted to take them over, out of the hands of the socialists and the anarchists. Official communist parties grew and spread across Latin America. By 1930 there were seventeen national parties. The communists organised among the peasants as well, frequently encouraging local dialect speakers to attend meetings to which the Indians had been invited. Throughout the continent the communists posed a serious challenge to the unions of the anarchists and socialists for control of the movements.

Throughout Latin America strikes and protest marches disrupted industry. The most bitter battle occurred in January 1919 in Argentina during the *semana tragica* (tragic week), when a metalworkers' strike degenerated into a battle between pickets, armed guards and strikebreakers. The national labour organisations called out their members in support. The police attended the funeral of those killed in the initial clash and massacred the mourners. The workers responded by calling a general strike which led to a small war between the army, police and vigilante groups and the workers. Within a week there were hundreds wounded, more than a hundred dead and thousands in jail. In 1920 and 1921 the military killed more than two thousand workers in Patagonia.[1] To a large degree, however, these militant strikes favoured the rise of socialism and communism among the workers rather than anarchism. The Latin American workers were growing tired of being called out on frequent general strikes and paying with their lives and property for abstract political ideals. The attraction of the communists and the socialists was not that they were the most militant unionists but rather that they offered the Latin American worker the thing that he felt he most needed: discipline.

The communist unionists were disciplined and tightly controlled. They, and their sometimes socialist allies, were able to win numerous economic and legislative concessions from the new group of Liberal governments which formed. They united with many of the forces of the centre-left to press for social legislation, which they were often able to achieve. By 1929 the communists in Latin America were able to bring together in Montevideo representatives of the communist national centres in a confederation, the *Confederacion Sindical Latino America* (CSLA) which became the regional affiliate of the Profintern. Although membership in some nations was purely notional, the communists controlled serious labour organisations in Uruguay, Brazil, Chile and Cuba. These organisations were often hostile to rival national centres promoted by the socialists and the Christians. Another ideological strain, *Aprismo*, was also opposed to the rise of communist unionism. The *Apristas*, developed from the Peruvian model of Haya del la Torre, called for a policy of broad social, nationalist reform, rejecting communism and religious domination. It had important adherents in Venezuela, Brazil, Costa Rica and the Dominican Republic, although under different names.

The success of the communists and their socialist allies was matched by the creation of an interamerican federation of national centres under the influence of the AFL, the Pan-American Federation of Labour (PAFL). After the fall of the Porfirio Diaz government in Mexico, the AFL had expanded its role in promoting peace between the US and Mexico. The AFL, long established in the corridors of Washington power, was a vital element in the tripartite American Alliance for Labour and Democracy (AALD). This AALD was an organisation of business, labour and the US government dedicated to the growth and expansion of the free enterprise system and the creation of the American model of industrial relations around the world. This American model was designed as a non-political model; pure 'bread and butter' unionism.

Another American model, the IWW's model of one big union, had spread to Mexico as early as 1906 when IWW organisers helped promote a Mexican mineworkers' strike. The AFL and the US government opposed the spread of radical US unionism south of the border. The government and the major business interests with holdings in Central and South America, encouraged the AFL to extend its stabilising influence in Latin American unionism. The opportunity for direct AFL–government action came when the chaos in Mexico had led to the Veracruz landing in 1914, and the cross-border attacks by Pancho Villa. The US was especially concerned that the Imperial German forces were gaining a foothold in the Americas and were threatening to disturb peaceful commerce in the area. To assist the AFL in building non-political unionism in Latin America was seen as an important tactical step to keep the trades union from causing disruptive strikes or demonstrations which might be harmful to US strategic interests. This extension to the labour field of the 'Monroe Doctrine' led to a widespread organising campaign by the AFL throughout Latin America, financed partially from government funds.

In 1918, the AFL was able to gather together in Laredo, Texas, representatives of unions from Latin America which joined together to form the Pan-American Federation of Labour (PAFL). Outside the US contingent, the largest body of representatives came from the newly formed Mexican confederation, the *Confederacion Regional de los Obreros Mexicanos* (CROM). The CROM, formed earlier in the year at Saltillo under the direct control of President Carranza, was an organisation which condemned radical unionism. Its leader, Luis Morones, formed a political party the following year, the *Partido Laborista Mexicano* (PLM), which entered into a coalition with the forces of Obregon, Carranza's successor. Between them they turned the CROM into a powerful political machine offering labour peace in exchange for political contributions. The government's support for the CROM and the CROM's support for the government was established on a firm political and economic foundation. Between the two, other forms of unionism were crushed or impeded. The unity of the CROM and the AFL within the PAFL provided the basis for interamerican activities. Also affiliated to the PAFL were representatives of union organisations from El Salvador, Costa Rica, Colombia and Guatemala, formed primarily from among unionists from these countries living in exile in the US.

The PAFL was given $50 000 by the US out of the president's special fund. The *Pan-American Labour Press* was funded through the AALD. Other funds were made available to promote travel by union organisers to help organise congenial unions elsewhere in Latin America. With the death of Gompers in 1924, the prime mover behind the PAFL was gone and the organisation only limped along until 1940. A major factor in its decline was the gradual rise of more militant unionism, led by the US labour forces grouped within the Congress of Industrial Organisations (CIO) and the newly formed Mexican national centre the *Confederacion de Trabajadores de Mexico* (CTM). These two national centres attracted the groups of unions throughout Latin America organised into popular fronts and built a rival interamerican federation to the PAFL, the *Confederacion de Trabajadores de America Latina* (CTAL), under the leadership of the CTM's president Vincente Lombardo Toledano. By the beginning of the Second World War there were strong leftist unions affiliated to the CTAL. The position of the AFL and the US government was hostile to CTAL. When the CTAL inherited the mantle of the communist CSLA it also inherited the fears of the US and some conservative governments in Latin America that the CTAL was a communist-dominated subversive organisation.

There had been an attempt by the anarchists to form a continent-wide federation of unions in 1919, the *Association Continental Americana de Trabajadores* (ACAT) but it was soon destroyed by government repression. Negotiations between the non-communist national centres of Argentina, Uruguay, Cuba and Venezuela with the IFTU about the affiliation of their Ibero–American Labour Federation (FIAT) in 1928 were never resolved. They affiliated separately. The growth of interamerican unionism was largely the result of strong overseas pressures from Moscow and Washington to promote the type of unionism in Latin America most sympathetic to its system.

Direct conflict between the CTAL and the PAFL was never very strong because, to all extents and purposes, the heart of the PAFL had gone out of its efforts with the withdrawal of US participation after 1927–8. The real conflict was between the CTAL and the AFL. The AFL condemned the CTAL both for its communism and for the fact that it maintained close ties to the CIO, although the CIO was not a CTAL affiliate. The principal bone of contention in the early days of this conflict was the support given by the CIO, the CTM and the CTAL to the Mexican regime of Lazaro Cardenas. Cardenas acted in March 1938 to nationalise the primarily American and British interests in the Mexican oil industry. Cardenas' methods in bringing about the pressures for nationalisation involved using the CTM. Cardenas had condoned numerous strikes in the oilfields by CTM oilworkers by permitting the oilworkers to air their grievances in a government-appointed commission. This commission found in favour of the workers and, despite appeals by the corporations to the Supreme Court, the workers' rights were upheld. When the corporations refused to obey the rulings of the Supreme Court, the CTM proclaimed a campaign 'on behalf of the Mexican masses'. Cardenas used this public support for the Expropriation Law of 1938 to take over the oil industry in Mexico.

The expropriation of the petroleum industry was strongly supported by the CIO under John L. Lewis. While the CIO supported the expropriation on the political grounds of solidarity with the Mexican unionists, Lewis had additional reasons for his support. Lewis maintained a close relationship with William Rhodes Davis, a US oilman whose partners in his Mexican oil business included Hjalmar Schacht of the German *Reichsbank*. After the expropriation of the Mexican oil interests Davis received $600 000 from Admiral Raeder to finance purchases of oil for Germany. Davis contacted John L. Lewis who called Lombardo Toledano to persuade him to use his influence with Cardenas to get Davis an oil allocation. Lewis could not reach Lombardo Toledano but did reach Alejandro Carillo, Toledano's assistant. Lewis introduced Carillo to Davis and arranged for Davis to be welcomed in Mexico City. During the prolonged negotiations Toledano was invited twice to Washington to meet with Lewis and Davis. In September 1938 the first of what was to be an allocation of 400 000 barrels of crude oil was sent from Mexico to Germany through the Davis–Lewis connection. This trade in oil, carried on Japanese and Italian ships, was controlled by the *Abwehr*'s main *Aussenstelle* in Mexico City. It was not until the British 'Intrepid' operation opened in New York that the monies to finance the *Abwehr*'s undercover operations in Latin America were curtailed and finally stopped.[2] The close alliance between the communists in Latin America and the axis forces following the Hitler–Stalin pact permitted the growth of sabotage and covert intelligence activities on behalf of Germany to flourish – not only in Mexico, but also in Argentina, Chile and Brazil. The CTAL provided a useful cover for some of the *Abwehr*'s agents.

The AFL supported Cordell Hull's demand for the immediate compensation to the oil industries for the assets nationalised by Cardenas. The State Department called in Matthew Woll and Chester Wright of the AFL to seek their support in an effort to drive a wedge between the communists of the CTM and the large bulk of its non-communist membership. The AFL delegates reiterated that they preferred to work through the remnants of the CROM of Luis Morones and requested State Department aid to intervene within the Mexican labour movement. The State Department was cautious about openly endorsing the AFL in these efforts because they feared the domestic political consequences of alienating the CIO. The AFL, nonetheless, attempted to rebuild the CROM and rejuvenate the PAFL. It did not succeed.

Government and labour co-operation proceeded apace with the US entry into the war. The State Department created an Office of Inter-American Affairs (OIAA) under Nelson Rockefeller, aided by labour intellectuals like Herling and Saposs. One of their concerns was the growth of strong pro-axis forces among the unions of Chile, Bolivia and Brazil: unions which threatened the supply of vital raw materials to the allies' war effort. The OIAA worked with both the AFL (with Green and Meany) and the CIO (with Jim Carey and Phil Murray) to sponsor visits of Latin unionists to the US. The Bureau of Labour Statistics began to publish a series of detailed analyses of the Latin union situation. In 1943 the first labour attachés were sent out under State Department supervision to maintain regular contact with foreign unionists along the model pioneered by Great Britain. The AFL suggested using its interamerican presence to build up an anti-CTAL labour force but the State Department, fearing the loss of co-operation with the CTAL that this might entail, held off on such a programme. With the formation of the Free Trades Union Committee, the AFL began to extend its representation throughout Latin America. Among the most successful of these organisers was Serafino Romualdi. Romualdi, having returned from Italy where he served in the OSS as a specialist operating among labour and socialist groups in the north, was initially attached to the OIAA. He travelled through Latin America working specifically on preventing too close a linkup between the large Latin American Italian community and the Mussolini forces in Italy. He augmented this effort with meetings with key Latin unionists. At the end of the war he was asked to stay on in Latin America where he represented the AFL and the FTUC.

Romualdi was convinced that the major Western unionists outside the AFL were preparing to form a world labour confederation after the war which would include the unions of the communist states. He was concerned that the continued existence of the CTAL would give this new labour international an opening to recognise the leftist unions of the CTAL as the sole legitimate representative of Latin American labour.

Romualdi was concerned that the many unionists he had met during his visits in Latin America who opposed the leftist elements who led the CTAL would be smothered after the war by the entrenched leadership of the CTAL unions. He proposed to Matthew Woll that the AFL strive to build a new interamerican labour federation to rival the CTAL.³

As a first step towards building a new interamerican organisation Romualdi began to generate pamphlets and other publicity warning of the dangers of the CTAL and Lombardo Toledano. George Meany of the AFL travelled to Mexico in 1944 to establish contacts with Mexican unions opposed to the CTM and to promise them his aid if they could build a rival Mexican federation. Romualdi contacted Bernardo Ibanez of Chile to cement a relationship between the AFL and the Chilean national centre which would parallel the CIO–CTM ties supporting the CTAL. This relationship was strengthened when Ibanez and Arturo Sabroso of Peru visited Washington, along with Albino Barra, and agreed with Romualdi on a plan to reconstitute an interamerican labour federation similar to the PAFL. The creation of the WFTU had brought about the very situation feared by Romualdi. The CTAL unionists did affiliate to the WFTU at its inception and constituted the regional arm of the WFTU. The AFL and its allies in Latin America were galvanised into promoting an anti-communist confederation of unions in the Americas. Ibanez returned home to work towards this end and found himself ousted from the Chilean national centre (CUTCh). He formed a new centre.

Romualdi continued his efforts at building a new interamerican organisation at the regional ILO meeting in April 1946, in Mexico City. He was successful in winning support from several delegations at the meeting (Chile, Peru, Canada and Venezuela) and especially from Father Nuñez of the Costa Rican federation. Romualdi's success in winning an initial assent to his proposal spurred the AFL to sponsor a trip by Romualdi throughout Latin America.

The efforts by Meany to build an anti-CTM coalition within Mexico from the CROM loyalists had succeeded in part. A loose and weak coalition had emerged, the National Labour Council, but was very much weaker than the CTM because of the close ties between the CTM and the ruling party in Mexico. Nonetheless, this achievement was hailed as a beginning for the AFL recruiting campaign. Romualdi, under the quiet aegis of the State Department, visited most Latin American countries. Once again the State Department, fearing a political backlash from the CIO, was very muted in its support for the Romualdi effort. In Peru, Romualdi met and won the support of Haya de la Torre and his *Apristas*. Similarly he won over Romulo Betancourt in Venezuela. In Chile he succeeded in persuading Ibanez to lead the new movement. The recent split in Colombia occurred at an opportune time for Romualdi who promised the anti-communist faction his support. They agreed to join. After many more meetings, and discreet lobbying in Washington by Nelson Rockefeller, Spruille Braden and the veteran US socialist Norman Thomas, the State Department was weaned from its timid pursuit of neutrality and gave its blessing to the AFL's efforts. In early 1948 the AFL's Lima Conference took place, with 156 delegates from seventeen nations in attendance. This conference created the Interamerican Confederation of Workers (CIT) which became the main rival to the CTAL.

Soon after, the Western unions walked out of the WFTU to form their own organisation: the ICFTU. The ICFTU had agreed at its founding congress to establish regional bodies. The first of these regional bodies was created in Mexico City in 1951 when President Aleman of Mexico and Oldenbroeck of the ICFTU welcomed labour delegations from twenty-one countries; primarily the CIT affiliates. The CIT reorganised itself as the regional organisation of the ICFTU under the name of *Organizacion Regional Interamericana de Trabajadores* (ORIT). From 1951 to the early 1980s ORIT has served to promote free unionism in Latin America. This included a major Cold War struggle against the forces of the WFTU and its CTAL. Its greatest battles consisted of the struggle against the forces of right-wing military dictatorships which devoured Latin unionism. To some degree, however inadvertently, the forces of the anti-communist unions and their interamerican organisations drove the free trades unionists of Latin America away from the clutches of the left, only to fall into the deadly embrace of the right.

The foreign policies of the AFL closely paralleled the foreign policies of the US government and the major business interests in Latin America. It would not be fair, however, to point at these congruities and assume that they were always part and parcel of the same effort. The US government and business interests were active in pursuing labour policies even without the active participation of the AFL. A good example was the Chilean crisis of 1947. In 1946 the presidency of Chile was won by Gabriel Gonzalez Videla of the Radical Party, a non-communist party but supported in the electoral coalition by the communists. Accordingly, Gonzalez Videla offered some Cabinet posts to the communists. The strikes in 1946 against the American copper mines led to much ill-feeling between Chile and the US. The US accused Gonzalez Videla of being 'too soft' on the communists and a danger to the hemisphere. Loans were blocked to Chile and trade sanctions were begun. In 1947 strikes, led almost exclusively by the Chilean communist unionists, threatened the coalfields. Gonzalez Videla was offered assistance by the Peronist government in Argentina and the Argentine unions began to expand their links with the CUTCh. The US, fearing that Chile would fall under the sway of Argentina, and fearing a communist success in the coal strike, offered support to Gonzalez Videla if he would sever his ties with his domestic communists and the Peronists. Gonzalez Videla agreed and the US began shipping coal from the US to Chile to break the strike. The rapid about-face of Gonzalez Videla led to increased investment in Chile and the imposition of strong government control over the unions (in fact the Chilean government tried to conscript the strikers into the army). The AFL, supporting Bernardo Ibanez, stayed very much on the sidelines in this crisis.

Nonetheless, throughout subsequent developments in Latin American unionism, the close ties between the US labour movement and the US government has created at least an image among Latin unionists that the AFL, and later the AFL–CIO, were more interested in fighting the Cold War battles than in permitting the development of a trades union movement within Latin American which was responsive to the wishes of Latin American workers. Additionally, the preoccupation by the AFL–CIO with the Cold War struggles created the type of domination of the trades unions that they professed they most feared.

A good example of the consequences of AFL involvement in the internal affairs of the delicate politico-economic relations which characterised the relations between governments and unions can be seen in the case of Guatemala. Guatemala was a poor nation largely dependent on the export earnings of its major crops, bananas and coffee, for foreign exchange. The major economic power in the land was the United Fruit Company which held a virtual monopoly on the production, storage and shipping of bananas, including a controlling interest in Guatemala's only railroad. Foreign domination of the economy was not Guatemala's only problem. During the depression of the early 1930s the government of General Jorge Ubico tightened its political control of the nation and pursued a determined policy of deflation; restricting credit, cutting social welfare programmes and impeding investment. This economic policy added to the large pool of unemployed and forced increased police and army efforts towards maintaining law and order.

A prime concern for US policy in Guatemala was the close ties between Ubico and the large German presence in Guatemala. Ubico himself and many of his Cabinet had maintained close ties with the Germans prior to the Second World War. With the outbreak of war, the US asserted its 'Good Neighbour' policy in Guatemala by forcing the liquidation of the German-owned coffee, banking and trading interests in Guatemala. FBI agents were sent to Guatemala to assist in the liquidations of these assets. Thousands of US troops were stationed in Guatemala to protect the Panama Canal and to keep an eye on Ubico.

Pressure continued to build within Guatemala during the war, resulting in a militant organising of clandestine unions. When the police fired on student demonstrators in June 1944, the clandestine unions called a successful general strike which paralysed the nation. Ubico resigned and tried to put a puppet in his place but the striking unions would not accept that solution. On 20 October 1944 the workers and the students installed a revolutionary triumvirate of Francisco Arana, Jacobo Arbenz and Jorge Toriello. After popular elections, Juan Jose Arevalo became president of Guatemala. Arevalo, long tied to the unions, undertook a series of social reforms. He legalised unions; he established a minimum wage; he brought in the eight-hour day; he created a social security system; and he built labour courts to which unions could appeal. He acted to abolish forced labour on the plantations and sought to diversify the economy away from its dependence on coffee and bananas. These activities were not viewed with complacency by the major plantation owners. In the case of United Fruit, the social security provisions alone cost the company more than two hundred thousand dollars annually. Frequent attempts were made on the life of Arevalo. Arevalo countered these threats by becoming even more closely linked with the force of the trades unions.

These trades unions had formed a national centre, the *Confederacion General de Trabajadores de Guatemala* (CGTG), in 1945. The CGTG affiliated to the CTAL and to the WFTU at the earliest opportunity. The CGTG was led by Victor Manuel Guitierrez, a communist member of the parliament. The communists closely allied themselves with Arevalo and were rewarded with many plum jobs in his administration and in the trades union movement. This important role of the communists in the national administration greatly concerned Washington. This concern grew even more pronounced as Arevalo insisted on collective bargaining agreements being negotiated with United Fruit and other US companies. In retaliation, the US cut off military assistance; the World Bank refused loans; United Fruit curtailed banana exports by 80 per cent. Problems did not improve as the nation prepared for the next election in early 1950. Contesting the election was Francisco Arana, head of the armed forces. Opposing him was the Minister of Defence, Jacobo Arbenz, an Arevalo loyalist. In July 1949 Arana was mysteriously assassinated. Arana's supporters took to the streets assisted by the military. Arevalo called upon his allies in the unions, arming them and turning them loose in the streets to fight the military. This popular militia of unionists and students succeeded in restoring order. After another coup attempt, this time by Colonel Castillo Armas, Arbenz was elected and took office as Guatemala's new president.

Arbenz took office in 1951 with the solid backing of the unions. He vowed to strengthen Guatemalan power over the foreign monopolies by building nationalised enterprises to compete with them. He attempted to build a giant hydroelectric plant; he started work on a highway to compete with the United Fruit's railroad; and he planned a new port on the Atlantic to compete with the United Fruit's port. The crunch came in March 1953 when Arbenz expropriated 234 000 uncultivated acres of United Fruit lands, offering to pay United Fruit for them at the value that United Fruit had claimed as their taxable worth: six hundred thousand dollars. United Fruit demanded almost sixteen million dollars. Arbenz refused to budge. The US government decided that Arbenz must go. They were encouraged by their recent success in preparing the coup in Iran which effectively installed the Shah on the Peacock throne and their efforts within Greek labour politics in fighting off a communist threat. One of the major agents of the Greek operations, 'Smilin' Jack' Peurifoy, was sent as Ambassador to Guatemala in 1953 to plan the overthrow of Arbenz.[4] The project, under the code name APB/Success, was directed by Raymond Leddy and Tracey Barnes. Part of the CIA's efforts to overthrow Arbenz depended on the activities of the American trades unionists. As early as 1951, Serafino Romualdi was writing and lecturing about the communist takeover of the Guatemalan trades unions. The CIA's anti-Arbenz campaign was co-ordinated among three elements: the military, the trades unions and the corporations. The opening move came with the invitation by United Fruit to Miguel Ydigoras Fuentes to meet CIA officers to discuss the overthrow of Arbenz. He was offered funds and an army to overthrow Arbenz but he refused. The CIA decided to change over to Castillo Armas who had an anti-Arevalo track record. On the labour front Romualdi and the ORIT established and funded the formation of a rival national centre in Guatemala, the *Union Nacional de Trabajadores Libres* (National Union of Free Workers – UNTL). This organisation existed primarily on paper and never claimed control or

The Development of Latin American Unionism

representation rights in any industry. Arbenz arrested its leaders and deported the UNTL's secretary back to Mexico. George Meany addressed open letters to Arbenz attacking him for permitting the growth of strong communist forces, especially in the trades unions. Romualdi led the tattered remains of the UNTL to Mexico and on to Momotobito Island where the CIA ran a training camp for Guatemalan insurgents.

On June 18, the 'Liberation Army' of Castillo Armas crossed over the border from Honduras into Guatemala. The small insurgent force of about 160 members (including the UNTL exiles) were supported by US pilots flying *P-47 Thunderbolts* on bombing missions over Guatemala. The *P-47s* bombed the port of San Jose and flew missions over Guatemala City. Over the next few days they flew repeated missions (they were known as '*sulfatos*' from their apparent laxative effect on Arbenz's generals). Throughout the short campaign the AFL and ORIT praised the invasion as the internal uprising of anti-communist Guatemalans. The CIO unionists opposed the US action. Jack Knight of the Oil Workers said that the reason that the State Department was supporting Castillo Armas was that the Dulles brothers (head of the State Department and the CIA respectively) represented the law firm which handled all of United Fruit's business. The most forthright was Emil Mazey, UAW's secretary-treasurer, who demanded that the State Department stop conducting coups against governments which represented the best interests of the people.

The military campaign resumed when the CIA was able to fly down more planes to replace the initial four damaged or destroyed. At the embassy Peurifoy laboured to get Arbenz to resign. On 27 June Arbenz gave in and stepped down in favour of Carlos Enrique Diaz. Colonel Diaz, a simple man, did not have a grasp of what exactly was happening. He went on radio to declare his intention to continue the fight against the mercenary invaders. That was too much for Peurifoy. He strapped on battle gear, put a pistol in his belt and personally went out to arrange the demise of Diaz. The next day, Diaz resigned at gunpoint. Peurifoy sent his plane to pick up Castillo Armas, who took over as Head of State on 8 July. The revolution was over.

The next phase of pacification involved the trades unions more directly. Following fulsome praise for the destruction of the communist-dominated regime in Guatemala the AFL 'rejoiced' at the victory of Castillo Armas. It offered to him the loyal support of the free unionists who were returning to build non-communist unions in Guatemala. Ten days after Castillo Armas took power, his labour advisor, Romualdi, led a mission to Guatemala. Dan Benedict of the CIO, Otero Borlaff of the ORIT and Raul Valdivia of the Cuban CTC accompanied Romualdi to help advise Armas and to supervise the building of a free trades union movement. Romualdi stayed in Guatemala for two months, sending back glowing reports of his progress to the AFL and ORIT. The AFL and ORIT channelled large quantities of money to Romualdi to build a national centre through the National Committee for Trades Union Reorganisation. Organisation proceeded slowly. Castillo Armas showed himself to be less than a devoted supporter of free trades unionism. He set up a National Committee for Defence Against Communism, with police state powers. Immediately, between five and eight thousand people were jailed.

In August the government passed the Preventive Penal Law Against Communism, which could declare anyone a communist and put him 'on the register'. Being on the register meant being subject to arbitrary jailings without trial. Within four months the register contained over 72 000 names. The government summarily cancelled the registration of 533 trades unions and passed legislation forbidding unionisation. The organisers of the CGTG unions at United Fruit and the several peasant organisations affiliated to the unions were rounded up and shot. The employers and landlords, encouraged by the return to them of 99.6 per cent of all expropriated land (including United Fruit) embarked upon a campaign of ferocious attacks on unionists and peasants. The election law was amended to disenfranchise the 75 per cent of the nation which was illiterate. Labour unions were forbidden and Romualdi left Guatemala a disappointed man. The US agreed to send over ninety million dollars in aid and military equipment in the first two years of the Castillo Armas regime.

The AFL's complicity in the destruction of unionism in Guatemala, including its desired destruction of the communist unions, caused much soul-searching on the part of the AFL. Even more, it drove a wedge between the AFL position on international labour and the position adopted by the other Western union centres of the ICFTU. After all, it wasn't just the AFL dabbling in the CIA's coup activities in Guatemala; the AFL claimed it was doing this on behalf of ORIT, the ICFTU's regional arm. Many European unionists were reluctant to give the AFL a free hand in Latin America but felt that there was no mechanism for exerting control over the AFL's programmes. They tried to insist that all aid go through the International Solidarity Fund but the AFL would not agree. These problems were exacerbated by the activities of the AFL in other areas of Latin America. Throughout Latin American unionism a strong current of nationalism was growing; a nationalism which transcended the Cold War divisions of East and West, and which manifested itself as the creation of domestic unionism closely tied to the political fortunes of a strong political leader. The most striking example of this phenomenon was Argentina where Peronism dominated the labour and political scene.

The growth of Argentine unionism stretches back to the FORA days when anarcho-syndicalist organisers succeeded in building a national labour organisation. In the mid-1930s immigration began to dry up. The new generation of Argentine workers began to take on a strong nationalist coloration and identified less with the political movements of Europe, concentrating on Argentina, and to a lesser degree, interamerican problems. Argentine politics and trades unionism became bound up in burgeoning Argentine populism. At the same time, the unions which were forming under socialist–populist influences were becoming successful in obtaining collective agreements from corporations. Most importantly, in the 1930s the British government imposed import controls; a move which severely reduced Argentina's ability to export to its traditional market. Argentine business and political leaders, battered by the financial crisis, embarked on a programme of import substitution industries. The agrarian interests which had seen a dramatic drop in their fortunes entered into an alliance with Argentina's nascent capitalist sector. They represented the major political power in the nation, under the strong economic direction of Frederico Pineda in the Ministry of Economics. His policies fostered the rapid expansion of domestic manufacture.

The government of Yrigoyen was overthrown in 1930 by a military coup led by General Jose Felix Uriburu who attempted to build a fascist state in Argentina along the lines of Mussolini's Italy. This was too much even for others in the army and Uriburu was soon replaced by a more popular figure, General Justo. The bulk of the union movement had recently reunited into a single labour confederation, the *Confederacion General del Trabajo* (CGT). This unified labour movement still excluded the remnants of the FORA. Most importantly, the leadership of a significant sector of the unions was in the hands of the Argentine communist party, although outside the CGT.

The CGT took an apolitical stance in relation to the military junta, preferring to let the forces of the state pursue the CGT's enemies in the communist labour and poltical movements. However, after an abortive counter-coup by the Radicals in 1932, the military junta became less discriminating in its repression of unions. Many unionists were jailed or deported. Many unions were dissolved by government decree. The military encouraged the formation of vigilante, paramilitary 'patriotic' groups which broke up workers' demonstrations and meetings. In 1935, with the dawn of the popular front the communists joined forces with the CGT, bringing with them their strong unions in the construction industry, the metalworkers and the textile workers. Unions gradually won recognition from the military and were permitted to carry out two important functions. Trades unions were permitted to negotiate collective agreements in industry. In some case these were national agreements; in others regional agreements. The negotiation of these collective agreements became an important union function and helped consolidate national unions in industries like the railroads, printing, the retail trades, etc. The second permitted function was the extension of social security and welfare programmes to workers through their unions. These programmes resulted in union-owned hospitals, recreation centres and clinics being built across Argentina. These were largely financed by the employers and supervised by the government, although the administration of these social welfare schemes was left to the unions.

The effect of these two functions was to revolutionise trades unionism. The collective agreements which developed were often quite complex, comprising in addition to wage bargaining, classification systems, pensions, fringe benefits and social welfare schemes. The skills required for these negotiations and the skills needed to administer the union hospitals and clinics were not those found among ordinary workers. Unions attracted professionals and skilled administrators. For many, trades unionism became a career opportunity. A professional class of trades unionists emerged; a bureaucratic group of union leaders operating increasingly centralised unions and controlling fairly substantial assets and dues revenues. After 1936 unionism spread across Argentina at a rapid pace, although strikes were still suppressed. These organised workers represented an aristocracy of labour. Through collective bargaining their wages were able to keep up to some degree with Argentine inflation. For the other, unorganised sector, real wages fell dramatically during the late 1930s.

In 1942 the CGT split over whether the unions should form their own political party or whether they should represent the labour arm of either the Socialist or the Communist Party. The faction of socialists, deriving their main support from the two giant rail unions, who supported the outgoing Secretary–General Jose Domench, preferred to keep clear of direct party ties. They were opposed by the faction headed by the head of the Municipal Workers' Union, Francisco Perez Leiros, and the head of the Commercial Workers, Angel Borlenghi. These pressed for affiliation to the Socialist Party. They were supported primarily by the communists who felt that they could win control over the movement. The two groups were distinguished as CGT–1 and CGT–2.

By the time of the 1943 coup there were four labour groupings in Argentina: CGT–1, CGT–2, the small group of FORA followers and a syndicalist group, the *Union Sindical Argentina* (USA) which had important affiliates in telecommunications and among the maritime trades. In 1943 a miltary coup took over control in Argentina from the leadership of Dr Castillo, an arch-conservative. Castillo had practised a strongly pro-axis neutrality. His close ties with Nazi Germany and with Italy were constantly condemned by the US which used its power within the hemisphere to isolate Argentina. Massive US military aid was sent to Brazil in an effort to maintain a capability to control Argentina. The difficulty of putting pressure on Argentina emerged from Churchill's refusal, after innumerable requests, to participate in a blockade of Argentina. Indeed, one of the most hostile encounters between Franklin D. Roosevelt and Churchill revolved around England's refusal to assist in blockading Argentina. Churchill needed Argentine foodstuffs and feared German reprisals if they interdicted trade with Argentina. Castillo, seeing the handwriting on the wall began to move more towards a pro-allied position. He chose as his successor, Dr Patron Costas, who was closely tied to US and British interests. The military, fearing the success of Dr Patron Costas, intervened. A small, tightly-knit military clique calling itself the *Grupo de Oficiales Unidos* (GOU), still believing in an axis victory, seized power on 4 June 1943. General Rawson lasted two days as president because he threatened to turn over power to the civilians. He was replaced by General Ramirez, the head of the GOU.

The new junta dissolved CGT–2 on the grounds that it was communist-dominated. It forced the two major rail unions to disaffiliate from the CGT–1, thus eliminating most of its membership. The union attitude began to harden against the junta and confrontation seemed inevitable. Then in October 1943 a prominent GOU member who was also in the war ministry asked for and was granted the job of running the labor department. The placing of the Colonel, Juan Domingo Peron, in charge of the labour department was an act which had dramatic repercussions in Argentina and on the rest of the world. Peron had decided that the trades unions were to be his vehicle to power and, during the next decade, the trades union movement in Argentina became the most potent force in the nation. Under Juan Peron and his wife Evita, Argentine labour was raised to a pinnacle of power unknown anywhere else in the history of trades unionism.

Peron took over control of the Ministry of Labour amidst widespread labour unrest. The government had placed military intervenors at the head of the two main rail unions and had acted swiftly against the communists in CGT–2. Peron, sensing that he could benefit from the ties with the unions continued to meet with the leadership of the CGT–1 and encouraged them in their activities. He rewarded the unionists who supported him and jailed, exiled and 'disappeared' any who opposed him (in Argentina 'to disappear' is a transitive verb). Most importantly Peron threw the power of his office behind a gigantic recruiting drive for new unionists. In the packing plants, for example, the meat workers had long been discriminated against. Their unions were non-existent. They were only seasonally employed and at low wages. Peron freed the meat workers' union leaders from prison. He put the force of the state behind their organising drive. He made welfare benefits available to them. Through these actions Peron was able to organise a powerful meat packers' union. There had been no more than 325 000 to 350 000 organised workers in Argentina before Peron came to power. Within a few years this number had more than quintupled. Peron personally led organising drives in the plantations and cattle lands of the interior, spreading his unique brand of welfare unionism to remote parts of Argentina. He aided the unions in building an organised labour force from the ranks of the 'descamisados' the 'shirtless ones' who had flocked to the cities to join the unemployment queues. He won the loyalties of the organised workers through a form of state–union welfare system not unlike the system used to gain the loyalties of the US poor and unorganised towards the New Deal programmes by Roosevelt. Peron also kept the loyalties of his fellow GOU members. By 1944 Peron was also Minister of War and Vice-President in addition to his labour duties.

Peron acted to promote the Statute of the Peon, extending legal recognition to farm workers' rights, including paid holidays, free medical service, job security and a fixed minimum wage. Peron personally intervened in innumerable labour disputes, settling strikes and decreeing collective bargains. This weakened the control by the unionists themselves as the workers looked to Peron rather than to their leaders for satisfaction. Peron continued to decry both socialism and communism as 'foreign imports' implying that a socialist or communist was unpatriotic. The workers became personally loyal to Peron and resistant to political agitation from the right or left which threatened Peron's position. By 1945 Peron had plenty of enemies from across the political spectrum. When the employers' federation tried to move against Peron through a petition calling for the revoking of the social legislation, Peron organised mass demonstrations through the CGT. Waving banners proclaimed that the workers were there 'In defence of the benefits received from the Minister of Labour'.

The power of Peron was immense. The military junta, sensing a growing discontent among the former political parties, attempted to lift the state of siege which had been in force since their takeover. The political forces demanded the restoration of the constitution and liberal freedoms. The socialists, too, joined the chorus of parties demanding an end to military rule. The socialist unions of the railroads, shoemakers and textile workers, as well as the communist unions, left the CGT to campaign for the restoration of civilian rule. Peron retorted by passing a new Law of Professional Associations which stated that only one union could be legally recognised as the bargaining agent for a particular industry. He then chose which union and which unionists should have legal status. He rewarded his friends and supporters and punished his enemies. The uproar among the parties at the lifting of the state of seige threatened to split the nation into battling factions. The military swiftly restored the state of siege and tried to put a lid on all political activity. At this juncture a contingent of the military rebelled at the reimposition of the state of siege and seized Buenos Aires. They arrested Peron and were trying to remove President Farrell from office. The employers announced that they were refusing to grant their workers a contractual paid holiday on 12 October (Columbus Day). The impression was clearly given that the restoration of constitutional liberties and the reinstatement of civilian government was at the same time an attack on the unions and the workers. Evita, who was with Peron when he was arrested, rushed off to the CGT headquarters to tell the unions what had happened. Cipriano Reyes, head of the packinghouse workers, called for a massive demonstration in Buenos Aires. Thousands of workers began making their way to the capital. A union Emergency Committee voted to call a general strike on 17 October to free Peron. On that day thousands of workers filled the streets of Buenos Aires and the other major cities. Civilian political leaders went into hiding and the military, swamped by the massive outpouring of unionists, feared to attempt to restore order. Juan Peron was brought to the balcony of the Casa Rosada, along with President Farrell, and from then on was the only real political force in the nation. The workers had put Peron back into power. The government announced new elections and Peron and the unions prepared to win them.

Peron first formed a labour party, the *Partido Laborista*, led by the trades union functionaries of the CGT. He persuaded a dissident group of the Radical Party to form a Renovated Radical Party under Peron. Finally, everyone else was lumped into his Independent Party. Peron's opposition grouped itself into the *Union Democratica Nacional* (UDN) which comprised the Radicals, the Socialists, the Communists, the Conservatives and the Progressive Democrats. These supported the candidacy of the old pro-British leadership of Tamborini and Mosca. The US, through Spruille Braden, tried to intervene on behalf of the anti-Peron forces by publishing a 'Blue Book' attacking Peron as a fascist sympathiser. Peron replied with a 'Blue and White' Book denouncing US imperialist efforts. In the election Peron won; his parties took control of the Senate and the Chamber of Deputies, every provincial governorship and most of the provincial assemblies. On 4 June 1946 Peron was inaugurated as President.

As Peron sought power he was aided by a remarkable woman: Maria Eva Duarte de Peron, his wife. Evita became the virtual head of the Argentine labour movement. She set up offices at CGT headquarters and spent her time convincing Argentine workers that all their benefits and advantages flowed directly from the Perons. A massive charitable foundation, the Eva Peron Foundation, which had a monopoly on all charitable work in Argentina collected millions of dollars which it used to build hospitals, schools, children's homes, orphanages, etc. It organised disaster relief and gave handouts to the needy. This foundation received innumerable 'gifts' from unions and employers. Even visiting dignitaries were expected to assist in this charitable work. The Perons did well out of doing good. They amassed a large sum of money with which they could buy friends, influence political movements and effectively lop off any branches of the tree of labour that might seem likely to bear anti-Peron fruit.

Evita held court at the CGT, often accompanied by Ministers sent over for the occasion. She would hear petitions two or three times a week and dispense justice, advice and cash to those who came to plead their case. In the meantime, she also supervised the unions. Within her six-year reign as Queen of Argentine labour virtually every major Argentine union was purged and new leaders were installed who owed their loyalty only to Peron. Even Cipriano Reyes languished in prison, only to emerge when Peron was overthrown. By 1950 there were very few organisations of workers not firmly in Peron's camp. When the railroad workers went out on strike in 1951, Peron drafted the strikers into the army and ordered them back to work.

Peron announced the ideology of *'justicialismo'* which emphasised the dignity of workers and their rights as unionists. He decreed the 'Declaration of the Rights of Workers' in 1951 which formulated ten key points which summarised his centrally-directed welfare populism. The only cohesive, if clandestine, opposition to Peron in the labour movement was the *Comite Obrero Argentino de Sindicatos Independientes* (COASI) formed among socialist and independent unionists outside of the CGT of Evita. The COASI received funds, publicity, and support from the AFL and the ORIT. The COASI was able to operate legally in Argentina until 1949 when Peron closed it down. It moved its headquarters to neighbouring Montevideo where it continued to operate clandestinely inside Argentina in an effort to break the control of Peron over the Argentine labour movement.

Peron's success in maintaining control over the unions and Argentina suffered with the economic difficulties that beset his regime after 1950. Real wages no longer outpaced prices. To spur growth Peron attempted to try and attract foreign capital. A principal attraction he offered to foreign investors was his control over a docile and obedient labour force. Resistance to the nation's economic woes by the workers threatened to destabilise the new directions of Peronism. Trades unionists were arrested with increasing regularity; the unions were placed even more closely under the direct control of the party. An effort by Peron to create a continent-wide rival to ORIT was begun in 1952 with the creation of the *Agrupacion de Trabajadores Latino Americanos Sindacalistas* (ATLAS).

Angered by the ORIT and AFL condemnation of his seizure of the independent newspaper *La Prensa* in 1951, Peron decided to counter-attack. He formed the ATLAS and staffed the Argentine embassies with ATLAS labour attachés who campaigned against the ORIT, the AFL and the CTAL. It was ATLAS who, through a well-financed campaign, attacked the AFL and the ORIT for being what it called tools of the State Department. The ICFTU was extremely sensitive to these attacks. It constantly attempted to reiterate the independence of ORIT from State Department influence. Latin American public opinion was difficult to convince, especially since the events in Guatemala.

Between 1953 and 1955 Peron had more pressing problems with which to contend. With the death of Evita in 1952, Peron was left on his own trying to keep control of the trades unions and the presidency. An attempt by the unions to nominate Evita as Vice-President in the 1951 election had enabled many anti-Peronists to gain strength. Evita withdrew her candidacy but an attempted military coup gave warning that things were not all well.

In September 1955 Peron was overthrown. Throughout 1954 and in early 1955 Peron had largely made his peace with the US and had invited in US business interests. In August 1955 Peron was faced with a tremendous pressure to resign by the forces of the centre and the Church. He addressed the workers gathered in a mass demonstration. His offer to resign was well stage-managed. The workers cheered him on to stay. This was too much for the military, however, and General Lonardi led the Cordoba garrison in revolt. Lonardi was supported by the middle and upper-class organisations. Peron boarded a Paraguayan gunboat and sailed into exile.

Peron's exile was followed by a period of strict military rule. Peronism had not died with the departure of Peron. It had been transformed into a class battle between the workers and the forces of the state. The new leaders were intent on wresting power from the hands of the CGT. They put intervenors within the organisation. The ICFTU sent six special missions to Argentina in 1956 trying to work with the authorities to build free unions again in Argentina. These efforts by the ICFTU led to direct conflict with Romualdi who complained that the Brussels headquarters was taking too great an interest in ORIT. He persuaded Meany to visit Latin America himself in 1956 where he attempted to improve direct AFL ties to Latin unionists. After Meany's visits the newly merged AFL–CIO generally bypassed the ORIT in favour of direct, bi-lateral ties with Latin unions.

The Argentine question was far from solved. Over the next decade Argentine unionists continued to dominate a major portion of Argentine political life. Under 'El Lobo', (Augusto Vandor's) leadership the CGT's main faction (the sixty-two loyalist unions) opposed the group of thirty-two anti-Peronist unions for control of the CGT. Later the union forces of John William Cooke's revolutionary band undertook urban guerrilla warfare in Argentina, only to find itself in conflict with Vandor. By 1965 Vandor proclaimed his independence from Peron. Jose Alonso split the CGT once again. When both Jose Alonso and Vandor were assassinated Ongaro took over as the Peronist loyalist in an effort to restore Peronism. The restoration of Peron to office did not solve the Argentine problem, nor did the temporary rule of his second wife, Isabelita. The military regimes of Ongania and Videla were firm in putting down opposition. Thousands have disappeared. Hundreds are imprisoned, but the trades union force created by Peron still exists as a major political force in Argentine life. Peron had demonstrated the latent power of Latin trades union movement. It was a lesson learned well in other Latin nations when military leaders faced a militant trades union movement.

The destruction of the ATLAS as a viable interamerican 'Third Force' in the trades union movement after the fall of Peron left numerous nationalist, and frequently anti-ORIT, unions without a focus. Many joined together under the auspices of the CISC, the Christian international, to form a continent-wide labour organisation, the Latin American Confederation of Christian Trades Unions (CLASC). The CLASC drew upon the rising success of Christian democratic parties in gaining political power in many Latin American nations and in the revolution in priestly concerns by concerned social activists inside the Church. The CLASC called for a 'Third Way' of trades unionism, much as the ATLAS attempted, and began its life in 1954 with strident attacks on both the CTAL and the ORIT. The CLASC called for an end to what it described as 'economic colonialism' in Latin America and denounced both the US and the Soviets for attempting to shape the destinies of Latin American nations through overt and covert pressure on the governments through the trades union movement. Under the leadership of Jose Goldsack Donoso and its secretary-general Emilio Maspero, the CLASC began a campaign within Latin America to organise unions and peasant bodies into a continent-wide federation. The parent CISC was unable to offer much support and the AFL was extremely hostile, so the bulk of its operating funds came from foundations and European Christian democratic parties. The Konrad Adenauer Stiftung, and the German Catholic Bishop's *Misereor* Fund provided the initial funding for CLASC. The CLASC has grown strong since 1954 and counted among its affiliates key national union centres in the Dominican Republic, Nicaragua and Guatemala which were at one time the largest national centres. The Christian democratic parties in Chile and Venezuela supported and nurtured CLASC. The CLASC, unlike its counterpart in Asia, the Brotherhood of Asian Trades Unions, grew even stronger than its parent organisation, the CISC.

Unfortunately, the success of the CLASC in organising a large chunk of its potential unions in Latin America has earned it the enmity and hostility of the AFL-CIO and the ORIT. Despite the efforts by CLASC to deconfessionalise (it changed its name to CLAT and dropped the Christian identification) it has posed a rivalry to the ORIT monopoly of anti-communist unionism in Latin America. The CLAT has also angered many of the ITSs by attempting to create Latin American committees of the CLAT in key sectors, attempting to set up a parallel ITS structure under its own auspices. This has been heavily criticised as foolish and counter-productive since most of the important ITSs have WCL affiliates within them. This type of dual unionism has made it difficult for the European unionists of the WCL to co-operate with the CLAT even though they share a similar ideology and promote similar programmes.

The rise of the CLAT as a 'Third Force' in Latin America posed many problems to the AFL–CIO, but were nothing in comparison to the effects on Latin unionism of the Cuban revolution and the rise to power of Fidel Castro.

The failure of the Bay of Pigs landing left Castro more tightly bound to the communists inside and outside of Cuba. Along with the foreign aid, the Soviet Union sent KGB specialists to Cuba to help organise the *Direcion General de Intelligencia* (DGI), the Cuban intelligence agency. These KGB officers included specialists in labour affairs. Through the DGI and the newly constituted CTC, the KGB and the Cubans built a base within the Western hemisphere to interact with the trades union movements of Latin America. Drawing upon the immense sympathy felt by the Latin American populace towards the Cuban revolution and Castro in particular, the Russians were able to mount a much more formidable attack against US labour activities in the area. Cuban labour attachés, cultural attachés and agricultural specialists trained by the KGB's labour offices soon dispersed across Latin America. A new stage of Cold War escalation in the labour field had begun.

At the same time the US had marshalled its forces into a new effort to deny the Cubans and their Russian allies a clear field in which to operate. By 1960 the AFL–CIO was facing difficulties within the ICFTU in winning support for its anti-communist crusade. Numerous European union centres resisted the AFL–CIO's assumption of the determining role in Latin America and were attempting to co-ordinate foreign assistance through the International Solidarity Fund. The AFL–CIO promised to refrain from bi-lateral activity but soon found that this was a promise it could not keep. The Cuban situation changed the AFL–CIO's thinking. As George Meany testified in Congressional hearings: 'In August 1960, when we came to a full realisation as to what happened to the Cuban workers and the entire Cuban people and Castro, the AFL–CIO appropriated $20 000 for the purpose of making a feasibility study of the establishment of a mechanism through which we could hope to strengthen the free labour unions of Latin America and develop trade union leadership.'[5] The vehicle that Meany and the AFL–CIO decided on was the American Institute for Free Labor Development (AIFLD) founded in 1961.

The AIFLD was created in a period in which the new Kennedy government was seeking to make its impact felt within Latin America. The Bay of Pigs invasion was not an isolated event in Latin America; it was only the most public act of a series of acts designed to strengthen anti-communism in the area. The reasoning behind setting up as powerful an anti-communist labour organisation as the AIFLD was best described in a report by George Cabot Lodge, Labour Department Assistant Secretary for International Affairs (and chairman of the ILO's governing body in 1960 and 1961):

> Since the October Revolution, the subversion and control of trade unions has been part of the international communist conspiracy ... Aided and inspired by Fidel Castro and his most significant export, *Fidelismo*, Communist leaders are now exerting serious pressures on the workers' organisations of Venezuela, Bolivia, Chile, Ecuador, Peru and Brazil among others ... On one side is a single effort, backed by the great resources of a bloc of nations, centrally directed, ably led, unbothered by principles of any sort, willing to adopt any guise, change any policy, go to any lengths to subvert and overthrow every non-communist system ... On the other side is a collection of organisations, largely unco-ordinated, certainly not centrally directed, each with separate interests, loyal to separate systems and states, unified by a general commitment to freedom, independence, and social justice, but divided as to the best methods of fulfilling this commitment.[6]

Beneath the hyperbole one can see that the type of organisation envisioned by Lodge and his colleagues in the Kennedy Administration was an organisation whose main function was to fight the international communist conspiracy. With the creation of the AIFLD these aspirations were achieved. Over the next twenty years the AIFLD has continued its battle against the forces of communism within the labour movements throughout Latin America. This battle was not conducted by the AFL–CIO on its own. It was joined in its efforts by the forces of the US government and the leaders of US multinational business with major investments in Latin America.

The AIFLD is a tripartite body, composed of AFL–CIO appointees,

US government appointees and businessmen. Meany was president, Joe Beirne of the Communications Workers and the PTTI was secretary–treasurer and J. Peter Grace (of W. R. Grace & Co.) was chairman. The W. R. Grace corporation owns shipping companies, sugar plantations, distilleries, box factories, textile mills, banks, etc., in Latin America – a scope of activity which keeps Peter Grace in close touch with the problems of Latin American workers. Also on the board was Bernd Friele, the vice-chairman, the Rockefeller family's specialist on Latin America. Other business members included Charles Brinkerhoff of Anaconda Copper, Juan Trippe of Pan American Airways, Henry Woodbridge of the True Temper Company, Robert Hill of Merck and William Hickey of the United Corporation. These directors were augmented by representatives of two foundations. Although the AIFLD is a tripartite body the bulk of its funds comes directly from the US government.

These funds are used in two major areas. The first area of activity has been the area of education. It trains Latin American unionists in trades unionism in local schools, regional schools and at their advanced training centre in Front Royal, Virginia. The Front Royal Institute was originally run as a PTTI training institute by the Communications Workers of Joe Beirne. At Front Royal, students are brought for extensive courses, usually ten weeks or so, and have their lessons supplemented by field trips throughout the US and Europe. Students are chosen by the AIFLD country directors. Classes are usually mixed although, in special cases, a whole class may be made up of students from one nation. In each country in which AIFLD operates it has established an institute through which courses lasting from one week to three months are undertaken to train local union leaders. Additionally the AIFLD arranges short courses or lectures on special subjects where it is felt a need exists. The AIFLD also runs special courses at Mount Vernon College in Washington for labour economists. As part of this educational effort the AIFLD publishes a wide variety of materials in Spanish and Portuguese to assist Latin American unions in training programmes of their own. The most important aspect of the AIFLD training programme is that, upon graduation, those trainees who have graduated from Front Royal or other US courses are put back in their own labour movements to apply their lessons. For nine months after graduation these trainees are kept on the AIFLD payroll and receive other expenses from the resident AIFLD director.

The second area of AIFLD activity has been in the field of social projects. Social projects assistance is rendered to local unions by the

AIFLD to help them provide tangible social benefits for their members. Through the provision of specialists the AIFLD assists local unions in building credit unions, co-operatives and workers' banks. Additionally AIFLD has been active in promoting workers' housing schemes. The social projects director, Billy Doherty, has travelled all over Latin America assisting unions there in long-term and short-term planning for assistance. In addition to the long-term projects (union housing), numerous impact projects, like providing sewing machines, have been undertaken by the AIFLD. Occasionally the AIFLD conducts educational projects and social projects on behalf of the ITSs as well as in joint projects with them. There has been some overlap with ORIT's training school for Latin unionists in Cuernavaca, Mexico, but most projects were kept strictly separate.

As might be imagined these projects are costly. AIFLD draws in about $8 million each year from the US government to assist in its work. Some of this money goes directly to the several national training institutes to meet their budget constraints (*the Instituto Cultural do Trabalho* – ICT – in Brazil draws over $500 000 per year, for example). Other funds go to maintain the institute graduates for nine months. There have been almost 600 000 graduates since the opening of AIFLD's training efforts, not all of whom have been subsidised. These funds are provided to the AIFLD by US AID under specific contracts. They are subcontracted to individual unions, like the Communications Workers, the Retail Clerks, the Brotherhood of Railway and Airline Clerks, the Oil Workers and some others. Occasionally these sums are subcontracted to an ITS, most notably the International Federation of the Petroleum and Chemical Workers (IFPCW) of Denver. The supervision of these funds is technically in the hands of the AID administrators but, as a 1962 Committee on Foreign Relations of the US Senate reported, such supervision is extremely difficult. Moreover this report, known as the Dockery Report, was critical of the basic structure of AIFLD assistance. It concluded: 'the programmes should receive government funds only to the extent of matching U.S. labour's own private funding of technical assistance abroad. In each and every instance, covert funding of labour activities must be rejected.'[7] It is in this last phrase that the problem lies. These government subsidies of the AFL–CIO's activities were not given on the basis of pure altruism. They were given to promote US foreign policy initiatives in Latin America.

This funding of AIFLD was supplemented by additional grants from charitable foundations and international institutes fronting for the CIA. CIA operatives were assigned to some of the labour programmes and the

CIA's International Organisations Division, whose Latin American section was run out of Mexico, supervised much of the AIFLD's programmes. Meany frequently denied ever having received money from the CIA. This is probably true, but is a trivial distinction. The CIA like any other US agency draws its funds from the public purse and derives these funds from tax revenues. Unlike other agencies its budget is classified. Its budget figures are buried in allocations to other US agencies and departments and made available to the CIA by the budgetary authorities. If a sum of money has been allocated to the CIA for one of its programmes and these funds have been buried in the State Department or Defense Department allocations, the State Department or Defense Department dispense these funds on behalf of CIA's programme. To choose to support a CIA Latin American labour programme through an allocation to the State Department is a question of accounting not politics. The fact remains that the AIFLD mounted a campaign with the US government in Latin America designed to strengthen anti-communist forces and to weaken or destroy union and political forces opposed to US foreign policy. It has been the results of these interventions which have disturbed the AIFLD's critics, not out of which budgetary allocations the enabling funds were paid.

The effects of this institutionalisation of co-operation between the US government and the American trades unions were felt throughout Latin America. They first received public attention as the result of the activities of these unionists in what was then British Guiana.

The development of trades unionism in British Guiana has been troubled by the recurring problems of racial separation and the close identification of the union movement with strong national political movements. The first union, the British Guiana Labour Union (BGLU), was formed in 1919 under the leadership of Hubert Critchlow but, apart from some sporadic strikes in September and October 1935 among the largely East Indian agricultural workers, it never played too great a role within the crown colony. The British government proposed a commission of enquiry to investigate labour unrest. The result of the enquiry was the formation, in 1936, of the Manpower and Citizens' Association (MPCA). The MPCA registered as a trades union and took on the task of union and political representation of the Guianese workers. Virtually all of the union members were from the East Indian community as were the officers of the union. The other workers organised in British Guiana were largely in small industry unions, but linked together in a British Guiana Trades Union Assembly. Both labour groups were part of a regional organisation, the British Guiana and West India Labour Congress.

Politics and unionism remained fairly dormant until 1943 when Dr Cheddi Japan, an East Indian dentist, returned to British Guiana. Together with his wife, Janet, he formed the People's Progressive Party (PPP). The PPP was a militantly nationalist and socialist party promoting independence for British Guiana. Along with many of the other West Indies national centres, the Guianan unionists joined the Caribbean Labour Congress (CLC) in 1945 and affiliated to the WFTU. With the creation of the split between WFTU and ICFTU in 1949 the unionists tried to get a consensus on disaffiliating from the WFTU. This agreement was not reached until 1952 when, under some strong pressure from the British TUC and the AFL, the CLC went out of business. In its place the ICFTU affiliates created the Caribbean Area Division of ORIT (CADORIT). After the split with the WFTU Guiana was beset by major political activities led primarily by Cheddi Jagan. By the early 1950s there were strongly divided feelings in British Guiana's trades union movement. On the one hand there were the combined forces of the militant left of Jagan's PPP and his own Guianese Industrial Workers' Union, composed mainly of East Indian sugar workers, allied to Forbes Burnham's, primarily black, British Guiana Labour Union. On the other side was the anti-Jagan MPCA supported by the colonial administration and the sugar growers' association. In the middle were the unionists of the Transport Workers' Union (mainly government ferry and railroad workers) and the British Guiana Mine Workers' Union. The miners were affiliated to the group of Caribbean unionists in the bauxite industry which comprised the Caribbean Federation of Aluminium Workers (CFAW). This CFAW had been created by the United Steelworkers of America (USWA) and funded and staffed by them. Under their guidance the aluminium workers of the Caribbean were united into a federation which promoted their mutual interests and co-ordinated their political activities within the CADORIT.

The British TUC and the TGWU sent down organisers and assistance to the Caribbean unions, particularly to British Guiana and Jamaica. In fact the MPCA, which virtually collapsed in 1953 after the general elections which put Jagan into power, was resuscitated only through frequent and direct contacts between the TUC and the MPCA.

In 1953 Jagan's PPP won a majority of seats in parliament, beating the National Democratic Party, led by Lionel Luckhoo of the MPCA. At the time of Jagan's accession to the premiership his Industrial Workers' Union (GIWU) was in the middle of a major strike at the Enmore factory. One of Jagan's first acts was to pass a Labour Relations Bill which provided for a regular process for union recognition: the subject of the strike at Enmore (where the GIWU was competing with the MPCA for recognition). On passing the bill the GIWU called off the strike. The opponents of Jagan accused him of using his political office to introduce communist control over the unions. The British government sent in gunboats to Georgetown and troops to the key cities. Jagan was dismissed; the constitution suspended; and direct rule was reintroduced. The intervention by the British government was warmly welcomed by the AFL and the Free Trades Union Committee. Its representative, Romualdi, wrote that the action was the only recourse left to prevent the setting up of a communist totalitarian state.

Jagan, having spent some time reorganising his forces, returned to the colonial government in 1957 and, in the general election of 1961, took over again as premier. When Jagan returned to political legitimacy in 1957 Romualdi's assistant, Harry Pollack, travelled to British Guiana to prepare the way for US assistance to the MPCA and to explore establishing ties to the former Jagan ally, Forbes Burnham, now head of the People's National Congress (PNC). The PNC, composed primarily of black urban workers and middle-class businessmen, were opposed to the East Indian sugar workers and agricultural labourers of the PPP. On the far right, Peter D'Augiar's United Force opposed both Burnham and Jagan. When Jagan took office in 1961 he was viewed as a threat by both the British and American governments. Jagan openly admired and praised Fidel Castro. Castro offered cheap rice to British Guiana and a $35 million loan which the British government refused to let Jagan accept. The British and American governments decided to remove Jagan. They feared that the 1963 planned independence day for the colony would leave a Soviet and Castroite ally in the Caribbean. The means they chose to use to destroy Jagan was the trades union movement.

In 1959 the American Federation of State, County and Municipal Workers (AFSCME) under its president, Arnold Zander, agreed to accept $60 000 per year from some CIA-funded charitable foundations and to put two CIA employees on the AFSCME payroll for international work. The AFSCME was a major affiliate of the London-based Public Services International (PSI), an ITS. Visiting British Guiana as delegates from the PSI and AFSCME, Howard McCabe and another PSI unionist met with Richard Ishmael, head of the MPCA and the Trades Union Council (TUC) to plan a co-ordinated campaign against Jagan. Ishmael, an AIFLD graduate, along with other AIFLD Guianan graduates, were still on the AIFLD payroll as 'interns' during these activities. Ishmael appealed to both ORIT and the ICFTU for help in combatting Jagan's 'Castroism'. The MCPA suddenly had numerous trades union visitors from the American labour movement. Many were unwitting of the covert efforts to oust Jagan but others, like Gerry O'Keefe of the Retail Clerks, were well aware of the covert battle being planned. In fact the secret report produced by Peter Owen (the British Police Superintendent) for the Foreign Office, lists Gerry O'Keefe as a lawyer from Annandale, Virginia, whose responsibility was to bring in money and supplies to the anti-Jagan forces. These supplies included stores of dynamite (code word 'cigarettes') and ammunition. Gene Meakins, ostensibly of the Newpaper Guild of the US, was another CIA officer assigned to labour cover in Georgetown. What these unionists needed was an issue to spark the dissent against Jagan.

The issue arose when Jagan introduced his labour bill, providing a government panel to supervise the registration of unions. Ishmael on behalf of the MPCA and the TUC demanded that the panel include a majority of TUC members and private business leaders. When Jagan refused, the TUC called a general strike; a strike which lasted eighty days. The strikers received strike benefits through a variety of agencies but virtually all of the funds for these agencies derived from the US government. Some estimates place this largesse at around $1.2 million. Unfortunately for the Guianese this strike was a catalyst to a major outburst of racial confrontation between the East Indian and the black communities. Widespread rioting throughout Georgetown, Demerara, and smaller concentrations of East Indians left many wounded. Explosions and fires destroyed property. The British moved troops in to patrol the cities but were unable to contain the violence. By the time the disturbance was over there were about 170 dead, about £10 million in damages and Cheddi Jagan was seriously discredited. When Macmillan and Sandys decided unilaterally to declare proportional representation for British Guiana for the 1964 elections, Jagan lost. Burnham became the new premier. The coalition of US union and government forces had succeeded in using the labour weapon against their enemy in the Caribbean. With the co-operation of the British government, the AIFLD and its cohorts showed that they were capable of challenging leftist governments in the area and by so challenging them, end their term in office. After the Guatemala effort, success had eluded the union–government nexus. Now the AIFLD and its associates had proved their worth and were called upon to undertake similar challenging assignments elsewhere in Latin America.

In the immediate pre-war period, Brazil was under the strong tutelage of Getulio Vargas, a populist leader who, like Peron, built a state-controlled labour movement as his political base. Vargas initiated his labour actions by closing down all trades union activity in 1931 and forcing all unions to reapply for registration. The communist, Christian, anarchist and socialist unions, which had been at daggers drawn with each other, either united under the new structure or were refused legal status. For the most part the Christian unions and the socialists remained legal. Vargas passed a series of laws raising wages, creating social insurance schemes, starting disability insurance, shortening the work week, establishing a minimum wage law, and providing government funds for social projects (like workers' housing and hospitals). The 1934 constitution guaranteed the right to join trades unions. Among the other aspects of the legislation was the right of the government to appoint intervenors who could replace elected union officers.

Vargas was re-elected president in 1934 and was opposed primarily by the parties of big business and the Brazilian Communist Party. With the era of the popular front, however, the communists attempted to create the *Alianca Nacional Liberatora* (ANL) a kind of popular front; calling for mass nationalisations, renouncement of foreign debt and land reform. This ANL was basically anti-Vargas and was outlawed in 1935. The communists went underground in an effort to build support among the workers, especially in Sao Paulo and Racife. Vargas decreed the *Estado Novo* (new state) and continued on his course of building a corporative state in Brazil.

The basis for this corporate state was the unions who were charged under the constitution with the duty 'to collaborate with the public authorities in the development of social solidarity; to maintain legal aid services for their members; and to promote conciliation in labour disputes'.[8] Strikes and lockouts were banned and an elaborate network of labour courts was created to oversee unionism. Unions received funds from a compulsory dues checkoff (the *imposto sindical*) paid by all workers, not just union members. These funds were controlled by the Minister of Labour. Vargas succeeded in forming a bureaucracy of urban labour. As part of the runup for the 1945 election, Vargas legalised the Communist Party and freed Luis Carlos Prestes, the leader of the party and an important Comintern agent. In return, the communists organised trades union support for Vargas. They formed the *Movimiento Unificador dos Trabalhadores* (MUT) which attempted to establish itself as a national labour centre. Vargas created a new national political party based on his loyalist unions, the *Partido*

Trabahalista Brasileiro (PTB). The PTB and the communists held mass rallies and demonstrations in support of Vargas. These succeeded in so arousing the army's fear of a leftist takeover that they intervened and ousted Vargas. General Eurico Dutra became president and promulgated a new constitution which maintained most of the labour rights permitted under Vargas but eased the restrictions on the right to strike and the powers of the labour court.

Dutra was opposed by a rapidly expanding Communist Party and labour movement under Prestes. Prestes continued to receive assistance from CTAL and WFTU organisers. In the 1945 election the communists had polled 9 per cent of the popular vote and had elected deputies to both houses. The communists provided the nucleus of the Brazilian workers' confederation through their strong support in the docks and among the metalworkers. Most importantly they expanded their political activities. Dutra banned the Communist Party in 1947 and sent government intervenors into 143 unions, ousting the leftist unionists. The communists then put their support behind Vargas and his PTB. The campaign for the 1950 election was marked by large numbers of illegal strikes by the left advocating the candidacy of Vargas. When Vargas won the election he restored his control over the nation by preaching the message of class warfare to his PTB and the unions. In 1953 the communists formed a mutual assistance pact with the PTB and together they engaged in strikes against what they called 'the imperialists'. Strikes were rampant. Vargas appointed the head of the PTB, Joao Goulart, as Minister of Labour. Goulart took an even softer line against militant strikes and refused to intervene when rank-and-file unionists ousted their bureaucratic union officials. Goulart's promotion of the 1953 general strike in Sao Paulo won him many friends among the labour left and the new union officials.

At the same time, these strikes were having a debilitating effect on foreign investment, especially US investment. The US, already upset by the strong role of the communists in the political life of Brazil, denied Brazil international loans. When Goulart announced, in 1954, a 100 per cent increase in the minimum wage a group within the military issued a manifesto against the increase and against Goulart. Goulart was dismissed. Finally, after further unrest following Vargas' insistence on legalising the increase, the military invited Vargas to resign. Vargas committed suicide. His successor, the Vice-President Cafe Filho, called new elections. These were won by Juscelino Kubitschek. Kubitschek attempted to maintain a generally centrist course but was unable to attract vital foreign loans at competitive rates because of the continued toleration by the Brazilian authorities of a growing communist presence in public life.

In addition to their continued strength in the unions the communists expanded their rural organising. By the end of 1959 the communists had succeeded in organising more than 250 000 peasant leagues under party control. Kubitschek's successor, Janio Quadros, fared little better. Quadros had inherited a severe debt-repayment burden from the previous administration and was trying to keep a lid on inflation. Quadros reinstated exchange controls and severely restricted credit. This angered many of the business and military leaders and precipitated a political crisis. Quadros resigned after only eight months in office, hoping that a new popular mandate would restore him to office with greater powers. He was succeeded by his legal successor, the Vice-President Joao Goulart. Goulart was allowed to succeed Quadros only after the opposition had passed a constitutional amendment limiting the presidential powers. Goulart later succeeded in holding a plebiscite which reversed this constitutional amendment. With the formation of the Goulart government in 1961, the forces of the left were mobilised and given strong support.

The ORIT had played an important role in keeping Quadros from returning to office. Romualdi had visited Brazil and established contact with the civilian leaders of the military movement: Carlos Lacerda, the governor of Guanabara State (the capital of which is Rio de Janeiro) and Adhemar de Barros of Sao Paulo. When Quadros resigned, the communists had called for a massive general strike to restore him to office. The ORIT, which happened to be having a convention in Rio at the time of the call for the general strike, invited Lacerda to address their meeting. He announced that he would resign his governorship to lead the campaign against Quadros if necessary. Romualdi and the AFL–CIO secretary–treasurer, Bill Schnitzler, lobbied among Brazilian unionists to persuade them to eschew the call for a general strike. When the call for the strike in support of Quadros came on 26 August 1961, the Railway Workers, the Maritime and Port Workers and a Trades Union Committee for the Defence of Democracy joined together to frustrate the strike call. The general strike failed. The activities of the ORIT in these manoevres prompted the Minister of Labour to try and ban ORIT from Brazil, but the change of government delayed the decree.

With the rise to power of Goulart the left movements united in support of his government. In 1962 the left unionists of the PTB and the communists joined together to form the *Comando Geral dos*

Trabalhadores (CGT), an illegal national centre but one tolerated and nurtured by Goulart. An attempt by the left unions to create a single national centre in 1962 at the Third National Labour Congress was frustrated by the activities of the centre and right unions who did not wish to be united with the CGT. These non-CGT unionists were assisted in their parliamentary manoeuvres by a labour specialist from the US who met with the Brazilian unionists and advised them of several parliamentary steps they ought to take to avoid an imposed unity with the CGT. Simultaneously the AIFLD began to expand its operations in Brazil. The *Movimiento Democratico Sindical* (MDS), a right and centre grouping of unionists, received training help from AIFLD. The AIFLD created the *Instituto Cultural do Trabalho* (ICT) as its local training institute and began training local unionists and rural leaders in democratic unionism. A particular fear was the strong growth of peasant unionism dominated by the Brazilian communists. When, in 1963, the government passed the Statute of the Rural Worker, the communists and some PTB organisers created the *Confederacao Nacional dos Trabalhadores na Agricultura* (CONTAG) uniting more than 1200 rural organisations.

In 1962, however, relations between Brazil and the US were growing progressively worse. The Brazilian government had expropriated an ITT subsidiary, had resumed diplomatic relations with the Soviet Union and had refused to condemn Cuba in the vote at the OAS. During the 1962 elections it is estimated that the US assisted anti-communist and anti-Goulart politicians with up to $20 million in an effort to break the communist hold on the Brazilian political scene. In a record turnout the pro-Goulart forces won a massive victory. Following the Goulart victory a determined effort was made by the US to oust Goulart. A principal vehicle for this activity was the trades union movement under the guidance of the AIFLD.

The AIFLD stepped up its training of Brazilian unionists inside Brazil and in Washington. In fact a special hand-picked class of thirty-three Brazilians was sent to Washington for training in an all-Brazilian class. The IFPCW sent down assistance to the Brazilian oilworkers to persuade them to break with their national confederation (which was CGT-led) and affiliate directly with the IFPCW. The IFPCW, using a $30 000 grant from the Andrew Hamilton Fund, began distributing assistance to Brazilian unionists in the petroleum unions and the labour ministry and press officials through their local representative. When reports of activities and copies of the receipts were published in the Brazilian press the IFPCW was asked to quit Brazil.[9]

When the special class of Brazilian trainees graduated from the Washington training school they travelled with Romualdi to Europe and to Israel. On their return to Brazil they went back to their unions, still on the AIFLD payroll as 'interns', to organise and conduct seminars on free unionism.

These pressures by the unions, combined with the cessation of loans by the US, and the interchange of military advice by the US to their Brazilian counterparts led to a military revolt against Goulart in early 1964. The unionists opposed to the CGT led their colleagues in demonstrations in favour of the new military junta. They assisted in purging the leftists from the trades union structure. The role of the AIFLD trainees in helping to bring about the anti-Goulart coup was stated publicly by Bill Doherty in a radio interview soon after the coup. He said that the AIFLD graduates returned to Brazil after their training and were active in organising workers and other projects.

> As a matter of fact, some of them were so active that they became intimately involved in some of the clandestine operations of the revolution before it took place on April 1. What happened in Brazil on April 1 did not just happen – it was planned – and planned months in advance. Many of the trade union leaders – some of whom were actually trained in our institute – were involved in the revolution and in the overthrow of the Goulart regime.[10]

Unfortunately for the Brazilian unionists who had plotted the demise of Goulart and the ousting of the communists from positions of strength in the union and peasant movements, the new military junta did not smile favourably on free unions. Within months the new government severely restricted all trades unionism, virtually ended all international union contact with Brazilian unions and ushered in a period of harsh repression. With the accession to power of Castelo Branco, the leftist leaders who supported Goulart were purged from political life. They were followed by many centrist political figures (like Lacerda and de Barros). The elimination of civil liberties under the military regime was extended to the trades union movement which discovered that many of their basic freedoms were eliminated. Military intervenors were placed in the unions. The unions were permitted to operate only within very strict limits. After the restoration of military rule in Brazil the AIFLD's local institute, the ICT, expanded its activities.

By the middle of 1973 the ICT had trained almost 30 000 unionists. Equally as important, the AIFLD had set up rural training schemes to help break the left's hold on the *campesino* movement, training over 4500 rural workers by the mid-1970s. AIFLD social projects have been set up in virtually every Brazilian state. While decrying the loss of trades union freedoms under the military regimes, the AIFLD continued to expand its operations in Brazil. The recent metalworkers strike in Brazil, led by the charismatic Sao Paulo metalworkers' leader, Luiz Ignacio da Silva ('Lula'), has shown that there still exists a strong union movement within the nation despite government intervention.

The Brazilian metalworkers' strike which lasted five weeks (the longest confrontation between Brazilian unions and the military since 1964) was finally settled in May 1980 when Lula and his fellow leaders were freed from jail. The government had attempted to take over the union, thrown its leaders in jail and harassed the members. Nonetheless, for the first time since the coup, the workers, demanding the right to organise unions within the factories and a higher cost-of-living increase within the contracts to keep up with Brazil's inflation, had demonstrated their independence from the government. Support for the metalworkers was forthcoming from the IMF who circulated much of the news about the strike. The metalworkers' strike is evidence of a new economic and political militancy among the Brazilian urban workers; not political in the sense of party politics but certainly political in the sense of a demand for greater freedom. The long night of union activities in Brazil ushered in by the 1964 coup may be ending.

The polarisation of Chilean politics emerged during the rule of Ibanez after 1952. Ibanez, a populist general along the lines of Getulio Vargas and Peron, attempted to build a mass following among the working classes and the peasants. Trades unions, ever since the Gonzalez Videla period, were strong but divided between unions loyal to the socialists, communists, radicals and Christian democrats. The communists had long held important strongholds in the copper mines and the coal mines. The maritime workers, however, were the unions most opposed to communist control. In 1953, under Ibanez, the socialist and communist workers organisations reunited into a new national centre, the CUTCh. They were opposed by the existing national centre (led by the AFL–CIO ally, Bernardo Ibanez), the CNT, whose major affiliate was the COMACH, the maritime workers. The economic policies of President Ibanez were leading Chile into difficulty. The US had sent a team of advisors to Chile (the Klein–Saks mission) which recommended a period of austerity. The economic dislocation which these policies created led to unemployment, a freeze on wages and general unrest.

These policies, moreover, united the left into a powerful and united force.

The forces of right and left clashed at the crucial 1958 elections where the candidate of the Conservative and Liberal coalition, Jorge Alessandrini, won the presidency against the Christian Democratic candidate and the candidate of the Socialist–Communist Alliance (FRAP), Salvador Allende. Allende had benefited from the legalisation of the Communist Party and its effective takeover of the CUTCh as a result of the widespread dissatisfaction with the Klein–Saks policies. Allessandrini continued to follow Klein–Saks recommendations and further polarised the nation. The strength of the FRAP was a constant worry for the US, especially as their recent efforts in Brazil and British Guiana had just prevented such a force taking power. In the run up to the 1964 election the US gave support to the candidate of the Christian Democrats, Eduardo Frei, in an effort to assist him in defeating Allende. From 1962 to 1964 Chile received $127 million a year in US foreign aid. Military aid jumped from $2.7 million in 1960 to $30.6 million in 1963. One observer estimated that the US was putting about $1 million a month into Frei's campaign augmented by around $20 million from Christian democratic parties in West Germany, Italy and Belgium.[11] Within the labour movement the AIFLD trained numerous Chilean unionists. Starting modestly with a training centre inside Chile which received a mere $30 000 in 1963, the figure was raised to $55 000 soon after. Between 1963 and 1967 the AIFLD spend $430 000 in Chile in addition to sums spent in training Chileans in the US. Virtually all of these funds were spent on COMACH. Additionally a further $5 million was budgeted for a COMACH housing scheme. To these sums must be added the monies made available to several ITSs through their US affiliates for work in Chile.

Particularly active in Chile was Serafino Romualdi who feared the strong communist role in the CUTCh. Romualdi and the leaders of the ORIT attempted to make common cause with the Christian Democrats whose unions were still largely under the CUTCh umbrella. Morris Paladino was sent down to Chile to meet with Jose Goldsack Donoso (head of the Christian democratic unions and president of CLASC). Paladino attempted to persuade Goldsack to get his unions to disaffiliate from the CUTCh at their upcoming convention in 1962. The two agreed that: (a) if the communists did not seat the rural workers (a strongly anti-communist union) the non-communists would walk out; (b) all unions opposed to the communists would form a coalition inside of the CUTCh to vote as a bloc (ORIT agreed to pay the delinquent dues payments of any union in arrears so that they could vote); (c) if the convention were split a new meeting place would be hired by ORIT to create a new national centre; and (d) any new centre would be given the choice of affiliating either to ORIT or to CLASC. In the event, the Christian Democrats pulled out of the agreement before the Congress.

In the election in 1964 the Christian Democrats of Frei won. The results illustrated the disappearance of the right as a political force in Chile with the Christian Democrats inheriting much of the Liberal and Conservative support against the increasingly strong FRAP of Allende. Additionally, in 1966, a new group formed on the left inspired by Castroite organisations of the peasantry and stirred by the prospect of guerrilla warfare: the *Movimiento Izquierda Revolucionaria* (MIR). The MIR began a series of assaults on banks and businesses after 1969 and created pockets of armed resistance in the cities. The CUTCh strengthened its hold on the left in the labour movement. They opposed the 1966 attempt to build a United Movement of Chilean Workers (MUTCh) under the auspices of AIFLD which provided money for seminars and the training of some of its leaders. It soon disappeared. Another unity attempt, in 1968, the *Union de Trabajadores de Chile* (UTRACh) fared no better. By the time of the 1970 election, despite efforts by the US government and the trades unions, Salvador Allende, the candidate of the *Unidad Popular* (UP) won 36.5 per cent of the popular vote. Since no candidate had a majority it went to the Congress to decide the outcome.

Despite efforts by Henry Kissinger, ITT and the CIA to foment a coup which would prevent Allende from winning the vote in the Congress they were unable to prevent his victory in October 1970. Allende was the first Marxist to be elected president in Chile and aroused deep fears over how he was going to proceed. Among Allende's projects were the nationalisation of the US-owned copper mines, the banks and the major industries. He increased wages but froze prices. Economic problems beset Chile. Demand outpaced production. Copper prices dropped and gross inefficiency and mismanagement gripped the economy. Frequent devaluations did not improve the situation. The communist control of the CUTCh was strengthened when Figueroa, a communist leader of the CUTCh, became Minister of Labour. Under the communist leadership, assisted by advisors from Eastern European communist states, the CUTCh asserted control over the unions in an effort to moderate their demands. When the miners at Chuquicamata went on strike for higher wages Allende denounced them as a 'labour aristocracy'. The CUTCh campaigned for an end to strikes, for higher productivity and for wage stability. In fact when the Chuquicamata strike was on, the president of the CUTCh announced that he was sending a number of 'teachers from the union school' to train copper workers to understand their responsibility to raise production and have their profits distributed for all of Chile. The CUTCh congress had as its first item on the agenda the damping down of wage demands. Allende and the leaders of the CUTCh continued to attempt to use nationalisations and union discipline to stop the rash of strikes in the public and private sectors. The workers insisted on maintaining their standard of living in the face of government and union hostility. Allende remarked: 'Neither revolutionary consciousness nor morality exists among the workers.'[12]

This ultra-conservatism by the CUTCh encouraged other unions to form. The MIR created its own union body, the *Frente de Trabajadores Revolucionarios* (FTR), which organised the occupation of plants. The MIR–FTR groups established *cordones industriales* around key plants. The Minister of Labour, Figueroa, demanded the return of illegally seized industries and attacked the MIR–FTR for their 'leftist adventurism' in their efforts to take over the direction of a large segment of industry. On the other hand the CUTCh and the FTR were both attacked by the Christian democratic unions as being 'another party of the government'. The revolution declared by Allende had heightened the aspirations of the trades unionists but raging inflation had denied them the fruits of their wage increases. The CUTCh had become a conservative bastion of the state intent on putting an end to high pay settlements. When workers went on strike the CUTCh led demonstrations and protest marches against the strikers, calling them 'traitors'.

In late September 1971 the Christian Democrats broke their working relationship with the Allende government, accusing it of attempting to set up a dictatorship of the left. Soon after, the first of a large number of demonstrations by the urban housewives protesting food and consumer goods shortages occurred. Allende declared a state of emergency which banned demonstrations. In April 1972 there was another protest demonstration, followed by a series of protest closings of shops by small shopkeepers distressed by high taxes and shortages. The largest demonstration was in October 1972 when the owner-drivers of the trucks (the major portion of Chile's internal transport system) went on strike to protest low rates and the lack of spare parts. The truckers were joined by dentists, engineers, shop owners, doctors, bus owners and several other middle-class groups. Allende declared martial law and ordered in the troops to open the shops. The polarisation caused by this strike marked the beginning of the end of Allende.

One of the principal organisations which assisted in channelling the frustrations of so diverse a group of demonstrators was the Chiliean Confederation of Professionals (CUPROCh). The CUPROCh was not really a union – it was more of a professional organisation. The CUPROCh was the recipient of an important series of training seminars organised by the US Retail Clerks' union on behalf of FIET (The International Federation of Commercial, Clerical and Technical Employees) through AIFLD in Chile. The AIFLD subcontracted the Retail Clerks (whose international affairs director was Gerry O'Keefe) to teach Chilean professional workers the elements of collective bargaining and other subjects. Leon Vilarin, the leader of the truck owners' strike, was a CUPROCh official. Through CUPROCh a nationwide federation for self-help among the professional groups and the middle classes, the National Command for Gremio Defence, was built. Two CUPROCh leaders were sent off to the AIFLD school in Front Royal. They were followed by others, including Jorge Guerrero, the head of the Gremio Defence. The AIFLD also granted subcontracts to the US Brotherhood of Railways and Airline Clerks (BRAC) who, on behalf of the ITF, held a conference in Chile in May 1973 on road transport with Chilean truckers and some airline personnel. The COMACH maritime union which had received such strong support from AIFLD over the years was not forgotten. Wenceslao Moreno, the head of COMACH, was an AIFLD board member and a vice-president of the ITF. Jack Otero of BRAC helped organise a new union of merchant marine professionals in Chile and assisted the COMACH by sending additional trainees to Front Royal. The American Federation of Teachers, through the International Federation of Free Teachers' Unions (IFFTU), whose interamerican representative was a US-nationalised Chilean, had expanded its contacts in Chile prior to the coup which ousted Allende. These unionists, operating with AIFLD funds, brought order to the chaos of discontent felt in Chile by those professional and other workers who were suffering from Allende's mismanagement and ineptitude. The visiting unionists did not create the unrest, the dissatisfaction or the despair at the political and economic course of the Chilean government: they merely showed those disaffected Chileans how they might best channel their energies to change the system.

Despite these initial protest demonstrations most Chileans were willing to await the outcome of the 7 March 1973 election to see if the

Allende government could be voted out of office. Allende actually increased his share of the popular vote to 43.4 per cent and gained sufficient seats in both houses of Congress as to make impeachment impossible. In response, the professional organisations in the *gremios* increased the tempo and the strength of their demonstrations. The truck owners carried out a twenty-four hour strike in May, followed by intermittent strike actions from July onward. In September the *gremios* demanded the resignation of Allende and begged for military intervention.

In response to the strikes by CUPROCh and the *gremios*, the CUTCh organised counter-demonstrations and plant sit-ins. CUTCh and the MIR–FTR ordered its members to defend the Allende regime by any means at their disposal. With the resignation of General Prats there was nothing that could save Allende. On 11 September 1973 Allende was removed from power and died in the Moneda in Santiago. The successor to General Prats as commander-in-chief of the armed forces, General Augusto Pinochet Ugarte, became president of Chile following the military coup. The new government was not slow in acting to stamp out the Marxist legacy of Allende. Just as in Brazil in 1964 and in Argentina in 1966, the new military government proceeded to carry out a counter-revolution. All political parties were banned. The CUTCh and the FTR were outlawed. Universities were purged of leftists. Congress was shut. Leftist books and newspapers were confiscated and forbidden to be published. Censorship was introduced. Thousands of leftists and suspected leftists were imprisoned, killed or 'disappeared'.

The role of the AIFLD graduates in the success of Pinochet was important. In fact the coup began by industrial action among the newly organised professional seamen in Valparaiso recently assisted by Jack Otero. It spread through the COMACH and the CUPROCh organisations. In return, the new government permitted these unions to continue to co-operate with the AIFLD, although all other unions were banned. Wenceslao Moreno of COMACH reconstituted the defunct CNT national centre after the coup, uniting most of the AIFLD-supported unions. The CNT is now the only tolerated union group in Chile. The ITSs continued to operate through their Chilean affiliates. Some of the ITSs, however, have refused to continued dealing with Chilean unions as long as they are not independent and as long as trades union rights are interfered with by the junta. Prime among these has been the IMF who rejected Chilean metalworkers from the government-controlled unions at its congress. The Chileans disaffiliated. Other ITSs have adopted similar policies. It has only been the AIFLD subcontracted ITSs or, to be more precise, only those ITSs whose major US affiliates have received and spent US government funds in the name of the ITSs, which have continued their ties to the Chilean unions.

Once again, the successful ouster of a leftist government in Latin America through the medium of the trades unions had led, not to a middle course of a mixed-economy capitalism in which trades unionism can flourish, but to a military junta intent on destroying the function of trades unionism in the name of national discipline and order.

The development of Latin American trades unionism has been largely a chronicle of the developing relationship between the military and the unions. The rise of populist generals (Peron, Vargas, Ibanez and others) with strong ties to their domestic labour movements is relatively unusual outside of Latin America. Throughout their early development trades unions tended to be created for political purposes by parties who saw in these movements a lever of power. The concomitant development of a responsive industrial relations system was much more difficult to achieve, largely because of the severe economic distress which has plagued Latin American economies since the 1950s. In Brazil, for example, a union contract is often devalued as it is signed by the forces of galloping inflation. Frequently collective bargaining has meant seeking a 150 per cent wage increase within months of signing an agreement because inflation has devoured the impact of wage rises. Social welfare schemes have suffered from the time lag between the setting of the levels of benefit and the drop in purchasing power of the currency in which these benefits are paid. Chronic dependence on primary product prices has made Latin American economies extremely vulnerable to the roller coaster of the cyclical fluctuations of supply and demand. Poverty and unemployment have been the frequent companions of rural workers in Latin America combined with a rising level of expectations.

Overshadowing all of these difficulties has been the growth of extremist movements of the right and left threatening the social order and the continuity of stable government. To some degree the presence of the US and its role as a special protector of the area has contributed to the instability of the political system. The US's interventionist role in Latin America has been justified as necessary to prevent hostile forces gaining or maintaining a political and economic foothold in the hemisphere. These efforts, however well-meaning or altruistic, have often resulted in the maintenance in power of political leaders who have not achieved the confidence of their people and in whom they are reluctant to place their trust. A principal actor in this US interventionist strategy has been the international trades union movement of ORIT, the AFL–CIO and the AIFLD. Almost without exception the result of this intervention to build free unionism has been the creation of a government whose policies are inimical to free unionism. The AFL–CIO justification has alway been that free unionism means anti-communist unionism. In fighting communism through the trades union movement they are strengthening free unionism. Unfortunately for the Latin American unions the struggle against communism has not only been conducted by democrats; it has also been conducted by those who dislike free unions almost as much as the communists. It is too frequently true that it has been the anti-democratic forces which have won.

For the most part the communist strategy in Latin America has moved away from the use of unions as principal agents of social change. Communist unions exist and, in some nations, they are strong. Nonetheless the primary tactics of the communists in Latin America have been to build revolutionary armed guerrilla bands in the countryside along the lines of the struggles of Castro. A principal reason for this type of guerrilla activity is a belated attempt by the communists loyal to the Soviet Union to catch up with the organisations of the left which have adopted this revolutionary course. Throughout Latin America the 'regular' communists have been a most conservative force within the Latin left. In Bolivia they have taken a centrist course (and refused support to Che Guevara); in Chile the CUTCh acted as a stabilising force under Allende; in Argentina there have been numerous attempts by the communists to wean away the left from Peronism but they have met with little success, especially amongst the terrorist groups to their left; in Brazil the sterile rhetoric of the communists led to a break with them by the urban guerrilla leader Marighella and his followers; similarly in Nicaragua, the victory of the Sandinistas was accomplished without the help of the 'regular' communists. It has been the Cuban communists who have provided the support, training and encouragement for the Latin American revolutionary activities. The close ties between the *Direccion General de Intelligencia* (DGI) and the KGB, and the Soviet's funding of the Cuban economy have not deterred these initiatives; rather the Soviets are kept informed about the nationalist/communist struggles which are occurring and assist, where possible, in supporting these revolutionary efforts. But the local domestic communist parties have largely been excluded from the revolution.

The conduct of the revolution through communist/nationalist/Castroite bands is important to the trades union movement in that there exists no major international labour body which unites or represents these organisations. The Sandinistas had allies among the leftist unions of Nicaragua but did not maintain a Sandinista labour union as such. Unlike the 'regular' communists whose labour unions affiliated to the CTAL (now the Permanent Congress of Workers of Latin America – CPUSTAL) and are associated with the WFTU, these Castroite guerrilla bands have no such ties. The primary focus of the left and ultra-left in Latin America is the revolution; not the winning of power through the democratic process in which control of the trades unions is vital. As a result, there has been a drop-off of concentration on labour activity within Latin America by the communists. The major antagonists of the AIFLD have been primarily the unions of the CTAL who see in the work of the AIFLD a force for centralisation and control too easily taken over by the government.

Equally opposed to the work of the AIFLD have been many US unions who feel that the American labour movement should not be advocating overseas policies for unions which it would not accept within the US. In Brazil the AIFLD was advising the unions to adopt a policy of wage control. A reporter asked Bill Doherty if the Brazilian workers would accept this and Doherty replied: 'the labour unions of Brazil . . . are perfectly willing to accept any type of wage freeze in order to control runaway inflation . . . There has to be some element of price controls . . . When these freezes and controls are put on the Brazilian people, they have to suffer equally.'[13] Until quite recently the idea of wage controls was anathema to US unionists. There are few unions in the US which feel that in a time of economic hardship rich and poor should suffer equally. This example is only one of a number of AIFLD proposals which incensed US unionists. Equally, they felt the presence of American industrialists, like Peter Grace, on the AIFLD board gave the wrong impression of US unionism. Most importantly, the union leaders in the US felt that their members would not approve of these activities if they became known. The 1967 exposure that many of these activities were being covertly funded by the CIA led to some rapid changes. Jerry Wurf, the new president of AFSCME, closed down his international affairs operation and stopped all covert subsidies of the PSI through his union. Juul Poulsen of the IUF suddenly discovered that his ITS had an eight-man Latin American regional office funded by AIFLD about which he know nothing. A reorganisation of the whole operation took place and AID was made the funding agency for what some journalists called the 'CIA's step-children'.

When the AFL–CIO pulled out of the ICFTU in 1969 it was allowed to maintain its affiliation and domination of the ORIT. Despite protests by the ICFTU, the AFL–CIO though not affiliated to the ICFTU still was a member and controlled the destiny of the ORIT. This matter was a subject of some discussion. In 1975 at the ICFTU Mexico City Congress an effort was made to make the ORIT an exclusively Latin American body (i.e. excluding the AFL–CIO and the CLC.) This effort failed because the ICFTU could not promise to match the financial contributions of the AFL–CIO to the ORIT budget. The Latin American affiliates asked where the funds were coming from to help them with their work. The ICFTU could not give them a satisfactory answer so they refused to vote out the AFL–CIO. The ICFTU's auditors created a flap when they refused to certify the ORIT accounts. The ICFTU cut off funds from headquarters to ORIT. Numerous Western European ICFTU affiliates withheld contributions. The Swedish unions, for example, informed the ICFTU that none of its contributions to the Solidarity Fund should be made available for any project in which the ORIT was involved. However by 1981 the ICFTU had resumed its payments to ORIT.

As part of the recent changes within the AFL–CIO after the death of Meany, the several aid organisations are undergoing review. The AIFLD will end the tripartism which has angered its critics and will be solely a union body (although still funded by the US government). This should mollify some of its critics, even if its policies remain the same.

These developments in Africa, Asia and Latin America were very important in the struggle for control of international unionism. Another struggle was also in progress in Europe as the nations there grew in economic strength and power, entering into new economic alliances. Both in Western and Eastern Europe trades unionism played an important role.

9 The Rise of Euro-unionism

After the initial period of reconstruction and consolidation following the end of the war and the early days of the Cold War, the nations of Europe began to concern themselves with the problems raised by the necessity of adjusting to a political system vastly different from that which preceded it. The initial set of problems, those which arose from the process of decolonisation, were largely internal problems although with international implications. The second problem, that of coming to grips with the realities of power in what was increasingly a bipolar world, was more intractable.

For the nations of Eastern Europe the options were few. Repeated purges and changes at the helm of government at the behest of the party leaders of Moscow and the sustained presence in Eastern Europe of the Red Army made certain that political liberties and freedom of choice were limited for those states. These informal military relationships between the Soviet Union and those nations with which it was allied were solidified in the Warsaw Pact, paralleling the unity of the West in the North Atlantic treaty pact; NATO. The end of the Korean War ended the open conflict between the two blocs but did not end the hostility between them.

The nations of Western Europe themselves faced a resurgence of nationalism in the early 1950s coupled with an increasing irritation at the need to follow the political and economic direction insisted upon by Washington. Despite their recognition of the need to preserve the credibility of the US nuclear umbrella as a cornerstone of Western defence, the nations of Western Europe felt that they had valid political and economic interests which diverged from those of the US. As the markets of Africa and Asia opened to them with the gradual independence of the colonial territories, they found themselves in competition with US producers and manufacturers in these and other markets.

Coupled with this competition with US producers was the fear of what was becoming the '*defi americain*' by which US corporations, lured by cheaper costs of production and labour, began to build enormous production and manufacturing centres in Western Europe. The nations of Western Europe began to explore the possibilities of recreating a powerful Europe through mutual economic treaties and political unity; both to create a 'Third Force' in the bipolar political sphere as well as a protective economic shelter from the winds of US competition.

This rising self-confidence of Western Europe generated a series of plans designed to further European unity in both the economic and political arenas. Some nations were more willing to talk of unity than others. Belgium, Holland and Luxembourg were early in developing customs unions among them. The Nordic nations followed their traditional practice of building economic unity among themselves. Substantive progress in reaching agreement on a more general unity in Europe began to develop as the nations of Western Europe grew to trust a new and powerful West Germany.

This rise of a separate Western European consciousness caused problems for US policy-makers as it was frequently coupled with a growing anti-Americanism. The spread of anti-Americanism, coupled with the new European consciousness, widened the political gap between Europe and the United States. The death of Stalin in 1953 and the different public face presented by the leadership of the communist movement which developed from the Eastern European purges of the Stalinists following the 1956 Krushchev speech led many in Western Europe to feel that a new Eastern Europe was developing; an Eastern Europe with which new contacts might be made. Even the brutal repression of the East German workers' revolt in 1953 or the Hungarian uprising in 1956 did not disabuse many Europeans of these beliefs.

One result of these developments was the increasing acceptance of Western European communist parties as legitimate political parties able to be considered as potential allies in the formation of government coalitions. The communist voting strength in Western Europe grew. In nations like France and Italy their share of the vote increased substantially. From the point of view of the trades unions, the rise of communist party legitimacy made communist-led unions more attractive to the workers. Competition between communist and non-communist unions for members caused some friction between the unions and their party allies because many parties of the left began to explore the possibilities of coalitions with the communists in local and national elections.

This reduction in friction between Western European parties and communist unionism had an important effect in reducing the participation of the AFL–CIO in ICFTU activities. There were two major areas of contention between the AFL–CIO and the Europeans. The first, and the most public dispute, was that which derived from the unwillingness of the Europeans to permit the AFL–CIO to conduct trades union development activities in the regions unilaterally but in the name of the ICFTU organisations. The second was the more fundamental conflict between them over the basic anti-communist commitment of the movement.

Postwar Western European governments often were led by socialist or social democratic parties. Those that weren't invariably had socialist or social democratic parties as the principal opposition parties. The role of the socialists in Europe was altered by this relationship. These parties had to involve themselves in areas of governmental affairs in which they frequently had had no tradition of experience or expertise. With these new duties came new responsibilities. Among these was the promotion of local industry and commerce, including participation in the promotion of international trade. The socialist parties and their trades union allies had created mechanisms during the reconstruction of their nations by which the unions, and through them the parties, participated in corporate decision-making. This took two forms. The first was the gradual accretion of union power by being permitted to name worker–directors onto the supervisory boards of companies. The second derived from the huge financial resources of the union members themselves. In order to tap this large pool of domestic savings during the reconstruction, schemes were devised by which trades union banks, savings institutions and pension funds were created whose asset bases were made available for both public and private sector industrial development. This often gave trades union institutions a direct say in the management of key corporations.

These trades union financial organisations operated with the co-operation of the political parties. In nations like Sweden or West Germany the parties themselves played a strong co-ordinating role. In other nations, like Italy, the parties divided the patronage of giant parastatal corporations among themselves and allocated jobs, responsibilities and power to their trades union allies within these parastatals. European unions took on an important role in the economic life of their nations; not only on the consumptionist side but also on the productionist side. Of course this development was taken to a far higher level of magnitude in Eastern Europe but the parallels were clear. In both cases trades unionism in Europe diverged sharply from the growth of trades union development in the United States.

Trades unionism in the US in this period was characterised by a growing gulf between the forces of labour and the forces of government. After the slump which followed the Korean War the election of a Republican leadership in the White House promised little access for labour at the highest levels. To this should be added the widespread political extremism of the American political right, whose major proponent was Senator Joseph McCarthy. Trade unions, even of the anti-communist AFL type, were suspect in the eyes of many on the right. The expulsion of the communists from the CIO in 1949 had made it a less easy target for the right but not one they chose to avoid in their attacks on the American labour movement. All these factors combined in 1955 to unite the two wings of American labour into the AFL–CIO – a united movement.

The unity of the AFL and the CIO was a fragile flower, blown by the hostile winds of an unsympathetic government and rooted in a very shallow base. Traditional enmities die slowly between opponents with real interests at stake. The redistribution of jurisdictions, the leadership battles at state AFL–CIO council levels and the establishment of a co-ordinated representation within the state and national Democratic Party councils was not easy to achieve. Equally difficult was the establishment of a united foreign policy. It would be wrong to assert that there was a battle within the American labour movement over anti-communism. Both the AFL and the purged CIO were strongly anti-communist. Both were intensely nationalistic (as are virtually all trades union movements). The differences between the Meany (AFL) and the Reuther (CIO) wings of the AFL–CIO on foreign policy were both ideological and personal.

For many years Meany, and his chief labour lieutenants Lovestone and Brown, had had an inside track in the formulation and application of US foreign labour policy. Through the Free Trades Union Committee, the Marshall Plan local offices and within the US government foreign policy establishment in Washington a continuing dialogue about foreign trades union policy had developed between the AFL and the successive US administrations. The CIO, although participants in the Marshall Plan programmes, had never developed the type of close ties to the US government which characterised the AFL. Prime among the reasons for this was the large left-wing caucus in the CIO and the participation of the CIO in the WFTU.

With the unity of the AFL and the CIO Meany found that he had to at least discuss foreign policy matters within his Executive Council. Discussions were occasionally heated, particularly with Reuther and Jim Carey. The issues were seldom over the questions of relations with the

Soviet Union or China. Rather they were most often concerned with the Reuther caucus' concern for the sensibilities of foreign labour movements likely to be offended by the bluntness and lack of tact shown in bombastic AFL–CIO resolutions. Occasionally, as in the case of India where Meany denounced Nehru as a communist because he had preached non-alignment, Reuther felt obliged to demonstrate to the Indians that Meany did not speak for the entire US labour movement.

Essentially the differences between the ideologies of the two parts of the AFL–CIO derived from the different feelings towards European socialism and social democracy. The Meany wing demonstrated the traditional hostility of the AFL to socialism, compounded by his dislike for Europeans who had initially joined in the WFTU against his express command. The Reuther wing felt that if any European trades union movement was to grow strong and prosper it must really reflect the needs and concerns felt by its members. Reuther frequently remarked that if nationalism was right for the AFL–CIO why should it be wrong for the TUC or the DGB? European unionists had no more right to tell the AFL–CIO how to behave in relation to the Democratic or Republican parties than the AFL–CIO had to tell Europeans how their domestic coalitions should be formed. Relationships with overseas unions should be conducted with full respect for the needs and responsibilities of those unions.

The divisions between the two were also personal. Meany looked upon Reuther as a someone who had himself been tainted by socialism. He resented Reuther's eloquence and the respect shown by the national and international community to him as the moral spokesman for US labour. Reuther had little respect for Meany's intellectual abilities and disliked the public links between the AFL and prominent groups and leaders of the American political right wing. Reuther also disliked Lovestone and Brown intensely; both from their early efforts to split his own union, the UAW, and from their successes in splitting several European and North African trades union movements. On the other side, Lovestone and Brown intensely disliked Victor Reuther, Walter's brother and specialist on international affairs, dating from the days when Brown ran the Paris office of the AFL and Victor the Paris office of the CIO. At the merger a compromise was reached and Mike Ross (formerly of the CIO) was put in charge of the International Affairs Department of the AFL–CIO. Nonetheless the effective control was still in the hands of Lovestone. The UAW set up its own International Affairs Department which was very active, particularly within the ITS structures.

The conflicts within the AFL–CIO were similar to the conflicts between the AFL–CIO and the Europeans which weakened the solidity of the ICFTU. The struggle within the ICFTU was largely the struggle to escape US domination. Throughout the late 1950s the AFL–CIO showed its displeasure with the ICFTU by using its muscle to oust one general secretary after another while continuing its unilateral aid policies in the Third World. The creation of an International Solidarity Fund in 1957 was designed to bring the AFL–CIO's aid policies within the structure (and presumably the influence) of the ICFTU. This was not successful.

Unity foundered on the reluctance of the European national centres to follow a policy of militant anti-communism. The early 1960s saw the growth of strong trade and commercial links between Eastern and Western Europe. As early as 1963 the British TUC had instituted a series of exchanges with unions from Yugoslavia. The printing ITS, the International Graphical Workers' Federation, had taken steps to admit into membership a French printing union affiliated to the CGT. Numerous trade delegations from Sweden, Denmark, Belgium and the Netherlands had visited Eastern Europe to promote trade links between their nations and those of the Eastern bloc. Many national centres had followed this up by exchanging fraternal delegations with the national centres of the Eastern European nations. Although this was against the letter of ICFTU policy it reflected the changing needs and responsibilities of Western European unionism.

By the early 1960s many Western European trades union movements had become very much a part of the national programme for expanded trade and international commercial contacts. Some, particularly the West German DGB, had become large commercial organisations in their own right. Like the Israeli national centre, the *Histadrut*, the German labour movement grew to encompass massive economic power. Initially, the DGB participated in German recovery through sponsoring its own trades union bank, the *Bank für Gemeinswirtchaft* (BfG). This bank grew to be one of the largest European banks. It participates in commerce throughout Europe, East and West, and has been the underwriter of many East–West trade, barter and buy-back deals. The BfG is the fourth largest bank in Germany. The DGB also began a self-help housing corporation, the *Neue Heimat*, which has expanded to major international proportions over the years. The DGB now runs the fourth largest German bank, the largest building society in Europe, the largest construction corporation in Germany, a major insurance company, a giant publishing house issuing over four hundred new titles each year, a giant travel company, an automobile club, a chain of over 5100 food and furniture shops including fifty-two supermarkets and nine large department stores stocked by thirty union-owned factories. DGB construction and banking groups are financing and building housing in Moscow, holiday resorts in Bulgaria and financing German corporate expansion in Poland, the Soviet Union and Hungary.

The DGB has more than a passing commitment to the West German government's *Ostpolitik*. Eastern European unionists like to joke that when DGB unionists visit Eastern Europe they spend a few days meeting unionists there and then a few more days checking on the state of their investments.

With this much investment and interest at stake the appeals of the AFL–CIO to the Europeans to stop any contact with Eastern Europe were doomed to failure. Ludwig Rosenberg, president of the DGB, told Meany that trades union anti-communism was not a programme; union policy could not be based on negativism.

The problems of the AFL–CIO's insistence on a militantly anti-communist stance carried over to the struggles within the ICFTU over aid to its regional programmes. Meany insisted that in the regions only anti-communist unions be eligible for assistance. Unions which claimed to be neutral or non-aligned were to be avoided. For many national centres such a policy would have put the union in direct conflict with its national government and ruling party. Equally distressing was the support given by the AFL–CIO to anti-communist unions which were also anti-democratic. The Europeans argued that to use anti-communism as the sole yardstick to measure trades union legitimacy would inevitably lead to giving support to unrepresentative and often anti-democratic national centres. This would both weaken the national centres with whom the Europeans sought to work and would earn the enmity of many of the Third World governments.

At the ICFTU's congress in Vienna in 1955 the conflicts over the question of aid to the developing world were raised by Meany. He demanded the right to continue his unilateral assistance programmes. A compromise was reached but there was a quite unpleasant campaign by the AFL–CIO to remove Oldenbroeck from his general secretaryship of the ICFTU. The next congress, in Tunis in 1957, took place in an atmosphere charged with tension following the repercussions of the Suez crisis. Meany's dual concerns of anti-communism and anti-colonialism were raised as key issues and only the compromise arranged by the Swedes to instal Arne Geijer of the Swedish LO as president reduced the tensions. Through his offices the ICFTU agreed to form an

International Solidarity Fund (ISF) to be the administrator of ICFTU aid to the regions. Meany himself, on the retirement of Tewson, took over control of the ISF.

Meany's chairmanship of the ISF did not lead to a marked diminution of the AFL-CIO's bilateral aid commitments. In 1961-2 the AFL-CIO set up the first of its tripartite aid programmes, the AIFLD. These were followed by the AALC and AAFLI. The activities of these bodies were conducted without any input from the Europeans and not subject to any supervision by them. The AIFLD, in particular, conducted its often controversial programmes under the umbrella of ORIT in Latin America, occasionally embarrassing the Europeans. Within the ISF itself problems arose over the allocation of funds. One problem was the sheer volume of money available to the ISF. Starting out in 1957 with assets of about five and one-half million dollars (or about half the money available in the ICFTU's General Fund), by 1965 the ISF had funds equal to more than double the money available in the ICFTU's General Fund. By the 1965 congress the ISF had reserves and contributions which yielded an annual income of about three million dollars. The interest on the ISF funds was taken by the ICFTU for its own use.

Meany demanded that the ISF be reorganised. He demanded that the ICFTU return to the AFL-CIO $880 000 which he claimed the ICFTU had not used and to account for $2 500 000 he claimed the ICFTU had mishandled. Many delegates, including the Reuther faction of the AFL-CIO, felt that this was only a convenient excuse to continue the unilateral AFL-CIO programmes and represented more Meany's pique at the ICFTU's toleration of the developing East-West trades union relations than any genuine distress at the ICFTU's financial condition.

The AFL-CIO's relationship with the ICFTU was marked by constant conflict. Following the 1965 congress the relations within the AFL-CIO itself were marked by an increasing reluctance of the UAW to continue to participate in programmes of the AFL-CIO with which it was in fundamental disagreement. In 1968 the UAW disaffiliated from the AFL-CIO and wrote the ICFTU that it sought affiliation to the ICFTU on its own behalf. Victor Reuther travelled through Europe, Latin America and Africa in pursuit of support for the UAW's application. The application for individual union affiliation by the UAW was not without precedent. Since its inception the ICFTU had accepted as an affiliate the United Mineworkers of America which was not an affiliate of either the AFL or the CIO. Additionally, the UAW had a long and vital history of international ties to the international trades union movement. The UAW had voted to allocate the interest earned on its strike fund towards international labour activities; an average of about three million dollars a year.

The UAW's international solidarity programmes were used to provide needed assistance to unionists throughout the world. The UAW provided a union clinic in Libya; jeeps and loudspeakers to Kaunda in Northern Rhodesia in his independence campaign; a blue-collar Peace Corps project in Guinea; a radio station for the Phillipines; and scores of similar assistance programmes around the world. These were paid for by the American autoworkers without one penny of US government assistance. In fact some programmes, especially in Latin America, were provided to democratic unions with whom the AFL–CIO and the US government were in less than total accord. This included assistance to the CLASC, the Christian international's Latin regional organisation.

The UAW's major objection to the foreign programmes of the AFL–CIO, and one shared by the majority of the European trades union leaders, was that it was not a genuine trades union programme. Rather they were AFL–CIO joint programmes with the US government designed to promote the policy ambitions of a fairly narrow band of US political opinion. In 1967 the US and world press was full of the revelations of CIA funding of student and labour groups. Just as many of the Europeans had suspected, it was shown that many of the trades union initiatives of the US unions and their respective ITSs were directly funded by grants from the CIA through a series of charitable foundations. Through bodies like the Kaplan Fund, the Gotham Foundation, the Michigan Fund, the Borden Trust Fund, the Edsel Fund, the Beacon Fund, the Kent Fund and many others the CIA poured millions of taxpayers' dollars into US unions for use in their overseas work, either directly or as contributions to their respective ITSs. In fact the founding and financing of one secretariat, the International Federation of Petroleum and Chemical Workers (IFPCW), as well as much of its staffing was directed and funded by the CIA.

Even such ostensibly neutral unions like the Newspaper Guild accepted money from the Warden, Granary, Chesapeake, Broad-High and Hamilton Foundations to contact and train foreign journalists. The Guild officers claimed that they didn't know this was CIA money. They were told that it came from the AFL–CIO and the ICFTU's International Solidarity Fund. The International Union of Food and Allied Workers (IUF), a major ITS, was surprised to learn in the press that it had a series of regional offices in Latin America. Juul Poulsen, the general secretary, found that the AFL–CIO had funded and staffed these offices without informing the IUF.

These revelations confirmed what many in the international trades union movement had feared since 1958: that the AFL–CIO was acting as a disbursement agent for US government, and the CIA in particular, projects in the Third World. Even more repellent to the UAW and the Europeans was the knowledge that the ostensible donor of these funds was claimed to be the ICFTU.

When the UAW pressed its own direct affiliation to the ICFTU the Europeans hesitated to either accept or reject the application. The AFL–CIO opposed the application of the UAW. The Europeans, fearing the loss of the AFL–CIO's 25 per cent contribution of the ICFTU's total budget, refused to make an immediate decision. The AFL–CIO declared a moratorium on dues to the ICFTU in 1968 and, despite the ICFTU's decision not to affiliate the UAW, itself disaffiliated from the ICFTU in 1969.

Despite its disaffiliation from the ICFTU in 1969 the AFL–CIO has maintained its role within the ORIT; to the great displeasure of the European unionists. The decision of the AFL–CIO to reaffiliate to the ICFTU in November 1981 and the reaffiliation of the UAW to the AFL–CIO in 1982 is more of a confession of weakness after the death of Meany than any sudden change in AFL–CIO's international posture.

This disassociation of the AFL–CIO from European unionism in 1968 marked the end of some very important changes in priority and emphasis within European unionism as well. European unionism turned inwards and concentrated on facing three major problem areas which enmeshed them in serious political difficulties. The first was the rising challenge of international industrial relations in the struggles against multinational corporations. The second was the increasing pressures to form a viable European trades union role within the expanding European Economic Community. The third was the adaptation of trades union activities to encompass a new and growing interaction with trades unions within Eastern Europe. For these three challenges the decline of the ICFTU was largely irrelevant.

The political developments which confronted the global internationals (the ICFTU, WFTU and WCL) were not absent within the structures of the international trades secretariats. With the formation of the ICFTU in 1949 the ITSs closely associated themselves with the ICFTU and maintained a regular liaison with the ICFTU at its Brussels headquarters and with the ICFTU's office in Geneva. For the most part, however, the ITSs were developing in a new direction in their efforts to build an international countervailing power to the power of the multinational corporation. What the ITSs were seeking was international recognition by the multinational corporations of their positions as the sole representative, on a world-wide basis, of those workers employed by the multinationals in the many countries in which they operated.

After the initial successes within Europe of rebuilding viable economies many major US corporations began to build production, distribution and sales facilities throughout Western Europe. The corporations began to employ in these enterprises many European workers and began collective negotiations with local European unions. The rapid growth of these corporations within Europe soon led to an emergence of a new type of corporation: a transnational corporation. What characterised these corporations was not only the fact that they produced their products in many countries, but also their creation of what amounted to an internationally integrated production process.

Perhaps the clearest examples of this were the developments within the Western European and US automotive markets. The giant auto firms, General Motors, Ford and Chrysler, set up extensive productive facilities in Europe in the late 1950s, and 1960s manufacturing separate European models in each of the countries in which they operated. The next stage in their development was the creation of uniformity of certain key components (engines, gear boxes, axles, etc.) for the European market as a whole, thus benefiting from economies of scale and enabling them to avoid duplication of facilities in each country of production. This dramatically lowered their costs and forced a major contraction of the numbers of automotive producers in Europe by making comparative costs a key measure of competition. By the late 1960s there were only very few major automotive producers in Europe.

The third stage in integration began in the late 1960s when these major automotive firms began designing 'European' cars; cars produced for the whole European market rather than any single country. Cars like the *Ford Escort* or the *Granada* began to appear in many countries of Western Europe, using some local components or occasionally only local assembly. This was taken even further in the production of agricultural machinery where production was integrated not only within Europe but also between Europe and North America. There was a replication of this process within Latin America and, to a smaller degree in Asia. There local governments passed numerous 'local content' requirements in an effort to control the internationalisation of their auto industries, but often to little avail.

By the early 1970s there was, within the auto industry, virtual international horizontal integration of production. This was replicated to a greater or lesser extent in most other productive industries. One impetus for this international integration was, ironically, the efforts by European and Latin American governments to build common markets or free trade zones. As barriers to international trade grew companies moved behind them. A good example is that of Ford tractors. Once made primarily in Highland Park, Michigan and exported world-wide from there, tractor production was set up in Basildon, England. Warehousing on the Continent was erected in Antwerp, Belgium. With the growth of the EEC of the original six nations and the European Free Trade Area of the other seven nations, it was reasonable for Ford to try to qualify as a local producer within these trading areas to benefit from lower duties. Production of engines was expanded at Basildon; gears and axles for the world market were produced at Highland Park; and other major components for the world market were made in Antwerp. By the early 1970s Ford of England assembled tractors from US and Belgian parts along with English parts and sold them from England to EFTA and the Commonwealth. Belgian tractors, assembled from the same parts, were sold within the EEC as local manufacture. US tractors, assembled from the same parts, were sold within the US–Canadian markets as local manufacture.

By the late 1960s the rise of the multinational corporations was a subject to excite the minds of the international community; none more so than the international trades union movement. The challenges posed by the spread of multinationalism were ones which affected unionists most deeply as they eroded the very foundations of bargaining strength by the unions representing workers employed in the multinationals. In order to fulfil their primary role of defending, maintaining and improving the economic fortunes of their members they had to find a method by which they could develop an international union solidarity capable of confronting their multinational employers on anything like an equal footing.

The unions were faced with the need to develop a working relationship with the trades unions in every country in which the transnational employer produced its products. The rise of the transnational corporation had created some important problems for the national unions representing the workers in these multinationals. The first of these resulted from the fractioning of the work content which occurred whenever international integration was undertaken. In some nations, whole job classifications were lost. In the auto industry, for example, as a 'European' car was developed, the building of tools and dies for the European car was consolidated in one location, thus disemploying tool and die makers elsewhere. The higher skilled jobs tended to be concentrated in one location and very few new assembly jobs were created.

A second problem derived from the corporation's development of an internal international sales operation in which components were sold from a subsidiary in one nation to a subsidiary in another nation. In addition to the disemploying aspects of specialisation, the pricing of these components was, within certain limits, left to the discretion of the corporation. This meant that a corporation could use the transfer-pricing mechanism of internal international sales to move funds from one country to another according to the priorities of the corporation or the vagaries of the currency markets. Indeed, most transnational corporations created their own currency speculation units or arbitrage departments to participate in the opportunities opened by having cash flows in many currencies. They experimented with 'leads' and 'lags'; paying bills to themselves over variable periods to benefit from foreign exchange fluctuations. The problems this caused for the unions derived from their inability to link productivity and profitability to the output of the workers they represented because it was no longer really related to an 'arms-length' pricing mechanism. For the most part, collective bargaining seeks to ensure a continuing participation of the unionised workers in the profitability of the company in which they are employed. When it was no longer possible to assess accurately the profitability of the corporations or to use traditional measures of deriving the workers' contribution to that profitability, the very foundations of collective bargaining were being undermined.

The third major obstacle created by the development of the transnational corporation was that which occurred when the corporations were presented with the opportunity of escaping from the constraints of the product cycle. Traditionally a corporation innovates and begins the manufacture of the innovation. Soon, competitors copy or adapt their products and make inroads into the markets of the original innovator. Then further innovation takes place and the product cycle is repeated. The aspect of the product cycle which interested the unions was that the innovating company traditionally produced the product in the country in which the innovation took place, thus maintaining employment in the innovating country and benefiting the local company from the rewards of the diminishing costs of the learning curve. With the growth of the transnational corporation innovation was frequently made in one highly developed country but initial manufacture was undertaken elsewhere, especially in the less-developed areas of the world where costs were lower and where host governments offered tax and start-up cost incentives. The international electronics industry is a prime example of this phenomenon. The mid-1960s saw the wholesale export of the US electronics industry (televisions, sound systems, etc.) to Asia.

These problems, and some others as well, confronted union organisations in Europe and North America seeking to play a role in protecting the jobs and welfare of their members and to assist trades unionists in the Third World in resisting exploitation. As early as 1956 Charles Levinson, then Assistant-General Secretary of the metal ITS, the IMF, pointed out the need for developing a world-wide union stance on confronting the transnationals. He convinced Victor and Walter Reuther of the need for such a policy and they, through the efforts of the UAW and the IMF, pioneered the development of world company councils. These world company councils brought together for mutual consultation the leaders of the unions representing workers employed within the transnational corporations.

In 1966 the IMF set up the first of a number of world company councils. These linked the unionists in General Motors, Ford and the Chrysler–Fiat–Simca–Rootes complex. Subsequently world company councils were created for other auto companies and later metal-producing, electronics and other corporations. Other ITSs as well set up company councils for their corporations (in the chemical, rubber, food products and other sectors).

The initial objects of these world company councils were to develop a data base about the international activities of the individual corporations. Copies of collective agreements were made available. Detailed studies on corporate labour policies and internal trade flows were developed. A comparative analysis of wage costs was made for corporations and intra-industry comparisons were made on a country-by-country basis. The avowed aim of the company councils was the creation of harmonisation of wages and working conditions within international corporations. This did not mean that wages would be equal around the world but rather that the comparative purchasing power of workers engaged in a similar job classification within a single transnational corporation would be roughly comparable. An example of this might be made by developing a common market basket for a General Motors headlight assembler (1 kilo meat, 1 white shirt, 1 month's rent, etc.) and dividing the costs of these commodities in local currency by the worker's hourly wage. The resultant figure (number of minutes of work needed to purchase a certain commodity) indicated the comparative remuneration of the headlight assembler and provided a crude international comparison of wages within a transnational.

Another aim of these world company councils was to support the weaker unions within the transnational corporation in achieving higher wages and better working conditions by assisting these unions in three important ways. The first was providing these unions with the necessary research about the corporation's earnings, prospects and remuneration in other countries so that a world-wide response to its world-wide earnings might be made. The second was an effort by the company councils to provide services to their fellow unionists within the corporations that the unions might not themselves be able to produce out of their own resources. The IMF and its world company councils created a network of teaching seminars instructing unionists in time and motion studies, monitoring for occupational hazards and preparing for collective bargaining. In one famous incident the IMF asked the UAW to send its chief negotiator with General Motors to Australia to assist the unions in General Motors–Holden in their effort to present a wage claim to the industrial court. After initial objections by General Motors that the UAW man was a foreigner the court ruled that he was no more foreign than the negotiators for Holdens who had come in on the same plane from Detroit as the union man.

The third, and perhaps the most important, endeavour to provide assistance to their fellow unionists in the world company councils was that of providing what was called 'solidarity assistance'. Solidarity assistance consisted of providing cash resources to assist unions in conducting strike actions, requesting workers in other countries to ban overtime work in support of the striking workers, calling consumer boycotts of struck products, and refusing to produce products which would be used to substitute for the products not being produced at struck plants. A corollary of this policy was the efforts to force the corporations to agree that their world-wide collective agreements would terminate on the same day so that the concerted efforts of the international workforce could be used to achieve a better settlement than that likely to be achieved on a purely national basis.

The world company councils sought to achieve the goal of building an effective countervailing international power to that of the transnationals. An early idea which gained some currency was the effort to begin to build an international collective bargaining relationship with the transnationals on the part of the councils. This was soon abandoned in the face of company resistance and the fundamental difficulties in establishing a united set of goals on the part of the individual unions. Instead what emerged was the success of the world company councils in utilising the openings presented to the labour movements of participating within management supervisory boards to install company council representatives on these boards. This was particularly true for transnationals operating in Germany or Sweden where key ITS officials were named to the supervisory boards to fill the seats reserved for the workers' representatives.

Today there are several ITS and company council representatives on the boards of many major transnationals. There they both assist these boards in providing an international input into the corporate decision-making process, as well as serving as a reporting group to unions employed in the transnational.

The economics of the development of the world company councils were fairly clear and straightforward. What was most complex was the intense political conflict the development of these councils generated. One of the first areas of discord resulted from the traditional union policies relating to admitting into membership of the ITSs only unions whose policies were generally in accord with what the ITSs described as democratic socialism. This had always excluded unions dominated by the communists as well as those affiliated to the Christian national centres. With the development of world company councils these exclusions had to be reconsidered. Throughout the subsidiaries of the multinational corporation around the world there were many unions which were not members of their respective ITSs. Some were independent; some were led by communists; some were led by Christians; and some were prohibited by their governments from affiliating to any international body.

The whole notion of developing countervailing power to the transnationals demanded the greatest possible universality of membership within the structure of the world company councils. On the other hand to allow into the council structures unions fundamentally opposed to the basic principles of the ITS was unlikely to promote the type of solidarity needed to carry out the basic programmes of the councils. The ITSs were forced to choose between allowing into the councils every union with membership in the transnational company or excluding their ideological opponents and thus diminishing the strength of the councils. In virtually all the ITSs the choice was made to allow into membership the Christian unions which professed adherence to the same democratic principles as the socialists and social democrats and to exclude the unions led by the communists. One result was the increased deconfessionalisation of European Christian unions which, as in the case of the French CFTC, dropped the word 'Christian' from their names.

A second result was the development of a large group of powerful unions in Western Europe led by communists who were effectively locked out of any real participation within the world company councils. The international trade departments of the WFTU with whom these communist unions were affiliated were virtually entirely Eastern European organisations and played no role within the structures of transnational corporate activities. The communist-led unions of the French CGT or the Italian CGIL found themselves without a role to play in one of the principal areas of European trades union activity. Despite their formation of new political caucuses with the Christian democratic parties and trades union national centres in their nations, their sectoral national unions were locked out of international activities within the framework of the ITSs.

This policy was far more important to the unions than it might appear on the surface. Not only could they not participate in developing an international trades union organisation in what was becoming the most vital sector of European industrial relations, but they also began to lose power and adherents at the very base of their organisations, the local plant committees, because of their inability to play a role in these international bodies.

The reasons for this lie in the very nature of trades unionism itself. The trades union movement has existed for at least a hundred years in most nations in one form or another. It has attracted to its leadership many gifted and devoted leaders, as well as some others less gifted and devoted. The continuity of the organisation has rarely been questioned. What is important is what impels a worker to seek trades union office. There have been numerous answers to this question. In its formative days most European unions were formed by those with a strong ideological commitment to social justice; either coming from the intellectual classes seeking to create a base for political action or from workers dissatisfied with what they considered oppression. The fact that this struggle was bound up with the struggle for political rights gave impetus and continuity for those who sought to play a role in its direction. However, the reasons for seeking union office are no longer exactly the same in modern Europe, at least for lower-level union jobs.

The reasons behind seeking union office on the lower levels of union activity relate principally to two distinct motivations. The first remains the traditional ideological commitment towards a cause or a social goal.

This is most frequently a goal expressed in a political movement rather than in the economic structure of unionism. Many lower-level leaders assume union office in an effort to achieve status within their political movements. Throughout the history of the European left, the assumption of union duties has been part of the *cursus honorum* of socialist, communist or Trotskyite politicians; a path to higher office and a proof of service to the party. This remains true.

For the most part, however, the payoff for assuming union office is not ideological. It is the winning of compensated time away from the workplace. It is the ability of workers to adjust their working day so that an increasing portion of the working day is spent away from the actual toil or labour for an employer. The benefit of winning union office has meant that the worker selected to be a shop steward, a committee person or a local union officer has been permitted, under the grievance procedures or collective bargaining procedures, to leave his or her work station for part or all of the compensated working day. The rewards of union office are the rewards of discretionary time.

The higher up the ladder of union office the worker moves the smaller the fraction of the working day is spent on working for the employing corporation. He or she may spend hours processing a grievance; or perhaps sitting on a works council planning company policy with the management; he or she may be asked to attend to local or regional union business which involves travel away from the workplace. Higher status accrues to union officers in direct proportion to time spent away from the workplace. This is not to say that they are not engaged in work whilst not in the workplace; most union jobs entail long and unsocial hours as well as tedious paperwork. Rather, this kind of union work is preferable to the job from which they have won time away. The payoff is greater personal power, greater job security (as most union officers accrue 'super seniority' with their union offices making them the last to be laid off), and a greater chance to participate in higher levels of union activities and travel.

For most trades union officers travel is the most common method of reward for service. Trades unionists travel from their workplaces to local, regional and national meetings and congresses. Higher levels travel internationally to meetings and congresses of labour bodies and non-governmental organisations in which the labour movement has won recognition. The reward of travel for a union officer is an increased sense of participation in union affairs, higher stature in the community and increased time away from the workplace. There are very many trades unionists world-wide whose principles would never permit them to receive favours or advantage from a party, a union or an international body who, nevertheless, will accept the gift of travel from these organisations as part of their just rewards for embarking on union service.

At the highest levels of union service the rewards include selection for high political office or, as in the case of Britain, retirement to the House of Lords. As unions become more involved in the workings of the state, union office leads to diplomatic posts, service within the EEC and its committees and even appointment to the board of directors of giant corporations. The union organisation which can deliver these rewards and emoluments to its leaders is one which commands loyalty and respect. When the unions can no longer offer the same levels of time away from work for its lower-level officers; when they cannot maintain seats for their adherents on plant and shop committees; and when unions cannot guarantee further steps up the ladders of power the union is in trouble. The best guide to trouble within a union is the turnover level of shop stewards. The higher the level the more difficulties being experienced by the union. The rise in the expansion of world company councils provoked just such a reaction within the trades union movements of the left in Europe.

With the creation by the ITSs of company councils a positive flurry of meetings were called to which unionists from across the globe were invited. These carried back to their own plants and factories the news of the development of the councils as well as massive documentation produced by the ITSs about their companies. Local unionists learned of what others had achieved in collective bargaining; they learned of solidarity campaigns in which unionists in Europe and North America campaigned for the solution to problems being faced by a national union representing workers in the transnationals. For those who were not members of these world councils the problems of non-membership were clear. The workers demanded from their stewards just what they planned to do about the multinationals. For many communist-led unions the answer was equivocal. They had not developed any response.

The communist-led unions of Europe eventually developed a strategy to both attack their ideological enemies in the Western European labour movements and to play a role in the development of a response to the growth of transnational corporations. They decided to build international shop stewards' committees representing workers within a transnational to carry out a parallel activity to the world company councils of the ITSs. Whenever a company council was formed for a particular transnational corporation by the respective ITS, the shop stewards' committees were then formed as well. Soon employers found they had two separate (and occasionally three) international labour groups seeking to discuss their world-wide and European labour policies, investment strategies, etc. Competition between the two groups was intense, but especially when the transnational corporation employed significant numbers of workers in Britain, Italy or France; the three countries in which there were substantial numbers of communist shop stewards and committee personnel. Later, when Portugal and Spain emerged into the early stages of democracy, it was these conflicting groups which played such a strategic role in the political development of trades unionism in these two nations.

Perhaps the clearest example of this kind of conflict between the company councils of the ITSs and the shop stewards' committees was that which surrounded the strike at Dunlop–Pirelli in 1972. As early as 1970 the shop stewards of the Dunlop and Pirelli rubber tyre companies established contacts between them on matters of common interest. When the two companies announced that they were going to merge in 1971 interest in expanding contacts between union organisations grew, both among the shop stewards and within the ITS with jurisdiction in the rubber industry, the International Chemical and General Workers' Union (ICF) of Geneva. In late 1971 and early 1972 the declining market for rubber tyres in Europe led to a contraction of the market share of the Dunlop–Pirelli combine. The introduction of short-time work, layoffs and redundancies by the company in response to the shrinking market were exacerbated by the rationalisation of the manufacturing plants by the two companies in the wake of their merger. The unions within the ICF requested that a world company council for the Dunlop–Pirelli corporation be formed in order that a co-ordinated response to the corporation could be made. They issued a call for unions representing Dunlop and Pirelli workers to come to Geneva to discuss this council.

Simultaneously the shop stewards of Dunlop and Pirelli in Britain and Italy, along with a representative of Dunlop–France, met to consider their action plans. The shop stewards from Pirelli's Italian operations were members of the CGIL rubber workers' union and had some support from local level shop stewards from the social democratic and Christian unions. The British unionists were stewards of the Transport and General Workers' union, whose national officer for the rubber industry was John Miller, a prominent member of the British communist party. The French delegate was a CGT steward. The co-ordinator of these meetings of shop stewards was Chris Gilmore, a British employee of the CGIL married to the daughter of Pietro Ingrao, the Italian communist party's theoretician.

This shop stewards' committee called for a 'Eurostrike' in June 1972 in which the European workers of Dunlop and Pirelli were called upon to stop work in order to manifest their opposition to the corporation's plans for job reduction throughout Europe. In Italy the Pirelli plants were closed for two hours as workers attended a protest meeting and demonstrations were held in some British plants (with the Speke plant closed for the day).

As this Eurostrike was going on the ICF's world company council for Dunlop–Pirelli, under the leadership of Bob Edwards of the Transport and General Workers (and a member of the British Parliament), was successful in arranging a meeting between the ICF and a representative of the Dunlop personnel department to discuss, informally, the demands of the company council. On the one hand the shop stewards of Britain and Italy, funded and directed in their work by the Italian and British communist parties, were conducting a Eurostrike whilst the recognised union leadership of unions in Dunlop and Pirelli were meeting with a Dunlop personnel executive to discuss essentially the same subject as that issue on which the strike was being called. To make things even more confusing the leadership of both sides of the union divide came from the same Transport and General Workers' union in Britain. To the executives of Dunlop–Pirelli, at least, it was clear that there were at least two separate international union organisations striving for recognition in their plants.

This conflict within Dunlop–Pirelli was not unique to this corporation. Soon other companies like Solvay, Michelin, Unilever, Ford, Continental Can and ITT found themselves in a similar position. Throughout European industry the communist unions sought a role within the transnationals by building international coalitions of shop stewards in opposition to the recognised union company councils of the ITSs. Frequently these shop stewards' organisations were aided by the WFTU and its trade departments which organised parallel union meetings to those conducted by the ITSs even when they did not concern individual corporations. In March 1977, for example, when the metal ITS, the IMF, was holding a congress to discuss the trades union role in facing the transnational corporation, the WFTU and its metal committee called a simultaneous meeting in Rome to discuss the same subject. The WFTU meeting was attended by the French and Italian communist federations and representatives from the national centres of Algeria, Egypt, Yugoslavia, Cyprus, Syria and the communist-led centres of Spain and Turkey. None of these has been overwhelmingly active in promoting free collective bargaining at home; still less on an international basis.

This conflict between the ITSs and their opponents has been the principal battleground of European labour. Behind the rhetoric of the global internationals about the multinational challenge lies a real battle for control of the European trades union movements. It is important to realise that the union organisations of North America, despite their absence from the ICFTU, continued to play a vital role within the ITS structures. It is here within the ITSs that the battle against European communist control of the trades union movement is being waged. The communist response to this battle has not been solely to build a strong shop stewards' movement. An important part of their programme has been the promotion of Euro-unionism; the development of a purely European trades union regionalism.

In this effort to build Euro-unionism the communist parties and unions of Western Europe have been aided by the creation and expansion of the EEC and its component committees. Euro-unionism has its roots in the trades union effort to participate in the recovery of Western European industry through the Marshall Plan. The Trades Union Advisory Committee (TUAC) which was formed as an advisory committee to the European Recovery Plan brought together most of the non-communist union national centres of Western Europe. The European Regional Organisation (ERO) of the ICFTU helped to coordinate this work and also co-ordinated the struggle against communist hegemony in the trades union struggles in Greece, Finland, Italy and France. However, unity on a lower level only emerged with the development of the European Coal and Steel Community (ECSC) in 1952.

In 1952 the metal and mining unions of Germany, Belgium, France, Holland, Italy and Luxembourg formed themselves into a Committee of Twenty-One within the ECSC to co-ordinate their work and to promote harmonisation of wages and working conditions in what was Europe's first major common endeavour. At the signing of the Treaty of Rome in 1957 establishing the EEC, this Committee of Twenty-One added representatives of the metal ITS (the IMF) and the mining ITS (the MIF) as well as an ICFTU–ERO representative and reconstituted itself as a metal and mining committee within the structure of the EEC and with a recognised consultative role. This committee excluded unionists from the communist-led centres of France, Italy, Luxembourg and Holland. This EEC committee pledged itself to the political and economic integration of Europe.

The Christian unions, too, were spurred by the creation of the EEC to try and build a European organisation. In 1958 the Christians founded their own European regional organisation, the CISC–EO to co-ordinate their efforts within the EEC and to try to get consultative status within the EEC committee structures. They were successful.

The communist unions were initially refused consultative status within the EEC. They formed their own Action Committee in 1958 which joined together the WFTU-affiliated national centres of France and Italy with the small *Eenheids Vakcentral* of Holland and the tinier *Freier Letzeburger Arbechter-Verband* of Luxembourg.

The ICFTU-affiliated national centres of Europe decided that it would be unwise not to include the national centres beyond the initial six EEC nations in its deliberations and expanded the membership of its ERO–ECSC Committee of Twenty-One to include them. They reconstituted themselves as the European Trades Union Secretariat (ETUS) in 1958. Thus by the end of 1958 there were three distinct trades union federations within Europe: the ETUS; the Christian CISC–EO; and the WFTU's Action Committee. Only the first two had recognised consultative status in the EEC.

These committees were mainly involved in the planning for the growth of the EEC institutions and remained fairly inactive for a number of years. The real spur for change of this gradual process of representation came after the cataclysmic events of 1968. The year 1968 represents a watershed in European history. There were few European institutions left unchanged in the wake of the turbulence of that year. The trades unions were no exception.

The events of 1968 in France, Czechoslovakia and elsewhere in Europe and North America radically changed the perceptions of the European trades union movements and political parties towards the role of the communist parties of Western Europe in the democratic process. The challenge to the communist parties of Europe posed by the radicalisation at the bases of their power, and the simultaneous need to distance themselves from their traditional close linkages with the policies of the Soviet party in the aftermath of the general world-wide revulsion following the Soviet repression of Czech communism, led these parties to a reappraisal of their strategy and tactics. The development of what became 'Eurocommunism' was a direct result of these upheavals.

If the term Eurocommunism has meant anything it has meant the development of what Palmiro Togliatti called 'polycentrism': the admissibility in party policy that there were different roads to communism, not only that decreed by Moscow. This was not a new discussion. Indeed the battles of Yugoslavia in 1948, the Polish Spring, the Hungarian uprising and the Sino-Soviet rift were largely about the same question. The split in the US communist party over the question of 'American exceptionalism' dated from the late 1920s. What was new, and important, was the willingness of European communist party leaders to take a public stand in favour of national autonomy and to promote the image of these Western European communist parties as genuinely committed to parliamentary democracy with all the responsibilities this entailed.

The reasons for the development of Eurocommunism are not only to be found in ascribing to the Western European communists cynical and opportunist motives relating to their changed circumstances – although this was certainly true in part. The reasons lay deeper in the very nature of the communist movement. When a political party or trades union is described as 'communist' this label is a useful and convenient shorthand for a political movement of far more convoluted complexity. It is convenient to say that the French CGT is a communist national centre or the CGIL represents the Italian communist trades union arm. In fact, in both cases there exists within the CGT and the CGIL numerous non-communist trends and leaders. Traditionally both these movements have drawn their primary leadership cadres from the ranks of their national communist party and have been in debt for resources to the party and to the international communist movement. Nonetheless, both the French and Italian national centres dominated by the communists have substantial and influential non-party members. Party membership and discipline is not the only requirement for office.

However, membership in the communist party is not a static thing. People join the party and leave it with surprising regularity in response to the policies of the party, its electoral successes and even the opportunities it offers its members to win and maintain attractive jobs. Every turn and change in party policy wins it new members and loses it others. Unlike Eastern Europe where party membership is considered a privilege, party membership in Western Europe has frequently been a liability. In order to attract new members the party has to continually offer its members incentives to join and remain in the party. An additional factor which concerns Western European communist parties is the rising generation gap between the party leaders and the young workers it seeks to attract to membership.

The Rise of Euro-unionism

After the Second World War the communists were successful in entrenching themselves and their party organisations in workshops, factories and offices throughout France and Italy. They installed in local office many of their most ardent supporters both grateful for their jobs and anxious to promote the cause of communist power. Many of these have grown old in their jobs, frustrated with the lack of success of their parties in winning wider electoral gains which would permit them better job opportunities and increasingly out of touch with the younger workers in the plants for which they are responsible. These younger workers regard the party apparatus as just another part of the bureaucratic structure of French and Italian industry; something that was there when they came in and something likely to outlast their time of employment. The local and regional party structures are generally viewed as part of the fabric of the national economic life; hardly as wild-eyed revolutionaries. Union membership as a whole in these nations is tiny. The West German I. G. Metall union has as members more workers than the CGT national centre claims as its membership. The TGWU and the AUEW have more members than the entire French organised workforce. Percentages in Italy aren't much higher. Even these figures are claimed members. Actual dues payers are about half the claimed members.

The dissatisfaction with the role of the Western European communists and the gap between the communist union bureaucrats and the workers came to a head in 1968; not only in France and Italy but across Europe. Significantly, the first open revolt came in France.

What happened in France in May 1968 illustrated to the political and trades union leadership of the communist and non-communist left in Europe just how far the gap between them and their members had widened. Within the French plants a new group of left activists had established themselves, drawing upon the support of the younger workers. Taking their lead from the student demonstrators in the universities the workers spread their industrial action across French industry, occupying their plants and offices. Just as the ideology of the movement in the university encompassed virtually every form of Marxism from Karl to Groucho, the ideologies espoused by the workers were equally as diverse. What the workers sat in their plants for was a demand for reforms. A working alliance between the students and the CFDT led to industrial unrest along the Loire and in Brittany. By mid-May there were more than ten million French workers on strike; that was almost one-half of the total French workforce and about five times the total national union membership.

In this massive outpouring of dissent the unions played only a marginal role. The student-labour coalition took a position much more radical than that of the *Parti Communiste Français* (PCF) or the CGT. They represented an anti-authoritarian reaction to the controls over French industry imposed by the government, the management and with at least the tacit consent of the unions. The unions rushed to keep up with their followers and to restore order.

The CGT met with the *Patronat* (the employers' federation) over the weekend of 27 May 1968 in an effort to resolve the conflict. The two parties agreed a compromise, the Grenelle Agreement, which they felt would restore order within French industry and which would not embarrass De Gaulle. The Grenelle Agreement was presented to the striking workers who rejected it. The workers, independent of their unions, chose to fight out local agreements plant by plant.

De Gaulle chose that moment to call a general election; an election in which the PCF lost a full 12 per cent of their electorate. Losses mounted within the CGT as local strike committees turned on their CGT stewards and representatives, supplanting them with leftist and revisionist plant committees. Most importantly, the traditional bedrock strength of the CGT in the plants of the nationalised industries (most notably plants like the Renault-Billancourt car factory) was weakened by the loss of safe seats to the young leftist groups.

Throughout French industry many loyal CGT unionists were faced with the threat of having to return to the shopfloor to earn their living. Local PCF councillors found that they could not return to safe seats in CGT posts now that they had been turned out of office in the election. Dissent within the party and confusion over the party's apparent loss of momentum was made even more apparent with the party's vacillating attitude to the Soviet invasion of Czechoslovakia in August 1968.

Throughout the world's communist movements, not only in France, the defeat of the Dubcek communist government by the armed forces of the Warsaw Pact was seen as a major break with the illusion of socialist unity. The Warsaw Pact forces dramatically proved to the European communist leaders that a gradual decentralisation of international communism was not going to be tolerated by the Soviet policy-makers. As in the case of Hungary twelve years earlier, communist party members left the party in substantial numbers. They also drifted away from activities within the communist-led unions. For most of the Western European parties the blow of Czechoslovakia came at a time when they, like their comrades in France, were already crumbling at the base. The inexorable propensity of the left, and especially the communist left, to form an intricate kaleidoscopic pattern of factionalism was boosted by this clear division over the justification for the Soviet invasion of a fellow communist state. These parties publicly had to declare their position on Czechoslovakia to retain any credibility with their followers; a declaration which inevitably led to more splits and factions.

Throughout the Western European communist parties a choice had to be made; and made publicly. Either the party declared itself loyal to Moscow in clear defiance of the general world revulsion against the Soviet invasion or the party declared itself opposed to the supremacy of the policies of the Russian party over national party policies. How the parties addressed this problem largely determined the parties' and their unions' commitment to Eurocommunism. Had there not been this widespread revolt at the base in 1968 throughout Europe the parties' choices might have been easier. As it was each party had to make the choice within the context of major unrest at the base; primarily the party base in the union organisations.

The PCF tried to be ambivalent about condemning the Soviet invasion. It was very slow and very conditional about venting its disapproval. On the one hand it had already been severely divided over the possibility of winning greater governmental power in an alliance of the broad left behind the candidacy of Mitterand in the 1965 election, when the Soviet party made clear its support for De Gaulle over Mitterand. When the 1968 election debacle showed the lack of grassroots party support for the Soviet view and the dramatic re-structuring of the trades union movement in the wake of the 1968 upheavals cost the party many local leaders, it was moved to take a different course. Yet, the continuing strength of the pro-Moscow faction in its strange alliance with De Gaulle (principally because of De Gaulle's anti-Americanism) made the party unwilling to cast its lot with the socialists in a broad anti-De Gaulle coalition. It issued the Manifesto of Champigny in December 1968 which took a much harder line against collaboration with the broad left. The PCF and the CGT decided to move back to the left in an effort to outflank the radicals who were threatening the party control of the union base.

The PCF, and the CGT, chose not to move further down the road towards Eurocommunism; it chose to follow the path outlined by the Soviet party. Despite its protests at overt Soviet interference (as in the 1974 elections when the Soviet ambassador publicly called upon Giscard d'Estaing and shunned Mitterand) the PCF has continued to follow the Soviet line fairly closely. It was the PCF which was the first Western

European party to renew contacts with Moscow after Prague and the PCF which was virtually alone among Western communist parties to identify itself with and support the Stalinist Portuguese communist party. It was this close identification with Soviet foreign policy which has been a major barrier to the PCF's participation in Eurocommunism and has been the major obstacle to the admissibility of the CGT and its constituent unions into the councils of the developing Euro-unionist structures.

The differences between the development of the French and Italian parties and unions have been dramatic. A major factor in this development has been the markedly different development of their trades union structures. Just as in France in 1968, there was a marked radicalisation of the base in Italian plants. A large-scale wave of *comitati di base*, rank-and-file committees, had begun to form in Italian industries in 1966 largely over the question of local autonomy when the 1966 confederal agreements barred local works councils, *commisione interne*, from participating in collective bargaining. Elections to these works councils were hotly contested by the unions affiliated to the three major Italian national centres, the CGIL, the UIL and the CISL. The successes and failures of the three rival unions in these elections tended to determine the national strength of the confederations.

To this extent the system was similar to that in France. The major difference between the systems emerged from the growth of co-operation on a national scale among the unions of all three confederations in collective negotiations in key industries. In 1962 and 1963 the three metalworker unions of Italy began to seek a joint nationwide agreement for their industry. This initial co-operation was expanded even more fully in the negotiations in 1968–9; particularly in the co-operation achieved in the 'hot autumn' strikes of 1969. There the three conducted widespread joint national strikes and demonstrations which won them improved contracts. This co-operation was extended to other national unions. By the end of 1970 the co-operation among the three national centres was well institutionalised and a virtual 'federation' of the three was truly established.

This co-operation within Italian industry had substantial results for the *Partito Communista Italiana* (PCI) and the CGIL. From 1972 onwards the party has added large numbers of new members. Despite a very high defection rate (about half the PCI's membership has joined since 1972) membership levels have grown. Many of these have come from among the ranks of the younger workers entering the labour market and the CGIL. The price of this high turnover has been the difficulty in creating an effective grassroots organisation but the benefits far outweigh the costs.

The unity achieved by the trades union federations won for the CGIL and the PCI a position of greater acceptability in the eyes of the Italian public. Through its electoral successes which brought the party a large number of local and regional offices, the PCI demonstrated itself as a party of moderation and discipline. Additionally, the weakness of its socialist opponents which grew even as they increased their participation in government in an alliance with the powerful Christian Democrats, created additional opportunities for the PCI to win greater support from the centre-left. The PCI leader, Berlinguer, pressed for a 'historic compromise': the creation of an Italian government in which the PCI would be invited to participate.

This movement towards a historic compromise was given greater impetus in the election of 1972. The non-PCI left cannibalised itself by factionalism and a strong Christian Democratic government took office. Unity on the left was achieved only in the trades unions when, on 24 July 1972, the three national federations combined. It was the trades unions which led the major battles against the Andreotti government. What prompted the PCI to forsake its traditional leftist stance and to declare itself in favour of seeking power through the ballot box was a combination of a number of factors: some concerned the need to preserve unity in the labour movement; some derived from the PCI's success in relegating the socialists to a secondary role which opened the way for the PCI to become the major Opposition party. By far the most important of these reasons was the PCI's interpretation of the impact on Western European communist movements of the overthrow of Allende in Chile.

Berlinguer and the PCI theoreticians felt that the events in Chile proved that even if the PCI were to win 51 per cent of the Italian vote against the Christian Democrats it would not be allowed to take office. A military coup, supported by the US and its NATO allies, would almost certainly rob the PCI of the fruits of its victory. For the PCI to attain power, a historic compromise with the Christian Democrats would be the only safe route. To achieve this goal the PCI had to be recognised as a party fully accepting the rigours of parliamentary democracy.

Accepting the rigours of parliamentary democracy and seeking to woo the Christian Democrats has not been without serious cost to the PCI. On the one hand the PCI has divided into three clear factions; each of which press for a more forceful role by the PCI in combatting Italy's economic woes. On the other hand the Christian Democrats have moved increasingly rightward, thus alienating a large segment of PCI thought. Until February 1979 the PCI seemed willing to follow a policy of support for the Christian Democrats in which they were consulted by the government but effectively were kept from direct participation in that government. This policy of moderation and compromise with the Italian government's drastically deflationary policy alienated the trades unionists of the CGIL and the other federations. Unrest grew more militant at the base. In February 1979 the PCI withdrew its tacit support for the Christian Democrats and new elections were held.

The results of the 1979 elections were as bad as the PCI had feared. They lost more than a million and one-half votes; their strength declined from 34 to 30 per cent. Most importantly, they did not lose these votes to the Christian Democrats; they lost them to the Radicals and to the ultra-left. The trades union movement again began to separate along the old lines of schism and many Italian sectoral unions began to reaffiliate to the ITSs from whom they had withdrawn after 1976. The historic compromise is not dead in Italy but the PCI has learned that no compromise is possible without taking into account the critical role played in the national arena by the trades unions and their shopfloor allies.

The spread of Eurocommunism and the commitment to developing Euro-unions reached even to the socialist strongholds of Scandinavia after their own minor upheavals in 1968. In Sweden, for example, where the Swedish Social Democratic Workers' Party (SAP) had governed Sweden as its majority party from September 1932 to October 1976, there was a marked radicalisation of the union base of the party in 1968. Traditionally the base of support for the SAP has derived from the party's organic links with the Swedish national centre, the LO. This LO organisation represents about 98 per cent of the organised workers in Sweden, with the rest affiliated to the white-collar TCO organisation or to the tiny group of unions affiliated to the Swedish Communist Party (VPK). The close links between the LO and the SAP provided the SAP with a solid majority for almost forty-five years.

Some of the problems which beset the LO in the mid-1960s were the same problems which confronted many of the other European unions: a growing feeling of disillusionment with the LO as an agent of social change because of its close ties to government economic policies; a growing age gap between the union members and officers; and an increased radicalisation at the base in which a wide variety of Maoists, anarchists, Trotskyites and left dissidents built local caucuses tied to splinter parties. Another factor, one which was more especially true for Scandinavia than elsewhere in Europe, was the growing public acceptance of a militant anti-American stance in reaction to the war in Vietnam. Peace committees, solidarity campaigns and similar mass movements united the centre, left and far left in Scandinavia into coalitions with the Scandinavian communist parties and their union allies which increased the sense of legitimacy by these parties.

The rapprochement achieved among the parties on the left in Sweden, however, was not immediately replicated within the labour movement. In 1968 the workers in Kiruna (the very heartland of the VPK stronghold, Norbotten, where the party exerts a strong influence on the mining and timber workers) went on strike against the LKAB company. This strike by the miners lasted fifty-seven days and was essentially a political strike rather than about economic issues. What the Kiruna strikers were complaining about was (in addition to a higher minimum wage and better health and safety rules) an end to authoritarian discipline by the management, speedup and piece rates. What made the strike important was that the mine was state-owned and representatives of the LO and the SAP sat on the mine's board of directors. The precipitating issue was the imposition of a contract in Kiruna by a SAP-dominated miners' union despite the contract's rejection by the local union branch in Kiruna. The strike, essentially a wildcat strike by the local union, raised serious questions about regional policy, union centralisation and the close ties between the LO and the SAP.

Just as the French workers rejected the Grenelle Agreement, the Kiruna strikers rejected the compromise agreed to by their central confederation. A settlement of sorts was arranged through the personal mediation of an LO official but the local strike committee retained its autonomy despite losing its battles for union reform at the branch and regional union levels. It became a source of financial and political support for waves of other wildcat strikes which swept across Swedish industry in the early 1970s. The strike at Kiruna and the similar strikes spawned by it illustrated the dissatisfaction with the tight centralisation of Swedish industrial relations and the resultant lack of initiative by the LO–SAP leadership in pressing for a radical programme of change, in part because of their fear of its electoral repercussions.

Partly as a response to the increased militancy at the union base the SAP and the LO gave support to the 'Meidner Plan' drawn up by a labour economist from their ranks. This plan envisioned the gradual expansion of the workers' participation in management to include a programme by which the trades unions would be permitted to gradually acquire the controlling interests in Sweden's top 4000 companies. A series of major reforms on unfair dismissal and equal rights for women were achieved. However, the price of this unrest and the disarray of the Swedish economy led to the ousting of the SAP from government and a rightward move of the Swedish electorate.

During this period of stress in the LO–SAP relationship with their collective base, the Swedish communists were engaged in presenting themselves as a party deeply committed to Eurocommunism. During the early 1970s the leaders of the Swedish VPK (and indeed the Norwegian Communist Party – NKP) opened a dialogue with the PCI and the Romanian party on the subject of Eurocommunism. The Spanish party (the PCE) set up an important liaison branch in Sweden to assist the Spaniards in their search for support in the internal struggles in Spain. The VPK aligned itself on a national basis with the SAP and was instrumental in keeping the SAP in power during the last faltering years of its governmental majority. This was of benefit to both parties, largely because it served to bridge the gulf between the trades union dissidents and their local party structures. The danger to the LO and the VPK unions was from the ultra-left anarchist, Maoist and Trotskyite factions across Sweden. A national pact between the two on the political front effectively cemented what amounted to a 'no-raiding' pact on the union level, thus securing their left flanks from any major or credible challenge.

This challenge on the left throughout Scandinavia was the principal impetus for the 'regular' communist parties to seek alliances with the union national centres and political parties of the Social Democrats. The effect of these alliances was to moderate the opposition of the Scandinavian national centres to the opening of membership opportunities for Eurocommunist unions seeking to affiliate to the Euro-union structures and the ITSs. This was of particular significance in the case of the Italian and Spanish communist unions' acceptance within the ranks of Euro-unionism.

Even in that bastion of social democratic strength, West Germany, the effects of the radicalisation of 1968 had their effect. Although the DGB is a wealthy and powerful organisation it relies for its strength on its role as the mediator between the SPD and the sixteen powerful national union sectoral federations. These industrial unions which comprise the DGB have only a limited presence at shopfloor level where power is exclusively exercised through the works council structure. Frequently these powerful unions have won majority representation on the works councils but they often have to share this power on the works council with councillors elected from the ranks of non-union workers (especially those with strong backing from the foreign, or 'guest' workers). Although collective bargaining takes place between the industrial union and an employers' federation on a regional basis, day-to-day representation of the workers takes place at shopfloor level through the works council structure.

Dissatisfaction among the workers with the 'economic miracle' of postwar German economic recovery began to grow as early as 1966 when the SPD joined with the Christian Democrats in what was in effect a national government, the *'Grosse Koalition'*. This coalition virtually eliminated any real parliamentary opposition. The growing forces of the left (mainly anarchists, Maoists and Trotskyites) within the student movements and the Young Socialists (Jusos) formed their own extra-parliamentary opposition movement which won them some considerable support among the ranks of the younger workers at the shopfloor level. These younger workers were dissatisfied with the centralisation of power in the DGB–SPD alliance and with the conservative role played by the union and party nexus in the field of moderating demands for higher wages and a reduction of the working day. These workers, and some trades union leaders at the regional level, were demanding a stronger and more direct union presence in the workplace; what they called a *betriebsnahe Politik*.

By 1968, when radical politics became very fashionable throughout Europe, the stage was set for a major upheaval in German left politics. The Jusos and their extra-parliamentary opposition joined forces with the dissident unionists to pursue a 'dual strategy' of working for change in the party at national level and through 'base organisations' like the unions to challenge the hierarchical and oligarchic structure of the SPD–DGB alliance. The SPD tried to respond by creating a committee of conciliation to study the demands for reform by the Jusos (the *Arbeitsgemeinschaft für Arbeitnehmerfragen*) but this body proved almost as radical as the Jusos. What emerged from the radicalisation of the German workplace organisation was the growth of dissident unionists at shopfloor level willing to co-operate with radical unionists elsewhere in Europe. It was largely from among the ranks of these radical unionists that the international shop stewards' committees, which were set up to combat the world company councils, drew their German representatives.

While never really growing strong enough to pose a real challenge to the unions of the DGB, these unionists did achieve a certain measure of distance in the relationship between the DGB and the SPD and played a role in the break-up of the coalition politics of the party. They also made the DGB union leaders very cautious in accepting the new structures of Euro-unionism as they feared the encouragement by these Euro-unions of their domestic opponents. It was mainly the DGB which opposed the expansion of Euro-unionism in its present form.

The radicalisation of trades union and socialist policies in 1968 was not absent in Great Britain, although it took a somewhat different form there than on the Continent. One major reason for the divergence from the Continental model was the strikingly different role played in trades union and Labour Party politics by the Communist Party of Great Britain (CPGB). After the schisms of the late 1950s and the victory of the 'technocrats' in winning control of the Labour Party after Gaitskell's death, the leadership of the CPGB is said to have actively encouraged some of its adherents to leave the party and join the Labour Party. In the late 1950s and early 1960s many CPGB unionists left the party to take up high office in the union structures. The CPGB, which could never muster more than a tiny electoral following, chose to make a virtue of necessity and prepared to 'bore from within' the Labour Party. Under Labour Party bloc voting rules, a trades union casts its bloc vote at Labour Party and TUC congresses on the basis of its claimed membership; a membership which also includes Conservative and communist members. In some unions, as in the now famous case of the Electrical Trades Union (ETU), the communists were able to control the voting procedures to gain effective control of the union. This gave them an important bloc vote within the TUC as well as in the Labour Party.

Labour's narrow victory in the 1964 election put the party in government; an event repeated in 1966 with a much greater majority. Under Wilson the party embarked on a search for the middle ground of British politics, seeking to shed its cloth cap image and to adopt a more social democratic posture (like the German and Swedish parties). This programme was supported by the leaders of the TUC which, as early as 1962, had agreed to 'move into Whitehall' (i.e. to move into the process of participating in government planning). Through the creation of the National Economic Development Council (the 'Neddy') and the sectoral planning councils, the 'little Neddies', the TUC was gradually integrated into the planning process.

As part of the reform of the Labour Party the Wilson government embarked upon a plan to modernise the trades union structure. In its policy document, *In Place of Strife*,[1] the Labour leadership proposed a series of reforms of the labour movement which, unlike the Donovan

Report which preceded it, sought to impose penal clauses for violations of the code. These included an imposed 'cooling off' period in strikes and an imposed ballot of union members. The TUC strongly resisted the legal sanctions of the policy and produced their own counter-proposals enshrined in their 'Programme for Action'. The TUC, in fact, did not totally reject the underlying principles of *In Place of Strife* or the Commission on Industrial Relations created to pursue its aims (headed by George Woodcock): the TUC rejected the departure from voluntarism.

What was complicating and embittering an already difficult situation was the wage restraints imposed by the Labour government. Following the sterling crisis in 1966 the government had imposed a six-month wage freeze, followed by a further six months of severe restraint. After that year of restraint it was clear that a wages explosion was about to occur. The Labour government tried to head off this wages explosion by seeking to introduce a statutory incomes policy and to renew its lapsed Prices and Incomes legislation but it was unsuccessful. Many in the trades union movement saw *In Place of Strife* as yet another way in which the government sought to impose restraint on the trades unions. The tough treatment of the seamen's union in 1966 by Labour was cited as an example of what might become practice. The crisis was resolved when the government agreed to withdraw *In Place of Strife* in exchange for a 'solemn and binding' agreement with the TUC to exercise moderation and to proceed with internal reform which would relieve the burden of continuous wildcat and inter-union disputes which were endemic in British industry.

One result of the disruption and discord between the Labour Party and the TUC was the mobilisation of trades union dissent at the base. Britain has always had a militant Shop Stewards' Movement since the early days of the First World War; a Shop Stewards' Movement led by the organised communist unionists. At various periods of its existence it threatened to displace the regular union structure in some key industries. In most major industries in Britain the shop steward is in a position of great power and authority. Because of the nature of British industrial relations much of the responsibility which normally rests with national or regional unions rests instead with the rank-and-file unionists and their elected representatives, the shop stewards. These stewards are elected by the shopfloor members and are responsible to them, not to the union or its national leadership. Between the stewards and the national leadership there exists only a very fragmentary structure. Full-time national union officials put in long hours on TUC committee work,

Labour Party councils and a wide variety of civic obligations, leaving much of the day-to-day running of the union to the shop stewards. During the period of great upheaval on the Continent which spawned the Eurocommunist movements, the growing conflict between the rank-and-file unionists in Britain and their national union leaderships over the Labour Party's repeated calls for wage restraint drove a wedge between the union leaders and their memberships. The national union leaders and the TUC were constrained by their responsibilities to the Labour Party to follow a path of moderation and restraint. Their rank-and-file members felt less of a responsibility. They turned on the stewards who fought for acceptance of national union policy and voted in more militant stewards to press their claims for higher wages.

The workforce tended to blame their unions as much as the government for what it felt was a decline in their living standards. Moderate stewards were voted out of office. Left caucuses in many key unions took over control of their union's national executive. The small and traditionally moribund white-collar and public sector unions grew rapidly as workers sought the protection of militant unionism. The traditionally conservative bloc votes of the miners, railwaymen and textile workers were lost to the Labour Party as militants won greater power in these unions. Other 'regular party' unions like the AEU and the TGWU were split between militant and conservative factions.

The Heath victory for the Conservatives in 1970 did not improve British industrial relations, although a reform of that system was the cornerstone of its policy. The Industrial Relations Act of August 1971 made law much of what was initially suggested in the *In Place of Strife* proposals. It sought to replace voluntarism in industrial relations by a series of legal rights and sanctions. These included making collective bargains enforceable by law; making unions responsible under law for the actions of their members; limiting the right to strike as an effort to suppress wildcats; and, most importantly, giving the government the right to register and deregister unions and by so doing control their rights of recognition as the recognised bargaining agent in a particular company or industry. It was this latter point which caused the most heated public debate as the TUC and its unions refused to register under the terms of the Act. It is ironic that this proposal should have generated such a heated debate, as it was precisely the issue of forcing unions to register under legislative sanction with a government body which alienated so many of the unions which had formed within the British Empire against the TUC labour advisors sent down to the colonies as labour attachés to administer colonial registration procedures.

The root of the division between the unions and the government was not the penal clauses of the Act. The problem lay in its extension of the Labour Party's policy of wage restraint. Initially the Tories sought to control wages through a voluntary system following an 'invisible' norm. In 1971 wage rises were kept to 8 per cent while prices rose by a mere 5 per cent. It was only when the miners' national strike in 1972 broke the trend of restrained wage rises that the government imposed a statutory incomes policy. This policy was administered by a Pay Board and was scheduled to take place in three stages. The first two proved loose enough to permit sufficient flexibility so that individual cases, when justified, were permitted to exceed the norms. Stage three, however, sought to close these loopholes and generated much unrest.

The failure of the Heath government to work out a successful relationship with the trades unions was a result of two major factors. One was outside the government's control; the astonishing rise of world prices and the concomitant world-wide galloping inflation which resulted from the oil price escalations of 1973. The second was the government's misunderstanding of the political realities of British unionism. Throughout the first years of the Heath government the TUC, while strongly resisting the constraints imposed by the Industrial Relations Act, nevertheless co-operated in building a social contract with the Tories and worked hard to restrain wage rises. In March 1973, at their Special Congress, the TUC voiced its opposition to a continued social contract with the government which would only cover an incomes policy. The TUC proposed that an effective social contract should include price and rent controls, adequate protection for the low paid and the retired, and a major alteration in the British tax system. The Heath government was unable to deliver on these and the co-operation of the TUC was withdrawn.

What the Heath government refused to recognise was that the TUC, in its co-operation with the first stages of the incomes policy, had seriously lost contact with the rank-and-file unionists of Britain because of its agreement to pursue wage restraint, and had alienated some key national unions by its less than militant stance against the Industrial Relations Act. It was clear by at least the end of 1972 that the TUC would be unable to deliver its side of the social contract as long as the Heath government insisted on pursuing its effort to impose the restraints contained in the Industrial Relations Act. If the government modified the Act the TUC might well have been able to deliver the social contract. As it was the government made continued co-operation impossible. The militancy at the shopfloor level, especially in the wake of the miners' strike, put the lower levels of the union structure firmly in the hands of the shop stewards. National unions became even more unable to control their members. Militant shop stewards took over control.

What is most important about this strengthening of the shop stewards' power is not only the domestic effects of this politicisation of the lower levels of trades union organisation but also the effects they provoked within the development of Euro-unionism. These shop stewards were not only militant about wage bargaining, they were militant about a whole range of policies. They became active in the creation of parallel world councils and, under their predominantly communist leadership, played an important role in winning acceptance within European labour circles for the Eurocommunist unions.

Despite the statements of the Western European communist parties meeting in Brussels in 1974 that they opposed the development of the EEC and the commitment of the socialists and social democrats to its progress, the Eurocommunist unions declared themselves more in favour of a pan-European policy.

However, it has been precisely in the area of intra-European trades unionism that the struggle between the communist and non-communist forces have been enacted. Following the events of 1968 the Eurocommunists developed a dual strategy to compete with their opponents in the trades unions. The first was the development of the shop stewards' committees to rival the company councils of the ITSs. When this proved ineffective and quite costly a new tack was embarked upon. The Western European communist unions utilised the existing structures of the EEC and the support of the political forces within the EEC committees to win for them a place in Euro-unionism.

In 1968 there were still the three European trades union bodies active within the structure of the EEC: the ICFTU's ETUS; the CISC–EO; and the WFTU's Action Committee which had changed its name to the *Comité Permanent* in 1966 which co-ordinated the work of the CGT–CGIL liaison with the EEC. The *Comité* was still refused consultative status. Later in 1968 these three organisations were joined by a new organisation linking the national centres of the European Free Trade Area (EFTA): the EFTA–TUC. This EFTA–TUC linked the national centres of Britain, Norway, Sweden, Denmark and Austria in an organisation which was separate and independent of the ICFTU–ERO.

There were major changes within the Christian union structures as they sought to play a wider role in European affairs. Under the strong influence of the French CFDT the Christian international changed its name to the World Confederation of Labour (WCL) and deconfessionalised. With this change many of the Christian unions were accepted into membership of the ITSs and played an active role within the world company councils.

By 1969 pressure by the Italian and French governments had led to the admission into consultative status of the *Comité Permanent*, thus giving the CGT–CGIL (and the small Dutch and Luxembourg federations) a voice in the councils of the EEC. There was much less objection to permitting the CGIL into the work of the EEC by the non-communist unions as the CGIL had won the support of the CISL and UIL in Italy in their tripartite arrangements. The sticking point was the CGT whose domestic political role was so fundamentally opposed by the CFDT and the CGT–FO.

The hostility to the CGT came to the fore with the creation of a new union body out of the expanding ETUS. The ETUS changed itself into the European Confederation of Free Trades Unions in the Community (ECFTU), a body external to the ICFTU. The ECFTU changed its voting rules from consensus to a two-thirds majority, thus blocking the veto power of any affiliate. This opened the door to possible affiliation of new national centres from nations with one affiliate already represented in the ECFTU. In fact the first test came when the CGIL was permitted by the ECFTU to join a trades union co-ordinating committee handling questions under study by the EEC's Economic and Social Committee. The CGT was blocked from this committee by the votes of the DGB and the CGT–FO.

It was largely this type of opening offered to the CGIL and just barely avoided in the case of the CGT which persuaded the AFL–CIO to withdraw from the ICFTU and to concentrate on its work within the ITSs. The European emphasis on developing a stronger form of Euro-unionism got a fillip in 1973 when three new members were accepted into membership in the EEC: Britain, Ireland and Denmark. To varying degrees the national centres of these three nations began to try to play a role within the structure of the EEC. In 1973, on the accession of the three nations to the EEC, the three national centres were also accepted into membership in the ECFTU.

The ECFTU felt that the cause of European unity would be fostered by broadening its reach to include the members of the EFTA–TUC. In 1973 both organisations merged into a blanket European body, the European Trades Union Confederation (ETUC), headquartered in Brussels. Its initial membership was the seventeen ICFTU-affiliated unions from fifteen European nations.

The British TUC wanted to go even further. It requested that all European trade unions be allowed to affilate, including affiliates of the WCL and the WFTU. This was defeated by the DGB which didn't want WFTU affiliates permitted and by the Belgians and Dutch who were not keen on accepting WCL affiliates. The ties with the ICFTU, however, were broken. The ETUC was made separate and independent. Although the vote against mass affiliation of WCL and WFTU went against the British the principle was adopted that any national centre which could be shown to be European and democratic would be permitted to affiliate.

The CFDT began to explore the possibility of affiliation to the ETUC. Its application was viewed favourably. The CFDT pressured the WCL–EO to discuss a mass affiliation to the ETUC by threatening to affiliate on its own. After some heated discussions an Extraordinary Congress of the ETUC in Copenhagen in 1973 accepted the eight national members of the WCL–EO into membership (along with four other unions).

The affiliation of the WCL–EO unions to the ETUC was achieved amid some heated controversy. This was not because the ETUC national centres generally opposed the Christians but rather because they feared that this was the thin end of the wedge to get WFTU members accepted. The chief reason for this fear was the efforts then being made by Jack Jones of the TGWU and head of the TUC's International Committee to build organic links with the trades union national centres of Eastern Europe. Under his guidance a series of 'informal' meetings were held in July 1973 in Vienna and January 1974 in Geneva between European unionists and representatives of the AUCCTU and other WFTU affiliates.

The ICFTU and the ITSs strongly objected to these exchanges. They questioned the motives behind such meetings, primarily because the TUC were still boycotting all EEC meetings until after the 1975 referendum. Vic Feather was made president of the ETUC despite the fact that the TUC refused to participate in any EEC business. The other Europeans questioned why the TUC was willing to sit down with the Soviet, Hungarian, Czech and Bulgarian unions to discuss European unity but refused to participate in the EEC. The DGB was particularly opposed to these talks as they threatened the unity of a common European stance towards the important political struggles in Spain and Portugal. The AFL–CIO, as might be imagined, was less than happy.

The May 1974 meeting which sanctioned the affiliation of the WCL–EO to the ETUC also gave the ETUC's Executive Committee the right to decide on the applications for affiliation made by the CGIL and CGT. After some long debate, the CGIL was accepted into membership in the

ETUC in July 1974 by a vote of 21 for and 7 against. The principal opponent to the CGIL was the DGB which doubted that the CGIL had really disaffiliated from the WFTU and had accepted only 'associate' membership in the WFTU. More importantly the DGB warned that the acceptance of the CGIL into membership might serve as a Trojan horse to permit other communist unions (like the CGT or the East German FDGB) to win membership in the ETUC.

Jack Jones and the TUC continued to plan joint events with the WFTU. In Geneva in 1975 the TUC, the Soviet AUCCTU and the WFTU were joint hosts to an East–West Conference on the hazards of work and toxic substances under the aegis of the ILO. This was followed by an official visit to Britain by the head of the AUCCTU, Alexander Shelepin, former head of the KGB and a noted defender of workers' rights. The TUC sent fraternal delegations to the national centres of Hungary and Czechoslovakia, presumably to congratulate them on their rapid achievements after the unpleasant events of 1956 and 1968. These visits to both Hungary and Czechoslovakia irritated the other unions in the ICFTU and the WCL so much that they issued statements condemning the TUC visits and affirming their view that the unions of Hungary and Czechoslovakia were still instruments of the Soviet state and definitely not genuine labour organisations.

Undeterred, the TUC proceeded with further meetings with the WFTU. The TUC was host to the second ETUC congress in London in 1976. At that meeting the new strategy to circumvent the strength of the ITSs was made clear. The ETUC agreed to pursue two simultaneous plans. The first was the promotion of the European Works Council as envisioned in the EEC Green Paper on Industrial Democracy in the Community.[2] The second was the commitment of the ETUC to create six major industrial committees, identical to the ITSs, to explore a European response to the multinational corporation. In both plans, the object was more than creating just another set of committees; the aim was to circumvent the restrictiveness of the ITSs in keeping out communist unions, by building parallel Euro-unions in which communist unions would be permitted to function.

The first of these plans relates to the proposals made as early as 1970 to create a legal mechanism by which the EEC could grant a corporate charter to a European Company (for example, a company operating in more than one EEC nation). This European company charter would provide for the creation of a European Company subject to EEC rules. It will have a two-tier management structure composed of an administrative body and a supervisory board. Power within the supervisory board will be shared by management with representatives elected by the workers joined together within a European Works Council. This European works council will be created for every European company and will have consultative rights on the day-to-day management of the plants. It will have the right of free information exchange with the management and the right to choose its representatives from among the workers and unions within the European works council to serve as liaison with the European company's management.

In October 1972 the EEC Commission presented the Council with a further delineation of its intent in the 'Fifth Directive' which added to the concept of a European works council by including the creation of 'co-determination' or 'worker's participation in management' to be enjoyed by these European works councils. The Fifth Directive posited a strong representation of the European workers' representatives on the supervisory board of the European company (based on the system of co-determination which had developed in Germany along the original outlines of the Coal and Steel Community practice of worker–directors). A Green Paper further outlining these proposals was issued in 1976.

The political implications of these proposals for the ITSs were clear. If the EEC mandated a European Works Council based on the Fifth Directive the representatives of the workers chosen to sit on this works council need not necessarily be from the trades unions. Even more importantly, these elected representatives need not be from the unions with bargaining rights in the plants. In France, for example, the unions, because of their plant-level strength, might win the seats on the works council but could not keep out the representatives of the CGT whose plant-level strength was proportionately greater than the FO or the CFDT. The creation of a European Works Council opened a back door through which the CGT and the CGIL could walk to take up seats on the works council as well as on the supervisory boards of the company. In some plants where CGT or CGIL strength was high (as in the north Paris industrial belt or Italy's Red Belt) the non-communist unions could actually be excluded from representation on the European Works Council.

A further danger to the position of the non-communist unions of Europe was created by the development of the European Works Council structure when these unions realised that the strong communist national centres of Spain and Portugal could win recognition in elections to the works council against the socialist and Christian unions locked in battle with the communists for control of their national labour movements. This opportunity was equally apparent for the leftist unions of Greece on Greece's accession to EEC membership. Despite the recognition of the problem the ETUC unions felt that the Eurocommunist process had sufficiently transformed the communist unions into apparently democratic organisations as to permit their inclusion into their deliberations.

Even this major step towards integrating the Eurocommunists into the mainstream of European unionism was not sufficient for the ETUC. The ETUC was, after all, an organisation of national centres. Its actual role in industrial relations was very small and it spoke only tangentially for the needs and aspirations of the European working classes. The development of a European Company and its European Works Council was still far down the road. The ETUC accepted the needs of the Eurocommunists and the blandishments of the EEC committees to make a more positive step towards integrating the communist unions into the day-to-day workings of European unionism.

The ETUC mandated the formation of six industrial committees to further the sectoral integration of European industry. It established and sanctioned the development of union bodies parallel to the ITS structures within the context of European unity. There are six of these committees in operation: the European Metalworkers' Federation (EMF); the Trades Union Committee of the PTTI; the European Regional Organisation of the FIET (EURO–FIET); the European Federation of Agricultural Workers; the Metal and Mineworkers' Committee; and the European Committee of the Entertainment Secretariat. All six are part of the ETUC and are responsible to that body and not the ITSs whose activities they parallel and with whom they share many joint members.

These bodies are composed of members of the ITSs as well as unions which maintain membership in the WCL and the WFTU. A series of research institutes and training colleges for these Euro-unions have been set up by the ETUC and funded primarily by the EEC directly. Many ITSs have set up European regional organisations on their own, separate from these Euro-unions. The primary efforts by these Euro-unions has been to try to take over the right to speak on behalf of the workers of the transnationals operating in Europe and to dislodge the ITSs from their traditional role.

As might be expected these Euro-unions have opened the door to the leftist unions of Spain and Portugal and have undertaken low-level discussions with the unions of Eastern Europe with whom they participate in sectoral committees of the ILO. Their successes have been negligible largely because of the continuing strength of the ITSs themselves. The prime motivator of the EEC and the ETUC in promoting this Euro-unionism was not only to respond to the new developments of Eurocommunism. The main reason lay in their efforts to displace the strong role played by US and Canadian unions within the ITSs and the company councils. It is this strength which the EEC and the ETUC see as their major impediment to the building of a European trades union movement.

When the ETUC and its committees speak of European trades unionism they are speaking in the broadest sense of the word Europe. Throughout the ILO and the ETUC the development of a programme of European regionalism has meant the development of a movement which encompasses both Eastern and Western Europe. The term 'European regionalism' has become a code word for détente among the unions of Eastern and Western Europe. This might be attractive to the national centres but is has certainly proved less than attractive to the national sectoral unions competing with the communist unions for the loyalties and support of shopfloor unionists. Even less attractive to these sectoral unions are the attempts to force a divorce between them and their North American union colleagues. This struggle is a very important aspect of the development of Western European unionism and has been the catalyst for the return of the AFL-CIO to the ICFTU and the return of the US presence in the ILO.

This struggle to dislodge the North American unions from activity within the world company councils of the ITSs has not been very successful, essentially because the largest number of transnational corporations covered by these company councils are North American based. To show any real effectiveness within the council structures has required that the union representing workers in the parent company plays the major role in company council activity. Indeed, on a global scale, the percentages of unionists organised by European communist unions within the total global employment of the transnational corporation, even those whose parent company is in Europe, rarely exceeds 5 to 6 per cent. The ITSs really don't need the communists to be effective but the communists need the ITS's European membership to claim representivity in Europe. Unable to win this support on their own merits the communist unions used the support of their own political representatives within the EEC and their national centre representatives within the ETUC to create a Euro-structure in which this aim could be made possible. The fact that it hasn't as yet been achieved is no guarantee that it might not be achieved later.

Euro-unionism is a phenomenon which emerged from the gradual coalescence of three separate strands of political development. The first was the radical transformation of European corporate structures which led the unions to seek to build a countervailing power to the rise of transnational corporations. The second was the change in expectations and support at the base which challenged the Western European communist parties after the upheavals of 1968; changes which led to the growth of Eurocommunism. The third was the growing self-awareness of Europe as an independent Third Force between the superpowers which, through the development of common markets and common institutions, tried to bridge the gulf between East and West through the policies of détente. All three combined to shape a movement in which politics, rather than economics, played the most important role.

The focus of Euro-unionism has begun to shift in 1980 and 1981 as new stresses have grown between the forces of the Western European political movements and the Eurocommunists over issues as diverse as Spain, Portugal and Poland. The return of the AFL–CIO to a more active international role after the death of Meany and the increased polarisation of Europe as a result of the policies of the Reagan Administration have had an important effect on the state of Euro-unionism. With the growing European debate over the stationing of nuclear weapons by the US in Europe new coalitions of the centre and left in Europe are rebuilding the links between the communists and the allies they attracted during the days of anti-Vietnam activism. In Scandinavia, Holland, Britain and especially West Germany, communists and the factions of the ultra-left are joining together with the younger political activists within the student and trades union movements to build national coalitions which threaten the stability of NATO and also threaten the continued political control of the trades union movements by the forces of the centre–socialists and social democrats. There are signs that the growing strength of these unilateralist activists is causing major disruption within many of the TUC, DGB and FNV (Confederation of the Netherlands Trades Union Movement) unions and may damage the stability, unity and electoral credibility of the British Labour Party, the German SPD and the Dutch socialists.

The victory of the Greek socialists, the Pan-Hellenic Socialist Party (PASOK), in the recent Greek election may bring into the EEC union debates, and perhaps into the ETUC itself, the representatives of the Greek communists. There is already growing resistance by the DGB and others to the presence in the ranks of the Euro-unions of the Spanish and Italian communists. As domestic pressures grow within Europe over issues like nuclear power, nuclear disarmament and the continued acceptance by the socialist centre of the legitimacy of Eurocommunism, the future of Euro-unionism may dramatically alter.

The most serious rifts will likely be over the most dramatic changes which have developed as a result of the important changes in Eastern European unionism and the death of the Polish Solidarity union. Of all the contemporary problems facing international labour the reopening of contacts with Eastern European unionism has been the most promising for revitalising the Euro-union dialogue with the East.

10 Current Problems in International Labour

Perhaps the most significant development in the world of international labour in the past eight years has been the growth of dissident unionism and political dissent among the organised workers in Eastern Europe. This growth of dissident unionism in Eastern Europe has seen the emergence of dissident unions within and without national communist parties whose strengths pose the most serious challenge to continued communist domination of the nations of the Soviet bloc. There have been numerous political issues around which this new unionism has formed, but fundamental to this process has been a serious economic fact which has been an almost universal determinant of trades union behaviour world-wide. This economic fact which the trades unions of the world have had to face is the effective removal from the world economy of over fifty-six billion dollars of hard currency by the oil-producing nations. Concomitant to this has been the unprecedented rise in world energy costs.

What this has meant on a world scale has been generally high levels of inflation, high interest rates, economic recession within the nations of Europe and North America, a staggering rise in oil prices which has severely impeded development plans in the Third World and growing levels of unemployment and underemployment world-wide. What the international labour movements have been facing over the past eight years has been the challenges of dealing with scarcity. How these unions have faced the challenges of scarcity has largely determined the political structures and thrusts of these movements.

One of the areas most severely affected by this scarcity has been the nations of Eastern Europe. The deficits run by the nations of the Comecon (the Eastern European parallel to the EEC) with the West are enormous. From a total debt of ten billion dollars in 1973 the present total has risen to around fifty billion dollars, and repayment costs of these debts absorb a very high percentage of annual hard currency earnings. Bloc average net real income has risen very slowly, if at all, and net foreign trade losses have amounted to around four billion dollars annually. Western banks and the International Monetary Fund have arranged numerous meetings to help reschedule Comecon debt and have provided short-term credits to cover immediate shortfalls. This has been true even for those nations, the Soviet Union and Romania, with access to oil and natural gas deposits. The Romanians, for example, arranged in 1980 to borrow a further billion dollars from the International Monetary Fund to help pay its debts of over ten billion dollars. Even though Romania produces oil, it has a refinery capacity which is more than twice as large as its domestic production. It must purchase oil for its refineries from OPEC nations (about sixteen million tons a year). This leaves Romania with a net shortfall in its petroleum account of over one billion dollars to OPEC nations annually.

The high prices for petroleum and many of its derivatives (ethylene-based fertilisers, etc.) have had a severely debilitating effect on the agricultural sectors as well. In Romania, where more than 90 per cent of agriculture is collectivised, the nation regularly suffers shortfalls of grain production and the resultant decline in meat production soon after. Soviet harvests have been consistently low and, despite massive grain deals with North America and Argentina, its supply of meat has dwindled. Participation within the Comecon has not been as valuable as many Eastern bloc nations had hoped, primarily because the Soviet Union has declined to provide cheap energy on a large scale and, as was particularly the case in Poland, has used the credit facilities of the Eastern bloc to purchase capital goods in the West to assist in Soviet development plans.

The effects of these shortages on the working people of Eastern Europe has been a major factor in discouraging their continued willingness to accept limits on their political freedoms in exchange for a promise of a gradual rise in their living standards. In the immediate postwar world the sheer devastation of the economies of Eastern Europe and the presence of the Red Army had a dampening effect on political dissidence. Nonetheless, the East German and Polish risings of 1953, the Hungarian uprising in 1956, the radical restructuring of the Czech Communist Party in 1968 and the Polish strikes of 1970 and 1976, all had at their root the same fundamental rage and frustration by the workers towards the governments which could not deliver a rising standard of living. Eastern European workers were willing to make the best of living under a repressive system of government as long as their prosperity also improved. After 1973 no communist government could assure its people that improvements were certain to develop. It was after 1973 that dissident movements cautiously began to spread across Eastern Europe.

It would be wrong to assume a one-to-one relationship between political dissidence and economic stagnation. Political dissidence, religious dissidence and artistic and literary dissidence have existed within Eastern Europe in an unbroken chain for the past three centuries. What was vital to the expansion of the power of these dissident movements was their forging of strong links with those who were becoming disenchanted with the lack of economic growth and the opportunities which arose for them to co-operate on programmes of mutual interest and benefit. Just as left-wing political idealism and activism thrives when it finds roots among the peasants and workers in Latin America, Asia and Africa, anti-communist dissident movements grow in strength and stature when they make common cause with the economic victims of the communist system. The dissident movements of Eastern Europe began to make common cause with the workers in their nations aggravated by shortages, high prices and shoddy workmanship.

A second aspect of the development of the linkage between political dissidence in Eastern Europe and the growth of non-party or anti-party unionism was the fostering of an international awareness of the problems facing dissidents in Eastern Europe, through the creation of local committees to follow up on the proposals agreed at the human rights meeting in Helsinki. The committees created to monitor the Helsinki accords have publicised the activities of political dissidents and unionists throughout the world. The struggle for free trades unionism within Eastern Europe which had, until then, only been discussed in arcane journals and in translations from the clandestine *samizdat* network suddenly became world news.

The first of these efforts at promoting free trades unions emerged from the struggles within the Soviet Union itself. In November 1977 Vladimir Klebanov and five other workers called a press conference in a Moscow flat to announce the formation of an Association of Free Trades Unions of Workers in the USSR. These unionists represented some of the millions of workers within the Soviet Union who had, for a variety of reasons, been sentenced to prison in the Gulag, sent to psychiatric clinics for 'treatment', or demoted and blacklisted for trying to pursue what would have been considered genuine grievances elsewhere. Klebanov, himself, had attempted to form a union of miners in his native Donetsk region to press for higher wages and shorter working hours when his official union refused to support those demands. For his pains, Klebanov was sent to a psychiatric ward and then prison.

These dissident Soviet trades unionists petitioned the ILO to win recognition as a genuine trades union. The Soviet Union had, as had all of the nations of the Eastern bloc, agreed to uphold Artilcle 87 of the ILO which guarantees the right of free association. The ICFTU also petitioned the ILO for a hearing on the Soviet Union's refusal to abide by Article 87; a petition joined in by many ITSs and national centres. The representatives of the Soviet government denied that such an organisation existed. Klebanov was rearrested and sent back to the psychiatric wards.

The dissident unionists made common cause with the rising group of political dissidents and Jewish 'refuseniks' to form a broader union organisation, the Free Interprofessional Association of Workers (SMOT) which attempted to win recognition as a legitimate representative of Soviet workers. In August 1979 the KGB arrested its three most prominent members (Nikolai Nikitın, Vladimir Borisov and Albina Yakoreva) on a charge of hooliganism. A wave of protest against these arrests followed. Borisov had in fact been invited to the annual convention of the AFL–CIO but the authorities did not grant him a visa. Many Western trades unionists cancelled planned visits to the Soviet Union as a protest against the KGB's actions.

In Czechoslovakia the dissident group surrounding the Charter 77 movement included a strong trades union presence. Many of these unionists, when their efforts were reported in the West, were fired from their jobs. When protests were made to the ILO by the ICFTU and others in the West the Czech government issued a directive to its unions that Charter 77 was a subversive document and all its signatories should be expelled from the union movement. The government also decreed that there could be no appeals to the employment board.

In February 1979 the prominent Romanian dissident, Paul Goma, announced the formation of a free trades union in Romania under the leadership of Goma, Dr Ion Cana and Georghje Brasoveanu. Their union, the Romanian Workers' Free Union (SLOMR), has concentrated primarily on labour relations (poor wages, unsafe working conditions, inability to obtain safety equipment, etc.). The SLOMR has petitioned the ICFTU to be accepted as an affiliate. These pressures from the SLOMR on the government-sponsored unions led to a strong reaction from the government which declared the union 'traitorous' and jailed most of its leaders. Similar unrest is growing in Hungary where the seeds of free trades unions are spreading as the economic climate worsens and Hungarian workers are being laid off their jobs.

Behind all of this dissent and unrest lay the economic realities of shortages, long queues for foodstuffs, poor working conditions and rising levels of inflation. The workers were made to realise that despite their years of hardship, deprivation and political repression the communist system had failed to create a workable mechanism by which their material needs could be satisfied. They joined forces with the political dissidents to create a challenge to the whole communist system. This challenge reached its fullest expression in the growth of the Solidarity union in Poland.

Polish workers were no strangers to dissent. In the early 1950s and throughout the late 1970s Polish workers protested against rising food prices and shortages, often incurring severe penalties for their riots. In mid-1979 the Polish unions joined with the political dissidents in massive demonstrations against low wages, the unavailability of foodstuffs in the shops, the government's unilateral raising of key commodity prices and the repression of political dissent. They formed an Organising Committee for Free Trades Unions in Silesia and a free trades union committee (KOR) to keep up the momentum of the 1976 strikes. The KOR spokesman, Kazimierz Switon, was arrested and others in KOR were siezed and tried.

The arrest of the KOR dissidents had three important results. The first was the world-wide publicity which focused attention on the strife in Poland; the second was the increased repression by the government on the KOR which made its leaders less able to maintain their momentum; and the third was the shift of the dissident union movement away from the predominantly middle-class and intellectual leadership of the KOR to the shopfloor workers in the key sectors of the economy (mines, metalworking and shipbuilding). These Polish workers were unhappy with the economic situation and especially with their state-run unions which, under their party-appointed leaders, refused to speak out for the demands of the workers. The economy of Poland was in disarray.

With the assumption of power in 1970 by Gierek, Poland began a sustained period of heavy capital investment, financed largely by loans from the West and from the Soviet Union. Although wages rose rapidly as industry expanded, the supply of consumer goods did not keep pace with the increased discretionary incomes of the workers. Most high-quality items were to be found only on the black market where only the privileged few (primarily party members, high-level functionaries or those with access to hard currency) were able to participate. The workers who were not entitled by virtue of some special status to participate in the black market had to do without, despite having the funds available to make the purchases. Equally annoying was the profligate spending by the party functionaries, police and security forces on luxurious offices, private villas and similar items of personal consumption.

This rapid build-up of massive international debt led Gierek to attempt to put a brake on increased capital spending. In 1976 the party ordered an increase in consumer goods production and, to finance this, imposed an across-the-board 40 per cent increase in the state-controlled food prices. The workers revolted at this measure and, despite the police crackdown on protest strikers in Warsaw and Radom, the party rescinded the price increases. Along with the public demonstration in Warsaw and Radom there were widespread sit-down strikes throughout Poland, but especially in Silesia and the workshops along the Baltic coast. It was largely from among the ranks of these sit-down strikers that Solidarity drew its first members. The KOR formed soon after the 1976 food riots as an organisation composed primarily of intellectuals seeking to protect the legal and social rights of the strikers. Jacek Kuron, a founding member of the KOR, became an important link between the two parallel protest organisations. He was later to become an advisor to Solidarity.

Between 1976 and 1980 the economic situation in Poland did not improve. There were increasing shortages of consumer goods and, most importantly, food. Polish agriculture has been in a parlous state since the late 1950s. More than three-quarters of Polish farm land remains in private hands. It is tilled by peasants. There are about three million separate farms. Capital equipment has been in very short supply; rural credit is unavailable; and fertiliser prices have skyrocketed. This has been as much the result of party policy as it has been the result of lack of funds. The party, in its efforts to collectivise Polish agriculture, has used its powers of capital rationing to persuade the peasants to release their lands to the state. As a result Polish agriculture has been woefully undercapitalised and inefficient. The response of the peasants to the demands of the state and party has been to produce even less than before. They retreated to virtual subsistence farming. The need to import ever greater quantities of food has placed a terrible burden on the Polish economy and has led to widespread shortages in the markets and shops. As a result of the 1976 strikes the government felt unable to raise the national food prices to a level consonant with the prices it had to pay for supply and so ran an ever increasing deficit on foodstuffs.

Two more events played an important role in creating a situation in which the Solidarity movement could thrive. The first was the accession of a prominent Polish Catholic activist to the Papacy. Poland has been a staunchly Catholic nation for hundreds of years. The links between the Church and the Communist Party have been strained many times in the past when the party has tried to replace the Church's hold on the Polish people with its own ideology. This has been an uphill task. Polish Catholicism has been the guardian of Polish nationalism and the two have developed an unusually deep syncretic relationship. With Pope John Paul II in Rome Polish Catholicism flowered. Key Church leaders felt they could speak out more boldly about the temporal problems of their followers. The Church gave its support to the workers' movemens then starting to mobilise.

A second event, which was less well publicised, was the food strikes within the Soviet Union in the late 1970s, where whole towns and villages made known their protests to the authorities that key foodstuffs were in short supply and, in some cases, unavailable. Usually these food strikes were dealt with by the soldiers and the KGB with the subtlety for which they are famous. However, in Novosibirsk there was a new development. Owing to severe food shortages there was what amounted to a general strike. The threat of sending in the soldiers and police did not work. The authorities capitulated. They declared Novosibirsk a 'Hero City': a title which not only confers honour upon the city but also entitles it to better rations. Foodstuffs were shipped into Novosibirsk and the strike ended. The ripples from that event spread across the Soviet Union and Eastern Europe. The Soviet system had capitulated to food strikers. Soon others tried to achieve the same result.

All these factors combined in August 1980 into sit-in strikes in Poland against the authorities' renewed attempt to raise food prices. These strikes were widespread but had as their central focus the Lenin Shipyards in Gdansk where militant workers had seized control of their plant. They held out against tremendous pressure and won a negotiated agreement with the authorities on a twenty-one point programme. Point number one was the right for these unionists to form their own trades unions, free from party control. Point number two guaranteed the workers' right to strike. Other points covered a variety of reforms in the Polish economy and improved working conditions. Perhaps the most important point (after the right to form free unions) was point four in which the civil liberties of those people who were sacked after the strikes in 1970 and 1976 were restored and students who were excluded from institutes of higher education because of their political beliefs were reinstated. Political prisoners were released and those responsible for the repressions of 1970 and 1976 were to be publicly named and punished. The government agreed to all the points and the strike ended. Gierek was dismissed and disgraced to be replaced, for a short while, by Kania until he, too, was replaced by General Jaruzelski.

The first year of Solidarity's existence was hectic. Solidarity grew amid wide international press coverage and under the continuing threat of Soviet intervention along the lines of Czechoslovakia and Hungary. Matters reached fever pitch during Solidarity's first annual convention in July 1981 when the union voted a special message to the 'working class people of Eastern Europe and the Soviet Union' offering them Solidarity's support in forming free trades unions of their own.[1] Solidarity leaders reported that strikes within the Soviet Union in favour of free trades unions had taken place in early 1981 and that there had been unofficial contacts between Solidarity and some Hungarian unions as well as some Czech unionists.

Solidarity and its leaders soon became popular folk heroes in the world's press; with none more famous than Lech Walesa, Solidarity's leader. Walesa and his comrades travelled the world, speaking at hundreds of labour gatherings, at the ILO, and to the Pope in Rome. Solidarity established links with the global internationals and the ITSs. A tentative agreement to affiliate Solidarity to the WCL was made and several ITSs established close contacts with Solidarity's sectoral unions. As Solidarity grew in strength within Poland it also grew in its popularity with the non-communist international labour movement.

One of Solidarity's main problems was that although it claimed to be only a trades union, its adherents and supporters viewed it as much more than a union. It became the vehicle for the full range of social idealism and reform within Poland, including in its midst those with widely differing ambitions as to the future constitution of the Polish state and its relationships with its Comecon partners. It became, inexorably, a political movement; a political movement which rivalled the paramountcy of the Polish Communist Party. A central feature of this expansion was the close links between Solidarity and the Polish Church. Throughout Poland's sad and turbulent history the Polish Church has been the custodian of Polish nationalism and has imbued that nationalism with a piety and sanctity which differentiates it from other nationalisms. The mantle of Polish nationalism assumed by Solidarity as a result of the close linkage between itself and the church leaders was both a strength and a severe weakness for the Solidarity movement. Piety, nationalism and dedication are tremendous mobilisers of social opinion, especially when they are fuelled by a justifiable resentment at patent injustice and incompetence. These emotions gathered together a broad spectrum of dissent, the diversity of whose aims were often contradictory or mutually exclusive. Furthermore, when these policies were couched in the highly emotive language of sacrosanct nationalism, compromise became almost impossible.

These cracks were evident in Solidarity very early and were exacerbated by the logistical problems which confronted the union. Solidarity, in addition to its lack of resources (printing presses, paper, ink, etc.) found itself without any effective means of bringing about central control. In a communist state like Poland, virtually all communications media are in the hands of the state. There are no private telecommunications networks, no private radio or television stations, and certainly no newspaper or journals not subject to government scrutiny. In order for Solidarity to communicate with its regional bodies it had to circulate mimeographed orders or make visits. This meant that communications were often slow, unclear and subject to government intervention. Originally, Solidarity was created to be a blanket organisation to co-ordinate the trades union initiatives of Interfactory Strike Committees (MKS) organised along the Polish *Wojewodztwo* (regional authority) boundaries. What emerged was an essentially regional autonomy for the separate components of Solidarity; a type of autonomy which allowed widely differing leaderships and policies to develop, all of which were put forward in the name of Solidarity.

What developed over the first year of Solidarity's existence was the creation of virtually autonomous regional organisations with local spokespersons, each of whom put forth their ideas as that of Solidarity as a whole. One in particular, Andrzej Gwiazda, became deputy chairman of Solidarity and took a far more radical political line than Walesa. Even further away from Solidarity's main political line were people like Jan Rulewski, who demanded that Poland should withdraw from the Warsaw Pact. At the Second Congress the deliberations began with a strident criticism of Walesa for moderating Solidarity's demands and his agreeing to a watering-down of the proposals to immediately bring about workers' self-management by which the workers would vote for their managers. The delegates proposed a thirty-four point programme including the creation of an independent judiciary, free news media, increasing private enterprise and a constitutional revision which would put Poland's second chamber in the hands of the workers. Even more newsworthy was Solidarity's call, proposed by Gwiazda, that the workers in Eastern Europe be encouraged to form Solidarity unions of their own. Later, the delegates voted for free elections to parliament and local legislative bodies. Walesa was challenged for leadership of Solidarity by Gwiazda, Rulewski and Marian Jurczyk but won with 55 per cent of the votes cast.

Yet another divisive element emerged during Solidarity's first year when the peasant workers demanded, and won, the right to form a 'Rural Solidarity' organisation of their own. Despite the political co-operation between the two Solidaritys their economic interests diverged. While Rural Solidarity sought higher prices for food and greater capital investment in rural areas, the Solidarity union sought to maintain current food prices and to restructure Polish industry. On some issues the two organisations were on opposite sides. Yet, despite all these internal problems and the chaos of the Polish economy which both created and sustained Solidarity, the fundamental problem lay elsewhere. It lay with the inability of the Polish Communist Party to achieve a viable economic or political system in Poland.

The takeover of the Communist Party apparatus by General Jaruzelski, and his purge of the civilian communist leaders (and indeed their public trials), marked the end of decades of party failure to deal with the economic and social woes of Poland. Despite the presence of Soviet and other Warsaw Pact troops in Poland, the party was unable to claim the loyalties of the bulk of the nation. This was less a result of any abstruse ideological fixation on liberty than it was a reaction to long queues for life's necessities. The party failed to perform. When Solidarity emerged and took root in Polish factories, shops and offices the advantages and perquisites which accrued to membership in the Polish Communist Party disappeared proportionately to Solidarity's growth. Whereas it used to be an advantage to be accepted as a party member (which gave one special rights, special consumption privileges, special holiday resorts and special electoral advantages), the rise of Solidarity made close identification with the party positively unattractive to factory workers. The party began to lose members.

When Jaruzelski took over as Prime Minister he had already installed military comrades in key political posts throughout Poland. In fact the military had placed military teams in more than two thousand Polish villages and towns, ostensibly to help them through the harsh winter. The party was being replaced by the only functioning Polish national institution, the military. Jaruzelski's assumption of the prime ministership and chairmanship of the party marked the end of civilian control of the Polish state and raised the problem of what Marx called 'bonapartism' in which the military and political roles become blurred. The stage was set for confrontation and Solidarity wasted no time in providing it.

Solidarity's successful one-hour general strike was met by a parliamentary resolution calling for the end to all strikes. Solidarity found itself trying to suppress wildcat strikes which spread across Poland as each region and local body decided to make its own protest to the continuing economic decline of Poland.

Lech Walesa rushed to Zielona Gora to try to contain a massive wildcat. In Szczecin over 40 000 construction workers walked off their jobs, followed by 120 000 more at Tarnobrzeg. Walesa failed to quell the wildcat at Zielona Gora or at the textile plants in Zyradow. Jaruzelski declared that Solidarity had gone out of control; not control by him but out of control of its leadership. The government began to take action against the militants, publishing a list of fifty-seven 'detainees' and sending in troops to oust strikers occupying a school. On 12 December 1981 at midnight, the government imposed martial law on Poland and imprisoned or 'detained' Solidarity's leaders.

Within weeks all protest was stifled within Poland except for sporadic and unco-ordinated pamphleteering by those Solidarity leaders who had avoided capture. The demise of Solidarity had dramatic repercussions within the nation and in the international communist movement. Within Poland, the first reaction, after the news had sunk in and people had adjusted to 400 per cent price rises imposed by Jaruzelski, was to leave the communist party in droves. In many factories large bins were placed for workers to throw away their party membership cards. Membership in the party dropped to a tiny fraction. The party, in effect, ceased to exist in Poland except in the central committee and politburo in Warsaw. It became impossible to hold regional, city or local party meetings. The army became the party. There are now no civilian leaders with sufficient national stature or support to whom the military can relinquish power. Even if the Soviet Union wished to restore civilian rule in Poland there is no one to whom they can delegate this power. They must deal with Jaruzelski.

Internationally the problems were even more complex. As might be expected the Polish moves evoked a massive outpouring of protest from the West. Some nations, under the lead of the US, called for immediate economic sanctions. Many US allies in Western Europe were reluctant to jeopardise their strong East–West trade links and declined to follow the US example. The attractions of a massive gas pipeline from the Soviet Union exceeded their moral outrage at the destruction of Solidarity. Even more, their bankers feared default on their loans if too much pressure was exerted against Poland or her eastern neighbours. One of the banks to whom the Poles were the most heavily indebted was the West German *Bank für Gemeinwirtschaft* (the trades union bank). Sanctions, such as they were, had only a marginal effect on Poland.

The most telling effect of the Polish intervention was on the Eurocommunist parties. Except for the French party, most Western European parties came out strongly against the destruction of Solidarity. None came out more strongly against the Soviets and the Poles than the Italian party whose leader, Enrico Berlinguer, condemned the 'force and repression' used by the Polish martial law authorities and blamed the Russians for compelling the Poles to act in that way. The Spanish party echoed these sentiments. Only the French party, which had been able to win four Cabinet places in the Mitterand Socialist Government, continued to defend the Russian role in Poland and congratulated the Poles for their destruction of Solidarity. The doglike devotion of Mr Marchais to the Soviet party line won him re-election as secretary–general of the party but cost the party a lot of support amongst trades unionists. Over 5000 CGT members defied their union to march in support of a demonstration in favour of Solidarity. Six CGT national federations declared their support for the Polish workers. They were joined by the top fifteen CGT lawyers. In the period following the Polish action the CGT has lost enormous amounts of support in shopfloor elections. This mirrors the tremendous drop-off in national support for the PCF. Party membership has dropped below 200 000 and the party daily has curtailed publishing and has laid off numerous journalists. The Polish affair has plunged the French party further into disarray.

The spread of free trades unionism throughout the rest of Eastern Europe was also impaired by this crackdown. Ironically, one of the key supports for Eastern Europe has been the Western banks and transnational corporations.

The growth and expansion of the transnational corporations within the framework of the Western economies and the Third World was not matched on a similar scale in their interactions with Eastern Europe. The nations of the COMECON (Council for Mutual Economic Aid) presented at least two key impediments to their integration into the world of the transnationals. One of the first problems was the highly artificial currency structure of the COMECON, in which a notional value was placed on a basket of non-convertible currencies, making prices, costs and values a very arbitrary exercise. The second major barrier was the restrictions imposed on a foreign corporation setting up a productive facility within the nations of Eastern Europe and the prohibitions against these foreign corporations either free-purchasing the necessary resources within these economies or having free access to their domestic markets. To overcome these barriers the transnational corporations and their bankers created a variety of alternatives to standard patterns of foreign commerce.

One of the first of these alternative strategies was the creation of large barter deals under which Western exports to Eastern Europe were financed, at previously arranged terms, by 'counter-purchases' of Eastern European exports. Perhaps the most famous of these deals was the sale of *Pepsi-Cola* in the Soviet Union in exchange for Russian vodka to be sold in the West. Chip Levinson's seminal study on East–West trade, *Vodka–Cola*, took its title from this pioneering transaction. These transactions, however innovative politically, were not an atypical response to dealing with nations with non-convertible or blocked currencies. What was unusual was the creation of later counter-purchase transactions in which component parts were made the subject of the purchase. In the auto industry, for example, the concomitant growth of licensing by Western automotive transnationals (such as FIAT, Renault and BMW) of productive facilities to Eastern European state corporations was paid for, in part, by the barter of components for inclusion in Western European production.

Particularly vulnerable to this type of counter-purchase arrangement have been the Western European producers of polyvinyl chloride products and synthetic fibres. In a recent ICF study statistics were revealed that over 7 per cent of the Western European market for polyvinyl chloride was filled from chemical plants built in Eastern Europe by Western chemical transnationals. These transnationals were able to market these products in the West since they received them as part of their buy-back arrangements made with Eastern European state trading companies in exchange for the capital investment and the technology transfer which made them possible. Even more sophisticated forms of co-production, cross-licensing and leasing are announced every day. While interesting to observe from a political and economic vantage point, the effects of these developments on European trades unionism have been less academic.

For many Western European unionists, the threats to their jobs and future job opportunities from the East have become severe indeed. The Western European car market has been invaded, not only by the Japanese, but also by the Eastern European car makers who sell Eastern European-produced FIATs (Lada, Zastrava, Polski FIAT, etc.) in the West at prices well below those of their competitors. Similar disemployment has arisen less visibly in the component business. The slump in the synthetic fibre business and the plastics industries has not caused restricted supply on the world's market, largely because of increased manufacture in the Eastern European plants of the same transnationals laying off workers in the West. The Scandinavian lumber and furniture industries have largely been subcontracted to Polish and other Baltic producers.

It is a little ironic that the first major victims of this transfer of job opportunities to the East were the Italian metalworkers united under the CGIL banner in the FIAT complex in Turin. While the Soviet authorities were praising Professor Valetta of FIAT for his creation of a massive Soviet FIAT complex at Togliattigrad, the unionists were locked in battle with Valetta for his hostile attitudes to the demands of the Italian unions for improved wages and working conditions in Italy. Now foreign-made FIATs threaten Italian jobs.

This penetration of Eastern Europe by the transnational corporations was undertaken largely because of two factors. On the one hand was the existence of a very large Eastern European market for the products of the transnationals as well as important sources of natural resources. On the other was a vast pool of docile and cheap labour strictly disciplined by their trades unions. It is not too surprising that the production of chemicals and plastics has been among the first of the international industries to move into Eastern Europe. A major factor in the siting and staffing of plants manufacturing substances like polyvinyl chloride or viscose yarn is the willingness of the workforce and the local public health officials to suffer prolonged exposures to the carcinogenic substances used in their manufacture. The growth of awareness of the health consequences and environmental implications of carcinogenic, teratogenic and mutagenic exposures in chemical productive processes by the trades union and environmental protection movements has precipitated a wholesale flight of these industries to Eastern Europe and the Third World.

This movement of the Vodka–Cola corporations into Eastern Europe has created numerous problems and opportunities for the trades unions in the West. In addition to the disemployment effects of these moves, both in terms of the current decrease in jobs as well as the future losses in employment likely to result from the transnationals' inclination to run down their existing plants in the West in favour of their newer plants in the East, these activities have made for closer co-operation between Western trades union movements and their governments in an effort to promote free unionism in Eastern Europe. It is clearly in the interests of Western governments to see the growth of free unionism within Eastern Europe, not only as a political ideal, but also for the practical reason that it tends to raise the costs of items sold by the East and subsidised by Eastern European governments while diminishing the attraction for further transnational corporate penetration of these markets. For the trades unions as well there is a real payoff in terms of job opportunities in building free unions in the East; unions which can press for higher wages, safer working conditions and shorter hours in Eastern European industry.

The building of Euro-unionism on a pan-European scale is a two-edged sword for the Russians and the Eastern European state unions. It gives them access to non-communist unions in the West but it also gives Eastern European unions access to the Western unions representing the transnationals from whom they learn about health conditions, methods of organising and the whole variety of trades union activities denied to Eastern European unions. Contact between the unions of the West and the East, as happened in Czechoslovakia in 1968 or in Poland in 1980, is not without risk for the communist governments of the East.

The increased activity in building bridges between Eastern and Western European unions is likely to cause further unrest in Eastern Europe, especially in nations in which free trades unionism is struggling to emerge. This is the most challenging feature of Eastern European dissident unionism and the one that offers the most fruitful field for international activity in that it need not necessarily be conducted as a political activity. There are a sufficiently impelling series of economic reforms to be undertaken by the unions of Eastern Europe in concert with unions in the West as to make this co-operation on the level of the transnationals difficult to prevent. The economic and political consequences will play an important role in the shaping of trades unionism in the nations of Eastern Europe.

The interaction between the forces of the East and the West in the trades union sphere have not been limited to only the creation of free unions in the nations of Eastern Europe. This conflict and competition has been most intense in the struggle for democracy and free trades unionism in Western Europe itself in the battles for the control of the Spanish and Portuguese trades union movements and, through them, the struggle for the control of Spain and Portugal. This is a continuing struggle.

The search for a stable Spanish government within a system of democratic pluralism has been influenced to a very high degree by the fight for the control of the Spanish trades union movement by the opposing socialist and communist forces. The Spanish socialists (PSOE) have had a long history of involvement in national government in Spain. Since its origins in 1879 the PSOE has been a workers' party which drew its support almost entirely from the ranks of the powerful General Workers' Union (UGT) and the intellectual community. In the elections for the Popular Front government in 1936 the PSOE won just under 20 per cent of the seats. The Spanish communist party (PCE), formed from a split in the PSOE in response to the formation of the Comintern in 1920, was much weaker nationally and its tiny trades union base, the United General Workers' Confederation (CGTU), was forced to merge itself into the UGT after attempting a futile revolutionary strike in 1934. In the Popular Front elections in 1936 the PCE won less than 3 per cent of the seats.

During the civil war which followed the creation of the Popular Front the socialists were deprived of resources and support in their war effort against Franco's armies by the nations of the West who took a hands-off policy towards Spain, and by the Soviet Union which threw its support to the PCE after the socialist and anarchist unions and military forces had been largely shattered. The Spanish Republican army and the International Brigades were placed in the hands of communist political commissars who gradually took over the controls of all levels of Republican administration. Interestingly, they undertook to follow a far more moderate policy than the PSOE and its anarchist allies, especially in reversing the process of collectivisation begun by the PSOE–CGT leader, Largo Caballero. The PCE and their foreign communist advisors became locked in a battle for the control of the Republic in a struggle which almost matched in intensity the battle raging with Franco.

The end of the Spanish Civil War in 1939 left the socialists and the anarchists in total disarray. The communists, although the victims of the Franco purges of the vestiges of the republic, tended to fare better than their allies largely as a result of the Hitler–Stalin Pact which won a grudging toleration of the communists by even such staunch Fascists as Franco. The two sections of the Spanish left split into a socialist–anarchist group and a communist group. With the severe repression of the left in the 1940s and 1950s the only presence within Spain of these two groups remained in their trades union organisations. The socialists in the underground UGT attempted a general strike in 1947 which failed, and similar strikes in 1951, 1953 and 1956. These strikes by the clandestine UGT were severely dealt with by Franco. In 1951 the strike leaders were executed; in 1953 the UGT's general secretary died from torture which he underwent in police custody.

The PCE re-established itself in Paris and Toulouse after the Second World War under the tight control of the Soviet communist party. It was a staunchly Stalinist party under the leadership of Dolores Ibarruri who had survived the war, as had most of the PCE leaders, by fleeing to Moscow. Unlike the socialists and anarchists who chose to fight on underground in Spain through trades union militancy, the PCE decided that its interests would be best served in the long run in Spain by infiltrating the corporate union structures which Franco and his Falange had created within Spanish industry. These Workers' Commissions (CCOO) were successfully infiltrated by the PCE and, after the 1957 trades union elections, became the PCE base inside Spain.

The PCE recognised that at some time in the future it would have to make an effort to attract the support of the socialists and anarchists in order to win effective national power, but as long as Franco lived there was no hurry. The PCE began to shift away from its Stalinist ideology gradually, following the takeover of the PCE by Santiago Carrillo in 1960. This shift was due partly to the ideological attractions of Eurocommunism, but more directly to the conflicts which arose within the PCE over the heavy hand of the Soviet Union in internal Spanish affairs. In October 1961 the PCE embarked upon a major campaign to remove the US bases in Spain and to prevent Spain's association with the EEC. The socialists supported Spain's bid to join the EEC in the hope that real political concessions would be the price of Spain's entry. The PCE was isolated on this issue. Similarly the party suffered when one of its clandestine central committee members, Julian Grimau, was arrested by Franco and executed. Many in the party felt that Grimau had been betrayed to the police by Santiago Carrillo to create a martyr on the orders of the Soviets who wanted a *'cause célèbre'* to ensure that Western revulsion at Grimau's execution would block Spain's accession to NATO and the EEC.

The PCE shifted its line in 1964. After expelling Fernando Claudin and Jorge Semprun for revisionism, Carrillo adopted their ideas and became a devoted Eurocommunist. In 1968 the PCE supported the Dubcek government in Czechoslovakia and publicly allied itself with Italian Eurocommunism. The PCE allied itself with the Spanish efforts to join the EEC and tried to use its Eurocommunist stance to win it allies within the Spanish left. It was less than totally successful as the socialists, anarchists and Christian democrats sought to maintain their underground strength in the trades unions. These attacked the communists for their collaboration with the Francoists in the state syndicates and refused to participate in elections to these vertical unions.

Like their Italian counterparts the PCE drew upon the lessons of the fate of Salvador Allende in Chile and decided that power could be won only through a 'historic compromise' with the existing powers of the state. They rejected the 'left alternative' and sought to win acceptance from the government rather than from the parties of the left. Following the unexpected admission of the Portuguese Communist Party (PCP) into the government after the fall of Caetano, the PCE euphorically announced the formation of a Democratic Junta for Spain. Ostensibly it joined some small social democratic parties and some businessmen in an alliance with the communists, but most felt it was basically a front for the political aspirations of the PCE. This Democratic Junta was opposed by the PSOE and the Christian democrats within Spain and by a major international coalition of political forces dedicated to preventing Spain from going the way of Portugal when Franco died.

The means by which support was channelled into Spain were the trades union movements. The DGB, the Swedish LO and many socialist and social democratic unions made available to the PSOE large sums of money to assist them in organising strong unions within Spanish industry. Benefiting from the presence of large numbers of expatriate Spanish workers in their nations and their trades unions the German unions, among others, began to prepare the way for a socialist presence in Spanish unionism when Franco died. The Christian unions of Europe also sent aid and assistance to the Christian trades union centre operating clandestinely inside Spain. Felipe Gonzalez, a young lawyer who had won recognition for his spirited defence of Spanish unionists, was elected head of the PSOE. This bridged the generation gap which had plagued the PSOE and the conflict between the exiled and internal wings of Spanish socialism.

On the other hand the PCE was aided by the Italian communist party and many of the other Eurocommunist parties and unions. After the death of Franco the communist unions in France, Italy, Great Britain and the left factions other European national centres sent down funds and organisers to Spain to assist the PCE and its CCOO unions. There were many multinational companies whose key shop stewards took their holidays in Spain as guests of the CCOO organisations. With the death of Franco in November 1975 and the installation of a new government under Juan Carlos the competition between the two groups was intense. Although the raid on the communist unionist meeting in June 1972 had captured the top leadership of the CCOO (including Marcelino Camacho, Francisco Garcia Salve and Nicolas Sartorius) the communist strength in the CCOO remained strong.

The hostile relations between the Democratic Junta and the *'Plataforma de Convergencia'* coalition led by the PSOE were made even more difficult by the struggles which broke out over the control of the labour movement. In December 1975 the PCE instructed its labour allies in the CCOO to undertake a series of *journadas de lucha* (days of struggle), a euphemism for mass mobilisations of workers by the party; particularly in the metalworking, transport and construction industries. At the height of this campaign in January and February 1976 these days of struggle involved well over a quarter of a million workers in Madrid alone and brought Madrid, Barcelona and other cities to a virtual standstill. The troops were called out to restore order in the public sector (mail, underground transport, municipal employees).

Even though the government tried to exploit the differences between the Democratic Junta and the *Plataforma* (which had united under the common banner of the *'Coordinacion Democratica'* in mid-1976), the right-wing intransigence of the Arias regime played into the hands of the PCE by making an alliance between the right and the moderates virtually impossible. Once again these problems focused on the labour movement. Throughout Spain the communists were active in winning control of local factory assemblies. As early as December 1975 Marcelino Camacho had pressed for general trades union unity within the structure of the CCOOs but the UGT, the Christian USO, the Basque STV and the remnants of the anarchist *Confederacion Nacional de Trabajadores* (CNT) refused. Competition among them, fuelled by support from outside Spain, kept them apart. In July 1976 a clandestine conference in Barcelona created a Coordination of Syndical Organisations (COS) with Marcelino Camacho as its head. Twenty of the twenty-seven members of the COS officials were PCE members. An indiscreet interview with Camacho on Radio Moscow raised questions about the COS's autonomy.

Despite the strength of the PCE within the CCOOs and the legalisation of the PCE, it was unable to muster more than twenty seats in the 1977 General Election (as compared to the 165 seats of the Christian Democrats or the 118 seats of the PSOE). With the PSOE as the main opposition party the PCE was effectively locked out of a major role in the determination of government policy. It tried to win power through the unions. The PCE, through the COS, tried to get the workers' commissions recognised as the sole union body, but Felipe Gonzalez threatened to pull out of the *Coordinacion* and the PCE was forced to dissolve the COS. Nonetheless the PCE remains strong within the trades unions. In the trades union elections of 1978 the CCOO won

35.8 per cent of the seats, compared to the UGT's 22.7 per cent. These results did not reflect the growth in support of the UGT in the major industries because the government, in its efforts to weaken the PSOE (which was its effective opposition party), juggled the rules of the election. It created two categories of delegates to the factory councils ('non-affiliated' and 'independent') which sufficiently clouded the loyalties of these delegates as to minimise the strong support given to the UGT.

This battle for control of the Spanish unions absorbed an enormous amount of manpower and resources of the international trades union movement, East and West. This struggle is still continuing as is the parallel battle for the control of the Portuguese trades unions.

The political development of Portugal remained essentially moribund for a period of thirty-five years. Under the *Estado Novo* of Antonio de Oliveira Salazar who took over power in Portugal in 1932 and promulgated the Portuguese constitution in 1933, Portugal was ruled with a heavy hand. Salazar created a highly authoritarian corporate state which guaranteed stability but not political liberty. Portugal was designed both politically and economically as a bulwark against modernisation. Elections were held periodically for a president and a National Assembly but without political parties. The only official organisation, the National Union (later the Popular National Action), was a movement rather than a party.

Industry and unions were organised on the corporative, vertical model and were part of the state administrative system. The main facet of national life through which Portugal interacted with the rest of the world was that of the Portuguese military in assisting the West by providing vital bases in the Azores and in antagonising the Third World through its colonial policies in Angola, Mozambique and Guinea. This grew ever more serious as colonial wars broke out in these Portuguese colonies after 1961.

It was largely these colonial wars which radically altered Portuguese politics. Faced by the enormous costs of these wars Salazar was forced to open up Portugal to foreign investment; an investment which grew dramatically and soon exceeded Portugal's ability to service its debts. If it were not for the remittances made to Portugal by its major export, Portuguese labour, Portugal would have been in an even worse state. Inflation reached high levels in Portugal even before the oil crisis of 1973. In the first quarter of 1974 inflation in Portugal reached an annual rate of 63 per cent. Salazar, who had suffered a stroke in 1968, had been succeeded in power by Marcelo Caetano who tried to continue Salazar's policies but proved unable to solve the difficulties of Portugal's economy and incapable of resolving the debilitating colonial wars.

Key elements in the military grew increasingly restive. An abortive rightist coup in 1973 threatened to topple Caetano but support from the military as a whole was not forthcoming. The catalyst for the military coup which did oust Caetano was the government's attempt to pack the officer corps with large numbers of new officers appointed from the universities under Law 353. This, coupled with the military's fear that it would be made the scapegoat for the disastrous military performances in Africa precipitated a military coup in April 1974. This coup was led by the Armed Forces Movement (MFA). It announced its programme to the nation; a programme which was designed to destroy the old regime and to foster modernisation. It envisioned a minor role for the army and an end to the colonial wars. Its leaders were politically naive and, with the exception of Major Melo Antunes and Commander Victor Crespo, had had virtually no contact with organised politics.

The only political organisation within Portugal at the time of the coup with any real national structure was the Portuguese Communist Party (PCP); and this was true only because of the continued interaction between the party and its trades union adherents during the Salazar years. At the time of the passage of the Corporative Constitution and its accompanying Labour Law (which banned strikes and independent unions) there were already some anarcho-syndicalist and communist unions established in existence in Portugal. In 1934 these fragmentary unions joined together in an attempted general strike against the Salazar government and its repressive legislation. The National Republican Guard put down the strike with great brutality. The anarcho-syndicalists were virtually wiped out, leaving the communist remnants as the only inheritors of the mantle of anti-Salazar unionism. The persecution of the PCP and its leaders over the years by the Portuguese secret police (PIDE) led to wholesale arrests and their incarceration in the special political concentration camp of Tarrafal in the Cape Verde islands. The present leader of the PCP, Alvaro Cunhal, was a graduate of the PIDE re-education schools.

Operating underground in Portugal under the direction of political advisers from Moscow, the PCP succeeded in building nuclei in the ports and shipyards of Lisbon and the workshops of the sole national conglomerate corporation, the CUF, with factories across Portugal. Rural organising amongst the peasants in the Alentejo was also fruitful. At the death of Salazar and the coup against Caetano the PCP had a strong presence inside Portugal and had, as well, a high degree of acceptance by the population as a consistent and organised foe of corporatism. There were other, non-communist, opposition groups and parties in Portugal under Salazar. They formed loose coalitions with the PCP in presenting candidates in the occasional elections, but they were weak, disorganised and poor. They relied on the centralised organisational structure of the PCP and its printing presses and resources for support. This gave even greater legitimacy to the PCP.

The Portuguese Socialist party (PS) had its origins in the late 1800s but virtually disappeared from Portugal in any organised sense after Salazar took office. It reappeared in embryonic form in the 1969 elections when it joined in an opposition coalition. Its present origins can be traced to a meeting called in Bonn, West Germany, in April 1973 when the Friedrich Ebert Foundation, the assistance foundation of the SPD, brought together the PS candidates in the 1969 election and other political activists. Under the supportive umbrella of the SPD and the DGB a reborn Portuguese socialism took form. It was perhaps symbolic of the nature of the Portuguese left that on the day the coup against Caetano took place Alvaro Cunhal was visiting Prague and Mario Soares (head of the PS) was in Germany.

When the MFA announced its programme in 1974 it pledged itself to a set of ideological principles which could have been accommodated by either the PCP or the PS. The MFA had first to contend with pressures within the military, led primarily by General Spinola, for far more centrist policies. The MFA's key priority was the ending of the colonial wars and to that end it appointed General Spinola to head the Junta of National Salvation (JSN). General Spinola was no stranger to the political process and quickly gathered together support from the centrist parties and the PS, as well as from the non-MFA wings of the military. He attempted to organise a national platform which would be far more temperate than the programme of the MFA; a platform which included a gradual liberalisation of the economy and a political solution to the wars in the colonies. The MFA leadership was split between those willing to support Spinola and those who formed a new organisation within the MFA, the Operational Commando of the Continent (COPCON), to press for a more radical programme. With the attempted right-wing coup in March 1975 the military was forced over leftward, delivering the momentum to the PCP.

The PCP moved into the vacuum of national politics and began to assert itself as a party of moderation. It chose to do this through its control of the trades union movement. After the coup workers called a rash of wildcat strikes throughout Portuguese industry. Many were fomented by the right but others owed their origin to the sheer feeling of liberation engendered by the removal of the strict controls on labour organisations. Utilising its nuclei in these newly forming unions the PCP was able to build a national trades union movement under its control, the Intersindical, which was recognised by the government as the 'sole representative of the workers'. The PS, which had been making a major effort to build socialist unions, found itself locked out in the trades unions.

With the destruction of the power of Spinola following the aborted 11 March 1975 coup, the new leaders of the Supreme Revolutionary Council, many of whom were PCP loyalists, felt secure enough to proceed with the scheduled elections to the Constituent Assembly in April. As a prelude to this election the MFA signed a pact with the six contending political parties in which they agreed to 'institutionalise' the role of the MFA in the government for a five-year period. The PCP overplayed its hand in the run-up to this election and the MFA, whose startling call to the Portuguese electorate to turn in blank ballots as a protest against civilian politicians, fared little better. To the great surprise of the PCP, the party only mustered 12.5 per cent of the vote, coming a poor third to the PS's 37.8 per cent and the PPD's 26.3 per cent. In response to this, the PCP and their allies in the MFA embarked upon a 'cultural revolution'.

This cultural revolution took the form of a massive propaganda barrage in the state-controlled media where revolutionary slogans and plays were broadcast to the nation. Travelling theatres were sent out to the Alentejo to perform Brecht for the masses. The PCP was able to force through the Agrarian Reform Act which sought to collectivise Portuguese agriculture. Unfortunately for them and their peasant supporters collective ownership of the farmland did not guarantee an instant economic miracle. Peasants lacked the skills, capital equipment and interest in collective ownership to produce a substantial crop. The agrarian reform was a total disaster. When, in late 1976, the government began to return the land to its former owners, the peasants, despite the rantings and threats of doom and disaster by the PCP, gratefully abandoned their occupation of the farms to owners who were willing to farm them.

However the PCP control of the media gave it great strength. This was accomplished by the forcible occupation of radio and television stations by the workers and the occupation of newspapers hostile to the PCP. In July 1975 the workers at the socialist paper, *Republica*, occupied the press rooms. This led to the walkout of the PS from the provisional government. Even the military itself was heavily propagandised by the PCP through its control of the Fifth Division and the Institute of Military Studies. The PCP rose in power through its close links with Vasco Goncalves who acted as its puppet – at least during his periodic bouts of sanity. Throughout July 1975 the PCP rode high on a wave of anti-PS propaganda and with the support of the COPCON. As the tensions rose even higher when refugees from Angola, Mozambique and Guinea flooded into Portugal needing housing, food and jobs, the PCP found a sympathetic ally in the military in Otelo Saraiva de Carvalho. Together they planned a classic left-wing putsch. This coup was planned for 25 November 1975 but the moderate leaders of the military, most notably General Ramalho Eanes, found out about the plot. The PCP withdrew its support and the planned uprising fizzled out.

The failure of the coup and the rise to power of the moderates in the army was reflected in the success of the PS in the elections in 1976 when they won a clear 35 per cent of the vote and formed a minority government. Similarly, General Eanes won the presidential contest by a massive 61 per cent. The PCP, however, retained its strength in the Intersindical and used this strength to force a deal with the PS to control industrial unrest, in return for the PS's reduction in the pace of de-collectivisation in the Alentejo. This deal cost the PS the support of the nation and, in 1978, the PS was forced out of government to be replaced by the Christian Democrats.

The socialists and the social democrats, with massive international support from unions and parties in the West, have attempted to break the lock held by PCP over the organised Portuguese workforce through its domination of the General Confederation of Portuguese Workers (CGTP–Intersindical). The CGTP–Intersindical still controls nearly 85 per cent of organised labour.

In 1979 the socialists were able to unite the non-Intersindical unions into one national confederation, the General Union of Portugese Workers (UGTP). The UGT, with about forty-five national unions affiliated to it, draws its major support from among the white-collar sections of the banking, insurance and service industries. It has recently had to distance itself from its support of the Democratic Alliance (the ruling coalition) in order to maintain its credibility in the face of the campaign of strikes and unrest spread by the Intersindical. When Alvaro Cunhal returned from a trip to Moscow in late 1980 he called for the overthrow of the Portuguese government; a threat which he began to carry out through the Intersindical. The Intersindical, which had begun negotiations with the government, withdrew from these negotiations when Cunhal returned. A wave of strikes lasting from just a few hours to four days hit the Portuguese economy. Just under half a million civil servants (both CGTP and UGT) struck simultaneously, paralysing government, the health service and schools. Lisbon found itself without deliveries of cooking gas for days on end and Oporto lost its public transport system for almost a week. This was extended throughout the economy. In the first week of April 1981 alone there were fifteen national strikes. The PCP seemed intent on bringing the government down.

The PS and its UGT allies remain in a very difficult position. The Democratic Alliance needs their support for the legislative changes which will be required to win acceptance by the EEC as a member; an event the PCP seems determined to prevent. Yet, if the UGT appears weak or lacking in commitment to the trades union militancy evinced by the CGTP–Intersindical it runs the risk of being permanently locked out of power within the trades union movement. This lack of a strong trades union base will condemn any future socialist party to a position of great weakness and vulnerability to PCP blackmail. It will certainly prevent the resurgence of the PS as the party of government.

Cunhal and his PCP have been the most unregenerate examples of Stalinism within the Eurocommunist movement. Most Eurocommunist parties have shunned the PCP. They fear that the anti-democratic activities of the PCP damage their credibility as parties committed to the democratic process. However the PCP has the support of the Soviet Union and its allies. These continue to support the PCP with more than rhetoric; they continue to send money and advisors to help build the trades union strength of the CGTP. The West has continued its support of the PS and the UGT. Numerous ITSs have set up Portuguese programmes and the ICFTU has built a separate Portuguese operation. It is in Portugal, above all, that the Cold War struggle for European labour is proceeding.

Europe has not been the only area in which the political activities of the trades union movements have continued to play an active role. One of the most important developments in the international trades union movement has been the growth of strong black trades unions within South Africa. The development of independent unions of black workers in South Africa has been strongly influenced by the interaction of these unionists with the international trades union movement and the international trades union movement continues to be a major force in the development of South African unionism.

Throughout the postwar era the government of South Africa has operated a policy of 'apartheid' (separate development) by which the different races within the nation were treated differently. Coloured, Asian and black citizens had markedly different civil rights in the areas of education, voting and free mobility than their white fellow citizens. This systematic policy of racial discrimination attracted a wide international press, especially after dramatic political events like Sharpeville or the treason trials. Recent developments of a militant black consciousness in areas like Soweto have threatened to disrupt the South African political system. What has received less public attention has been the developments within the South African industrial relations system and the increased politicisation of the trades union movement which has resulted from the changes in South Africa's labour legislation. The struggle within the trades union movement continues to be at the very heart of the controversy which now troubles South Africa.

South African trade unions have, until recently, been divided between two competing national centres: the all-white South African Confederation of Labour and the multiracial Trades Union Council of South Africa (TUCSA). Some of the TUCSA unions are multiracial in that they accept as members coloured and Asians, although the leadership remains firmly in white hands. Until the late 1960s TUCSA atttempted to act on behalf of a number of unregistered African unions but, under threat of legislative action by the government, TUCSA expelled its African members and refused to continue to act on their behalf. Two earlier multiracial confederations, the South African Confederation of Trades Unions (SACTU) and the Federation of Free African Trades Unions of South Africa (FOFATUSA) were banned in the fifties because the government claimed, with some justification, that they were communist-led subversive organisations. Because of the peculiar form of the South African industrial relations system the expulsion of Africans from TUCSA virtually excluded the African workers from any regular interaction with the process of industrial relations.

The South African system of industrial relations is largely based on an institutionalised interaction between the government, the employers and the unions sharing representation on industrial councils. The industrial councils decide the broad issue of wages and employment policy for key sectors of the economy. Only registered unions, whose registration is closely controlled by the government, are permitted to participate in these industrial councils. This industrial council structure is the backbone of the South African system.

Despite the intentions of the government to keep to a policy of separate development it found that without employing non-white labour it could not run its factories, operate its mines or till its fields. It tried to resolve this contradiction by creating a rationing system for jobs through its policy of job reservation. Under job reservation white employment within South African industry was protected from competition from non-white labour by 'reserving' a range of jobs only for whites. As whites vacated these posts they could only be replaced by other whites. Only coloured workers could fill coloured job slots, etc. Initially this policy served its purpose but soon it began to cause more problems than it solved. An expanding South African industry created new jobs faster than the whites could fill them, either by population increase or by immigration. Many companies had to get exemptions from job reservation; others chose to automate. Similarly, this policy created a labour market in which the whites occupied only the highest skill levels. This inevitably meant that the unions representing white workers became organisations of the privileged and the highly paid. Combined with the broad nature of collective negotiations under the industrial council structures, South Africa was left without any real trades union presence at the factory or shopfloor level.

This lack of a shopfloor presence was not too disturbing for the managers of South African corporations but caused innumerable headaches for the managers of the South African subsidiaries of the transnational corporations. They were under a great deal of pressure from trades unions in North America and Europe, as well as a broad coalition of religious and political organisations, to make changes in their South African industrial relations policies to minimise racial discrimination. Their task was made even more difficult with the outbreak of strikes in Durban in late 1972 and early 1973 in which black workers used their non-recognised union structures at plant level to strike for higher wages. The government responded to the Durban strikes by banning and arresting the leaders and trying to squash nascent black unionism.

The repression of black unionism after the 1973 strikes had a number of serious effects. First, it raised a world-wide outcry from the international trades union movement against South African industrial apartheid. For a change this was not idle rhetoric on their part as they were in a position to force important changes within the power structures of the transnationals through their world company councils. Above all, they were able to promote change within the transnationals because in key nations, especially West Germany and Sweden, the trades unionists held seats on the supervisory boards of these corporations.

There they could raise the issue of company policy in South Africa and were in a position to influence this policy by action domestically and through the company councils. After the 1973 strikes numerous ITSs sent delegations to South Africa to meet with local unionists and to offer their solidarity and assistance. The metal ITS, the IMF, took the lead in accepting into affiliation numerous black South African unions. Since 1970 the IMF has sent more than ten missions to South Africa and has accepted eleven affiliates with over eighty-five thousand members.

A second result of the 1973 strikes was the effective lobbying within Europe and North America by the trades unions and their allies to create a code of behaviour for the transnationals operating inside South Africa. The EEC and the Sullivan Codes were introduced to monitor transnational activities within the republic. A third result was the creation of parallel unions by TUCSA, in which the several affiliated TUCSA national unions organised unions of African workers in parallel to their own unions and sought to represent them within the industrial council structures.

Perhaps the most important result, however, was the growing awareness after 1976 by the South African government that by refusing to permit black trades unions they were creating an effective link between African trades union activists and the African community leaders. The government began to reconsider its labour policies in the light of the report of the Reikert Commission which highlighted many of the disturbing developments in South African industrial and social relations. The government appointed the Wiehahn Commission to study the situation within the trades union movement. This Wiehahn Commission reported its findings in 1979. Its major recommendation was that job reservation should be abandoned and that black worker unions should be recognised under the law, thus permitting these unions representation rights in the industrial councils, the conciliation tribunals and the industrial courts.

The report of the Wiehahn Commission was followed by legislation putting most of its findings into law. A new trades union national centre, the Federation of South African Trades Unions (FOSATU), was formed from the black unions which accepted registration. There were large numbers of black unions which refused to register under the act. A struggle has developed between the parallel unions and these independent unions. This conflict between the parallel unions and the independents is largely over the issue of shopfloor representation. If the unions register and participate in the industrial councils they become subject to the wider agreements made with the white unions and the government at that level, including a 'cooling off' period in industrial disputes. Most of the independent unions are already recognised as the *de facto* plant representatives anyway and would gain very little by seeking recognition. Most importantly, they would lose contact with their base and, through them, their support within the wider black community.

FOSATU unions point out that these same industrial councils are the bodies which denied Africans their rights for so many years. The shopfloor unionists have little trust in these bodies. In fact, events have shown that the shopfloor unionists place only a limited trust in the leadership of the black unions. In the wave of strikes in 1979 and 1980 it became clear that one of the key demands of the black unionists was the right to choose their own leaders and the right to reject the black unionists which the management sought to choose for them. In some key strikes, like Ford, it became clear that the strikes were directed not only at Ford management or government policy; they were also directed at their own black unions by the shopfloor unionists in league with the political activists of the Port Elizabeth Black Community Organisation (PEBCO). In fact their union, the National Union of Motor Assembly and Rubber Workers, did not know of the Ford strike call until the strike was actually underway.

The government fears that the establishment of a linkage between shopfloor union militants and community organisers in Soweto, Pinetown and Port Elizabeth bodes ill for civil peace and has taken to jailing local union leaders like Thozamile Botha, even when the Ford management was happy to continue dealing with him and PEBCO. In this the government is placing itself in direct conflict with the needs and policies of the transnationals. The activities of the international unions are critical to resolving this conflict by keeping up the pressure on the transnationals. A good example of the kinds of pressure which can be exerted was demonstrated in the case of the Volkswagen strike at Uitenhage in the eastern Cape. There, more than three and one-half thousand black workers went out on strike; a strike for recognition as much as for a higher standard of living. They called upon the IMF for support. The president of the IMF, Eugen Loderer, who is also president of Germany's giant metalworkers' union the I. G. Metall, and happens to serve as a vice-president of Volkswagen's supervisory board, made several trips to South Africa. He played a crucial role in bringing this conflict to a successful end. The IMF also made available more than fifty thousand Swiss francs to the strikers as solidarity assistance. Similar union interactions took place in Ford and in many other multinationals.

The struggle for free unionism is far from over in South Africa, much as the African's battle for equal rights under the law has a long way to go. In these battles the trades union movements, both domestic and international, will play a vital and continuing role. The conflict continues. In June 1981 alone there were more than forty strikes throughout the republic. More ominously these strikes have provoked a strong backlash amongst the white unions. Union leaders like Arie Paulus of the Mineworkers and Gert Beetge of the white Building Workers have allied themselves with the ultra-right *Hereformeerde Nasional Partie* (HNP) whose leader, Jaap Marais, has been attacking Prime Minister Botha on the issue of permitting black workers to organise. There is a significant growth of white workers' resentment to what the white unions consider leniency to blacks. This has led to a government crackdown on all unions and new powers being given to the Minister of Manpower Utilisation to discipline unions (black and white) which take an overtly political line.

Trades union activism has been the source of internal unrest in Zambia where the entire leadership of the movement had its party membership suspended. Strikes throughout Zimbabwe are causing the new government serious difficulties. The recent general strike in Sierra Leone called by James Kabia of the Labour Congress over the issues of high commodity prices, scarce food supplies and poor housing led to the arrest of over ninety unionists. The continuing battle for control of Tunisia is being fought within the trades union movement. After the 'Black Thursday' uprising of the Tunisian unionists in January 1978 and the attack on Tunisia by Libyan-supported dissidents in Gafsa in January 1980, the organic links between the *Union Générale de Travailleus Tunisiens* (UGTT) and the ruling *Parti Socialiste Destoerien* (PSD) have been strained. The election of Taieb Baccouche to head the UGTT in April 1981 has widened this breach even though the UGTT's administrative commission voted to maintain its ties to the PSD (by a narrow 53 per cent vote in September 1981). Throughout Africa the trades unions have been forced by unrest at the base to take a militant stance against the problems of scarcity, high inflation and general corruption.

This has been true even in relatively rich countries like Nigeria. With the restoration of civilian rule in Nigeria under President Shagari (National Party of Nigeria – NPN) the trades union movement reformed and united into a single national centre, the Nigerian Labour Congress (NLC). On 22 February 1980 the NLC presented the President with a Workers' Charter of Demands, listing the social priorities of the trades unions. This was followed up by a series of demands for better educational opportunities, better housing, better roads, regular electricity supplies and an end of the endemic corruption. The NLC, while not aligned with any political party, has in its leadership many of the pro-Awolowo (United Party of Nigeria – UPN) trades unionists from the past. In fact the Workers' Charter was largely written by the anti-Shagari faction and was praised by the Lagos State (UPN) government and the Kano State government (under Aminu Kano's PRP – Peoples' Redemption Party). When the NLC demanded a national minimum wage of 300 Naira a month, and called a general strike to back up its demands, Shagari agreed to a 100 Naira minimum.

The NLC has continued to antagonise the government and its ruling party. Even before the new government took office the NLC threatened a general strike in May 1979. In January 1980 the NLC threatened a general strike if Shagari did not agree to repeal the 1975 Trades Union Disputes Decree and to agree to the 300 Naira minimum wage. When the NLC did call a two-day general strike in May 1981 many felt that the NLC was playing too political a role and was evidencing the same problems of previous Nigerian labour organisations; especially manipulation from abroad. The Nigerian government is preparing legislation which will remove the NLC's monopoly of the labour movement. There has been a breakaway of several key unions from the NLC who have formed a rival Congress of Democratic Trades Unions (largely supported by the NPN). It seems highly likely that the Nigerian labour movement will, once again, divide along party political lines and may very well provoke a major crackdown on all unionism within Nigeria.

The pace of trades union interaction with national governments has provoked innumerable crises elsewhere, but most conspicuously within the Caribbean. There the struggles within the trades union movements have been the battlefield on which far more serious wars are being waged. The Bermuda Labour Party has used its control over the blue-collar labour movement to try and bring down the United Bermuda Party government of J. David Gibbons through a wave of strikes during the tourist season. The government of Michael Manley in Jamaica was turned out of office by Edward Seaga largely as a result of the success by Seaga in winning away the support of the organised workers from Manley on the key questions of combating inflation and maintaining employment. The government of Morris Bishop was threatened with serious disruption by the forces of the remaining centrist unions led by former CLAT organiser Stanley Cyrus. Even Forbes Burnham of

Guiana has adopted a markedly less pro-Cuban line after serious strikes in the bauxite industry.

In areas as remote from the mainstream of international labour as the islands of Dominica, St Kitts and Antigua the battle for the control of the national political structure is being waged through the struggle for control over their trade union movements. Similar battles rage in Central America, New Zealand and Australia. What is important in all these struggles is not only their domestic political effect but also their relationship to the increasing pace of international activity by the government–trades union nexus.

If there is one area of current problems in international labour relations which is likely to serve as a catalyst for political change it certainly will be the deep involvement of the world's intelligence services in the field of international trades unionism. Rather than fade away under a blanket of stale rhetoric on détente, the conflicts within the sphere of international trades unionism have remained the unabated core of the non-military Cold War effort. The world's press is full of exposés of attempted intelligence coups through the trades unions. Even more miss the attention of the world because they are successful.

The intelligence interest in the trades union movements is not only a function of their activity in national politics, although this is of vital concern. Their interest lies as well in the role of the trades unions, and key trades unionists, within the economy. Trades unionists act as agents of influence within national union bodies, political parties and social groups. They are frequently used as agents of access to key political figures in whom the intelligence service maintains an interest, and are most frequently used as utility agents providing information to one or more principal agents with access to intelligence officers. Throughout industry utility agents serve to provide a whole range of data on their corporations (sources of supply, markets, financial status, etc.). In many cases these utility agents are unaware of the fact that they are being used to gather information for a foreign intelligence service. They think they are promoting a cause or acting to strengthen their union or political caucus. They are never told that their information is being provided as well to foreign intelligence services. In fact, in some notable cases, even when they do know that the material is being provided to a foreign intelligence service they are never told to which foreign government the information is actually being transmitted. The history of several cases of intelligence penetration indicates that they have been conducted as 'false flag' operations. In these the collector of data does so thinking that he or she is assisting one government whose operatives pose as agents of that government although they are actually working for another.

One reason why the trades union movement has been such a fertile field for intelligence operations is that it has within it numerous trades unionists who are motivated by ideologies and a commitment to abstractions. The question of motivation is crucial for mounting a successful intelligence operation. The art of building a successful intelligence operation does not lie in coercing or blackmailing into service unwilling agents: it consists of finding agents already committed to a goal shared by the intelligence operatives and providing them with the resources in order for them to achieve this goal. If, for example, there exists a trades union or political party faction opposed to a key policy or programme of the targeted party or government, intelligence operatives would be very foolish to try and start their own opposition movement to this policy. It is wiser and more useful to offer to the dissident faction their covert assistance by providing funds, printing presses, media access and subsidised travel so that they can achieve their goals.

This has been a traditional method of operation. No intelligence organisation or government ever had to coerce European social democrats to build anti-communist factions in postwar France or Italy. No intelligence body ever had to force Eastern European trades unionists to resist being placed under the control of Soviet-trained political commissars intent upon eradicating collective bargaining in Hungary, Czechoslovakia or Poland.

Similarly, no Eastern European intelligence service has had to put undue pressure on a Latin American urban guerrilla to continue his opposition to the government hunting him. What is serendipitous about this type of operation is its long-term utility. Once an intelligence service has provided the needed assistance to a key unionist or political group it is then capable of using that fact to ensure a longer-term loyalty through the threat of exposure. Another useful aspect of utilising allies in the trades union movements is the access it gives intelligence agents to parallel organisations which it seeks to penetrate. Through its strength within sections of the trades union movements in Britain, Sweden, West Germany and Holland the intelligence services of the East have been able to build contacts and influence in the variety of 'peace movements' which have grown to such prominence; first in the anti-Vietnam campaign and now in the renewal of the unilateral disarmament movements.

This is why one of the most vital jobs for an intelligence operative is that of a 'spotter', by which he can pick out those individuals or groups who are susceptible to receiving assistance by virtue of their political outlook, ambition or position of access. One of the best posts for a spotter to operate from is in the personnel section of an international agency. In June 1978, just after Vladimir Bukrayev was asked leave the publications department of the ILO in Geneva because of British revelations of his KGB connections, his colleague Grigory Miagkov was similarly expelled from his key job in the training department of the ILO where he handled the personnel files of all the ILO specialists. After Arkady Shevchenko, the highest-ranking Soviet UN defector, left the UN in 1979 he pointed out several high-ranking KGB officers operating inside the UN, including the personnel chief of the UN Secretariat. The former Soviet labour attaché, Berdennikov, who was expelled from Britain with 104 of his colleagues, was noted for his ability to spot suitable subjects within the British trades union movement. Once spotted, other officers can move in to make contact with the subjects.

One of those who was active in the field of labour penetration in Britain was Josef Frolik. Frolik, who subsequently defected from Czech intelligence, spent his years in Britain 'running' a number of trades unionists and high-level union officials along with colleagues from Poland and the Soviet Union. This type of activity occurs elsewhere as well; particularly in West Germany where officers of the East German intelligence organisation, like Hans Faltermayer, Gunter Guillaume and others, have been discovered in high posts in the SPD and the DGB. Other unionists have acted as agents for East Germany and numerous quiet enquiries have been undertaken in Pullach into the extent of Mischa Wolf's penetration of the West German labour movement. The Scandinavian countries are full of intelligence operatives from the East, usually in their early stages of training, who are targeted on middle-level trades union penetration operations.

One other facet of this relationship between the international trades union movement and the intelligence community is the cover these trades union programmes offer to intelligence organisations to place their operatives abroad in a role which gives them access to foreign unionists and government bodies. Places like Geneva, Brussels or Mexico City are full of trades unionists who also work for one or more intelligence organisations. This type of activity is even more widespread within the Third World where trades union solidarity organisations send down specialists to operate local and regional assistance programmes. These have often included intelligence specialists utilising the wonderful cover opportunities offered by the trades union programmes. Depending upon the sensitivity of the country and the nature of the programme, there may be in any one programme several intelligence officers using trades union cover, several trades unionists actively co-operating with one or more intelligence services, one or more agents of an opposing intelligence organisation as well as local host-country intelligence officers and trades unionists keeping an eye on the programme and its local contacts for the national counter-intelligence service. Occasionally even this number is increased by the participation of local police and military agents. This has had its effect on the nature and impact of these programmes.

In the Third World, some trades union solidarity assistance has been used to achieve ends which tended to be less altruistic than might appear. In one famous case in Latin America there was a trades union leader who was in a position of great strength in his national labour movement. He led a militant faction of the national centre, opposed to the government in power. It was also rumoured that he was 'friendly' to Eastern bloc agents. Western trades unionists and their intelligence service observers, along with the leadership of the host government, decided to remove the leader from his post. They were unsuccessful in dislodging him through the union ballot box, so they decided to 'help' him instead. The local Western trades union assistance body offered to build a massive housing project for his union. They sent down architects to do drawings and scale models, one of which was set up in the union's headquarters. Specialists in credit union development were sent down to create a credit bank to finance the workers' purchases. The local union membership was involved in every stage of the planning. Finally, on the day when the final contracts were to have been signed, the assistance organisation presented the documents to the union leadership for their signature. They noticed that title to the land was to remain with the assistance body. They pointed out that this was a violation of local land tenure rules and that they couldn't sign. The assistance body officers said they could not proceed further. They pulled out of the scheme and told the union membership that its leader had refused to sign the contract because he wanted to control it all himself (and inferred that he was trying to get rich in the bargain). The local unionists were so incensed at the collapse of their housing scheme that they ousted the leader. The housing scheme was never built. For the price of a few architects' drawings and the services of two credit union specialists the assistance organisation and the intelligence organisation achieved their aim. They ousted the union leader and won support from the local union. It was a most successful operation.

Not surprisingly, many Third World unionists have grown suspicious of trades union charity and assistance. Sometimes this has catastrophic results. In late 1979 two employees of the AIFLD, Michael Hammer and Mark Pearlman, were sitting in the coffee bar of the Sheraton Hotel in San Salvador when they were gunned down. A third victim, Jose Rodolfo Viera, who headed the Agrarian Reform Institute, was killed as well. The AIFLD had been active in attempting to foster desperately needed land reform in EI Salvador and had sent Hammer and Pearlman as specialists to assist Viera in this activity. There was no evidence that any of the three were connected with anything other than what they were sent down to EI Salvador for but the suspicion that the AIFLD was engaged in more than mere solidarity work was sufficient to endanger the lives of its local representatives.

For the most part the interaction between intelligence organisations and the trades unions are conducted quietly, behind the scenes. Occasionally, as in the scandal in New Zealand, in 1981, the Russian ambassador himself was caught giving money to the left-wing trades union leadership. For the most part the monies needed for large-scale assistance (financing journals, buying equipment, subsidising conferences) are transferred to union organisations through the travel corporations of the East. For example, many union organisations in the West and the Third World run extensive programmes of worker travel. They send travelling parties all over the world, including Eastern Europe. They maintain substantial financial positions with the national airlines of the Eastern bloc (Aeroflot, Malev, Balkan, etc.). It is very easy for these airlines to claim as paid substantial bills incurred by these travel companies although monies were never sent, although collected. Other forms of transfer include straight cash or grants, but these are usually sent on a union to union basis. This is why the recognition of union national centres like CGTP–Intersindical by the national centres of the WFTU is so important. While the Portuguese government might blanch at their national centre receiving cash from the Soviet or Czech governments, they are more at ease with solidarity assistance from the Soviet or Czech union national centres to Intersindical. Similarly, despite Soviet protests that these funds are subversive, the donation of cash, printing equipment and supplies by the AFL–CIO and other Western unions to Polish Solidarity are very difficult to stop, lest Soviet assistance be similarly blocked. The trades union vehicle is an excellent method of channelling assistance abroad; particularly to the Third World where items like loudspeakers, printing presses, typewriters and vehicles are so hard to come by and are so useful for political, as well as trades union, campaigns.

It would be a mistake to see intelligence activities behind all trades union activity; or indeed to see the monitoring of international trades union activities by the world's counter-intelligence services as evidence of some diabolic plot. Nonetheless, particularly on the level of the national centres, this type of activity is a major part of the international trades union scene. Most governments, East and West, have established close organic links between their security and intelligence services and their trades union movements. This symbiosis continues to increase as the threat of direct military conflict diminishes. The trades union movements, more than any area outside the military, are prime actors in the continuing Cold War.

With the rejoining of the ILO by the US and the restructuring of the ICFTU and its regional programmes which will occur now that the AFL–CIO has rejoined that organisation, a new chapter in the story of international labour is beginning. It will likely be no less interesting or less conflicted than previous periods. Just as the rise of the transnationals radically altered the very nature of the international trades union movement, the changes which can be foreseen within the political alignments of Eastern European unionism after the emergence of Solidarity in Poland seem likely to prove as dramatic a change. In all these political and economic adaptations to a new international order the trades union movements, on all levels of abstraction from the workplace, will play a vital role.

Notes and References

CHAPTER 2: EARLY TRADES UNION INTERNATIONAL ORGANISATIONS

1. Lenin, V. I. in '2.S'yezd Kommunisticheskovo Internatsionala', Moscow, 1920.
2. Fournier, N. and Legrand E., *E . . . Comme Espionnage*, p. 9.
3. Farago, L., *The Game of Foxes*, pp. 336–76.

CHAPTER 3: THE LABOUR–GOVERNMENT NEXUS

1. Snow, S., *Samuel Gompers and the Pan-American Federation of Labor*, pp. 68–71.
2. Ibid., pp. 56–7.
3. Lahey, E., *Chicago Daily News*, 1958.
4. Persico, J., *Piercing the Reich*, p. 24.
5. Ibid., p. 39.
6. Smith, R. Harris, *OSS*, p. 106.

CHAPTER 4: INTERNATIONAL LABOUR IN POSTWAR EUROPE

1. Zinner, P., *Communist Strategy and Tactics in Czechoslovakia 1914–1948*, ch. 11, pp. 196–223.
2. Jecchinis, C., *Trade Unions in Greece*, ch. 11, pp. 86–96.
3. Lens, S., *The Military–Industrial Complex*, ch. 6, pp. 99–121.
4. Radosh, R., *American Labor and U.S. Foreign Policy*, ch. 10, pp. 304–47.
5. Montaldo, J., *Les Secrets de la Banque Sovietique en France*, p. 45.
6. Smith, R. Harris, op. cit., pp. 107–8.
7. Windmuller, J. P., *American Labor and the International Labor Movement 1940–1953*, p. 148.
8. Quoted in 'Report of the First Congress – ICFTU' (Brussels: ICFTU) p. 90.
9. Quoted in ibid., p. 95.

CHAPTER 6: THE DEVELOPMENT OF AFRICAN UNIONISM

1. Suret-Canale, J., 'The French West African Railway Workers Strike 1947–1948' in Gutkind, P., Cohen, R. and Copans, J. (eds) *African Labor History*, pp. 129–51. See also Sembene, O., *God's Bits of Wood*.

2. 'The Great Conspiracy in Africa', *Trud*, (AATUF, 1960).
3. Ibid.
4. Tettegah, J. K., 'Press Statement', 6 June 1961 (Accra).
5. Richards, L., 'The Military and Trades Unions as Initiators of Political Stability in a Selected Number of West African Polities' in *The Military and Trades Unions as Vehicles for Political Change*, p. 188–9.

CHAPTER 7: THE DEVELOPMENT OF ASIAN UNIONISM

1. Trotsky, L., *Summary and Perspectives on the Chinese Revolution*, p. 334.
2. Goulden, J. C., *Meany*, p. 127.
3. Masani, M. R., *The Communist Party of India*, p. 37.
4. For the role of the AFL in these activities see Goulden, J. C., op. cit., p. 357.

CHAPTER 8: THE DEVELOPMENT OF LATIN AMERICAN UNIONISM

1. Corradi, J. E., 'Argentina' in Chilcote, R. H. and Edelstein J. C., *Latin America: The Struggle With Dependency and Beyond*, p. 340.
2. Farago, L., *The Game of Foxes*, p. 337.
3. Romualdi, S., *Presidents and Peons: Recollections of a Labor Ambassador in Latin America*, pp. 7–8.
4. Corson, W. R., *The Armies of Ignorance*, p. 357.
5. US Senate, Committee on Foreign Relations, Subcommittee on American Republics Affairs, *Survey of the Alliance for Progress*, 15 July 1968, p. 9.
6. Lodge, G. C., *Spearheads of Democracy: Labor in the Developing Countries*, p. 52.
7. US Senate, op. cit., p. 21.
8. Spalding, H. A., *Organized Labor in Latin America*, p. 181.
9. Garvey, E., 'Meddling in Brazil' in *Commonweal*, 9 February 1968, p. 553.
10. US Senate, op. cit., p. 14.
11. See particularly US Senate, Senate Committee on Foreign Relations, *Hearings on the International Telephone and Telegraph Company and Chile 1970–1971* (two volumes), p. 22 et passim.
12. *Ercilla*, 24 January 1973, p. 8.
13. Quoted by Reuther, V., in his address to the Chicago Peace Council, 5 April 1968.

CHAPTER 9: THE RISE OF EURO-UNIONISM

1. *In Place of Strife – a Policy for Industrial Relations*, Cmnd. 3888 (London: HMSO).
2. Presented by the Commission to the Council in October 1972.

CHAPTER 10: CURRENT PROBLEMS IN INTERNATIONAL LABOUR

1. *Newsweek*, 21 September 1981, p. 8.

Glossary of Commonly-used Abbreviations

AAFLI *Asian–American Free Labor Institute.* The US Government–AFL–CIO joint assistance body for Asian unions.

AALC *African–American Labor Center.* The US Government–AFL–CIO joint assistance body for African unions.

AALD *American Alliance for Labor and Democracy.* The AFL co-operative effort with the Wilson Presidency for Labour peace in 1915.

AATUF *All-African Trades Union Federation.* The Pan-African labour international linking the national centres of the Casablanca Group.

ACFTU *All-China Federation of Trades Unions.* The mainland Chinese national centre at one time affiliated to the WFTU.

ACLI *Associazione Cristiani dei Lavoratori Italiani.* The Christian-Democratic labour faction within the CGIL before the CISL split.

ACWA *Amalgamated Clothing Workers of America.* The CIO-affiliated garment workers' union led for many years by Sidney Hillman.

AEU *Amalgamated Engineering Workers' Union.* A major British engineering workers' union merged with the Foundry and TASS to form the AUEW.

AfA *Arbeitsgemeinschaft für Arbeitnehmerfragen.* The SPD-sponsored German committee of workers and unionists designed to minimise the Jusos' role.

AFL *American Federation of Labor.* The US national centre led for many years by Samuel Gompers.

AFL–CIO *American Federation of Labor–Congress of Industrial Organizations.* The US national centre formed in 1955 and led by George Meany.

AFRO *African Regional Organisation.* The African Regional Organisation of the ICFTU formed after the rise of independent African states in 1960.

AIFLD *American Institute for Free Labor Development.* The tripartite US Government–business–AFL–CIO assistance body for Latin America.

AITUC *All-India Trades Union Congress.* The Indian national centre with close ties to the Indian Communist Party led by S. A. Dange for years.

AMG *American Military Government.* The legal body created to administer the US zone of postwar Germany.

ARU *American Railroad Union.* The socialist-led independent federation of railway workers active in the Pullman Strike under Eugene Debs.

ATLAS *Agrupación de Trabajadores Latino Americanos Sindicalistas.* The 'Third Force' Pan-American labour federation created by Peron.

Glossary of Commonly-used Abbreviations 267

BCEN *Banque Commerciale pour l'Europe du Nord.* The Moscow-owned French bank which acts as a conduit for covert subsidy of the CGT and PCF.
BfG *Bank für Gemeinwirtschaft.* The West German trades union bank with major commercial links with Eastern Europe.
BRAC *Brotherhood of Railways and Airline Clerks.* An AFL–CIO affiliated union active in overseas work through the AIFLD.
CCOO *Comisiones Obreras.* The Spanish trades union national centre closely allied with the PCE, led by Marcelo Camacho.
CDU *Christian Democratic Union.* The West German Christian-Democratic Party which participates with the CSU of Bavaria in a coalition.
CFDT *Confédération Française Démocratique du Travail.* The French Christian-Democratic national centre formed after the CFTC deconfessionalised.
CFTC *Confédération Française des Travailleurs Chrétiens.* The French Christian-Democratic national centre until 1964.
CGIL *Confederazione Generale Italiana del Lavoro.* The Italian national centre with close ties to the Italian Communist Party.
CGT *Confédération Générale du Travail.* The French national centre with close ties to the French Communist Party.
CGT–FO *Confédération Générale du Travail – Force Ouvrière.* The French Socialist national centre formed in 1948 as a split from the CGT.
CGTG *Confederacion General de Trabajadores de Guatemala.* The Guatemalan national centre associated with the Arbenz regime.
CIA *Central Intelligence Agency.* The US Government Agency formed in 1947 out of the Central Intelligence Group as a successor to the OSS.
CIO *Congress of Industrial Organizations.* The US labour centre founded in 1936 among industrial unions, led by Lewis and then Reuther until 1955.
CISC *Confédération Internationale des Syndicats Chrétiens.* The Christian global international until 1968.
CISL *Confederazione Italiana Sindicati Lavoratori.* The ICFTU-affiliated Christian-Democratic Italian national centre.
CLN *Comitato di Liberazione Nationale.* The post-invasion six-party coalition of anti-Fascist parties in Italy south of Rome.
CLNAI *Comitato di Liberazione Nazionale dell'Alta Italiano.* The anti-Fascist coalition in effective post-invasion control of Northern Italy.
Cominform *Communist Information Bureau.* The nine-nation, communist party mutual help organisation founded in 1947, largely anti-Yugoslav in nature.
Comintern *Communist International.* The Leninist Third International formed in 1919 to organise world communist support for the Bolshevik revolution.
CPGB *Communist Party of Great Britain.* The British Communist Party with a substantial membership within the TUC-affiliated unions and cadres.
CROM *Confederacion Regional de los Obreros Mexicanos.* The Mexican national centre allied with the AFL in the PAFL.
CTAL *Confederacion de Trabajadores de America Latina.* The Pan-American Labour Organisation led by Lombardo Toledano; now a WFTU regional body.
DAF *Deutsche Arbeitsfront.* The German national labour centre closely tied to the Nazi Party on a corporatist model.

Glossary of Commonly-used Abbreviations

DGB *Deutsche Gewerkschaftsbund.* The West German national centre with close ties to the Social Democratic Party.

EAM *National Liberation Front.* Greek political organisation formed by the Greek Communist Party and other left parties under German Occupation.

ECFTU *European Confederation of Free Trades Unions in the Community.* The co-ordinating body for ICFTU affiliates in the EEC.

EEAM *Workers' National Liberation Front.* Greek clandestine labour organisation dominated by the Communist Party during the German Occupation.

EMF *European Metalworkers' Federation.* The European industrial committee set up by the ETUC as a rival to the IMF.

ERO *European Regional Organisation.* The European regional organisation set up by the ICFTU in 1950 to co-ordinate work within Europe.

ERP *European Recovery Programme.* The agency set up to administer the various Marshall Plan assistance activities in postwar Europe.

ERP–TUAC *European Recovery Programme–Trade Union Advisory Committee.* The trades union advisory group to the ERP led by the AFL against the WFTU.

ETU *Electrical Trades Union.* The TUC-affiliated union for the electrical trades whose communist election-rigging was exposed in the late 1950s.

ETUC *European Trades Union Confederation.* The European labour international linking the ICFTU, the WCL affiliates and the CGIL within Europe.

EWC *European Works Council.* The planned intra-European works council structure for the EEC's new European Company.

FDGB *Frei-Deutsche Gewerkschaftsbund.* The WFTU-affiliated East German national centre.

FGTB *Fédération Générale du Travail de Belgique.* The Belgian national centre affiliated with the Belgian Social Democratic Party.

FIET *International Federation of Commercial, Clerical and Technical Employees.* The Geneva-based ITS led by Heribert Maier.

FIL *Federazione Italiana del Lavoro.* The socialist and republican Italian national centre formed form the CGIL split in 1948.

FTUC *Free Trades Union Committee.* The main US labour assistance arm during the war which worked with the OSS in support of European labour.

GSEE *Greek General Confederation of Labour.* The Greek national trades union centre closely allied to the leading faction of any current government.

ICF *International Chemical, Energy and General Workers' Federation.* The Geneva-based ITS led by Charles Levinson.

ICFTU *International Confederation of Free Trades Unions.* The predominantly Western-oriented global international based in Brussels.

IFBWW *International Federation of Building and Wood Workers.* The Geneva-based ITS led by John Löfblad.

IFFTU *International Federation of Free Teachers' Unions.* The Brussels-based ITS led by Andre Braconnier.

IFPAAW *International Federation of Plantation and Agricultural Workers.* The Geneva-based ITS led by Stan Correa.

IFPCW *International Federation of Petroleum and Chemical Workers.* The defunct ITS based in Denver, Colorado led until recently by Curt Hogan.

IFTU *International Federation of Trades Unions.* The 1913 Amsterdam international organisation closely linked with the socialist international.

Glossary of Commonly-used Abbreviations 269

IGF *International Graphical Federation.* The Bern-based ITS led by Heinz Coke.

ILGWU *International Ladies Garment Workers' Union.* The American needle trades union affiliated to the AFL led for many years by Dave Dubinsky.

ILO *International Labour Organisation.* The League of Nations and United Nations tripartite labour organisation based in Geneva.

IMF *International Metalworkers' Federation.* The Geneva-based largest ITS led by Herman Rebhan.

Intersindical The Portuguese national trades union centre controlled by the Portuguese Communist Party, recognised until recently as the sole legitimate union.

IRI *Istituto per la Riconstruzione Industriale.* The controlling body of the Italian parastatal corporations and the largest dispenser of patronage.

ISF *International Solidarity Fund.* The voluntary assistance fund of the ICFTU controlled until 1969 by George Meany.

ITF *International Transport Workers' Federation.* The London-based ITS led by Harold Lewis.

ITS *International Trade Secretariat.* International labour body of unions representing workers in an economic sector; associated with the ICFTU.

ITUS *International Trades Union Secretariat.* The early labour global international set up in 1903 and dominated by the German unions.

IUF *International Union of Food and Allied Workers' Associations.* The Geneva-based ITS led by Dan Gallin.

IWW *Industrial Workers of the World.* The North American syndicalist labour federation also known as the Wobblies.

KGB *Committee for State Security.* Soviet secret police and border guard force long active in international labour activities.

KKE *Kommonistikon Komma Elladas.* The Greek Communist Party, closely tied to the Soviet Party and the cominform; major protagonist in civil war.

KPD *Kommunistische Partei Deutschlands.* German Communist Party; once a major political force in Germany and German unionsim.

LCGL *Libera Confederazione Generale del Lavoro.* The ACLI-led split from the CGIL in 1948.

LO *Landesorganisationen Sverige.* Swedish national trades union federation closely allied with the Social Democratic Party.

MFA *Armed Forces Movement.* The Portuguese armed forces political organisation which seized power in 1974–5 after the fall of Caetano.

MIF *Miners' International Federation.* The London-based ITS led by Peter Tait.

NKP *Norges Kommunistiske Parti.* The Norwegian Communist Party.

NVV *Nederlands Verbond van Vakvereiningen.* The Dutch national labour centre which has recently merged with the Catholic national centre.

ORIT *Interamerican Regional Organization of Labor.* The interamerican regional organisation of the ICFTU.

PAFL *Pan-American Federation of Labor.* The interamerican labour federation formed by the AFL and the Mexicans in 1918.

PCE *Partido Communista de Espana.* The Spanish Communist Party operating underground since its defeat in 1936 and tied to the CCOO unions.

PCF *Parti Communiste Français.* The French Communist Party tied closely to the CGT unions.
PCI *Partito Communista Italiana.* The Italian Communist Party closely tied to the CGIL unions.
PCP *Partido Communista Portugues.* The Portuguese Communist Party closely tied to the unions of the Intersindical.
PPR *Polska Partia Robotnica.* The immediate postwar Polish Workers' Party which was a euphemism for the Polish Communist Party of Gomulka.
Profintern *Labour Union International.* The Russian abbreviation for the Red International of Labour Unions, the labour arm of the Comintern.
PSI *Public Service International.* The London-based ITS led by Carl Franken.
PSOE *Partido Socialista Obrera de Espana.* The Spanish Social Democratic Party with close ties to the UGT.
PTTI *Post, Telegraph and Telephone International.* The Geneva-based ITS led by Stefan Nedzynski.
ROH *Revolucni Odborov Hnuti.* The Czechoslovak national trades union centre reconstituted under Zapotocky after the war.
SAK *Suomen Ammattiyhdistysten Keskusliitto.* The Confederation of Finnish Trades Unions; the Finnish national trades union centre.
SED *Sozialistische Einheitspartei Deutschlands.* The East German Communist Party with close ties to the FDGB.
SFIO *Section Française de l'Internationale Ouvrière.* The French Socialist Party with ties to the CGT–FO and the CFDT.
SPD *Sozialdemokratischepartei Deutschlands.* The West German Social Democratic Party with close ties to the DGB.
SSA *Sveriges Social demokratiska Arbetarparti,* The Swedish Social Democratic Workers Party closely tied to the LO.
STV *Solidaridad de Trabajadores Vascos.* The Basque regional confederation of unions which co-operates with the UGT.
TCO *Tjänstmännens Centralorganisation.* The Swedish white-collar and civil service national labour confederation.
TGWU *Transport and General Workers Union.* The largest affiliate to the British TUC and an important factor in Labour Party politics.
TUC *Trades Union Congress.* The large British national centre closely allied with the British Labour Party.
TUI *Trade Union International.* One of a number of WFTU departments set up to parallel and compete with the ITSs of the ICFTU.
UAW *United Automobile, Aerospace and Agricultural Implements Workers.* The large North American union led for many years by Walter Reuther.
UGT *Union General de Trabajadores de Espana.* The large Spanish national centre closely linked with the PSOE and the Christian democratic unions.
UIL *Unione Italiana del Lavoro.* The Italian trade union national centre closely tied with the Italian Socialist Party.
USO *Union Sindical Obrera.* The mainly Christian-Democratic Spanish trades union centre which has merged with the UGT.
VPK *Vänsterpartiet–Kommunisterna.* The Swedish Communist Party linked in an informal alliance with the SSA.

WCL *World Confederation of Labour.* The Christian global international which dropped its confessional ties and labels in 1968.
WFTU *World Federation of Trades Unions.* The largely communist-dominated global international from which the Western unions split in 1948.

Select Bibliography

Abou Alam, A. R., *Labor Movement in Eygpt* (Washington: Embassy, 1955).
Abramova, A. A., *Sovetskoe Trudove Pravo* (Moscow: Profizdat, 1957).
AFL–CIO, *To Clear the Record* (Washington: AFL–CIO, 1968).
Afrifa, A. A., *The Ghana Coup* (London: Frank Cass, 1961).
Agee, P., *Inside the Company* (Harmondsworth: Penguin, 1975).
Ameen, M. F., *Le Histoire du Mouvement Syndicale et Legislation Ouvriers en Eygpte* (Cairo: Almal-Kutob, 1961).
Anananba, W., *The Trade Union Movement in Africa* (London: Hurst, 1969).
Angell, A., *Politics and the Labour Movement in Chile* (London: Oxford University Press, 1972).
Attwood, W., *The Reds and the Blacks* (New York: Harper & Row, 1967).
Ayusawa, I., *A History of Labor in Modern Japan* (Honolulu: East–West Center, 1966).
Badaoui, Z., *Les Problèmes du Travail et les organisations Ouvrières en Eygpte* (Alexandria: Societies, 1948).
Baily, S. L., *The U.S. and the Development of South America* (New York: New Viewpoints, 1976).
Baily, S. L., *Labor, Nationalism and Politics in Argentina* (New Brunswick: Rutgers University Press, 1967).
Barkin, S. (ed.), *Worker Militancy and its Consequences* (New York: Praeger, 1975).
Barkin, S., *International Labor* (New York: IRRA, 1967).
Barnet, R., *Intervention and Revolution*, New York: Meridian, 1969).
Beling, W. A. (ed.), *The Role of Labor in African Nation-Building* (New York: Praeger, 1968).
Beling, W. A., *Modernization and African Labor* (New York: Praeger, 1965).
Beling, W. A., *Pan-Arabism and Labor* (Cambridge, Mass.: Harvard University Press, 1961).
Bentum, B., *Trade Unions in Chains* (Accra: Liberty, 1966).
Bernstein, I., *Turbulent Years* (Boston: Houghton Mifflin, 1970).
Bernstein, I., *Lean Years* (Boston: Houghton Mifflin, 1968).
Beshir, M. O., *Revolution and Nationalism in the Sudan* (London: Rex Collings, 1974).
Bidwell, B. W., *History of the Military Intelligence Division* (Washington: US Army, 1961).
Bowen, W., *Colonial Trade Unions* (London: Fabian, 1954).
Brown, A. C. (ed.), *The Secret War Report of the OSS* (New York: Berkeley, 1976).
Brown, B. E. (ed.), *Eurocommunism and Eurosocialism* (London: Cyrico, 1979).

Brunschwig, H., *French Colonialism* (New York: Praeger 1966).
Brzezinski, Z., *Africa and the Communist World* (Calif.: Stanford University Press, 1963).
Buell, R. L., *The Native Problem in Africa* (New York: Macmillan, 1928).
Buhkbinder, N., *Istoriia Yevreiskogo Robochego Dvizhenia v Rossii* (Leningrad: Star, 1925).
Busch, G. K., *Political Currents in the International Trade Union Movement* (London: Economist Intelligence Unit, Special Report No. 75, 1980).
Busch, G. K. *Pan-Africanism and Pan-African Trade Unions* (Washington: American University, 1969, dissertation).
CMB–FGTB, *Etudes No. 7* (Brussels: FGTB 1973).
Cadbury, W. A., *Labour in Portuguese West Africa* (London: Routledge, 1910).
Carew, A., *Democracy and Government in European Trade Unions* (London: George Allen & Unwin, 1976).
Chalmers, W. E., *Crucial Issues in Industrial Relations in Singapore* (Singapore: Donald Moore, 1967).
Chilcote, R. H. and J. C. Edelstein, *Latin America* (Cambridge, Mass.: Schenkman, 1974).
Clegg, H. A., *The System of Industrial Relations in Great Britain* (Oxford: Basil Blackwell, 1972).
Cockburn, C., *Union Power* (London: Kimber, 1976).
Colby, W., *Honorable Men* (London: Hutchinson, 1978).
Cole, R. E., *Japanese Blue Collar* (Berkeley: University of California Press, 1971).
Connor, E., *Global Unionism* (Old Bridge: Blinker, 1967).
Cook, A., *Japanese Trade Unionism* (Ithaca: Cornell University Press, 1966).
Cormier, F. and W. J. Eaton, *Reuther* (Englewood Cliffs, NJ: Prentice-Hall, 1970).
Corson W. R., *The Armies of Ignorance* (New York: Dial, 1977).
Crawley, A., *The Spoils of War* (New York: Bobbs-Merrill, 1973).
Dahl, R. (ed.), *Political Oppositions in Western Democracies* (New Haven: Yale University Press, 1966).
Dahrendorf, R., *Class and Class Conflict in Industrial Society* Calif.: Standford University Press, 1959).
Davies, I., *African Trade Unions* (Harmondsworth: Penguin, 1966).
Dogadov, V. M., *Istoriia Profsoiuznogo Dvizhenia v SSSr* (Moscow: Profizdat, 1955).
Dubofsky, M., *American Labor Since the New Deal* (Chicago: Quadrangle, 1971).
Dulles, A. W., *The Secret Surrender* (London: Weidenfeld, 1967).
Dulles, F. R. *Labor in America* (New York: Crowell, 1955).
Dziewanowski, M. K., *The Communist Party of Poland* (Cambridge, Mass.: Harvard University Press, 1959).
Farago, L., *The Game of Foxes* (New York: McKay, 1971).
Fawzi, S. E. D., *The Labour Movement in the Sudan* (London: Oxford University Press, 1957).
Fine, S., *Sit-Down* (Ann Arbor: University of Michigan, 1969).
Fonseca, A. J., *Wage Determination and Organized Labor in India* (Bombay: Oxford University Press, 1964).

Ford, C., *Donovan of the OSS* (Boston: Little, Brown, 1970).
Foster, W. Z., *American Trade Unionism* (New York: International, 1947).
Fournier N. and E. Legrand, *E . . . Comme Espionnage* (Paris: Alain Moreau, 1978).
Friedland, W. H., *Unions and Industrial Relations in Underdeveloped Countries* (annotated bibliography) (Ithaca: Cornell University Press, 1963).
Galenson, W. (ed.), *Labor in Developing Countries*, (Berkeley: University of California Press, 1962).
Galenson, W., *The CIO Challenge to the AFL* (Cambridge, Mass.: Harvard University Press, 1960).
Galenson, W., *Labor and Economic Development* (New York: Wiley, 1959).
Galvin, M., *Unionism in Latin America*, (Ithaca: Cornell University Press, 1962).
Gamba, C., *The Origins of Trade Unionism in Malaya* (Singapore: Eastern University, 1962).
Geiss, I., *Gewerkschaften In Afrika* (Bonn: Friedrich Ebert, 1965).
Gil, F., *Political System of Chile* (Boston: Houghton Mifflin, 1966).
Gilly, A., *La Nueva Nicaragua* (Mexico City: Nueva Imagen, 1980).
Godson, R., *The Kremlin and Labor* (New York: Crane, Russak, 1977).
Godson, R., *American Labor and European Politics* (New York: Crane, Russak, 1976).
Goldman, W. E., *I.C.F.T.U. 1949–1962* (Los Angeles: University of Southern California, 1967, dissertation).
Goldwert, M., *Democracy, Militarism and Nationalism in Argentina* (Austin: University of Texas Press, 1972).
Gompers, S., *Seventy Years of Life and Labor* (New York: Dutton, 1925).
Gott, R., *Guerilla Movements in Latin America* (London: Nelson, 1970).
Gottfurcht, H., *Die Internationale Gewerkschaftsbewegung* (Cologne: Bund Verlag, 1966).
Goulden, J. C., *Meany* (New York: Atheneum, 1972).
Grieg, I., *The Ultra-Left Offensive Against Multinational Companies* (London: Foreign Affairs Research, 1979).
Grossholtz, J., *Politics in the Philippines* (Boston: Little, Brown, 1964).
Gutkind, P., Cohen, R. and Copans, J. (eds) *African Labor History* (London: Sage, 1978).
Hammond, T., *Lenin on Trade Unions and Revolution* (New York: Columbia University Press, 1957).
Harada, S., *Labor Conditions in Japan* (New York: Columbia University Press, 1928).
Harrod, J., *Trade Union Foreign Policy* (New York: Anchor, 1972).
Hazama, H., *Nihon Romu Kanrishi Kenkyu* (Tokyo: Diamond, 1964).
Hero, A. O. and E. Starr, *The Reuther–Meany Foreign Policy Dispute* (New York: 1970, manuscript).
Hirsch, F. and R. Fletcher, *CIA and the Labour Movement* (Nottingham: Spokesman, 1977).
Hodges, D. C., *The Latin American Revolution* (New York: Morrow, 1974).
Horowitz, D., *The Italian Labor Movement* (Cambridge, Mass.: Harvard University Press, 1963).
Horowitz, I. L. (ed.)., *Cuban Communism* (Chicago: Aldine, 1970).
Horowitz, I. L., *Latin American Radicalism* (New York: Vintage, 1969).

Horrell, M., *South African Trade Unionism* (Capetown: IRRA, 1961).
Hulse, J. W., *The Forming of the Communist International* (Calif.: Stanford University Press, 1961).
Hymoff, E., *The OSS in World War II* (New York: Ballantine, 1972).
Ianni, O., *Politica e Revolucao Social no Brasil* (Rio de Janeiro: Edicciones Civilizacao Brasileira, 1966).
Ind, A., *Allied Intelligence Bureau* (New York: McKay, 1958).
Jackson, D. B., *Castro, the Kremlin and Communism in Latin America* (Baltimore: Johns Hopkins Press, 1969).
Jacobs, E., *European Trades Unionism* (New York: Holmes & Meier, 1973).
Jecchinis, C., *Trade Unionism In Greece* (Chicago: Roosevelt, 1967).
Josey, A., *Trade Unionism in Malaya* (Singapore: Donald Moore, 1954).
Kamplelman, M. M., *The Communist Party vs. the CIO* (New York: Praeger, 1957).
Karnik, V. B., *Indian Trade Unions* (Bombay: B. K. Desai, 1960).
Kassalow, E. (ed.), *Trade Unions and International Relations* (New York: Random House, 1969).
Kassalow, E., *National Labor Movements in the Postwar World* (Chicago: Northwestern University Press, 1963).
Kassalow, E. and Damachi, U. G., *The Role of Trade Unions in Developing Societies* (Geneva: Institute For Labour Studies, 1978).
Kautsky, J. H., *Moscow and the Communist Party of India* (New York: Wiley, 1956).
Kendall, W., *The Labour Movement in Europe* (London: Allen Lane, 1975).
Knoellinger, C. E., *Labor in Finland* (Cambridge, Mass.: Harvard University Press, 1960).
Knowles, W. H., *Trade Union Development and Industrial Relations in the British West Indies* (Berkeley: University of California Press, 1959).
Kujawa, D., *American Labor and the Multinational Corporation* (New York: Praeger, 1973).
Kurihara, K., *Labor in the Phillipine Economy* (Calif.: Stanford University Press, 1945).
Kusnetsov, V. V., *Partiia i Profsoiuizy* (Moscow: Profizdat, 1945).
La Palombara, J., *The Italian Labor Movement* (Ithaca: Cornell University Press, 1947).
Lador-Lederer, J., *International Non-Governmental Organisations and Economic Entities* (Leyden: A. W. Sythoff, 1963).
Laskaris, G., *Democratic and Communist Trade Unions* (Athens: GSEE, 1958).
Latin America Bureau, *Unity is Strength* (London: Latin American Bureau, 1980).
Lefranc, G., *Les Expériences Syndicales Internationales* (Paris: Aubier, 1952).
Legum, C., *Pan-Africanism* (New York: Praeger, 1962).
Lens, S., *The Military–Industrial Complex* (London: Kahn & Overhill, 1970).
Lens, S., *The Crisis of American Labor* (New York: Perpetua, 1961).
Levine, S., *Industrial Relations in Postwar Japan* (Urbana: University of Illinois Press, 1958).
Levinson, C., *Vodka–Cola* (London: Gordon & Cremonesi, 1987).
Levinson, C., (ed.), *Industry's Democratic Revolution* (London: George Allen & Unwin, 1974).

Levinson, C., (ed.), *International Trade Unionism* (London: George Allen & Unwin, 1972).
Lewis, A., *Labour in the West Indies* (London: New Beacon, 1977).
Lewis, A. H., *Lament for the Molly Maguires* (New York: Pocket, 1969).
Lodge, G. C., *Spearheads of Democracy* (New York: Harper & Row, 1962).
Lopez, Aparicio, A., *El Movimiento Obrero en Mexico* (Mexico City: Jus, 1952).
Lorwin, L., *The International Labor Movement* (New York: Harper, 1953).
Lorwin, L., *Labor and Internationalism* (New York: Macmillan, 1928).
Lubembe, C., *The Inside of the Labour Movement of Kenya* (Nairobi: Equatorial, 1968).
Lynd, G. E., *The Politics of African Trade Unionism* (New York: Praeger, 1968).
Mahmud, K., *Trade Unionism in Pakistan* (Lahore: University of the Punjab, 1958).
Maier, C. S., *The Origins of the Cold War and Contemporary Europe* (New York: New Viewpoints, 1978).
Mandel, E., *Kritik Des Eurokommunismus* (Berlin: Olle & Wolter, 1978).
Markakis, J. and N. Ayele, *Class and Revolution in Ethiopia* (Nottingham: Spokesman, 1978).
Marchetti, V. and J. D. Marks, *The CIA and the Cult of Intelligence* (New York: Knopf, 1974).
Masani, M. R., *The Communist Party of India* (New York: Macmillan, 1954).
Mathur A. S. and J. S. Mathur, *Trade Union Movement in India* (Allahabad: Chaitanya, 1962).
McGarvey, P. J., *CIA: The Myth and the Madness*, (New York: Saturday Review, 1972).
McInnes, N., *Communist Parties of Western Europe* (London: RIIA, 1975).
Meier, A. A., *Rukovodstvo Bol'shevistkoi Partii Profsoiuzami v Period Stalinskoi Piatiletki* (Moscow: Academy Social Science, 1951).
Meyers, F., *European Coal Mining Unions* (Berkeley: University of California Press, 1961).
Meynaud, J. and A. Salah-Bey, *Trade Unionism in Africa* (London: Methuen, 1967).
Millen, B., *The Political Role of Labor in Developing Countries* (Washington: Brooking, 1963).
Mintz, J., *Mohammed, Marx and Marhaen* (New York: Praeger, 1965).
Montaldo, J., *Les Secrets de la Banque Sovietique en France* (Paris: Albin Michel, 1979).
Montaldo, J., *Les Finances du P.C.F.* (Paris: Albin Michel, 1977).
Morrell, E. B., *Communist Unionism* (Cambridge, Mass.: Harvard University, 1965, dissertation).
Morris, G., *CIA and American Labor* (New York: International, 1967).
Morris, J. O., *Elites, Intellectuals and Consensus* (Ithaca: Cornell University Press, 1966).
Neufeld, M. F., *Poor Countries and Authoritarian Rule* (Ithaca: Cornell University Press 1965).
Olle, W. (ed.), *Einfuehrung in die Internationale Gewerkschaftspolitik* (Berlin: Olle & Wolter, 1978).
Orde Browne, G. S. J., *The African Labourer* (New York: Barnes & Noble, 1967).

Ornati, O., *Jobs and Workers in India* (Ithaca: Cornell University Press 1955).
Orri, F. S., *Theories and Solutions of National Trades Unionism* (Madrid: Prensa, 1950).
Panettieri, J., *Los Trabajadores* (Buenos Aires: Jorge Alvarez, 1967).
Pelling, H., *A History of British Trade Unionism* (Baltimore: Pelican, 1963).
Pelling, H., *American Labor* (New York: Popular, 1962).
Persico, J. E., *Piercing the Reich* (London: Michael Joseph, 1979).
Petras J. and M. Zeitlin, *Politics and Social Forces in Chilean Development* (Berkeley: University of California Press, 1969).
Pierson, F. C., *Unions in Postwar America* (New York: Random House, 1967).
Plum, W., *Gewerkschaften im Mahgreb* (Hannover: Friedrich Ebert, 1962).
Price, J., *The International Labour Movement* (London: Oxford University Press 1945).
Prouty, L. F., *The Secret Team* (Englewood Cliffs, NJ: Prentice-Hall, 1973).
Radosh, R., *American Labor and U.S. Foreign Policy* (New York: Random House, 1969).
Ramos, J. A., *Revolucion y Contrarrevolucion en la Argentina* (Buenos Aires: Plus Ultra, 1965).
Rayback, J. G., *A History of American Labor* (New York: Macmillan, 1964).
Rebhan, H., *Trade Unions and the World* (London: Anvil, 1980).
Renshaw, P., *The Wobblies* (Garden City, NY: Doubleday, 1967).
Reuther, V., *The Brothers Reuther* (Boston: Houghton Mifflin, 1976).
Rhemus, C. M. and D. McLaughlin, *Labor and American Politics* (Ann Arbor: University of Michigan Press, 1967).
Richards, L., *The Military and Trades Unions as Vehicles for Political Change* (Honolulu: University of Hawaii, 1974, dissertation).
Rigola, R., *Storia del Movimento Operaio Italiano* (Milan: Domus, 1947).
Roberts, E., *Worker's Control* (London: George Allen & Unwin, 1973).
Rolph, C. H., *All Those in Favour* (London: Andre Deutsch, 1962).
Romualdi, S., *Presidents and Peons* (New York: Funk & Wagnalls, 1967).
Roper, J. I., *Labour Problems in West Africa* (Harmondsworth: Penguin, 1958).
Rositzke, H., *The CIA's Secret Operations* (New York: Reader's Digest, 1977).
Ross, A. M. (ed.), *Industrial Relations and Economic Development* (London: Macmillan, 1966).
Sandbrook, R. and R. Cohen, *The Development of an African Working Class* (London: Longman, 1975).
Saposs, D., *Left Wing Unionism* (New York: Russell, 1967).
Sarti, R., *Fascism and the Industrial Leadership in Italy* (Berkeley: University of California Press, 1971).
Schneider, R., *Communism in Guatemala 1944–1954* (New York: Praeger, 1958).
Schwarz, S., *Labor in the Soviet Union* (New York: Praeger, 1952).
Scott, R., *The Development of Trade Unions in Uganda* (Nairobi: East Africa Publishing House, 1966).
Seidman, J., *American Labor from Defense to Reconversion* (University of Chicago Press, 1953).
Sembene, O., *God's Bits of Wood* (Garden City, NY: Dubleday, 1952).
Seton-Watson, H., *From Lenin to Khruschev* (New York: Praeger, 1960).

Singh, M., *History of Kenya's Trade Union Movement* (Nairobi: East Africa Publishing House, 1969).
Skidmore, T., *Politics in Brazil* (New York: Oxford University Press, 1967).
Smith, R. H., *OSS* (New York: Dell, 1973).
Snow, S., *Samuel Gompers and the Pan-American Federation of Labor* (Richmond: University of Virginia, 1960, dissertation).
Spalding, H. A. (Jr), *Organized Labor in Latin America* (New York: Harper, 1977).
Spitaels, G., *Le Mouvement Syndical en Belgique* (Brussels: Free University of Brussels, 1967).
Stenson, M. R., *Industrial Conflict in Malaya* (London: Oxford University Press, 1970).
Sturmthal, A., *Comparative Labor Movements* (Belmont: Wadsworth, 1972).
Sturmthal, A., *Unity and Diversity in European Labor* (Glencoe, Ill.: Free Press, 1963).
Sturmthal, A. and J. Scoville (eds), *The International Labor Movement in Transition* (Urbana: University of Illinois Press, 1973).
Suarez, A., *Cuba, Castroism and Communism* (Cambridge, Mass.: MIT, 1968).
Sufrin, S., *Unions in Emerging Societies* (New York: Syracuse University Press, 1964).
Sweet-Escott, B., *Greece: A Political and Economic Survey* (London: RIIA, 1954).
Tachau, F., *Politics and Modernization in South and Southeast Asia* (New York: Schenkman, 1973).
Taft, P., *Defending Freedom* (Los Angels: Nash, 1973).
Taft, P., *The AFL from the Death of Gompers to the Merger* (New York: Harper, 1959).
Taft, P., *The AFL in the Time of Gompers* (New York: Harper, 1957).
Tedjasukmana, I., *The Political Character of the Indonesian Trade Union Movement* (Ithaca: Cornell University Press, 1959).
Thompson, D. and R. Larson, *Where Were You, Brother?* (London: War on Want, 1978).
Toriello, G., *La Batalla de Guatemala* (Mexico City: Cuaderna Americanos 1955).
Totten, G., *The Social Democratic Movement in Prewar Japan* (New Haven, Conn.: Yale University Press, 1966).
Tulatz, H. A., *Die Gewerkschaften Nigerias* (Hannover: Friedrich Ebert, 1963).
Tyler, G., *The Labor Revolution* (New York: Viking, 1966).
Urban, G. (ed.), *Euro-Communism* (London: Maurice Temple Smith, 1978).
Van der Slice, A., *International Labor, Diplomacy and Peace* (Philadelphia: University of Pennsylvania, 1941).
Vargas, G., *A Nova Politica* (Rio de Janeiro: Jose Olympio, 1938).
Viklund, B. and G. Edgren, *Fackligt Samarbete Over Graenserna* (Stockholm: LO, 1967).
Wallerstein, I., *Africa, the Politics of Unity* (New York: Random House, 1967).
Warmington, W. A., *A West African Trade Union* (London: Oxford University Press, 1960).
Wedin, A., *Internationell Fackling Solidaritet* (Stockholm: Prisma, 1974).

White, L., *International Non-Governmental Organizations* (New Brunswick: Rutgers University Press, 1951).
Wigham, E. L., *Trade Unions* (London: Oxford University Press, 1969).
Windmuller, J. P., *Labor Internationals* (Ithaca: Cornell University Press, 1969).
Windmuller, J. P., *Labor Relations in the Netherlands* (Ithaca: CornellUniversity Press, 1969).
Windmuller, J. P., *American Labor and the International Labor Movement* (Ithaca: Cornell University Press, 1954).
Yusufu, T. M., *Industrial and Labor Relations in Nigeria* (London: Oxford University Press, 1962).
Zammit, J. A. (ed.), *The Chilean Road to Socialism* (Austin: University of Texas, 1973).
Zartman, I. W., *Man, State and Society in the Contemporary Mahgrib* (New York: Praeger, 1973).
Zetlin, M., *Revolutionary Politics and the Cuban Working Class* (NJ: Princeton University Press, 1967).
Zinner, P., *Communist Strategy and Tactics in Czechoslovakia* (New York: Praeger, 1963).

Index

AALD, 34, 137
AAPO, 91–2
AATUF, 104
   competition with AFRO, 92–5
   competition with ATUC, 95–6
   formation, 92–4
Abad Santos, Pedro, 121–2
Abwehr, 35, 140
ACAT, 139
ACFTU, 41
ACLI, 63
Adebola, Alhaji Haroun Popoola, 94
Adler, Friedrich, 14
Adoula, Cyrille, 76
AFL, 65
   competition with IWW, 17–18, 34
   founding, 7–9
   Free Trade Union Committee, 36–9, 48, 132, 141
   German trades union reconstruction, 53–6
   in Africa, 88
   in Latin America, 33–5, 137–44
   relations with ICFTU, 68–72
   relations with IFTU, 18–20
   relations with WFTU, 26
   split in French trades union movement, 57–60
   split in Italian trades union movement, 64–5
   ties to U.S. government, 32–4, 137–8
AFL-CIO, 2, 40
   AAFLI, 123–4, 131–3
   AIFLD, 138–61, 169–80
   formation, 184
   Meany–Reuther conflict, 184–6
   relations with CIA, 189–90
   relations with European unions, 186–9
Afro-Asian Training Institute, 40
Ahmed, Muzzafar, 110
AITUC, 109–16, 132
Akumu, Dennis, 99
Aleman, Miguel, 143
Alessandrini, Jorge, 172
Allende, Salvador, 172–6, 244
Alonso, Jose, 156
American Labour Union, 17
American Military Government, 53–4, 56
Anastasia, Albert, 94
Ansari, Farid-ul-huq, 111
Antunes, Melo, 247
Appleton, J., 20
Apristas, 137
Arana, Francisco, 145–6
Arbenz, Jacopo, 145–7
Argentina
   development of trades unions, 149–50
   under Peron, 151–7
Arias, M., 245
Armas, Castillo, 147–8
ATLAS, 41, 155
ATUC, 95–6
AUCCTU, 26–7, 51, 107
Awab, M., 95

Baccouche, Taieb, 256
Badoglio, Pietro, 61
Bakunin, Mikhail, 6–7, 135
Banque Commerciale pour l'Europe du Nord, 58–9
Barnes, R., 20
Barnes, Tracey, 146
Barrra, Albino, 142
Baruch, Bernard, 34

Bauer, Otto, 14
Becu, Omar, 38, 88
Beetge, Gert, 256
Beirne, Joseph, 160
Ben Ezzidine, Mahmoud, 94, 98
Ben Seddick, Majoub, 93, 95
Benedict, Daniel, 148
Benes, Edouard, 43
Bennett, William, 112
Berdennikov, Nikolai, 260
Berlinguer, Enrico, 209
Betancourt, Romulo, 143
Bevin, Ernest, 29, 32, 58, 94
Bidault, Georges, 58
Bishop, Morris, 257
Blankenhorn, Herbert, 37
Blum, Leon, 14, 32
Boeckler, Hans, 52, 72
Bonomi, Ivanoe, 62
Borisov, 230
Borlaff, Otero, 148
Borlenghi, Angel, 151
Borodin, Mikhail, 105, 109, 136
Bose, Subhas Chandra, 112–14
Botha, Piet, 256
Botha, Thozamile, 255
Bothereau, Robert, 57
Bowden, George, 37–8
Braden, Tom, 60, 70
Braden, Spruille, 154
Bradley, William, 110–11
Brasoveanu, Georghje, 230
Brazil, 166–71
Brecht, Berthold, 249
Brinkerhoff, Charles, 160
British Guiana, 162–5
British TUC, 2, 55
   conflict with government, 214–17
   creation of labour attachés, 78
   founding, 6, 9
   in British Guiana, 163–5
   mission to Germany, 52–3
   relations with ICFTU, 69–72
   role in WFTU, 29–30, 68
   search for Allied unity, 24–7
   ties to government, 31–2
Brophy, John, 30
Brown, Irving, 36–7, 54, 57, 59–60, 64–5, 119

Bukrayev, Vladimir, 260
Bulgaria, 48
Burnham, Forbes, 163–5, 257
Buu, Tran Quoc, 131

Caballero, Largo, 242
Caetano, Marcelo, 244, 246–7
Cafe Filho, M., 167
Camacho, Marcelino, 244–5
Cana, Ion, 230
Canini, Giovanni, 64, 66
Cardenas, Lazaro, 35, 139–40
Carey, James, 66, 68, 141
Carillo, Alejandro, 140
Carillo, Santiago, 243
Carranza, M., 136
Caribbean unions, 257–8
CASL, 90
Castelo Branco, F., 170
Castillo, Ramon, 151
Castro, Fidel, 158–9, 164, 178
CATC, 81
CFTC (CFDT), 59, 87
CGIL, 62–5
CGT (Argentina), 149–54
CGT
   control by PCF, 27
   external funding, 58–9
   founding (Charter of Amiens), 9, 16
   in Africa, 73, 78–9, 84–7
   in Germany, 51–2
   role in WFTU, 27
   split, 56–9
   strike in 1947, 58–9
CGT–FO, 57–61, 79, 86–9
CGTA, 87
CGTG, 145
Chile, 171–7
Chilean Confederation of Professionals, 175–6
China, 104–8
Churchill, Winston Spencer, 151
CIA, 69, 131
   and charitable foundations, 164, 169
   and ITSs, 189–90
   inheritor of OSS, 39, 56
   in Guatemala, 146–8
   relations with AIFLD, 161–2, 173

Cid, Cypriano, 122
CIO
  and German reconstruction, 53-4
  formation, 24-5
  relations with ICFTU, 69-71
  role in WFTU, 27-30
  split, 67-8
CISC (WCL), 92-3, 190
  CISC-EO, 203
CLASC (CLAT), 157-8, 203
  formation, 20-1
  relations with ICFTU, 71-2
CISL, 65
Cisse, Alioune, 94
CIT, 143
Citrine, Walter, 24-5, 29-32, 36, 68
Clark, John Magnus, 112
Claudin, Fernando, 243
Clay, Lucius, 53
Cominform, 83
Comintern
  and Profintern, 23
  formation, 12-14
  in India, 109-14
  in Latin America, 136
Communist Party of India, 110-17
Cooke, John William, 156
Cope, Elmer, 60
Costas, Patron, 151
Crespo, Victor, 247
Critchlow, Hubert, 162
Croizat, Ambrose, 57
CROM, 35, 138
Cruz, Hermanigildo, 120
CSLA, 137
CTAL, 26, 29, 139-42, 155
CTM, 35, 139
Cunhal, Alvaro, 247-8, 250-1
Cyrankiewiecz, Jozef, 49
Cyrus, Stanley, 257
Czechoslovakia
  Charter 77, 230
  model for Eastern European unions, 47-8
  postwar political crisis, 43-7
  Prague Spring, 203, 206-7

D'Aguiar, Peter, 164
D'Estaing, Valerie Giscard, 207

Da Silva, Luiz Ignacio, 171
Dan, Phan Quang, 132
Dange, S. A., 110, 115-16
Daniels, Gerry, 119
Davis, William Rhodes, 140
De Barros, Adehmar, 168, 170
De Caux, Len, 68
De Gasperi, Alcide, 63
De Gaulle, Charles, 206-7
De La Torre, R. Haya, 137, 143
De Los Reyes, Isabelo, 120
Deakin, Arthur, 62, 68-9, 72
Debs, Eugene Victor, 17
Delaney, George Phillip, 70
DeLeon, Daniel, 17
Deshpande, S. V., 111
Deverall, Richard L., 107
DGB, 2, 186-7, 212-14
Di Vittorio, Giuseppe, 63, 66, 68
Diallo, Abdoulaye, 87
Diallo, Seydou, 87
Diaz, Carlos Enrique, 147
Diaz, Porfirio, 75, 137
Doherty, William, 170, 179
Domench, Jose, 150
Donovan, William, 37
Dubcek, Alexander, 243
Dubinsky, David, 36-7, 71
Duclos, Jacques, 22, 59
Dulles, Allen, 37
Dutra, Eurico, 167
Dutt, Rajni Palme, 112, 169

Eanes, Ramon, 250
Eberlein, Hugo, 12
Edwards, Robert, 201
Eisner, Kurt, 11
EITUC, 31
Emmanuel, Victor, 62
Erban, Evzen, 44
ERP-TUAC, 64, 66-8
Eurocommunism, 205-11
European unions
  competition in Western Europe, 181-3
  Eastern European dissidents, 227-31
ETUC, 219
Euro-secretariats, 223

Index

European unions (*Contd.*)
  inter-union competition, 218–26
  relations with governments, 181–3

Faltermayer, Heinz, 260
Fantomas Affair, 22
Farrell, Edelmiro, 153
Feather, Victor, 220
Fernandes, George, 117
Ferri-Pisani, Pierre, 60
FDGB, 51, 53–4
Fierlinger, Zdenek, 44–5
Figueras, Jose, 123–4
Figueroa, Luis, 172–4
Fimmen, O., 20
Finet, Paul, 71
Frachon, Benoit, 57
France
  events of 1968, 205–6
  postwar political crisis, 56–60
  role of communist unions, 23–4
Franco, Francisco, 242–3
Frei, Eduardo, 172–3
Friele, Bernd, 160
Frolik, Jozef, 260
Front organisations, 102–3, 121

Gaitskell, Hugh, 214
Gandhi, Indira, 117–18
Gandhi, Mohandas, 76, 108, 113, 115
Garcia Salve, Francisco, 244
Geddes, Charles, 119
Geijer, Arne, 187
Germany
  political conflicts, 212–14
  postwar political crisis, 50–6
Gibbons, J. David, 257
Gilmore, Chris, 201
Goldberg, Arthur, 37–8
Goldsack Donoso, Jose, 157, 172
Goma, Paul, 230
Gomez, Dominador, 120
Gompers, Samuel, 7, 17–20, 32–3, 139
Gomulka, Wladyslaw, 48–9
Gonzalez, Felipe, 244–5
Gonzalez Videla, Gabriel, 143–4, 171
Gori, Pietro, 135
Gottwald, Klement, 45–7

Goulart, Joao, 167–70
Grace, J. Peter, 160, 179
Great Britain
  colonial military policy, 97
  in Africa, 87–8
  in India, 113–15
  national relations, 214–18
'Great Conspiracy Against Africa', 94
Greece, 49
Green, William, 25, 72, 141
Grimau, Julian, 243
GTUC, 97
Guatemala, 144–7
Guerrero, Jorge, 175
Guevara, Che, 178
Guillaume, Gunter, 260
Guitierrez, Victor Manuel, 145

Halim, Abdul, 111
Hammer, Michael, 262
Hallsworth, R., 27
Heath, Edward, 216–17
Herling, John, 141
Hickey, William, 160
Hilferding, Otto, 14
Hill, Robert, 160
Hitler–Stalin Pact, 23
Hoffa, James Riddell, 94
Howlen, Helen, 112
HMS, 115–17
Huang, Tran Van, 132
Hull, Cordell, 140
Hungary, 47–8
Hutchinson, Lester, 110

IAW, 14
Ibarruri, Dolores, 243
Ibanez, Bernardo, 72, 142, 144, 171
Ibanez, Carlos, 171, 177
ICATU, 92
ICFTU, 65
  AFRO, 90, 93–6
  ARO, 118–20
  ETUS, 203
  formation, 69–72
  in Africa, 88–9
  ISF, 148, 187–8
  ORIT, 148, 155, 168–70

ILGWU, 36
ILO, 13, 20–1, 69
India, 108–19
Inglesias, Santiago, 33
Ingrao, Pietro, 201
INTUC, 115–18
Ishmael, Richard, 164–5
IRI, 62
IMF, 194–5
Italy, 61–6, 208–10
ITF, 31, 38
ITS
    and Euro-secretariats, 223
    formation, 15–16
    in Chile, 175
    relations with AIFLD, 161–2
    relations with ICFTU, 72
    relations with multinationals, 191–201
    relations with WFTU, 28–9
    role in Germany, 55
    rules of affiliation, 60
ITUS (IFTU)
    disruptions of First World War, 18
    effects of Second World War, 24
    founding, 16
    name change, 18
IWA, 6–7
IWW, 17–19, 80, 135, 138

Jagan, Cheddi, 163–5
Jagan, Janet, 163
Jallow, Mamadou, 93
Japan, 124–30
Jeffrey, Newman, 54
Jensen, Einar, 72
Johnstone, J. W., 111
Jones, Jack, 220–21
Joshi, N. M., 110–11
Jouhaux, Leon, 20, 58–9, 72
Juan Carlos, King of Spain, 244
Justo, Augustin P., 149

Kaba, Mamady, 95
Kabia, James, 256
Kano, Aminu, 257
Kai-Shek, Chiang, 106
Karl, Albin, 118
Katayama, Sen, 124, 136

Katju, Kailash Nath, 111
Kawawa, Rashidi, 76
Keenan, Joseph, 54
KFL, 91–3
KGB, 158, 230
Khan, Amir Haidar, 112
Kilsky, Jozef, 44
Kissinger, Henry, 173
Klebanov, Vladimir, 229–30
Knight, Jack, 147
Knights of Labour, 7
Kossa, Stephen, 48
Kovacs, Bela, 48
Kraina, Vladimir, 44
Kubitschek, Juscelino, 167
Kun, Bela, 11
Kupers, Evart, 66, 69
Kusnetsov, Vassily V., 67–8
Kuu, T. C., 131
Kweit, William, 112

Lacerda, Carlos, 168, 170
Landauer, O., 11
Lansdale, Edward, 122
Largentier, P., 57
Lausman, Bohumil, 45
Lawther, Will, 52
Leddy, Raymond, 146
Legien, Karl, 16, 18
Lenin, Vladimir Ilyich, 10, 22, 49
Levinson, Charles, 194, 239
Lewis, John L., 25, 94, 141, 194
Liebknecht, Karl, 11
Liu, S., 68
Loderer, Eugen, 255
Lodge, George Cabot, 159
Lombardo Toledano, Vincente, 35, 139, 142
Loveira, Carlos, 33
Lovestone, Jay, 36–7, 69–70, 89, 132, 184–5
Luckhoo, Lionel, 163
Lulchev, Kosta, 48
Lumumba, Patrice, 91
Luxemburg, Rosa, 11
Lynd, Henry, 112

Maachou, Abdelkader, 95
Macarthur, Douglas, 127

Index

Macmillan, Harold, 165
Macrae, G., 94
Majer, Vaclav, 45
Malatesta, Enrico, 135
Manley, Michael, 257
Mannheim Declaration, 16
Marais, Jaap, 256
Marchais, Georges, 238
Marcous, Mbilla, 94
Marighella, Carlos, 178
Marshall Plan (ERP), 55, 58–60, 63–6
Martens, C., 20
Martov, Julius, 49
Marx, Karl, 6–7
Masaryk, Jan, 46
Maspero, Emilio, 157
Maxwell, Reginald, 114
Mazey, Emil, 147
May Day, 8
Mboya, Tom, 76, 91–4
McCabe, Eugene, 164
McCarthy, Joseph, 184
McGuire, Peter, 7
Meany, George, 37, 69–70, 88–9, 132, 141–2, 147, 156, 159–60, 162, 180, 184–5, 187–8
Meiji, Emperor, 125
Mendoza, Democrito, 123
Meskinen, John, 89
Meyer, Cord, 70
Miagkov, Gregory, 260
Mikolajczyk, Stanislaw, 49
Millard, Charles, 89
Miller, John, 200
Mirajkar, S. S., 115
Mitterand, François, 207
Moch, Julius, 59
Molotov, Vyacheslav M., 58, 116
Moreno, Wenceslao, 175–6
Morones, Luis, 33, 35, 138, 141
Mosca, E., 154
Moumie, Felix, 91
Murray, Phillip, 72, 141
Mussolini, Benito, 61

Nambiar, S., 111
Narayan, P., 112
Nefishi, H., 99
Nehru, Jawarharlal, 13, 76, 111–12, 185
N'Gom, Doudou, 94
Nigeria, 256–7
Nikitin, Nikolai, 230
Nkomo, Joshua, 76
Nkrumah, Kwame, 92
Nunez, Father, 142
NUTA, 97

OATUU, 98–9
OAU, 98
Obregon, Alvaro, 138
Oca, Robert, 123
Ochwada, Arthur, 93
Odayemi, E. O. A., 99
O'Keefe, Gerald, 132, 165, 175
Olalia, Felixberto, 122
Oldenbroeck, Jan, 29, 71, 94, 119, 187
Ongania, Felix, 156
Ongaro, Raimundo, 156
OSS, 37–8, 56
Osugi, Sakae, 125
Ota, H., 129
Otero, Joaquin, 175–6
Oudegeest, Jan, 18, 20
Owen, Peter, 165

PAFL, 33, 137–40
PAFMECA, 91
Paladino, Morris, 132, 172
Parri, Enrico, 64
Pastore, Giulio, 64–5
Paulus, Arie, 256
Pearlman, Mark, 262
Perez Leiros, Francisco, 151–7
Peron, Evita Duarte, 152–6
Peron, Juan Domingo, 151–6, 177
Petkov, Nikola, 48
Peurifoy, John, 146–7
Philippines, 120–3
Pineda, Frederico, 149
Pinochet Ugarte, Augusto, 176
Pissas, Michael, 88
Poland
    KOR, 231–2
    postwar political crisis, 48–50
    Solidarity, 233–7
Pollack, Harry, 164
Pollitt, Harry, 114

Pongault, Gilbert, 92
Portugal, 246-51
Poulsen, Juul, 179, 189
Prats, Carlos, 176
Pratt, George, 38
Pressman, Lee, 68
Prestes, Carlos, 166-7
Profintern (RILU), 21-3, 110-11, 136
Punniah, Basava, 116
Puzak, Kazimiercz, 49

Quadros, Janio, 168

Rai, Lala Lajpat, 110
Ramirez, Pedro P., 151
Ranadive, S. A., 113, 115
Rao, Rajeshwar, 116
Rawson, Arturo, 151
Reuther, Victor G., 118, 185, 188
Reuther, Walter Phillip, 60, 70, 184-5
Reyes, Cypriano, 153-4
Reynaud, Pierre, 57
Roberto, Holden, 91
Robinson, Howard, 119
Rockefeller, Nelson, 38, 141, 143
Romualdi, Serafino, 141-2, 146-8, 156, 164, 168, 172
Roosevelt, Franklin Delano, 151
Rosenberg, Ludwig, 187
Ross, Michael, 70, 185
Roy, M. N., 109, 112, 136
Rusinek, Kasimiercz, 48
Rusk, Dean, 132
Russian revolution, 11-13
Rutz, Henry, 54
Ryan, J., 111

Sampo, 126
Saillant, Louis, 28, 30, 57, 62, 67-8
Saklatvala, S., 111-12
Salazar, Antonio, 246-8
Salema, S., 95
Sandys, Duncan, 165
Saposs, David, 141
Saraiva de Carvalho, Otelo, 250
Sargent, Constance, 112
Sartorius, Nicolas, 244
Schacht, Hjalmar, 140
Schevenels, Walter, 26-7, 30

Schmidt, August, 52
Schnitzler, William, 168
Seaga, Edmund, 257
Sekondi-Takoradi Strike, 98
Semprun, Jorge, 243
Shagari, Shehu, 256-7
Shelepin, Aleksandr, 221
Shevchenko, Arkady, 260
Shop Stewards' Movement, 22, 215-18
Shulter, John, 107
Shusui, Kotoku, 125
Sidorenko, V., 66
Singh, Prem Lal, 111
Sino-Soviet split, 102-4, 107
Sissoko, Famady, 95
Slansky, Rudolf, 46
Soares, Mario, 248
Socialist International, 8-14
Sohyo, 129-30
Soumah, David, 95
South Africa, 79-80, 251-6
Spain, 242-6
Spinola, Antonio, 248-9
Spratt, Phillip, 110-11
Stalin, Joseph Vissarionovich, 116
Stauffenberg, Count von, 52
Steinhardt, Karl, 12
Stevens, Siaka, 76
Stramek, Jan, 44
Stransky, Jaroslav, 44
Strasser, Adolph, 7
Sulyok, N., 48
Suzuki, Bunji, 74, 125
Svoboda, Ludvik, 46
Sweden, 210-12
Switon, Kazimiercz, 231

Taft, William Howard, 120
Takano, Minoru, 129
Tamborini, Jose P., 154
Tanner, Jack, 52
Tarasov, Mikhail, 20
Taruc, Luis, 122
Tata, Naval, 118
Tepper, Lazar, 38
Tettegah, John Kofie, 90, 93, 95
Tewson, Victor, 68-9, 88, 118, 188
Thomas, Norman, 143

Tlili, Ahmed, 95
Togliatti, Palmiro, 62, 64, 204
Tokugawa, Ieyasu, 126
Tokugawa, Iyesato, 126
Toriello, Jorge, 145
Touré, Ahmed Sekou, 76, 86–7, 90–1
Trippe, Juan, 160
Troitino, Adriano, 135
Trotsky, Leon, 106
Trades unions
  colonial unions, 79–80
  decolonisation, 81–2
  links with intelligence organisations, 4–5, 258–63
  links with political parties, 3–5
  nature of, 1–2
  nature of in Third World, 73–8
Truman, Harry S, 67
TUAC, 202
TUCP, 123

Ubico, Jorge, 144–5
UGTAN, 87, 91–2
UMW, 24–5
UPTC, 95
Uriburu, Jose Felix, 149
Usmani, Shaukat, 110

Valdivia, Raoul, 148
Valletta, Vittorio, 240
Van Arkel, Gerald, 37, 56
Vanderveld, G., 20
Vandor, Augusto, 156
Vann, T. P., 131
Vargas, Getulio, 166–7, 171, 177
Videla, Jose, 156

Viera, Jose Rodolfo, 262
Vilarin, Leon, 175
Villa, Pancho, 138

Wadia, B. P., 74, 109–10
Wallace, Henry, 67
Webb, Sidney, 78
WFTU
  competition with ICFTU, 69–71, 104–5
  founding, 27–30
  in Africa, 83–4
  in Europe, 203
  in German reconstruction, 50–1
  Sixth Congress, 104
  split, 66–8
Wheeler, George Shaw, 53–4
Wilson, Woodrow, 19, 32, 214
Wolf, Mischa, 260
Woll, Matthew, 25, 36–7, 53, 140, 142
Woodcock, George, 215
Woodridge, Henry, 160
Wright, Chester, 140
Wurf, Jerry, 179

Yakoreva, Albina, 230
Ydigoras y Fuentes, Miguel, 146
Yrigoyen, Hipolyto, 149

Zack, Joseph, 136
Zander, Arnold, 164
Zapotocky, Antonin, 44–5, 47
Zenkl, Peter, 44, 46
Zorin, Valerian, 47
Zulawski, 49